Seeking Redemption

Seeking Redemption
The Real Story of the Beautiful Game of Skee-Ball

NoMoreBoxes LLC • San Jose

Skee-Ball is a registered trademark of Bay Tek Games, Inc., iPhone is a registered trademark of Apple Inc., all other trademarks are property of their respective owners.

© Thaddeus O. Cooper and Kevin B. Kreitman 2016.
SeekingRedemption@NoMoreBoxes.com

All rights reserved. This book or any portion thereof may not be reproduced or used in any manner whatsoever without the express written permission of the authors except for the use of brief quotations in a book review.

To Mao Mao, Dorian & Angel, mommy and daddy are sorry for all the late dinners and missed cat presents...

Mommy & Daddy

CONTENTS

Foreword *ix*
Preface *xiii*
Acknowledgements *xvii*
Cast of Characters *xxiii*
Prologue *xxix*

Chapter 1
The Beautiful Game of Skee-Ball *1*

Chapter 2
The Origins of Skee-Ball *5*

Chapter 3
Birthing Skee-Ball *29*

Chapter 4
Launching Skee-Ball *51*

Chapter 5
The Struggle For Redemption *87*

Chapter 6
The Resurrection *153*

Chapter 7
The Tournaments *189*

Chapter 8
A Challenger *195*

Chapter 9
The Competition   *219*

Chapter 10
Interlude   *249*

Chapter 11
Flying High   *255*

Chapter 12
Stealth Transition   *275*

Chapter 13
The Clone Wars   *295*

Chapter 14
Manufacturing Elegance   *311*

Chapter 15
Full Circle   *355*

Chapter 16
Full Circle and Beyond   *387*

Skee-Ball Ownership Chronology   *393*
End Notes   *395*
Photo Credits   *419*
Index   *423*

FOREWORD

The story behind this book is a fascinating tale that began in 2011. As Thaddeus would later explain, he had been working on another project, a documentary, when the subject matter expert with whom he was collaborating became consumed with work at her day job and the film was indefinitely placed on hold. An examination of alternative topics failed to inspire another project, but one evening, while enjoying a game of Skee-Ball on his iPhone, he was suddenly struck by an idea. "I jokingly suggested that the history of Skee-Ball might be an interesting short documentary that might be fun to work on, since it's been so popular, and around for so long -- and it even made it into electronic gaming," he later confided in the first of several interviews with me for the Vineland, New Jersey newspaper The Grapevine.

The electronic version of the game, he admitted, brought back memories of his youth and his family's trips to the Jersey shore, which is where many of the state's residents had been introduced to this popular form of entertainment during the 20th century. The following evening he undertook some preliminary research and concluded that "it looked like the history was pretty cut and dried -- that is, until I started looking for the patent that was supposed to have been issued to J. D. Este and I couldn't find it." A more aggressive search of patents uncovered one "that appeared to be what I was looking for, but it was the Simpson patent. At this point I decided there might be a story. I started doing some more digging and found two articles that suggested that Simpson was in fact the inventor of Skee-Ball. Those articles were by Michelle Moon and Vince Farinaccio. So that's when the project really got legs."

My article had appeared in the August 19, 2009 edition of The Grapevine under the headline "The Origins of Skee Ball." In it, I examined Vinelander Joseph Fourestier Simpson and his registered patent for Skee-Ball, crediting him as the creator of the game and not Jonathan Dickinson Este who had traditionally been recognized as the inventor.

Seeking Redemption

The patent, I discovered, had been filed in 1907 and preceded any claims made by Este by two years.

Vineland has a considerable list of accomplishments and recognition, from its establishment in 1861 as a planned community by Charles K. Landis to the progressive outlook that made it a hub for women's suffrage and other movements in the 1860s and 1870s. It was a successful center for manufacturing and agriculture and a haven for those seeking a healthy climate and a temperance-based existence. It has served as a home for such distinguished individuals as entomologist/botanist Mary Treat, industrialist John Gage and Jewish Holocaust Museum creator Miles Lerman as well as a stopover for such luminaries as President Ulysses S. Grant, Frederick Douglass and Susan B. Anthony. It's also where Welch's Grape Juice had originated. Simpson's role as the inventor of Skee-Ball wasn't such a surprise and the fact that history had not preserved his name as its originator wasn't so unusual either. It's only recently that Oberlin Smith, the inventor of the magnetic recording process and resident of the nearby town of Bridgeton, has been properly acknowledged after nearly a century during which another individual enjoyed the credit.

My Simpson research ended with that article as I pursued other historical topics about Vineland and the surrounding area. However, on April 21, 2011, my editor received an email from Thaddeus inquiring about my Skee-Ball piece and stating that "the article that Mr. Farinaccio wrote actually supports my theory as to the origins of Skee-Ball, bucking the current and oft-repeated version of the history that is currently being told (i.e., J. Dickinson Este invented Skee-Ball). If it is possible I would very much like to be able to contact Mr. Farinaccio to correspond with him and find out more about his research in this area."

The email was forwarded to me that day, and in my response I inquired as to how I could be of assistance. On May 1, I received an email in which Thaddeus gave an account of the work he had already undertaken for the project, which at that point was still intended only as a documentary. He had already amassed approximately 4,000 citations and was actively sorting and cataloging them. After bringing me up-to-date on his endeavors, he informed me that because my article "was more than just restating the oft repeated history, I used it as a jumping-off point to support my research, but I'm having some trouble locating some of the information resources you mention." Of particular interest was an article by Del Brandt I had referenced that had appeared years earlier in a Vineland newspaper. "Unfortunately, I have been unable to find a copy of this article or even the newspaper it appeared in," he wrote. "I was wondering if you would be willing to share a copy of that article, or give me a reference so that I can retrieve it." He closed the email with the hope his work would "eventually be pulled together into a documentary about Skee-Ball."

The Brandt piece had been the starting point for my article, a springboard that had allowed me to examine Simpson's role in developing the game. Brandt had been the leading authority on Vineland history and a local journalist whose name was familiar to anyone who lived in the town during the second half of the 20th century. Well before computers offered us the convenience of searching databases from home and surfing the web for information, he had researched and collected his information old school fashion. His files, which I am assured still exist, consisted of hard copy items: clippings, notes, and documents. They were essential in keeping Vineland's history alive.

Thaddeus's email sent me scurrying to my own files and I scanned the Brandt article, sending it along with photocopies of Simpson's funeral notice, the family genealogy Simpson wrote for the Vineland Historical Magazine and a request to interview Thaddeus by email so he could inform the readers of The Grapevine about his Skee-Ball/Simpson project. I also recommended he contact Patricia Martinelli, the curator of the Vineland Historical and Antiquarian Society and a published author. He agreed to the interview, answering a series of questions over the month of May, and he also contacted Martinelli. By this point, I was quite impressed with his research and the information he imparted in the interview made it clear that this project had the right person in charge.

Some of Thaddeus's interview answers illustrated his working methods and the insight he had gained. When queried about how much time he had already spent on the project and what his findings entailed, he explained that three months of work consisted of examining "patents, genealogical information, corporate records, newspaper articles, and books. As I've been collecting information I've started putting it on a time-line so that I can begin to see how the events are related. I think that the corporate records are really interesting, and there have been one or two things that have popped in the newspaper research that I've been working on."

I had been interested in how Simpson's role would influenced the angle his project would take, and he explained that "Simpson is central to the documentary because it completely changes the way the early history of Skee-Ball is currently told, i.e., Este invented it. The idea behind the documentary is to unravel the history of Skee-Ball and try to figure out what really happened."

Vineland was in the midst of its sesquicentennial that year as Thaddeus had begun learning about the town and its background. It was a period in which Vineland's history was being re-examined. I asked Thaddeus about what he had discovered about our locale. "I didn't know much at all about Vineland before I started my research, but the more research I'm doing, especially about Simpson, the more interesting it sounds," he confessed. "The town seems to have more than their share of high-profile people, and some unique features in that it is apparently the first 'planned community,' so that's an ongoing learning process for me and the documentary, one I plan to pursue." And he did.

Over the following years, my wife and I shared more than a few meals with Thaddeus when he visited Vineland to spend hours at the Historical Society. Breakfast, lunch and dinner included updates about his research, and his accounts, derived from poring over material from multiple sources around the country, gradually formed an image of how detailed and extensive his project had become. The eventual decision to complete a book about Skee-Ball prior to a documentary is more than warranted and, I believe, considerably welcomed.

Thaddeus and Kevin have put together an authoritative account of one of America's most beloved pastimes. If you've ever been even remotely interested in the real story behind the game of Skee-Ball, this is it.

Vince Farinaccio
June 2016

PREFACE

We never intended to write this book.

Thaddeus was looking for a small documentary project when he was faced with some free time from work. Because of his day job, he could not revert to his normal hobby, writing software. So he shifted his focus to this other passion and former profession: Theatre and film. In this case, a documentary.

Playing an electronic game of Skee-Ball on his iPhone gave him an idea. Perhaps he could do a short history of the game of Skee-Ball, looking at how it moved from being ubiquitous at amusement venues onto the electronic device. After a few days of Internet research, he came across at least three different stories of how Skee-Ball originated. None of them, it turned out, were true. Then he ran across an article by Michelle Moon discussing how Skee-Ball was actually developed by a little known inventor from Vineland, New Jersey. With a little more exploration, he discovered a similar piece by Vince Farinaccio. Vince, in turn, referred Thaddeus to Patricia A. Martinelli at the Vineland Historical and Antiquarian Society. And the rest, as they say, is history.

Actually, not quite.

This was originally supposed to be a short 10-minute documentary for YouTube. However, like many other endeavors that Thaddeus has undertaken, it grew to somewhat mammoth size fairly quickly. We've done this before. Find a fact, and as you verify it, you discover a whole context that leads to ten more facts, and so on. For five years.

The reason we have a real story is that the Vineland Historical and Antiquarian Society (VHAS) was the recipient of all of inventor Joseph Fourestier Simpson's personal papers, donated by his sister Alice upon his death. Patricia Martinelli graciously gave us access to his notes, correspondence, drafts, sketches, bills and records. That led us to the rest of the resources we'd need: The Billboard and other amusement and technology journals; ancestry.com; Fold3; Genealogy Bank and

Newspaper Archives; research with other historical societies all over the East Coast; the National Archives; Library of Congress; the United States Patent Office; and the Canadian Patent Office. In short, what was supposed to be a simple 10-minute video on the origins of Skee-Ball turned into a five year research project that became a labor of love, or perhaps a full-blown obsession.

It's led us to meet wonderful, brilliant people who helped us understand the history and context of life in Philadelphia and Vineland during Simpson's lifetime, and to provide a backdrop against which his personal story and the story of Skee-Ball unfolded. Originally, we focused on Simpson as the inventor. But other characters, like John W. Harper, the co-owner of the original Skee-Ball Alley Company, were equally compelling. Harper had a major hand in keeping the fledgeling game alive, at great personal cost. In addition, we discovered so many of the characters involved in the early history of Skee-Ball who were impressive and powerful, from J. D. Este to Layman M. Sternbergh, Morris Goldberg and Herman Bergoffen.

By the end of 2015, after hundreds of inquiry letters, several trips to VHAS, and many weekends spent in front of the microfilm reader at the San Francisco Public library, we decided we probably had enough information. Thad had transcribed all of Simpson's personal papers, notes and letters, extracted stories and ads from microfilms of journals, created extensive timelines and synopses on the characters, and wound up with 5,622 documents.

Not that we were counting.

By early 2016, we were in pre-production on the documentary, having done preliminary interviews with our historical experts, and some storyboarding, and lining up the other professionals we needed. But were still struggling somewhat with the story.

And then, serendipity struck.

When Skee-Ball was sold to Bay Tek Games Inc., it once again became a news story. Patt Martinelli referred Martin DeAngelis from the Press of Atlantic City to interview Thad as the expert on Skee-Ball and Joseph Fourestier Simpson. It was a great article. And it motivated us to get moving. Book first. Documentary second. We realized that putting the book together would focus and deepen the story for the documentary. And we could write the book from his research rather quickly. So that's what we've done.

As we "finished up" the research, one more opportunity emerged. We discovered the rich archive, lovingly maintained by Tom Rebbie, owner of Philadelphia Toboggan Coasters, Inc. since 1991 (successor to the Philadelphia Toboggan Company). Tom's generosity allowed us unfettered access to that archive, which shed so much light onto the history between 1936 and 1985 that we had to add a new chapter. His support is deeply appreciated.

We have focused here on the early history of Skee-Ball, because it is the least well understood, and the richest story in many ways. Watching the people, identifying with their struggles and disappointments, being in awe of their resourcefulness and, indeed, being touched by their humanity has been a deeply moving experience for both of us. In many ways Skee-Ball began as a typical start-up company, with all of the issues, challenges, potential and pain of start-ups today, and it has weathered a whole series of economic and social changes almost unprecedented in the game world.

We hope you enjoy this saga as much as we've enjoyed writing about it. The beautiful game of Skee-Ball turned 108 this year.

One of our favorite quotes from Joseph Fourestier Simpson was unbelievably prescient:

> "Games that are played when they become old are rare. Of those that remain, their origins are lost in antiquity."

He certainly couldn't have been referring to the game he was in the process of launching. But he was right. The stories of the origins of Skee-Ball have been varied and many, but not detailed or accurate.

It's been our privilege to shine a light on the origins of this beautiful game that has been played and loved for over a hundred years.

Thank you, Joseph Fourestier Simpson for the beautiful game of Skee-Ball, and thank you J. D. Este for not letting it die an untimely death.

ACKNOWLEDGEMENTS

Historical books that are breaking ground for the first time relying on primary sources require the assistance of a vast army of people. We've been extremely fortunate to have had help from so many wonderful organizations and people, many of whom started as colleagues and have wound up as friends.

Patricia A. Martinelli, Curator at the Vineland Historical and Antiquarian Society (VHAS), has been more help than we can adequately describe, and without her support, this book never would have been possible. Joseph Fourestier Simpson's sister Alice donated all of his papers to VHAS after his death, and Patricia and her team unearthed the boxes one by one, and graciously hosted us for multiple weeks to review and scan stacks of documents and other artifacts, from personal letters to sketches, business correspondence, patent drawings and blueprints. She still calls every time they unearth another goodie, and we are thrilled when she does.

Tom Rebbie, President and CEO of Philadelphia Toboggan Coasters, Inc. (successor to Philadelphia Toboggan Company, Inc.) and owner of the PTCI Archive gave us unfettered access to what can only be called a treasure trove of resources. The archive shed enormous light on the early history of the Philadelphia Toboggan Company, owner Henry Auchy, as well as the middle years of Skee-Ball history. Tom also favored us with his personal knowledge including his insider insights and historical corporate stories. We're especially grateful for hard to come by photographs of Henry Auchy, and Skee-Ball alleys through the years, not the least of which was the photo of the first National Skee-Ball Tournament in 1932 at Skee-Ball Stadium in Atlantic City, New Jersey. He provided so much in the way of information, business notes, legal documents and records regarding the middle years of Skee-Ball, from the 1930s to the 1980s, that we added an extra chapter for the fascinating material we discovered there. We can't adequately express our thanks for giving us access to these amazing resources.

Two Philadelphia historians contributed enormously to our understanding of the early years of Skee-Ball through personal interviews.

Thomas H. Keels, author of the forthcoming book "Sesqui! Greed, Graft and the Forgotten World's Fair of 1926," provided us valuable and colorful insights into life in historical Philadelphia especially the fascinating stories of the origins, success and demise of Chestnut Hill Park, as well as owner Henry Auchy himself and his unique business practices.

John H. Hepp, Associate Professor of History at Wilkes University, supplied a rich context for the Philadelphia region, helping us understand the growth of the electric trolleys and other industries, the Philadelphia Centennial Exposition, the changes in work, economics and amusements, and the neighborhoods of turn of the century Philadelphia.

Their generous contributions of time and their willingness to answer all our questions, and to provide background information when we didn't know enough to ask, has brought more depth than we thought possible to the story.

Vince Farinaccio is author of the book "Nothing to Turn Off: The Films and Video of Bob Dylan," and the forthcoming book "Before the Wind," a biography of Charles K. Landis, founder of Vineland, New Jersey.

Vince is a wealth of knowledge about the Vineland area and is the source of one of the original articles identifying Simpson as the inventor of Skee-Ball. He also led us to Patricia Martinelli and VHAS, as well as other sources of local information in Vineland and Philadelphia.

Alex Bartlett, Archivist, of the Chestnut Hill Historical Society, Librarian, Archivist and Curator at Germantown Historical Society. Springfield Township Historical Society was a huge help in providing background research on countless persons of interest in the Philadelphia area.

Ed Zwicker, former President and Board Member, Springfield Township Historical Society, author of "Springfield Township, Montgomery County" which features a chapter on White City (Chestnut Hill Park), was also generous in his support of the project, helping with information, access to photographs and generally bending over backward to support the research in countless ways.

Other archivists and Historical Societies have been of tremendous help, and the source of unexpected and deeply appreciated enthusiasm for this project.

One area of particular interest for us was identifying who bought the very first Skee-

Ball alleys in 1909. Shirley Russell, docent at the Lincoln Area Archives Museum deserves special mention. She is informally credited with being a moving force behind the Museum, and she has provided us information about Allen & Sparks, some of the earliest customers of the Skee-Ball Alley Company. Shirley is one of those people who keeps her eyes open for interesting tidbits which she's fed us multiple times, to our delight. Thanks also goes to Linda Steele, Registrar at the Historical Society of Western Virginia, Edwina Parks at Roanoke Public Library, and the staff at Mendocino County Historical Society who all provided information about the very early buyers of Skee-Ball Alleys.

National Archives and Records Administration at Kansas City provided copies of the original patents that were key to unravelling the early history of Skee-Ball and deepening our understanding of Simpson, his inventions, and his dogged determination in pursuing his patents. Special thanks to Chris McGee for going above and beyond to help us.

Jill Rawnsley, Archives and Preservation Consultant at Philadelphia City Archives, provided valuable information about Simpson and the Philadelphia Centennial Exposition.

Ms. Kate Scott, Collection Assistant, Reference Services at the William H. Smith Memorial Library, Eugene and Marilyn Glick Indiana History Center, provided a wealth of information about Briant Sando and the Briant Manufacturing Company, later the Briant Specialty Company.

David Haugaard, Director of Research Services and Shannon Hadley, Researcher at the Historical Society of Pennsylvania, provided a wealth of material on family genealogy and personal information on some of the early people of interest in Skee-Ball, including unearthing moldy disinterment records and patiently going through them looking for Joseph Fourestier Simpson's father.

James G. Mundy Jr., Director of Library and Historical Collections at The Union League of Philadelphia, provided us records about purchase of Skee-Ball alleys that were some of the first sold by J.D. Este and installed at The Union League of Philadelphia.

James Smith, acclaimed author of the classic books "Playland at the Beach: The Early Years" and "Playland at the Beach: The Golden Years," generously provided images of Skee-Ball alleys and Whirl-O-Ball alleys installed at Playland in San Francisco, CA., a real find.

Kirk Hastings, President of the Wildwood Crest Historical Society, provided us images of Wildwood Crest Pier in the early 20th century, site of some of the earliest Skee-Ball installations.

Jim Waltzer, author of "Tales of South Jersey: Profiles and Personalities," provided us with early information about the first National Skee-Ball Tournament in 1932 and pointed us to Heather Halpin Pérez, Archivist, Atlantic City Heritage Collections at the Atlantic City Free Public Public Library, who provided additional information about the tournament.

Nancy R. Miller at University of Pennsylvania Archives provided information about Frederick E. Okie, Simpsons's cousin and co-inventor of the ratchet wrench.

Amanda Fontenova, Librarian/Archivist at Luzerne County Historical Society provided a wonderful image of Harvey's Lake Skee-Ball Alleys and the people about to play the game.

Rosalba D. Varallo Recchia, Special Collections Assistant at Princeton University, Seeley G. Mudd Manuscript Library, provided us information about J.D. Este from their alumni records, including facts about his military service.

National Archives and Records Administration Still Picture Reference Team, Special Media Services Division, supplied photographs of J. D. Este's military service.

Historical Society of the Tonowandas provided images of the Rudolph Wurlitzer manufacturing facilities and Skee-Ball management in North Tonawanda, New York, site of the manufacturing of Skee-Ball Alleys in the late 1930s and early 1940s.

To San Francisco Public Library, Microfilm Division and Special Collections, thanks for supporting our research in countless ways.

Thanks to Michelle Moon, the author of one of the early articles on Simpson and Skee-Ball that led us to the true identity of the inventor, which kicked off this project.

A lot of our insights into the who's who of Skee-Ball, and its lineage originally came from corporate records. Thanks to Jo Anne Matthews, at the Delaware Secretary of State's office, for her help in providing corporate records of many of the companies who were involved in the early manufacture and sale of Skee-Ball Alleys; to the New York Department of State Division of Corporations; to the State of New Jersey, Department of the Treasury, Division of Revenue and Enterprise Services; and to the Commonwealth of Pennsylvania, Department of State, Corporation Bureau all of whom provided corporate records that helped us understand the lineage of companies that were involved with Skee-Ball.

Understanding the people and their family histories was important as well. Laurel Hill Cemetery provided us with genealogy information about John W. Harper. The Woodlands cemetery provided us with genealogy information about Joseph Fourestier Simpson and his family.

Philadelphia City Archives provided information about 1876 Centennial Exposition, and Simpson's participation in it.

Manlius Pebble Hill School information about J. D. Este and his father Charles Este.

New Jersey Department of Health, Office of Vital Statistics and Registry provided Simpson's death certificate.

Commonwealth of Australia Patent Office provided a copy of Simpson's patents.

And thanks to Martin DeAngelis, staff writer for the Press of Atlantic City. Martin wrote the article about the latest sale of Skee-Ball to Bay Tek Games, Inc. It was Martin's interview with Thad that kicked this book project into high gear.

Special Thanks

A number of people reviewed all or part of the manuscript and provided invaluable feedback.

Patricia A. Martinelli graciously read the entire manuscript—multiple times—and provided us with significant feedback and creative suggestions as well as the extra added attraction of copy editing suggestions (thank you!). We take full responsibility for any errors which may remain. We are in her debt.

Tom Rebbie, President and CEO of the Philadelphia Toboggan Coasters, Inc. and owner of the PTCI Archives, also read the entire manuscript and provided us additional valuable insights and feedback based on his inside knowledge. We deeply appreciate his commitment to this project.

Thomas H. Keels and Dr. John Hepp both reviewed the early sections of the manuscript, providing corrections, additional color and further insights. We are so grateful for their assistance on understanding what life was like in Philadelphia over a hundred years ago, and the significance of some of the life circumstances of Simpson, Harper and other people involved with Skee-Ball.

Many thanks to Vince Farinaccio who graciously took time away from working on his own book to write the Foreword to this manuscript.

Thanks to Kevin Kreitman for her herculean effort in pulling the book together and getting it out the door.

Thank you to Argun Tekant who took time out of his busy schedule to photograph bears and Skee-Balls, and also to Jack Carr, Vice President of the Board of the Vineland Historical and Antiquarian Society, for photographing the original Skee-Ball blueprint so that we could include it in this book.

Finally thanks to all of our friends and family members who have patiently listened to me prattle on about this project for the past five years. And a special thanks to our cats, who have constantly provided reminders about what is really important in life…fresh cat food, belly rubs and cat treats.

CAST OF CHARACTERS

Chapter 2

Joseph Fourestier Simpson • Inventor of Skee-Ball, Bridge Ball, over center trunk latch, a ratchet wrench, egg shipping carton; also attorney, real estate agent, business owner and sales agent.

Henry Evans Simpson • Father of Joseph Fourestier Simpson.

Josephine Marion Simpson • Mother of Joseph Fourestier Simpson, married to Henry Simpson, descendant of Jean Baptiste Brognard.

Josephine Simpson • Sister of Joseph Fourestier Simpson.

Alice Simpson • Sister of Joseph Fourestier Simpson, donated Simpson's papers and other artifacts to the Vineland Historical and Antiquarian Society.

Henry Rowland Simpson • Brother of Joseph Fourestier Simpson.

Gardiner Simpson • Brother of Joseph Fourestier Simpson.

Sophia Maria Brognard • Joseph Fourestier Simpson's aunt, keeper of the Brognard family genealogy, funder of some of Simpson's endeavors.

Mary Brognard • Sister of Sophia and Josephine Brognard.

Joseph Barkham • A sawyer that was a principal in Simpson & Co., Joseph Fourestier Simpson's first company.

Frederick E. Okie • Cousin of Joseph Fourestier Simpson, co-inventor and co-patentee of a ratchet wrench, owner of the Okie Ink Company, of which Joseph Fourestier Simpson became general manager.

Charles A. Rutter • Mechanical engineer and Joseph Fourestier Simpson's patent attorney.

Chapter 3

Mr. Hyatt • Initial patent examiner for Joseph Fourestier Simpson's Skee-Ball patent.

Dr. William Wilder Townsend • Principal patent examiner for United States Patent Office, who oversaw and finally granted Joseph Fourestier Simpson's Skee-Ball patent.

Chapter 4

William Nice Jr. • Former owner of William Nice Lumber, owner Pressed Steel Manufacturing Co., fifty percent owner of the Skee-Ball patent, business partner of John Washington Harper in the Skee-Ball Alley Company.

John Washington Harper • Owner of John W. Harper Lumber, successor to William Nice Lumber, principal in the Skee-Ball Alley Co. with William Nice Jr., later general manager of The J. D. Este Company, and Vice President of the Skee-Ball Company.

D. Walter Harper • Brother of John W. Harper, car racing enthusiast, racer of Stanley Steamer steam powered cars, owner of a Cameron automobile dealership, employed John W. Harper when Harper was out of money.

Anna Harper • Sister of John W. Harper.

Susan Harper • Sister of John W. Harper.

Joseph Oyen • Carpenter who worked for John W. Harper building Skee-Ball alleys.

James T. Noell • First and second purchaser of a Skee-Ball alley, first repeat customer, lived in Roanoke, Virginia.

John Clifford Warren • Third purchaser of a Skee-Ball alley, and cigar store owner in Ukiah, California.

Andrew F. Gustav • Fourth purchaser of a Skee-Ball alley, lived in Gloversville, New York.

Mark Inman • Fifth purchaser of a Skee-Ball alley, lived in Pana, Illinois.

F. J. Williamson • Sixth purchaser of a Skee-Ball alley, lived in Burlington, North Carolina.

Budd Nice • Son of William Nice Jr., became funder of Skee-Ball after his father's sudden death, President of the Pressed Steel Manufacturing Company.

Allen and Sparks • Two men from Lincoln, California who collectively were the seventh and ninth purchasers of a Skee-Ball alley, second repeat customer.

Fred J. Cossey • Eighth purchaser of a Skee-Ball alley, lived in Benicia, California.

Mrs. M. E. Lombard • Tenth purchaser of two Skee-Ball alleys, lived in Denver, Colorado.

J. E. Langford • Eleventh purchaser of four Skee-Ball alleys, which were probably installed at Saltair amusement park near Salt Lake City, Utah.

Edson • Landlord to Skee-Ball manufacturing shop for Skee-Ball Alley Company, the owner of a livery stable and hauling company in Vineland, New Jersey.

Henry B. Auchy • Owner of the Chestnut Hill Amusement Park, Philadelphia Carousel Company, Philadelphia Toboggan Company.

C. J. Enochs • Business advisor to John W. Harper, and Joseph Fourestier Simpson.

Chapter 5

Arnold Aiman • Business partner with Henry B. Auchy in the Chestnut Hill Amusement Park.

Philip Baker • Founder of Wild Wood Crest, New Jersey, had one Skee-Ball alley operating at the Pier in Wildwood Crest, N. J. in 1910 and possibly 1911.

William F. Boogar • Owner of the Dreamland Theatre in Philadelphia, Pennsylvania and operator of the Skee-Ball alley at the Pier in Wild Wood Crest, New Jersey for Philip Baker.

Fred Hoke • Principal in Holcomb & Hoke, owners of the American Box Ball Company.

J. J. Holcomb • Principal in Holcomb & Hoke, owners of the American Box Ball Company.

John Merrill • General Manager of Chestnut Hill Park, informal marketing person when prospective clients came to see Skee-Ball alleys at Chestnut Hill Park, and co-marketeer along with John W. Harper.

I. N. Levi • A potential investor in Skee-Ball.

Chapter 6

Jonathan Dickinson Este • Owner of The J. D. Este Company which manufactured Skee-Ball between 1913 and 1919, one of the incorporators of the Skee-Ball Operating Company, Civil Engineer, businessman, pilot and military aviator, decorated with the Distinguished Service Cross in WWI.

Charles Este Sr. • Lumberyard owner, father of Jonathan Dickinson Este.

Edward Browning • Cousin of Joseph Fourestier Simpson and potential investor in Bridge Ball.

Joseph M. Doebrich • Employee of The J. D. Este Company and holder of a United States Patent for "Scoring Mechanism For Game Apparatus."

John T. Byrne • Operator of Skee-Ball alleys in Wildwood, New Jersey.

Charles "Chief" Bender • Pitcher for the Philadelphia Athletics, owner of a sporting goods store at 1309 Arch Street, Philadelphia, operator of Skee-Ball alleys, first organizer of a formal Skee-Ball tournament.

Arthur Ledlie Wheeler • All American football player at Princeton, stock broker, Vice President and Secretary of The J. D. Este Company.

Herbert Wheeler • One of the incorporators of the Skee-Ball Operating Company. After the death of his brother Arthur, he would become the Vice President of The J. D. Este Company.

Celeste Captell • One of the incorporators of the Skee-Ball Operating Company, former organ dealer, President of the Canarsie Coaster Co., Inc. in New York.

Richard Walford • One of the incorporators of the Skee-Ball Operating Company.

Chapter 7

Hilda M. Kolar • Winner of the Skee-Ball tournament held at Young's Old Pier in Atlantic City, New Jersey in 1915.

Paul B. McKinney • Owner of McKinney's Market Square Billiard Parlors, Philadelphia, Pennsylvania, owner of a second parlor at Spruce and Mifflin Streets, Philadelphia, owner of a Skee-Ball parlor in Palmyra, Pennsylvania, Skee-Ball operator, Skee-Ball tournament host.

Chapter 8

Evelyn Parker • Friend and confidant of Joseph Fourestier Simpson.

Newlin Trainer • The partner of Edward Browning and potential investor in Bridge Ball.

Briant Sando • General Manager of the American Box Ball Company, Vice President and General Manager of Briant Manufacturing, built and sold Bridge Ball Alleys, and Whirl-O-Ball alleys.

George A. Bittler • President Briant Manufacturing Company, Vice President of Merchants National Bank, Indianapolis, Indiana.

Isaac A. Lewis • Vice President Briant Manufacturing Company.

Mark E. Archer • Secretary / Treasurer Briant Manufacturing Company.

Chapter 9

Charles Este Jr. • Brother of Jonathan Dickinson Este, Treasurer of The J. D. Este Company,

Edwin V. Dougherty • Jonathan Dickinson Este's Princeton schoolmate, fellow WWI aviator, business partner in The J. D. Este Company, President of the Skee Ball Company started in 1919.

Chapter 10

Lydia Richmond Taber • Wife of Jonathan Dickinson Este.

Edward H. LeBoutillier • Secretary of Skee Ball Company started in 1919.

Chapter 11

Morris Goldberg • Real estate mogul, General Manager, Secretary/Treasurer, and motive spirit of The J. D. Este Company, later owner of the Skee-Ball Sales and Security Company.

George V. Tonner • Premiered Skee-Ball in London, England at the prestigious London Olympia Christmas Carnival in 1921.

Harry E. Tudor • An agent who represented many prominent American and European amusement devices. Highly enthusiastic about Skee-Ball.

Arnold Neble • President of the Kentucky Derby Company, first brought Skee-Ball alleys to England.

Minnie Goldberg • Wife of Morris Goldberg, director of Skee Ball Sales and Security Company, Inc. founded in 1921.

Frank Montsko • Director of Skee Ball Sales and Security Company, Inc. founded in 1921.

Herman Bergoffen • Director of National Skee-Ball Company, Inc., real estate mogul, teacher, attorney, activist, Vice President and General Manager Coast Holding Company, President Hershbeck Building Corporation, member of the Board of Directors of the Coney Island Chamber of Commerce, officer in the National Association of Amusement Parks, executive committee member of the tournament committee for the First National Skee-Ball Tournament in 1931, philanthropist.

Hugo H. Piesen • Director of National Skee-Ball Company, Inc., member of the Coney Island Chamber of Commerce, officer in the National Association of Amusement Parks,.

Maurice Piesen • Son of Hugo Piesen, Director of National Skee-Ball Company, Inc., member of the Coney Island Chamber of Commerce, officer in the National Association of Amusement Parks.

Chapter 12

Layman M. Sternbergh • Built and operated Skee-Ball Stadium in Atlantic City, New Jersey, executive committee member of the tournament committee for the First National Skee-Ball Tournament in 1931; operator of two Skee-Ball Alley arcades in Asbury Park, New Jersey, operator of Skee-Ball Alleys at the North-End Pavilion in Ocean Grove, New Jersey; inventor and patentee of an improvement to Skee-Ball Alleys making it easier to change the rubber buffers on the targets.

Dominick Peccerillo • Inventor and patentee of a pinball version of Skee-Ball.

Rolland K. Strong • First Prize winner of the First National Skee-Ball Tournament held in Atlantic City, New Jersey, 1931.

Laurence Lipkin • Second Prize winner of the First National Skee-Ball Tournament held in Atlantic City, New Jersey, 1931.

Al Schoenfeld • Third Prize winner of the First National Skee-Ball Tournament held in Atlantic City, New Jersey, 1931.

Harry M. Gardner • Fourth Prize winner of the First National Skee-Ball Tournament held in Atlantic City, New Jersey, 1931.

Mrs. R. G. Phelps • Winner of the Women's National Championship at the First National Skee-Ball Tournament held in Atlantic City, New Jersey, 1931.

Chapter 13

George Ponser • A distributor of various arcade games including Genco Bank-Roll, and the manufacturer of Roll-A-Ball.

Chapter 14

Julian Bergoffen • Attorney and principal in the National Skee-Ball Company, Inc.

Paul Fuller • Rudolph Wurlitzer cabinet designer, redesigned classic Skee-Ball Alleys in 1936.

Paul Bennett • Head of Games Division of the Rudolph Wurlitzer Company, organizer of party for the formal presentation of the first Skee-Ball game built by Wurlitzer.

Homer E. Capehart • Vice President in charge of sales of the Games Division of the Rudolph Wurlitzer Company, organizer of party for the formal presentation of the first Skee-Ball game built by Wurlitzer.

Joe A. Darwin • Organizer of party for the formal presentation of the first Skee-Ball game built by Wurlitzer.

Chapter 15

Samuel High Jr. • Majority stockholder in Philadelphia Toboggan Company and corporate attorney.

Samuel High Sr. • Attorney for the Philadelphia Toboggan Company, who took all of his payment in corporate stock and gained controlling interest in the company in 1930.

Frank D. Johns • Inventor and patenter of the Automatic Ticket-Dispensing Skee-Ball Machine.

Samuel High III • President of Skee-Ball Inc. 1971-1985.

Chapter 16

Joe Sladek • Manager and later President of Skee-Ball Inc. until 2016.

Eric Pavony • "Skee-E-O" of the Full Circle Bar, located in the Wilmington District, Brooklyn, New York, founder of the BrewSkee-Ball League.

Ray Carannante • Also known as Skee Diddy, the first National Skee-Ball champion of the BrewSkee-Ball league.

Joey Mucha • Also known as Joey the Cat, the second National Skee-Ball champion of the BrewSkee-Ball league.

Tracy Townsend • Also known as Trace Face, the first woman to win the National Skee-Ball championship of the BrewSkee-Ball league.

PROLOGUE

The Beautiful Game of Skee-Ball

"Games that are played when they have become old are rare. Of those that remain, their origin is lost in antiquity. Our interest in games when analyzed, is found to rest in three human elements, namely: the love of planning or cold calculation, the excitement of the imaginative and emotional faculties and the stimulation of the blood circulation by physical effort.

"A game combining the exercises of these elements in moderation, may be considered to be the ideal in games. In the beautiful game of Skee-Ball, these are equally joined and a new game has been brought into existence which from its nature must come into both permanent and universal use. The principle is an absolutely new appeal to the imagination in its application to games and the mental skill and physical exercise that it affords renders it a completion.

"It is the only game which is a game of skill that is quick enough in play to be used in connection with prizes." [1]

From an early article about Skee-Ball, published in The Billboard in December 11, 1909.

Chapter 1

THE BEAUTIFUL GAME OF SKEE-BALL

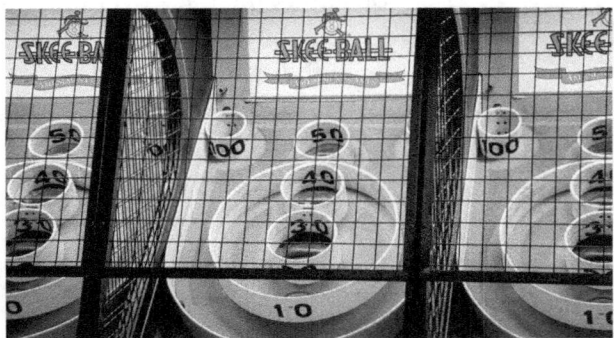

That's what it was called in the first major article published about the game in The Billboard on December 11, 1909: "The Beautiful Game of Skee-Ball." [1]

Skee-Ball is one of the most beloved and widely played alley games in history. You can find Skee-Ball alleys on boardwalks, in arcades, at amusement parks and in kid-friendly restaurants all over the country, as well as in some bars and retail venues. Something about the game is fascinating and almost addictive.

Skee-Ball is one of the first "redemption" games. You insert a coin into the game coin box and it releases nine balls. You roll each ball up the alley over a hump, which launches the ball into the air toward a target of concentric circles. Depending on which area of the target the ball lands in, you're awarded a number of points. You play all nine balls, collect tickets or tokens that represent your score, and redeem them for prizes.

Walking into the arcade, whether it be at an amusement park, on the boardwalk, or at a kid-friendly restaurant, you can't help but notice all of the prizes that abound for you to take home—if you get enough tickets. The prizes include pencil erasers and pencils, trivets with bird pictures, ash trays, condiment plates with garish colors, glitter balls, pot holders, watches, piggy banks, decks of cards, Chinese finger traps, the small, medium, large and extra large teddy bears. Ah, the

ginormous teddy bear. THE prize to get.

Normally, most of us would just walk past most of these items in our local five and dime store and not give them a second thought. But something happens when you step into the arcade. Suddenly, those prizes become something that you fixate on. You must have them. You scope out how many tickets you need, and go off to the Skee-Ball alleys to win your fortune in tickets so you can bring home THE prize. Your heart rate goes up, and your hands get just a little sweaty. At the end of the day, most people will leave with a pencil and an eraser. But what fun you've had with the challenge. And if you're patient and save your tickets, you can come back over and over again until you have enough for the ultimate prize — the ginormous teddy bear!

Almost everybody has played Skee-Ball at one time or another, even if they don't remember the name of the game. They'll remember the cacophony of the arcade, the sound of balls rolling up adjacent alleys, of picking up a three and a half inch

Chapter 1 • The Beautiful Game of Skee-Ball

ball as they intently consider the target just out of reach about ten feet away. Then swinging an arm back, they rapidly bring it forward and release the ball. The ball rolls up the alley, flies into the air and lands in the target as the scoring device advances their score.

Or they might just grab the balls and roll them quickly, with no real attempt to control where they go, as a child might. But that's one of the great things about Skee-Ball. You can play it any way you want. Because at the end of the day there are only two rules: You get nine balls; You roll them up the alley. That's it.

Simplicity!

Few games have shown the staying power of Skee-Ball. Patented in 1908 and first sold in 1909, it is a story of more than a hundred years of profitable recreation.

Stories abound about the game, who invented it, why and how it was invented, but the true story is by far the most interesting. It not only provides a fascinating look into the creative mind of the inventor, and the dogged determination of partners to bring it to market, but also the age of invention itself.

Seeking Redemption

Chapter 2

THE ORIGINS OF SKEE-BALL
Joseph Fourestier Simpson

"Games that are played when they are old are rare, of those that remain, their origin is lost in antiquity."

Skee-Ball, one of the oldest arcade games in the business, was the brain-child of an inventor who grew up in Philadelphia and moved to Vineland, New Jersey, in the last half of the 19th century.

The mid-19th century marked a turning point in our nation's history. It was the beginning of the end of slavery, and the falling away of the dominance of agriculture in favor of industry and invention. In 1850, Joel Houghton was granted the first patent on a dishwasher. The following year, Isaac Singer is credited with inventing the sewing machine. In 1852, Jean Bernard Leon Foucault invented the gyroscope. That was the year our inventor was born.

Joseph Fourestier Simpson was born October 31, 1852, six months after his parents married. [1] He grew up in Philadelphia, Pennsylvania,

Joseph Fourestier Simpson
(Courtesy Vineland and Historical and Antiquarian Society)

at his parents' home on North 4th Street, part of a tight-knit family. His father, Henry, and his mother, Josephine, were Quakers, and Henry Simpson Sr. was a prosperous cotton duck merchant before the Civil War. [2] Joseph was the oldest of five siblings. He grew up with sister Josephine, born in 1855, sister Alice, born in 1860, and brother Henry, born in 1863. Their youngest brother, Gardiner, was born in 1866 but, sadly, died in 1878 before he turned 13. [3]

Simpson went by the nickname Foury, short for his middle name, Fourestier. He was named for a close friend of the family who gave him a silver spoon, knife and fork, housed in a handsome wooden box. Joseph Martin de Fourestier, who also lived in Philadelphia, was very likely his god-father.

In the mid-1800s, Philadelphia was a bustling industrial city, known as "the workshop of the world," with a thriving lumber industry and a broad range of commerce. It was served by multiple rail lines, as well as overseas and domestic shipping lines, with ships traveling up the Schuykill River to the docks. A cotton duck merchant like Henry Simpson could sell into multiple industries, since cotton duck fabric could be fashioned into work clothing and protective gear, tarpaulins, sails for ships, canvas bags, awnings and more. It was a critical component of many industries that formed the backbone of the economy.

The neighborhood where Foury grew up, on Chestnut St. above 40th, was a classic, middle-class West Philadelphia neighborhood. There was public transit in the form of horse-drawn streetcars to take people into the city center, tree-lined residential streets with broad lawns, and a wide variety of shops within easy walking distance. Life was good. Everyday life in this moderately well-off Quaker household seemed pleasant and uneventful. Although the Civil War raged nearby from 1861-1865, Philadelphia was largely untouched by the battles. However, it was battered by the awareness of the fighting, and affected by the shift away from commerce with the agricultural South toward an ever-more industrial focus, and a national and international trade environment.

As the war wound down in 1865, and the front pages of newspapers turned from war back to everyday life, Henry Simpson ceased to identify himself as a cotton duck merchant. [4] Many cotton-based industries previously supplied from the American South were badly impacted by the war and reconstruction. For the next few years, Henry Simpson listed his occupation as "Gentleman" in the Philadelphia City Directory.

Generally, people of this merchant class, like

Foury's father, could expect to send their sons to college. After graduation, parents could exploit their connections with other merchants and people of reasonable means to place their sons as managers in other companies, or position them to take over the family business. That was the future that Foury had been raised to expect.

But everything changed for young Foury when in 1869, at the age of 41, Henry Simpson died suddenly, just as his son was turning 17.

His father had closed the cotton duck business after the war, and was not alive to help him get started on his career. So in 1870, Foury took a job as a clerk at the ticket office in the main station of the Pennsylvania Railroad, located at North 31st. and North Market streets. The railroad had hundreds of clerks working for them, at jobs like accounting and ticket-selling. The term "clerk" applied to thousands of jobs whose main requirement was that the candidate be able to read, write and do simple sums, rather than just perform physical labor. These were low-paying, entry level opportunities, the lowest rung on the middle class ladder. However, the position was respectable enough to get him started on his quest to redeem himself and his position in society, and become a successful businessman like his father.

In the meantime, his mother marshaled the entire family, and moved a few blocks away to Spruce Street in West Philadelphia to live with her sisters, Sophia and Mary Brognard. Foury developed a special bond with his aunt Sophia. They shared a passionate interest in family genealogy, and he spent an inordinate amount of time working on it with her, putting intensive effort into independent research into the genealogy, and making copious notes over the years. She also continued to support him by lending him money in his later life. She had inherited the family wealth, and held the purse strings of the extended family.

While living with his aunt Sophia, Simpson began to help her answer letters about the genealogy of the Brognard side of the family. The Brognard family could trace their ancestors back to Jean Baptiste Brognard who fought in the Revolutionary War on the side of the Colonists. The Brognards also included some impressive relationships with famous figures. One of these was the marriage of Varina Howell, Simpson's second cousin, to Jefferson Davis, President of the Southern Confederacy.

Years later, when the city claimed some of aunt Sophia's property by eminent domain to the street widening in front of her property, Foury was the first one there to defend and protect her interests. As favorite aunt, favorite nephew,

Seeking Redemption

Pennsylvania Railroad Building, Philadelphia, Pennsylvania
(Courtesy Library of Congress)

they shared a powerful bond. Her support to Foury proved invaluable as he sought to make his way in the world.

In 1870, the family bought a cottage in Atlantic City, New Jersey, facing the ocean. [5] They vacationed there each summer until 1875, traveling by train between Camden and Atlantic City. 1870 was a particularly significant year for Atlantic City. This was the first year of the Atlantic City Boardwalk, which would soon become an institution in its own right. Although Foury wasn't aware of it at the time, that boardwalk would be of great importance to his future endeavors.

Foury was in many respects an exceptional young man, extremely meticulous and highly observant. He made copious notes on whatever his current interests were, and was as much an engineer as anything else. He had an obsessive streak which served him well in terms of perfecting his designs and single-mindedly pursuing projects, though sometimes well past their reasonable conclusion. He also spent a lot of time sketching and doodling to help him work out his ideas. In appearance and presence, he was memorable, with a twinkle in his eye and a clever sense of humor. He sported a bushy mustache, prided himself in being well dressed, and was something of a clothes horse with his impeccable three piece suits, complete with a vest and a pocket watch,

Joseph Fourestier Simpson
(Courtesy Vineland Historical and Antiquarian Society)

and topped with a bowler hat.

Foury inherited some of his father's focus on business, and he certainly started life expecting to be a successful businessman. But he also had something that his father did not: a passionate drive to create and invent. In that, he was a child of his age.

The Age of Innovation and Industry

In the early years of its nationhood, U.S. industry had a reputation for stealing ideas and copying industrial machines invented in England and Europe. All that changed around the time of the Civil War. Although there were notable inventions starting in the mid 1800s, the Civil War accelerated both innovation and industrial development.

Between the London World's Fair (The Great Exhibition of the Works of Industry of All Nations) in 1851, and the Philadelphia Centennial Exposition in 1876, there was a huge growth in patents in the U.S.

One way for ordinary but intelligent people to make a mark on the world was to develop patentable inventions. To create real value, and benefit financially from their patents, they had to license them, and get their patented devices manufactured and sold. But getting a patent was the first step.

This era was the beginning of the U.S. focus on industrialization, and created a huge wave of innovation. The number of patents issued between 1851 and 1875 exploded, with the Civil War driving the need for for new equipment. This included mechanical devices to make agriculture a more productive and less backbreaking endeavor. It also focused on building machinery and equipment to produce new goods faster and cheaper, supporting fabrication and assembly lines. This period between 1860 and 1900 also saw the invention of equipment to support commerce, including the typewriter, cash register, and adding machines. There were other more personal and creative inventions, like the first Kodak camera. And there were leaps forward in technology for communication and transportation that supported the inexorable expansion and development of the country. In 1876, Alexander Graham Bell (1847–1922) patented the telephone. In this era, Thomas Alva Edison (1847–1931) invented the electric light. Nikola Tesla (1856–1943) developed systems for long-range, high voltage electricity transmission, and the electric motor, which saw uses from home automation to the development of electric trolleys and railroads. The invention of the trolley, based on Tesla's groundbreaking work, would prove important to Simpson as well, in ways he could not have fathomed.

With that shift from copying and improving, to

innovation and creation of the new, the patent became a pathway for people to try to make a profit on their inventions, spawning brand new business opportunities. This was the world in which young Foury found himself.

While he labored daily as a railroad clerk, the enterprising young man had a yearning to be more than just another worker. He worked steadily, living with his mother and siblings, saving up his salary. In a few years, he was finally on his way back to a life of prosperity, and thinking of having his own family. He met a woman named Ellen in 1873, who was to be the love of his life. Simpson proposed. Sadly, she rejected his proposal, and although he had many women friends over the years, he never considered marriage again. He lived with his extended family his entire life. This seems to have freed his mind to concentrate almost obsessively on innovation, as he bounced from career to career to support himself.

In 1874, Foury struck out on his own. He bought a planing mill and started his own business, Simpson & Co., on Washington Street in Philadelphia, with Joseph Barkham, a sawyer. Planing mills take seasoned cut lumber and turn it into finished, dimensional lumber suitable for building and construction. Against the daily din of the saws and amidst the sawdust on the floor of the mill, Simpson conceived his first patent-worthy idea for an invention. Frustrated by how hard it was to close a trunk with the leather closures popular at the time, he hit on the idea of a new kind of trunk closure based on a lever and hook arrangement: the "over-center" latch.

The frustration probably came as a result of his summer travels back and forth from Philadelphia to the Jersey Shore with an over-packed trunk. This over-center latch allowed the trunk lid to be closed effectively even when the trunk was somewhat overfilled, an idea ripe to support the burgeoning shipping and travel industry.

Foury applied for a patent on the trunk latch in early September 1874. After waiting expectantly for nearly a year, he finally received the notification of his first patent, U.S. Patent Number 168,677 in October 1875. [6] for "Improvement in Trunk-Fastenings."

The timing was perfect.

Reflecting the excitement of a nation at the dawn of industrial innovation, on March 3, 1871, Congress passed "An Act for celebrating the one hundredth anniversary of American Independence, by holding an international exhibition of arts, manufactures, and products of the soil and mine, in the city of Philadelphia, and State of Pennsylvania in the year eighteen hundred and seventy-six." This

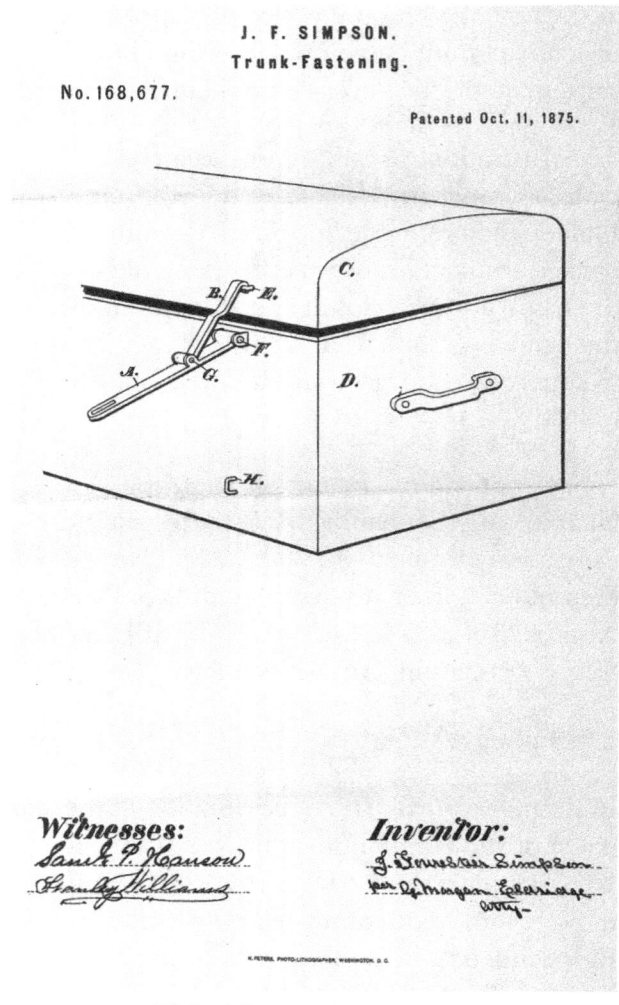

United States Patent 168,677
(Courtesy National Archives and Records Administration)

was the Philadelphia Centennial Exposition.

A Centennial Commission was organized, and plans for the Centennial Exposition were begun in earnest. By May 10, 1876, when the Centennial Exposition opened in Fairmont Park, there were 249 buildings, 5½ miles of railroad track, 16 bridges, 3 miles of fencing with 179 stiles and gates, three separate telegraph systems and 153 acres of lawns and flower beds. The Centennial grounds were the size of a small city, accommodating 250,000 people at a time. The mammoth buildings were made of cast iron and glass, with soaring ceilings and light streaming in. They were filled with fascinating exhibits, including enormous working machines that towered over visitors' heads, working steam engines, and complexes of manufacturing equipment linked with belts and pulleys, operated by huge levers. This was the first time most people had a chance to see how factories produced the goods that improved their everyday lives. It was a thrilling environment, an international sensation as well as a regional mecca for a populace fascinated with the wonders of the industrial age.

After receiving his patent, Simpson submitted his newly patented trunk latch to the Centennial Commission. Acceptance meant that his invention would be displayed at the Centennial and judged by an international panel. Simpson's trunk latch was accepted by the Centennial Commission and was put on display in the Shoe and Leather building.

This budding inventor must have been over the moon with pride and excitement to be one of the movers and shakers represented at the event. The committee that reviewed each of the entries in the exposition reported that Simpson's new trunk latch was:

"Commended for novelty, utility, and low cost." [7]

One of the key advantages of being featured at the Centennial was that it was a place to get the broadest visibility to potential clients, investors and manufacturing partners without having a standing personal network of business and industry contacts.

Shoe and Leather Building, 1876 Centennial Exposition.
(Author's collection)

Unfortunately, Simpson seemed unable to reap those benefits in spite of the timing and the potential of his invention. Although the concept of the over-center latch appears in many forms from that day forward, none is credited to Simpson.

After the Exposition, Simpson returned to his work at the planing mill and remained there until 1879, when he sold the business. He returned to working as a clerk for the William D. Rogers Carriage Business at 1009 Chestnut Street, where he stayed until 1885. It was there that Simpson conceived of a second patent-worthy invention, this time working with Frederick E. Okie.

Okie, Foury's second cousin, had attended the Massachusetts Institute of Technology between 1870 and 1872, but returned home to Philadelphia without finishing. Upon his return, he attended the University of Pennsylvania for almost two years, but again did not graduate. That did not seem to dampen his enthusiasm for engineering and design, though. Working together, Simpson and Okie conceived of a new type of ratchet wrench. In mid-February 1883, Frederick E. Okie and Joseph Fourestier Simpson applied for a patent for this clever and useful device.

In mid-June of that year, Okie and Simpson were granted U.S. Patent No. 279,271, Simpson's second patent. [8] Although it was a sound design, and similar in many ways to ratchet wrenches in use today, it appears that this patent failed to get Simpson and Okie the traction they needed to turn that useful invention into income.

Foury went to work for Okie, who had opened

an ink manufacturing company in 1885. [9] The following year, he was promoted to manager of the company. [10] In 1888, Okie and Simpson moved the company to new quarters on Carter Street. [11]

In February 1889, Josephine Simpson, Sophia Brognard, and the rest of the family including Foury, moved from Philadelphia to Atlantic City, New Jersey. They never returned to the house in West Philadelphia again. [12]

The next year, Josephine and Sophia moved the family to their final destination, settling in Vineland, New Jersey. [13] Founded in 1861 by Charles Landis, Vineland had grown into a small but thriving town, with broad streets and pleasant homes with generous lawns. It was surrounded by fields of scrub oak and pines, and linked to Philadelphia and the Jersey shore by rail lines.

The house in West Philadelphia was finally sold in 1894 along with the other scattered lots. [14] After occupying a succession of temporary lodgings, Foury moved with his mother, aunt, and siblings into the Gage house at 919 Landis Avenue. It was a lovely, large two story home, with peaked gables, many windows and a generous screened-in porch, nestled among the trees, where Foury spent the rest of his life.

In Vineland, in 1892, Foury started his

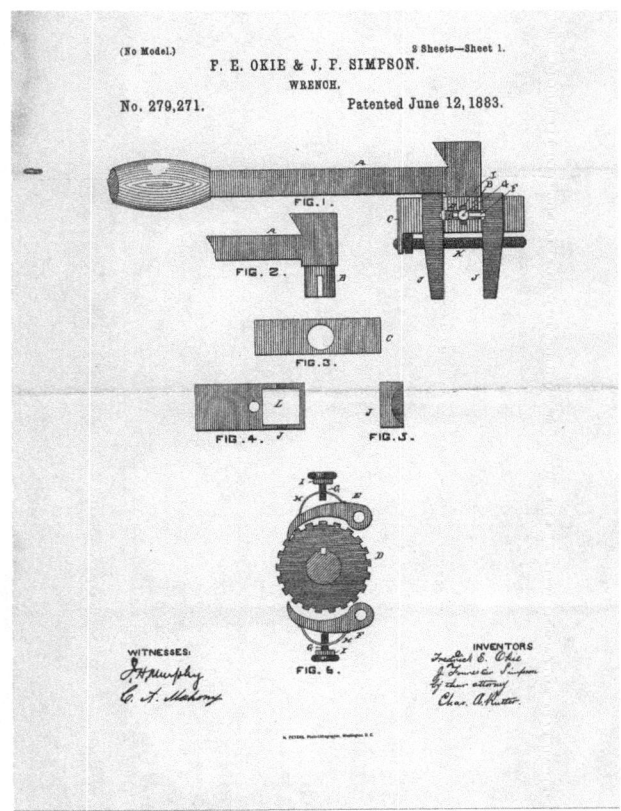

United States Patent No. 279,271.
(Courtesy National Archives and Records Administration)

second business, the Vineland Knitting Mills Company, along with principals William S. Watson and W. H. Ramsay. The purpose of the company was broad, and showed their high hopes for success and expansion. In their articles of incorporation, they described their intention:

Seeking Redemption   15

Shoe and Leather Building, 1876 Centennial Exposition.
(Courtesy Library of Congress)

Simpson residence at 919 Landis Ave., Vineland, NJ.
(Courtesy Vineland Historical and Antiquarian Society)

"to buy cotton and wool; buy and spin all kinds of yarne [sic]; manufacture and knit all kinds of under wear hosiery blankets and other cotton and woolen fabrics and other like materials; sell the same at wholesale and Retail [sic] and to rent and build factories and other buildings necessary to carry out said business." [15]

William S. Watson, whom Foury likely met while he was working in the ink business, was the major stockholder. He invested $18,000 in the business, receiving eighteen shares of stock. Simpson was president of the company and invested $2,000, receiving two shares of stock. W. H. Ramsay, the Simpson family attorney, also invested $2,000 and received two shares of stock.

No one knows exactly what happened to the company in those early years, but two years later, on October 23, 1894, the State of New Jersey filed an injunction against the Vineland Knitting Mills Company to restrain the company from conducting transactions, for non-payment of the license fees and taxes in the amount of $50, owed to the State. [16]

Unfortunately, the knitting mill was no more successful than Simpson's other businesses, and he began to look for other opportunities to make a living.

Over the next eight years, Simpson tried his hand at many careers. He became a self-educated attorney dealing in real estate and small claims. This included handling a protracted battle defending his aunt's property from a government declaration of eminent domain against part of her property in Philadelphia, reducing the property value at a particularly inauspicious time.

He became a stockholder in the Western Loan and Trust Company. He was involved in buying and selling real estate in New Jersey. He also became involved in investment management in gold dredging and mining. He joined the Paul S. Keller Brokerage, trying to extend rail lines, and working tirelessly to evaluate opportunities and obtain loans on behalf of various railroad projects from banks and investors.

He seemed to be working hard, and not making much progress. The sheer volume of correspondence with potential investors he dealt with, and the limited success he had would be enough to wear a lesser man down. Working on commission meant that his income was limited to the rare positive results from these engagements, and subject to being negotiated away. His papers show reams of letters, financial analyses he prepared, correspondence and sales calls to convince investors in the soundness and potential for these endeavors, month after month and year after year.

He also borrowed family money and invested in multiple endeavors, with often disappointing results. In 1903, he discovered that the hefty loan he had made back in the mid 1890s to the Dakota Wyoming and Missouri River Railroad Company, which was backed up by stock, was likely never to be made good. The railroad was so tied up in litigation that it became obvious no one was ever going to be repaid. [17] This was a story echoed across the financial industry of the times.

In truth, the writing was on the wall much earlier than that. Around 1899, as he was nearing 50, began a time of reckoning. He had struggled his whole life to redeem himself in his own eyes and his family's, to strike out on his own and be a successful businessman and succeed through his own considerable efforts. Now, as he faced the half-century mark within a few years, the game changed. Those years between 1899 and 1908 were perhaps more desperate, but also more creative.

Discouraged but resolute, he turned back to inventing, while finding ways to produce income, including marketing cash registers, to keep body and soul together. In this period, he conceived of ideas for a "Postal Check", an improved shock-absorbing bicycle seat, a candy company, and a railroad board game. And, of course, the game that was to become Skee-Ball.

He had not given up entirely on having his own business. Typically, he focused on the opportunity for innovations. He became obsessed with the idea of starting a candy company after sugar became a commonly available commodity. At the time, sugar was actually touted as a health food because it was known to provide energy to the body. Simpson tried and refined dozens recipes to perfect the "healthy candy" product. He engaged professionals to refine the recipes so they could be produced in large batches. It was frustrating at every turn. Eventually, he looked closely

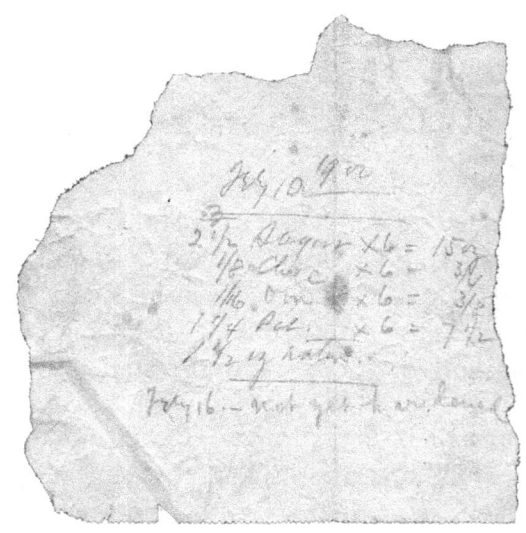

Candy recipe
(Courtesy Vineland Historical and Antiquarian Society)

at the business and labor costs, and resigned himself to the fact that recipes might not scale to provide sufficient quantities of quality product. He reluctantly concluded that the candy company would not be a viable business endeavor.

He was still highly enthusiastic about his idea for a "Postal Check." He spent three years, and wrote countless letters to the Postmaster General describing the superiority of his idea for Postal Checks over the system that was already in place to transfer small amounts of money via the mails. [18, 19, 20, 21, 22, 23] Foury's Postal Check used stamps that were to be purchased for the amount to be transferred, affixed to a postcard, so they could be redeemed on the other end. He convinced the local Vineland Postmaster of the value of his idea, which lead the local postmaster to introduce Foury to many influential people. Even those advocates were unable to convince

Candy box drawings.
(Courtesy Vineland Historical and Antiquarian Society)

Candy Business Cost Analysis
(Courtesy Vineland Historical and Antiquarian Society)

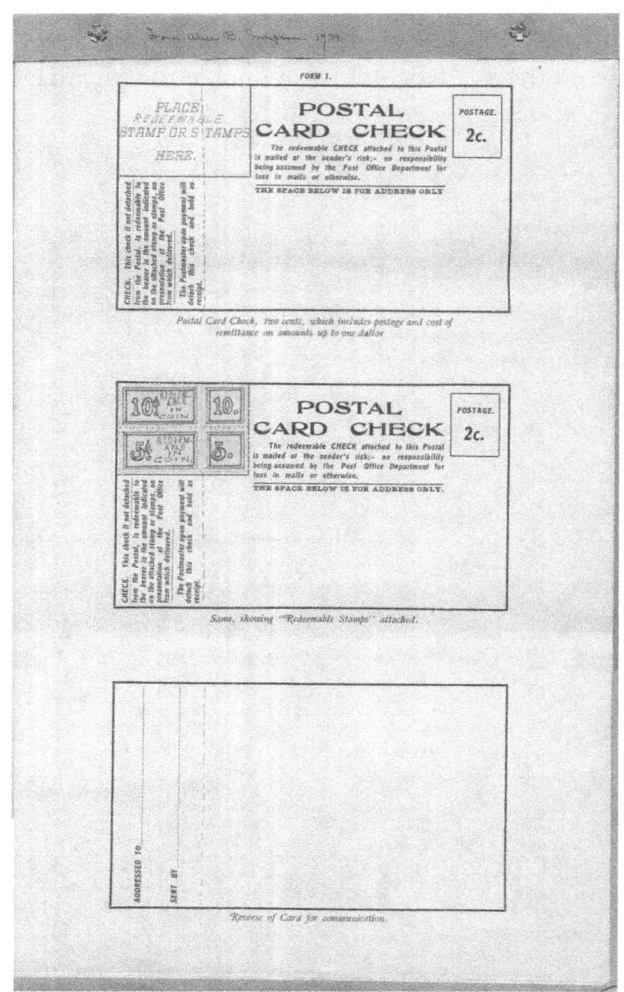

Postal Card Check proposal.
(Courtesy Vineland Historical and Antiquarian Society)

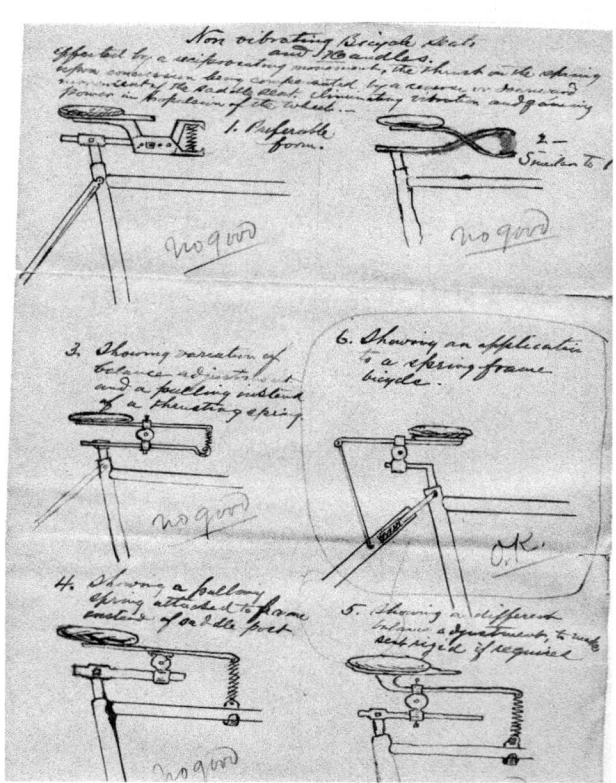

Bicycle seat designs
(Courtesy Vineland Historical and Antiquarian Society)

CHARLES A. RUTTER,
MECHANICAL ENGINEER
AND SOLICITOR OF PATENTS,
IMPERIAL BUILDING,
411 AND 413 WALNUT STREET.

Cable Address: Rutter, Philadelphia.
TELEPHONES:
Bell and Keystone Telephones.

PHILADELPHIA, November 6, 1905.

My dear Forrie:-

    I have been giving very considerable thought to the arrangement of springs that you left with me a few days ago and to save my life I cannot see that you can accomplish anything more that can be accomplished with the ordinary arrangement. The shock of any obstruction against the wheels has to be taken up in all cases by the spring whether it be arranged as in the usual construction or whether it be arranged as you have it. The two levers carrying the spring seem to me to exercise no useful function except that their length may act as an additional spring and so far as any shock transferred to the body of the vehicle is concerned it must be the same in both cases. The resultant of the forces acting upon the two levers will not result in the shock being absorbed in a horizontal direction, at least so far as I can see.

    Under the circumstances I feel that you will be wasting your money in making an application for patent on this device and I would like to be relieved of any responsibility in this line. I hate to have to inform you of my conclusions but I am certain that you will appreciate my reasons.

                        Sincerely

J.F. Simpson Esq.   Chas. A. Rutter

Letter from Charles A. Rutter to Joseph Fourestier Simpson, November 6, 1905.
(Courtesy Vineland Historical and Antiquarian Society)

the U.S. Postmaster General, George B. Cortelyou. Each time Foury or one of his allies approached Cortelyou over a period of three years, the proposal was soundly rebuffed. It was turned down for the last time in 1905.

Finally, attempting to cash in on the ubiquitous bicycle craze at the turn of the century, Foury spent years designing and redesigning a shock absorbing mechanism for bicycle seats. He hoped to have something not only effective, but original enough to be patent-worthy. He continued to develop and refine drawings for designs that had little apparent advantage over existing seats for several years. Sadly, no patentable ideas presented themselves. Foury persisted. It finally got to the point where his Patent Attorney, Charles A. Rutter, a mechanical engineer by training, flatly refused to have anything more to do with it.

At some point in the early 1900s, his idea began to form for an arcade game. He began to make sketches of the game that would eventually become Skee-Ball. This idea was different, and he knew it. To understand the fascination and potential of Skee-Ball, and what made it a wonderfully timed business opportunity, one need only look at the history of the amusement park.

The Boardwalks and Amusement Park Industry

In the late 1800s, there was a real shift with the rise of industrialization and the emergence of the middle class. Suddenly, enough people had enough money and time to expand their leisure pursuits, and a new business opportunity arose: Amusement parks.

The 1893 World's Fair in Chicago, boasted huge buildings housing a variety of exhibits. The centerpiece was a large midway running through the fairgrounds, prominently featuring a Ferris Wheel, and lined with vendors, amusements and games. That midway became the model for all the amusement parks that followed.

The popular phenomenon of boardwalks had started in Atlantic City in 1870, the year that Foury's family bought a cottage at the shore. The very first boardwalks began literally as a set of 1½ inch thick boards nailed to joists two feet wide and built in twelve foot long sections so they could be moved back from the storm tides. They were laid down on temporary foundation piers over the beach, so that people could stroll over the sand, wearing their street clothes and shoes, and enjoy the ocean. Initially, these boardwalks were laid down at the beginning of the season, and picked up and stored at the end of the season. This method continued for fourteen years.

Midway Plaisance and balloon, World's Columbian Exposition, Chicago, Ill., 1893.
(Courtesy Library of Congress)

Ferris Wheel and view of the midway at the World's Columbian Exposition, Chicago, Ill., 1893.
(Courtesy Vineland Historical and Antiquarian Society)

[24] They gradually became more permanent installations, along with piers with vendors and permanent enclosures, and lined with amusement games that were simply shuttered during bad weather. Boardwalks continued to pop up all along the East Coast and soon after, in cities and towns along the West Coast of the United States.

Then there were the regional Trolley Parks. The rise of trolleys as public transportation was transforming life in the city in the late 1800s. Thanks to the brilliant work of Nicola Tesla, the horse-drawn streetcars were being replaced with electric trolleys. Trolley lines were an expensive investment, however, and required significant capital for rolling stock and tracks, as well as the expense of ongoing maintenance. While trolleys were popular and heavily used during normal work and shopping hours, on evenings and weekends they sat idle. That was a concern from the trolley companies' perspective, because they were not making any revenue during that time. In order to draw people out, especially that new middle class with leisure time and money, they needed to extend their hours of productive operation. The trolley companies hit on a solution. They created amusement parks at places far enough from the city center to give people a reason to ride the trolley on weekends.

These trolley parks featured live music, Ferris Wheels, carousels, food and drink stands so guests could eat on the go, lakes with boat rides, and midways lined with arcades and games. Most trolley parks were operated by the trolley companies at a financial loss, and they leased space to vendors to operate the games and rides. The trolley companies made plenty of money just ferrying people to and from the parks on weekends.

Trolley parks became a huge draw for families, and for young men and women, as well as courting couples. In the very formal and conservative Victorian era, these amusement parks were a respectable way for young women, in particular, to get away from their chaperones, and spend time with young men in a socially acceptable environment.

One of the more famous trolley parks was Willow Grove Park, owned by the Widener family who operated the People's Traction Company. They were making their money from their trolley lines as well as other business investments, so they didn't mind losing money on Willow Grove by hiring big name attractions like John Philip Sousa and his famous orchestra for outdoor concerts that would attract more crowds.

These venues would be a perfect opportunity for games like Skee-Ball.

Willow Grove Park, Philadelphia, Pa., owned by the Widener Family.
(Courtesy Library of Congress)

Chapter 3

BIRTHING SKEE-BALL
The Patent For The Game

Foury continued with his sketches and designs, and experimented with building the mechanisms the game would require. He created prototypes of the game, refining it until he found one that satisfied him. He finally reached a point in late 1907 when he was ready to submit the patent and launch the business.

What's critical for any patent is that it represent some unique and different feature than those already covered by existing patents, so as to secure for a period of time the sole right to use that particular design. It is a way of acknowledging the value of the period of development and early sales, so that inventors can reap the financial benefits of their design before it can be copied by competitors. The applicant must prepare a "patent letter" describing each feature to be patented, supported by drawings showing how the features will operate together, and submit it to the patent office. Professional patent examiners then research existing patents to see whether the feature, or something sufficiently similar, has already been patented by somebody else. If the design is found to be sufficiently novel, the U.S. Patent Office grants a patent giving the applicant sole permission to control and license the design for a period of time. In this period, the duration of patent protection was 17 years.

It was a good thing that Foury had developed persistence to a fine art in his previous endeavors. Otherwise, Skee-Ball would never have seen the light of day.

Foury and his patent attorney, Charles Rutter, prepared his first patent letter in November 1907:

TO ALL WHOM IT MAY CONCERN;

BE IT KNOWN, that I, Joseph Fourestier Simpson, a citizen of the United States, and a resident of Vineland, Cumberland County, New Jersey, have invented a certain new and useful improvement in Game of which the following is a specification.

My invention relates to improvements in

game apparatus, and the object of my invention is to furnish a game, to be played with a ball or projectile, in which both skill and chance will play a part and which will give to the player a considerable amount of exercise.

My invention consists of a board or alley, which may be varied greatly in length to suit different conditions or requirements, along which the ball or projectile is rolled or slid. The board or alleys is arranged to cause the ball or projectile in its passage to be projected in the air. This may be done in a number of ways, but I prefer to accomplish it by means of an obstruction, which will give to a ball or projectile passing it a range. To the rear of the board or alley is a target, preferably furnished with a number of spaces or holes into one of which the ball or projectile falls, each of the holes or spaces represents a value and the game is counted by adding the value of the successive shots of each player. In order that there may be no disputes as to the value of the several shots the apparatus may be furnished with a counting device to be actuated by the ball as it passes through or out of the holes in the target. This counting device may simply indicate the value of each shot or it may be arranged to indicate the value of the sum of several shots. [1]

He itemized seven features to be patented: (emphasis ours)

1. In a game apparatus, in combination, a board along which a projectile is adapted to travel, <u>an obstruction upon said board for causing said projectile to be projected into the air</u> in a direction which will be a continuation of its original movement, and a target in the line of the trajectory of said projectile.

2. In a game apparatus, in combination, a board along which a projectile is adapted to travel, an obstruction for trajecting said projectile, <u>and a perforated target</u> in the line of the trajectory of said projectile.

3. In a game apparatus, in combination, a board along which a ball is adapted to be rolled, an obstruction for trajecting said ball, a target in the line of the trajectory of the ball, and <u>an inclined base or floor for returning the ball to the player</u> after it has been played.

4. In a game apparatus, in combination, a board along which a ball is adapted to be rolled, an obstruction for trajecting said ball, a target in the line of the trajectory of said ball, and <u>an indicator</u> for showing the part of said target engaged by the ball.

5. In a game apparatus, in combination, a board along which a projectile is adapted to travel, an obstruction for trajecting said projectile, a target in the line of the trajectory of said projectile, <u>screens for limiting side movements of said projectile,</u> and an inclined base for returning said projectile to the player.

6. In a game apparatus, in combination, a board along which said ball is adapted to be rolled, an obstruction for trajecting said ball, <u>inclined gutters to the sides of said board, an inclined base to the rear of and leading to said gutters,</u> a target, and screens for limiting side movements of said ball.

7. In a game apparatus, in combination, a board along which a projectile is adapted to be rolled, an obstruction for trajecting said projectile, a perforated target in the line of the trajectory of said projectiles, <u>pivoted levers connected with said perforations adapted to be engaged and depressed by the projectile after passing through said perforations,</u> and an indicating device adapted to be operated by the movement of said levers. [2]

Thus, he described:

1. the "skee-jump" to launch the ball into the air;
2. the target at the far end with holes into which the ball would fall;
3. an inclined board to direct the ball to the gutter so it could roll back and return to the player;
4. a score indicator that would register the number of points associated with the hole the ball passed through in the target;
5. the side screens at the target end, to keep the ball from bouncing out of the alley;
6. the gutters at the side of the alley that would catch the ball after it was played, and return it to the player end;
7. the lever that would act as a registering device to detect which hole in the target the ball had passed through so it could be registered on the score indicator.

The acting examiner in the patent office, Mr. Hyatt, replied [3], beginning with general comments about corrections needed:

Please find below a communication from the EXAMINER in charge of your application, Game, filed Nov. 12, 1907, Serial #401,786.

E. B. Moore. Commissioner of Patents. Case has been examined. The title

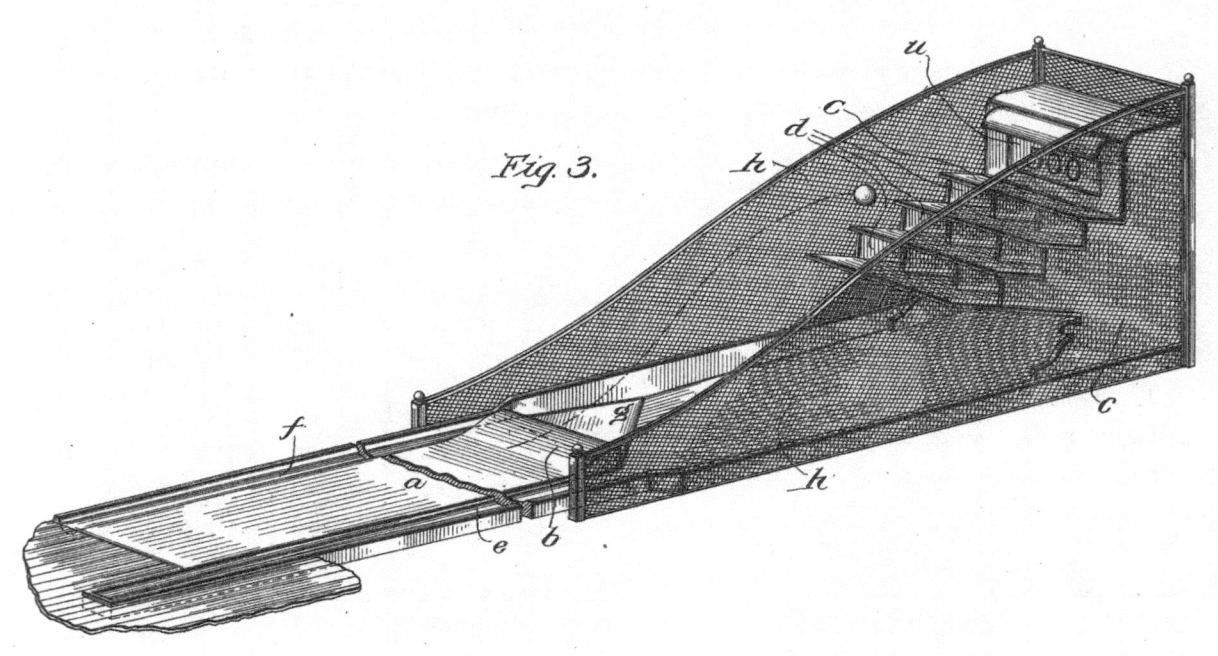

Early Skee-Ball game design
(Courtesy United States National Archives and Records Administration, Kansas City)

of the invention should be changed to Game Apparatus.

In the 5th line from the bottom of page 1, "Fig.1" occurs twice, and correction is required.

A fuller and more specific description of the construction and operation should be given than is contained in lines 4 to 7, of page 4. It should be brought out how the several levers bring different cards opposite the window.

The projectile is not projected in a direction which is a continuation of its original movement, and claim 1 is accordingly rejected because inaccurate.

Claim 7 does not clearly define the invention, and it is suggested that a target having perforations be substituted for a perforated target, line 3, and the words arranged in substituted for "connected with", line 5.

He continued, discouragingly, with the actual findings about each of the patent claims:

Claims 1 and 2 are substantially anticipated by Bush #836,561, Nov. 20, 1906; and are rejected.

Claim 3 involves no invention over Bush, in view of Rollert, #660,460, Oct. 23, 1900; or Kary, #754,456, March 15, 1904;

Claim 3 is accordingly rejected.

Claim 4 is substantially anticipated by Fahl, #787,161, April 11, 1905, and is rejected.

Claim 5 involves no invention over Bush, cited, in view of Rollert, or Kary, cited and Griebel, #768,600, Aug. 30, 1904; the latter patent showing screens for limiting side movements. Claim 5 is accordingly rejected.

Claim 6 involves no patentable merit over Griebel cited, in view of Rollert, and is rejected.

Claim 7, if amended as indicated, may be allowable.

R. H. Hyatt. Acting Examiner.

Although the Patent Office rejected six out of the seven claims, and required amendment of the last one, Foury was undaunted. Unwilling to give up all of what he perceived were his innovations, he redrafted the patent application, and resubmitted it with amendments.

He re-crafted the patent request into five claims [4]:

1. In a game apparatus, in combination, a board along which a projectile is adapted to travel, an elevated target at the rear of said board, and an obstruction upon said board, in front of said target adapted to engage and elevate said projectile in its flight.

2. In a game apparatus, in combination, a board along which a projectile is adapted to travel, a perforated target at the rear of and at the rear of and above said board, and an obstruction upon said board, in front of said target.

3. In a game apparatus, in combination, a board along which a ball is adapted to be rolled, a target at the rear of said board, an obstruction upon said board in front of said target adapted to traject said ball, and an inclined base or floor for returning said ball to the player.

4. In a game apparatus, in combination, a board along which a ball is adapted to be rolled, an obstruction upon said board in front of a target, said target, and an indicator for showing the part of said target engaged by said ball.

5. In a game apparatus, in combination, a board along which a projectile is adapted to be rolled, an obstruction for trajecting said projectile, a target having perforations in the line of the projectory of said projectile, pivoted levers arranged in said perforations adapted to be engaged and depressed by the projectile after passing through said perforations, and an indicating device adapted to be operated by the movement of said levers.

He closed with a justification for why his claims were unique, and should be allowed.

It is thought that the claims as amended will not conflict with the references of record none of which show a board with an obstruction in front of the target adapted to traject the ball. Bush shows a game table the rear of which is curved upwards so as to cause a ball to follow along it and be projected in a direction opposite to its original line of flight.

Rollert and Kary show means for returning the ball to the player. Fahl shows a means for causing the ball to reverse its line of flight and an indicator adapted to be engaged by the ball. None of these references show the construction claimed by me and therefore favorable action upon my claims is asked. [5]

This time, Foury's letter went to the Principal Examiner at the Patent Office, who was not nearly as impressed with his new claims. Examiner William Wilder Townsend was not an easy man to impress. He had earned two medical degrees, one from Howard University, and a second one from Harvard University in 1879, and had practiced medicine in Washington, D.C. for two years. He became a third assistant examiner at the U.S. Patent Office in 1881, rapidly rising in the ranks to Principal Examiner in less than five years. He took over review of the claim and replied on February 1, 1908, rejecting ALL of the claims:

> *Claim 1 is substantially anticipated by Wise, #304,286, Aug. 26, 1884; or German patent to Kiebitz, #46,070 Feb.6,1889;*
>
> *Claim 1 is accordingly rejected.*
>
> *Claims 2 and 5 are rejected on Wise, cited, in view of Walk, #797,244, Aug. 15, 1905;*
>
> *There would be no invention in mounting a board having perforations at the top of the construction of Wise through which the balls may roll, in view of the perforated target of Walk.*
>
> *Claim 3 involves no intervention over Wise, or Morgan, #722,603, March 10, 1903; in view of Walk, cited, and is rejected.*
>
> *Claim 4 is substantially anticipated by Wise, and is rejected.* [6]

Foury, however, was not a quitter. He responded somewhat forcefully on Feb 12, 1908:

> *Sir:-*
>
> *In the matter of my application for patent on Game, No. 401,786, filed November 12, 1907, and in answer to Examiner's letter dated the 1st instant, I hereby amend my specification by striking out claims 1, 2, 4, and 5 and by substituting the following claims:*
>
> *1. In a game apparatus, in combination, a board along which a projectile is adapted to travel, an elevated target to the rear of said board, and an obstruction upon said board, in from of said target, adapted to cause said ball to leave said board and continue its flight towards said target in the air.*
>
> *2. In a game apparatus, in combination, a board along which a projectile is adapted to travel, a perforated target to the rear and above of said board, and an obstruction*

upon said board, in front of said target, adapted to cause said ball to leave said board and continue its flight towards said target in the air.

4. In a game apparatus, in combination, a board along which a ball is adapted to be rolled, an obstruction upon said board, in front of said target, adapted to traject said ball, said target, and an indicator for showing the part of said target engaged by said ball.

5. In a game apparatus, in combination, a board along which a projectile is adapted to be rolled, an obstruction for trajecting said projectile, a target having apertures placed to the read of said obstruction, pivoted levers arranged in said apertures adapted to be engaged and depressed by the projectile after passing through said apertures, and an indicating device adapted to be operated by the moment of said levers. [7]

He then began his argument by emphasizing the single most important and truly unique aspect of the game, the "skee-jump" obstruction that launches the ball into the air, and followed it with a discussion of the other relevant patents, which did not include that feature.

The claims have been amended for the sake of clearness and it is thought that they do not conflict with the references of record none of which contemplate trajecting the ball, that is causing it to continue its flight from the obstruction to the target through the air.

Wise distinctly states that to play his game the ball is rolled up the front piece a of his board, over the apex and down the rear piece a1. The ball is not projected through the air but from the construction of the device, and from the description of the manner of using it, is simply rolled up one side and down the other.

In German patent to Kiebitz the ball is rolled up a band or belt from which it rolls to the platform f which carries the ten pins. He says that the belt b will diminish the velocity of the ball without causing it to jump as would be the case if the rising surface were simply rigid.

It appears from this that he seeks to prevent any trajecting of the ball, his statement to this effect could not be more clear.

In the Walk patent a perfectly level board is shown, the ball being adapted to engage the target while still on the board. Return chutes for the balls are shown and are common with games of this class. I make no claims upon this latter feature except in combination with parts not shown by any of the references.

In the Morgan patent the parts f, which the Examiner seems to consider equivalents of my obstruction, are for another purpose. Their real function is that of pockets to engage and hold the ball at certain stages of the game, they are so described and it will be found that they are numbered so as to assist in the counting. The ball is struck by a mallet and driven from one to another of the stops f and thence down through hollow post A to the ground.

<u>*None of the references so far cited have shown a game in which a ball is engaged by an obstruction causing it to rise in and fly through the air towards a target,*</u> *hence the applicant beleives [sic] that he is entitled to claims covering a game in which the ball passes from the player to a target first along a board and finally through the air. The precise details of applicants game as illustrated and described would be of no value without the main feature upon which, he believes, he is entitled to protection. [8] (emphasis ours)*

Principle Examiner Townsend responded on March 2, 1908, with some routine corrections and the following terse comments about his claims. Foury's persistence paid off in some

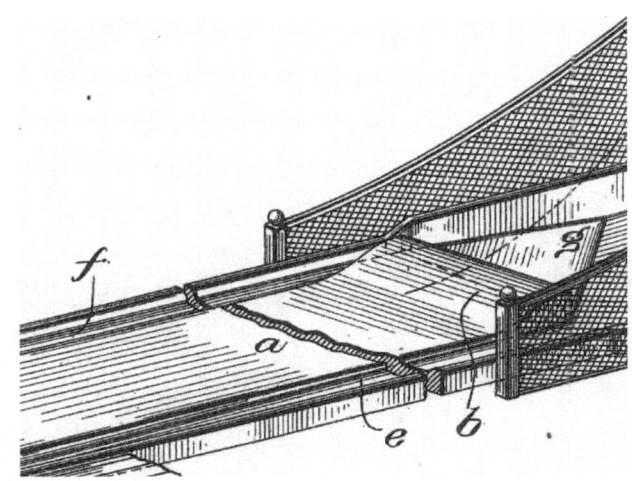

Closeup of the skee-jump or "obstruction" in the Skee-Ball alley.

measure, leaving two of the claims intact, but Townsend rejected the other three:

Claims 1 and 3 are anticipated by Miller, #809,715, Jan. 9, 1906; and are rejected.

Claim 4 is substantially anticipated by Wise, of record. It also defines nothing patentable over Miller cited, and is rejected. In the ltter [sic] patent the pins themselves are the indicator. [9]

Foury replied on March 17, trying once again to expand the patentable material, and passionately defending the uniqueness of Skee-Ball, particularly the obstruction, the "skee-jump" that launched the ball into the air

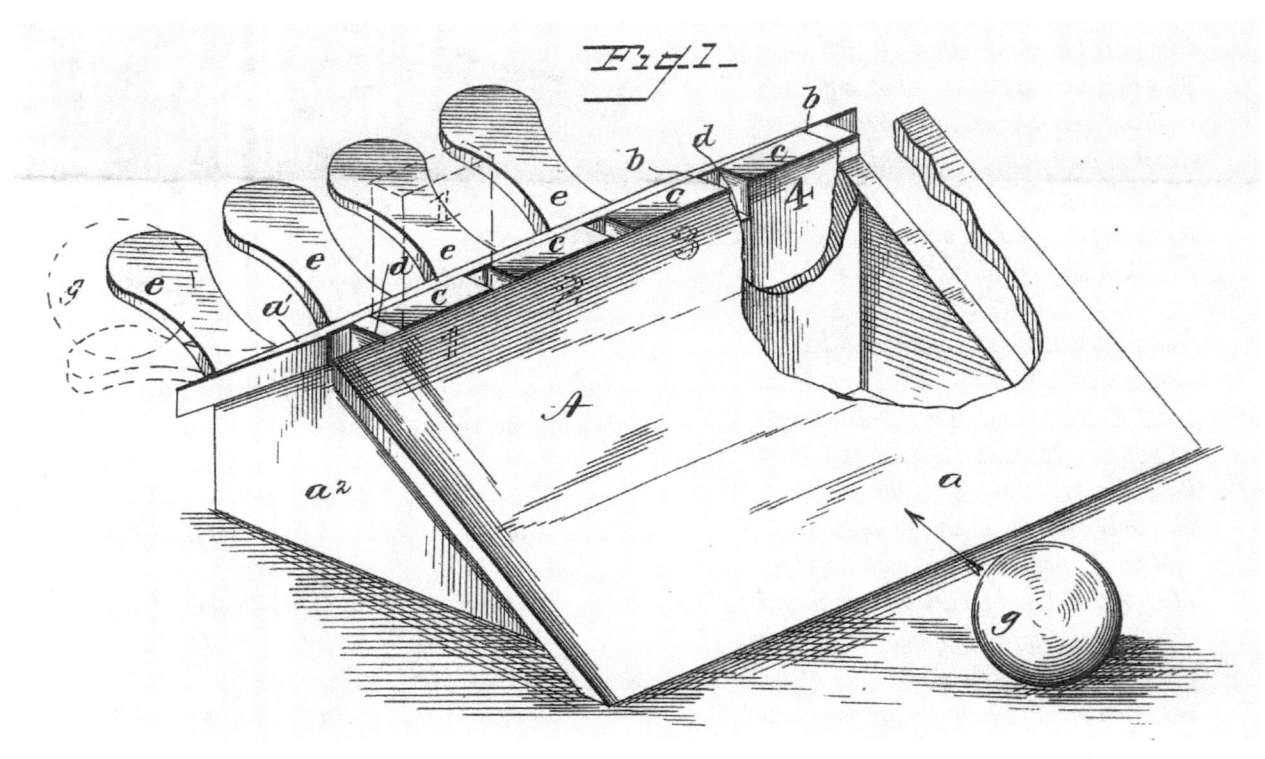

Detail from the Wise Patent.
(Courtesy National Archives and Records Administration, Kansas City)

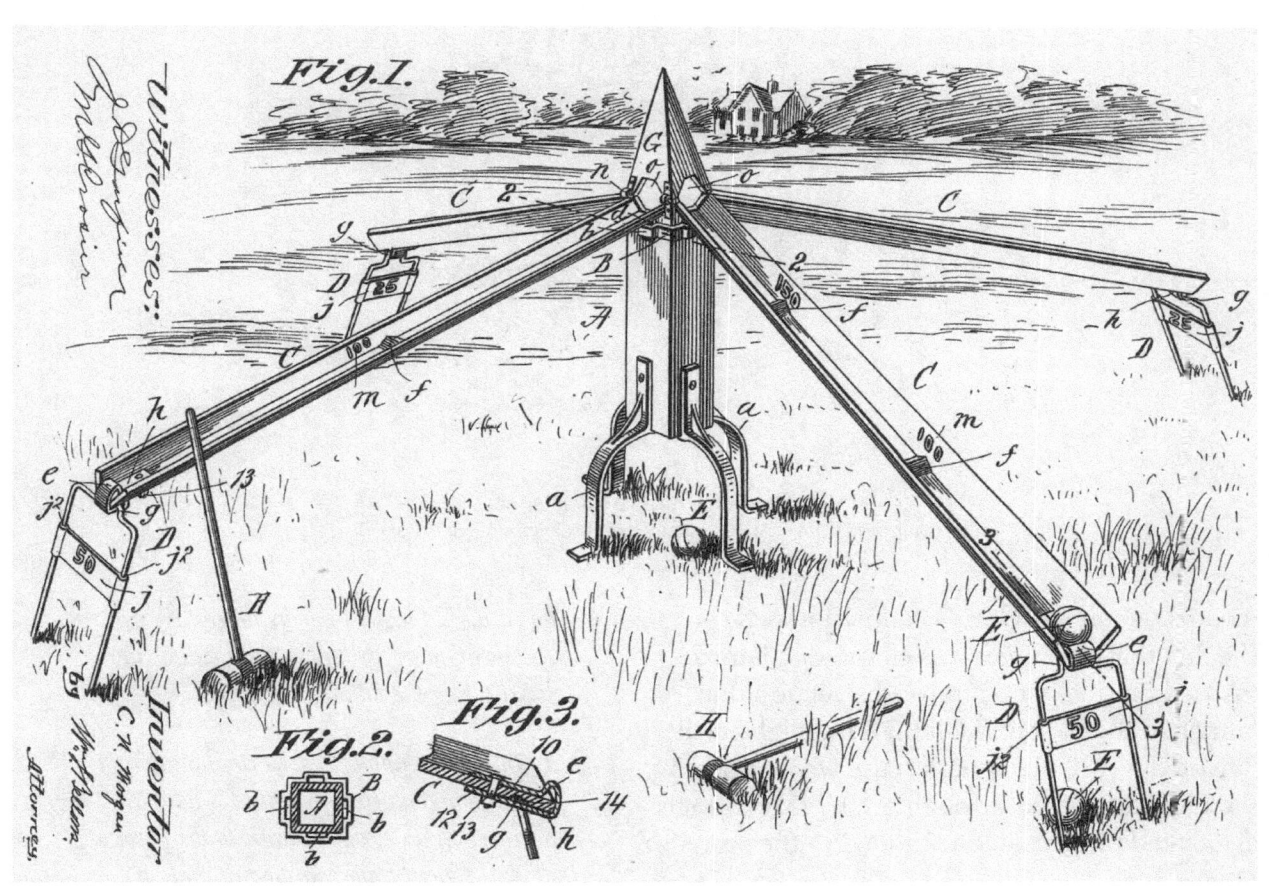

Detail from the Morgan Patent.
(Courtesy National Archives and Records Administration, Kansas City)

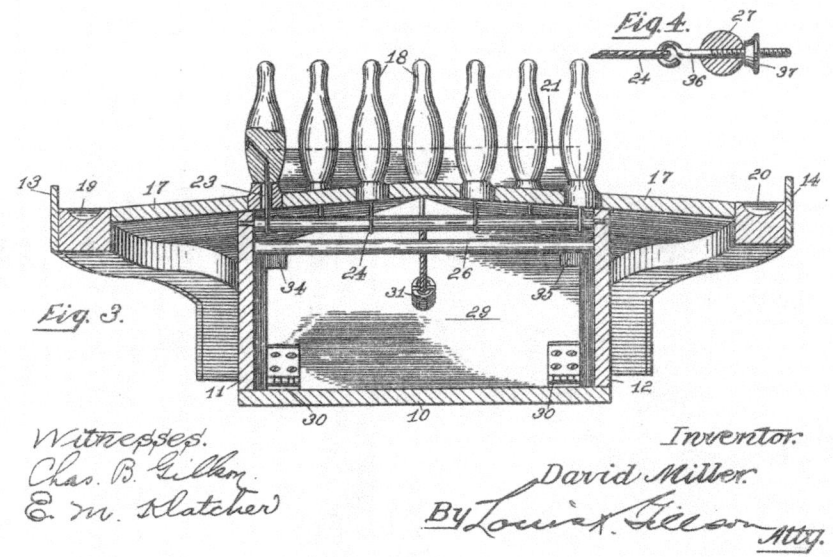

Detail from the Miller Patent.
(Courtesy National Archives and Records Administration, Kansas City)

toward the target. Here, Claim 1 focused on the fact that the target was elevated; Claim 2 focused on the "skee-jump" obstruction that launched the ball; and Claim 3 highlighted the "pivoted lever" that would sense which opening the ball had passed through on the target, so its associated points could be added to the score.

Sir:-

In the matter of my application for patent on Game, No. 401,786, filed Nov. 12th, 1907, and in answer to Examiner's letter dated the 2d inst., I hereby amend my specification by striking out the claims and substituting the following claims:-

1. In a game apparatus, in combination, a board along which a projectile is adapted to travel on an elevated target to the rear of and spaced from said board, and an obstruction upon said board, in front of said target, adapted to cause said ball to leave said board and continue its flight towards said target in the air.

2. In a game apparatus, in combination, a board along which a projectile is adapted to travel, an apertured target to the rear of and above and spaced from said board, and an obstruction upon said board, in from of said target, adapted to cause said ball to leave said board and continue its flight towards said target in the air.

3. In a game apparatus, in combination, a board along which a projectile is adapted to be rolled, an obstruction for trajecting said projectile, an apertured target to the rear of and above and spaced from said obstruction, pivoted levers arranged in said apertures adapted to be engaged and operated by the projectile after passing through said apertures, and an indicating device adapted to be operated by the movement of said levers.

It is believed that the above claims will not conflict with the references of record, none of which show a board furnished with an obstruction and a target to the rear of and spaced from said board and obstruction. [10]

W. W. Townsend replied on April 4, 1908, with more amendments and findings:

In claim 1, line 3, at should be substituted for "to" and the words "and spaced from", canceled; line 4, the comma between "board" and "in" should be canceled and the words and spaced from inserted after "front of".

In claim 2, line 3, at should be substituted for "to", and the words "and spaced from", canceled, and the words and spaced from, should be inserted before "said target".

In claim 3, line 3, elevated, should be inserted before "apertured"; and, line 4, "and above" should be canceled.

Claim 1 defines no invention over and is substantially anticipated by Miller, of record. Claim 1 is accordingly rejected.

Claims 2 and 3, if amended as indicated, may, as at present advised, be allowed. [11]

Foury made one more attempt to convince Dr. Townsend of the validity of claim #1, the uniqueness of the elevated target:

Claims 2 and 3 have been amended as suggested by Examiner - claim 1 has not been amended as suggested as it is believed that to do so would clearly put the claim in shape to be met by Miller, of record.

Attention is called to the fact that in Miller the targets, which are ordinary ten pins, are carried upon a board that is not spaced from the ball track but which is a continuation of this track.

In the Miller game the pins are not "elevated targets", in the sense that my target is elevated, they are carried by the pin table and the ball is adapted to strike their tops so that it may not be impeded by the pins and the cords attached thereto. In my case the target is separate and distinct from the table or board along which the balls are rolled. Broadly speaking this target might not be perforated but it should be elevated above the level of the ball table and entirely separate therefrom and it is this construction that I claim. [12]

Dr. Townsend was not impressed by his passionate defense of claim #1, replying rather tersely on April 20:

Applicant's statement that claim 1 has not been amended as suggested is not understood, unless it refers to the retention of the comma in line 4 of the claim, which could not possibly define a distinction over the references. The claim is still held to be substantially met in Miller, of record, and is again rejected. [13]

Finally, having gotten as much as he was likely to in the way of patent protection for the features of the game, Foury submitted his final letter:

Sir:-

In the matter of my application for patent on Game No 401,786, filed November 12, 1907 and in answer to Examiners [sic] letter dated April 20, 1908, I hereby amend my specification by striking out Claim 1.

Very respectfully

Joseph F. Simpson [14]

Foury began by trying to patent the entire game and all its features: The alley with the obstruction that launched the ball toward the target; the target; the screens at the side of the target; the slanted board that vectored the balls back after they hit the target; the lever actuator, and the automatic score display, which was originally a set of cards in a rolodex-like mechanism.

In the end, he was able to patent two features. The first, and probably the most important, was the obstruction, the "skee-jump" in the middle of the alley. The second was the automatic scoring mechanism, the levers which were triggered by the balls passing through the target to record the score for hitting that part of the target. It was enough to do the job. Foury would later be grateful that the patent was so narrow.

The Patent Office accepted those two claims and informed him of the final requirements for granting the patents:

> SIR:
>
> Your APPLICATION for a patent for an IMPROVEMENT IN Game apparatus, filed Nov. 12, 1907, has been examined and ALLOWED.
>
> The final fee, TWENTY DOLLARS, must be paid, and the Letters Patent bear date as of a day not later than SIX MONTHS from the time of this present notice of allowance.
>
> If the final fee is not paid within that period the patent will be withheld, and your only relief will be a renewal of the application, with additional fees, under the provisions of Section 4897, Revised Statutes. The office aims to deliver patents upon the day of their date, and on which their term begins to run; but to do this properly applicants will be expected to pay their final fees at least TWENTY-SIX DAYS prior to the conclusion of the six months allowed them by law. The printing, photolithographing, and engrossing of the several patent parts, preparatory to final signing and sealing, will consume the intervening time, and such work will not be done until after payment of the

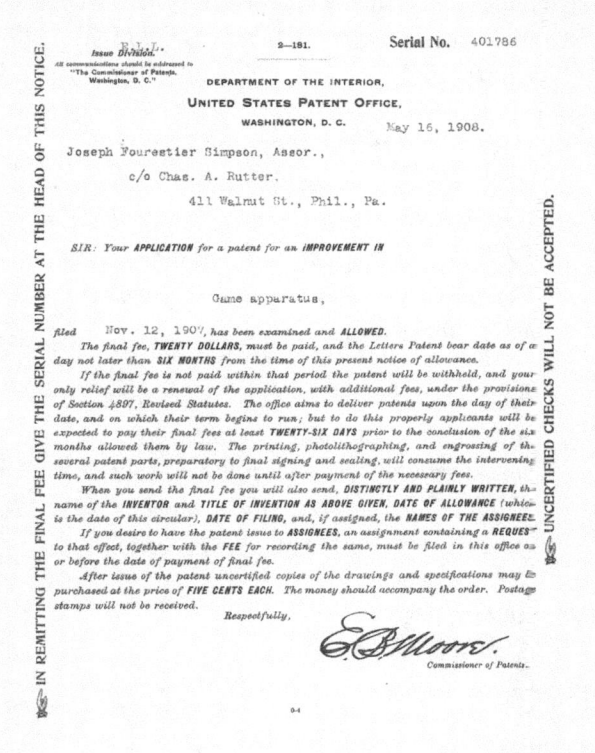

Letter from United States Patent Office
(Courtesy National Archives and Records Administration, Kansas City)

> necessary fees.
>
> When you send the final fee you will also send, DISTINCTLY AND PLAINLY WRITTEN, the name of the INVENTOR and TITLE OF INVENTION AS ABOVE GIVEN, DATE OF ALLOWANCE (which is the

Seeking Redemption

date of this circular), DATE OF FILING, and if assigned, the NAMES OF THE ASSIGNEES.

If you desire to have the patent issue to ASSIGNEES, an assignment containing a REQUEST to that effect, together with the FEE for recording the same, must be filed in this office on or before the date of payment of the final fee.

After issue of the patent uncertified copies of the drawings and specifications may be purchased at the price of FIVE CENTS EACH. The money should accompany the order. Postage stamps will not be received.

Respectfully,
E. B. Moore.
Commissioner of Patents. [15]

Finally, on November 6, 1908, Foury's patent attorney Charles A. Rutter sent a letter, along with a check for $20 to The Honorable Commissioner of Patents for payment of the final fee.

CHARLES A RUTTER
MECHANICAL ENGINEER
AND SOLICITOR Of PATENTS,
IMPERIAL BUILDING

411 AND 413 WALNUT STREET.

Cable Address: Rutter, Philadelphia
TELEPHONES
Bell and Keystone Telephones

PHILADELPHIA, November 6, 1908.

The Hon Commissioner of Patents,

Sir:-

Please find enclosed my check to your order for twenty dollars in payment of the final fee upon the application of Joseph Fourestier Simpson for patent on Game, No 401,786, filed November 12, 1907 and allowed May 16, 1908.

A one-half interest in this invention has been assigned to William Nice Jr and the assignment duly recorded. The patent is to be issued jointly to the inventor and Mr Nice and sent to

Very respectfully

Chas A Rutter. [sic] Attorney. [16]

The Patent was finally granted and published December 8, 1908. Skee-Ball was officially ready to be presented to the public.

The first Skee-Ball alleys were a far cry from the compact, 10 foot alleys of today. They were 32 feet long, about half the length of a

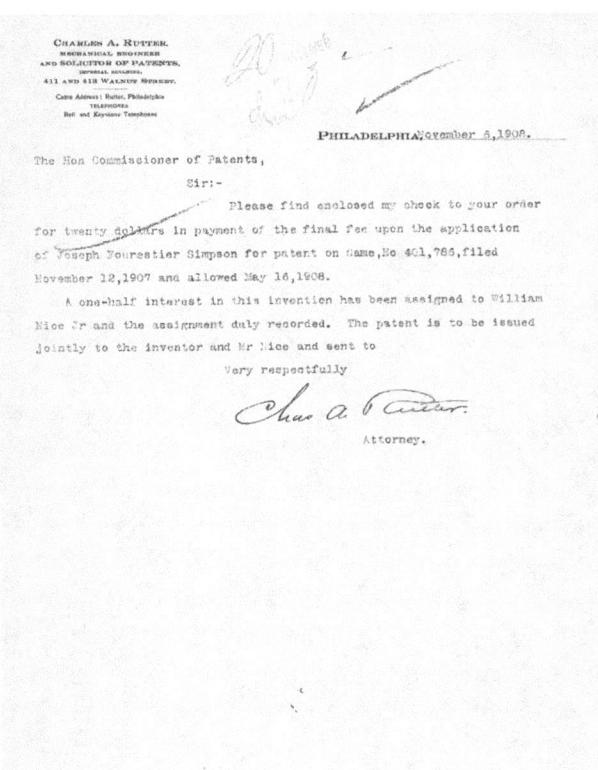

Letter from Charles Rutter to the United States Patent Office
(Courtesy National Archives and Records Administration, Kansas City)

Victorian era, but women would soon prove that they were perfectly capable of launching those balls as well.

All that was required now was a business to manufacture and offer the alleys for sale. This time, Simpson had a plan that would open the floodgates, and Skee-Ball would be well on its way to exceeding even its inventor's highest expectations—eventually.

That road, however, would have more than one obstruction in its way, and the path would be a far cry from the smooth straight alley to the target.

standard bowling alley. They were constructed in two sections, with the "skee-jump" at the mid-point of the alley, not at the far end, close to the target. It required some strength to launch the balls with enough energy to make it to the target. These early alleys were marketed as "a man's game" for a reason, late in the

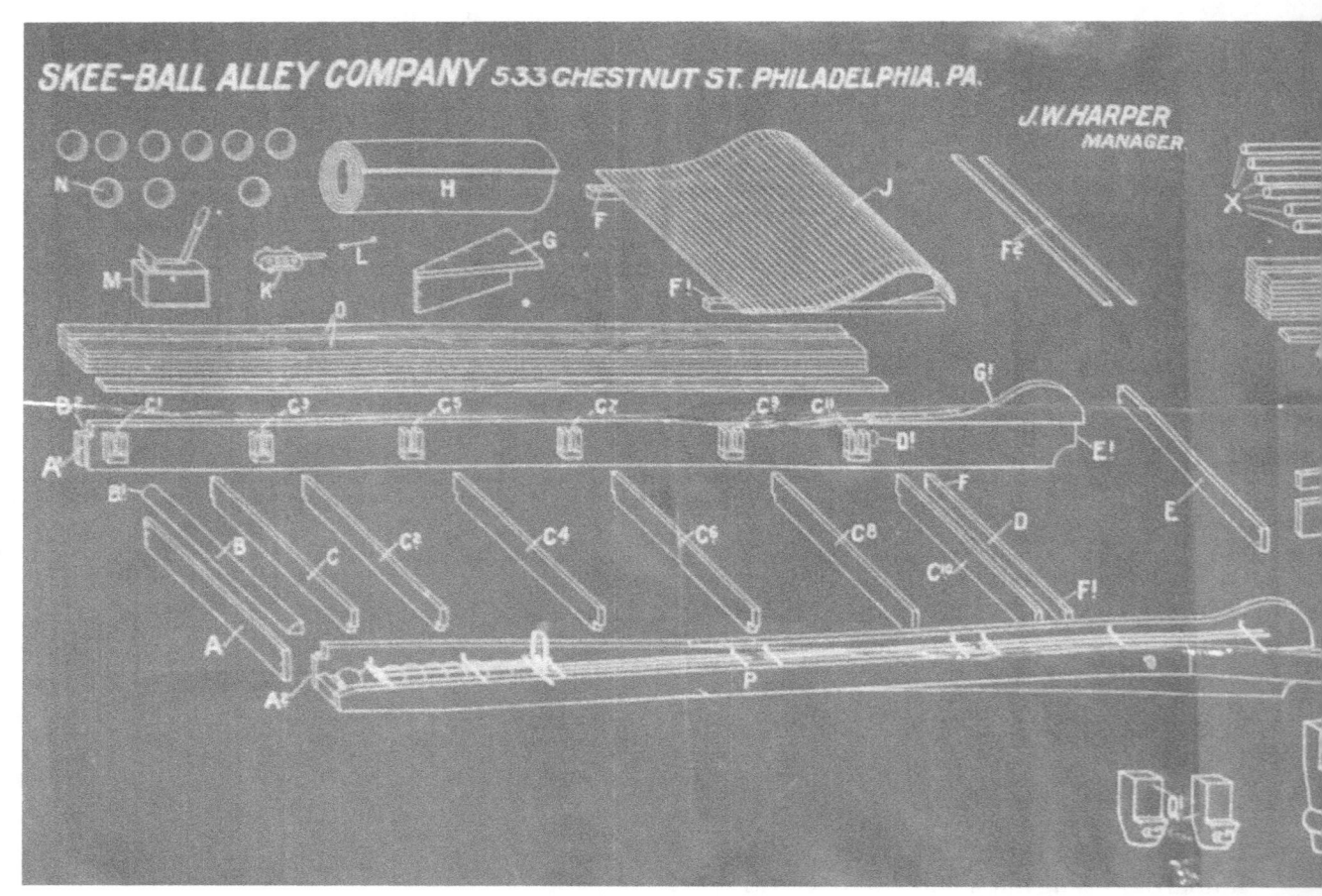

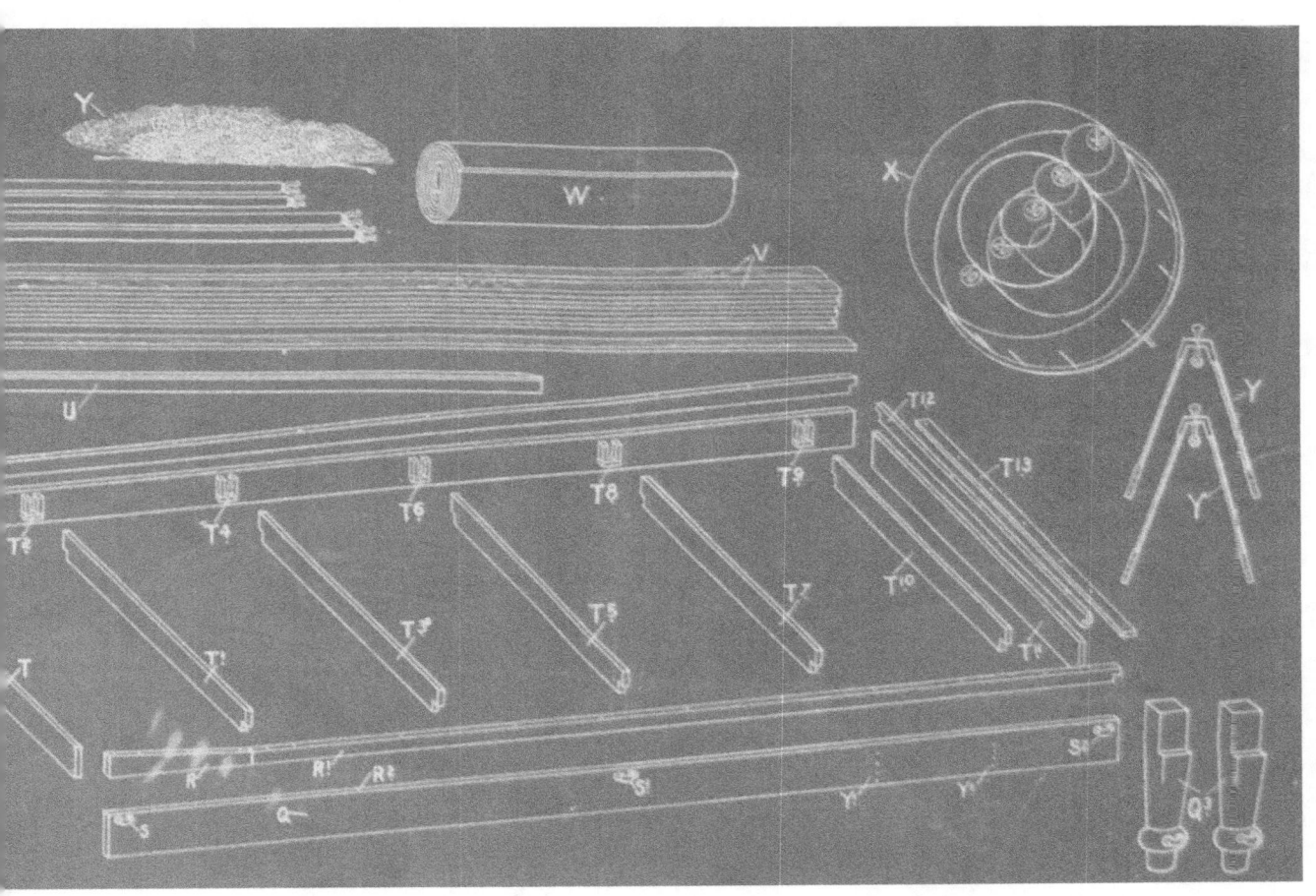

Skee-Ball Alley blueprint circa 1909.
(Courtesy Vineland Historical and Antiquarian Society)

Parts list for Skee-Ball alley, circa 1909, p. 1.
(Courtesy Vineland Historical and Antiquarian Society)

P – hardwood finished 7/8 × 4 3/4 – 16 ft long (when finished this would be a couple inches less than 16 ft. This forms outside of trough for balls to roll. The bottom piece is 7/8 × 4 same length with groove in center [illegible]. Cover with "2" poplar board instead of wire shown.

The sides of this section of the alley are hardwood – finished 1 1/8 × 7 3/4 16 ft. long, or an inch or two less.

Q hardwood finished 7/8 × 5 1/4 – 16 feet long.

Q 1–2–3 legs – the largest highest point about 29 inches (Q3) the lowest about 11"

Q1 – Turned poplar 4 × 4 or 5 × 5 – cut as shown – sides (Q) fit flush.

R strip 7/8 × 1 3/4 16 ft. to fasten cord carpet to floor, and bored 1/4" hole about every 5" apart to lash net to.

S – Pipe hangers to fasten pipe marked X with – see on legs also.

T. 7/8 × 5 3/4 16' or planed on top edge or all over when sections are to be joined have the center of E and center of T join exactly and fasten with about 2 – 1 3/4 No 12 screws.

Parts list for Skee-Ball alley, circa 1909, p. 2.
(Courtesy Vineland Historical and Antiquarian Society)

SKEE-BALL ALLEY CO.,
PHILADELPHIA, PA.

U - runs across alley to guide balls into trough or runway 7/8 × 1 3/4: beginning at centre post on left hand side of alley and running diagonally across to meet inside side of ball runway.

V 1/8 flooring to cover upper or further section of alley: 16 ft. length.

T 1 × 3 - 5 × 10 same thickness and width as C - 1 - 4 - 6 × 8 but 46 1/2" long (Basswood) (used rough on both sides to get thickness)

W Cork carpet 1/4 thick 4 8" wide 16 ft. long

Y - net made in 4 pieces - 2 sides, back & top: good cotton cord, mest 1 1/2 or 1 3/4", the back net should be one half again as heavy as sides & top.

X - pipe 1 1/4" wrought iron 2 pieces each { 2' 5" / 7' 4" / 8' 0" } the tops are castings that are fit in

Would have to explain target separately.

Parts list for Skee-Ball alley, circa 1909, p. 3.
(Courtesy Vineland Historical and Antiquarian Society)

Chapter 4

LAUNCHING SKEE-BALL
The Skee-Ball Alley Company

It was 1909.

Henry Ford had just launched the Model T, costing less than one-third what other automobiles on the market sold for. Admiral Peary and Matthew Henson were about to become the first people to reach the North Pole. The ball dropped in Times Square to mark the beginning of the new year. And Simpson was finally ready to launch the best, most marketable invention of his life.

At the time he finally received the patent for Skee-Ball, Simpson had just turned 57 years old. This time, he acknowledged he was not going to succeed alone, and he was not about to try to manage his own business. He finally seemed to realize that his true calling was that of envisioning and inventing. But he had a plan. His new partners in the Skee-Ball endeavor were William Nice Jr. and John W. Harper.

William Nice Jr. was three years Simpson's senior, the son of William Nice Sr. and Mary Haslam. The Nice family descended from the Huguenot family of the same name, who arrived in the colonies about the same time as William Penn. His ancestor, John Nice, was granted a tract of land in Philadelphia, subsequently known as Nice Town. William Nice Jr. operated sash mill, cutting raw lumber stock, with his partner John Good from the early 1870s to 1880, when his son Budd Good Nice was born. From 1880 on, he operated a planing mill, producing smooth dimensional pieces from the raw stock, and the lumber yard selling finished goods, until 1900, when he sold his lumber yard to John W. Harper. Restless in retirement, he became fascinated with the future of mechanics, and a new material: Steel. He bought the rights to two patents for ball bearings, and founded the Pressed Steel Manufacturing Company in New Jersey in 1902. When the purchased patents failed to perform after manufacture, he put his own mechanical genius to the test, developing and patenting a number of other ball bearings which proved more successful. William Nice Jr. was in the process of handing the business over to his son Budd in 1909, right after he bought a fifty percent interest in the patent rights to Skee-Ball.

John Washington Harper was a young man, ready for a new adventure and highly enthusiastic about Skee-Ball. Born February 27, 1877, in Philadelphia, he was the son of lumberman Henry Clay Harper, and Abby Young, with three older siblings: D. Walter Harper, five years his senior, and sisters Anna and Susan, three and two years older than he, respectively. The family resided at 812 Cumberland St. in the middle of Philadelphia. Following in his father's footsteps, he made his living the lumber business.

His mother passed away in 1896, followed by his father in 1898, so as a young man of 21, he was on his own fairly early in life. Short in stature, and somewhat stout, with piercing gray eyes, he had some experience starting at the bottom of the trade. One of his early jobs was counting lumber at his father's lumber yard, outside, in all weather: rain; the heat of summer; and the bitter cold of the Philadelphia winters. He was well schooled, and wrote in a fine hand, although he grew to prefer the typewriter. Aided by family money, around 1900 he bought the lumber yard formerly owned by William Nice Jr. In 1909, at the age of 32, he sold the lumber yard, and invested part of the proceeds into the Skee-Ball Alley Company, based on his enthusiasm for the game, and his belief in Foury's vision.

Harper and William Nice Jr. became principals in the Skee-Ball Alley Company, with Harper taking on the day to day management role. It was a compelling vision. Foury's prospectus laid out the entire business plan in some detail, including anticipated costs and income and finished off with the bold observation "at this point we will all be rich." [1]

The company was started on a shoestring, with Harper, carpenter Joseph Oyen, and occasionally Foury doing most of the manufacturing work, and sub-contracting out the crafting of scoring devices as they were needed. The alleys were hardly refined in finishing details and fine craftsmanship, but for the time being, they were enough.

Simpson remained in his role as the inventor and patent licensor, not formally affiliated with the Skee-Ball Alley Company as an officer or owner. However, a murkier and more entwined relationship emerged out of necessity in those early years, as two former lumber merchants and Simpson, the former manufacturer, inventor, self-educated attorney and businessman, attempted to sell the game into an amusement market with which none of them had any prior experience.

Early Skee-Ball alleys
(Author's Collection)

Seeking Redemption

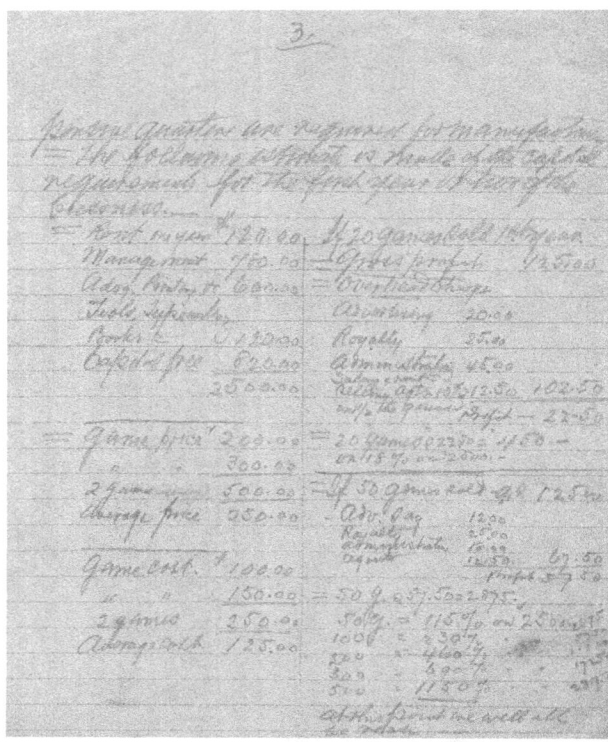

Part of the prospectus of the National Skee-Ball Alley Company showing cost of manufacture, projected sales and anticipated profits.
(Courtesy Vineland Historical and Antiquarian Society)

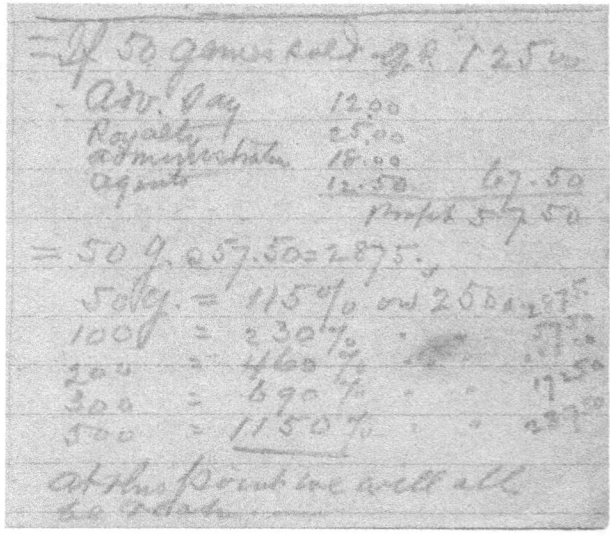

Closeup of the prospectus, and its conclusion: "At this point we will all be rich.--"
(Courtesy Vineland Historical and Antiquarian Society)

The first year of the business was off to a promising start. At the beginning of 1909, they had a manufacturing location in Philadelphia, and an office in Vineland. The game was not only fun to play, or as Foury preferred to describe it, "fascinating," but it also had powerful business selling points.

Play was controlled by a coin box which, when fed, would release nine balls. It featured automatic cumulative scorekeeping for the entire play of nine rolls, so no attendant was required to operate the game itself, saving on labor costs. This was business genius. The only thing an attendant might need to do would be to dispense tokens for high-scorers to play free games. Perhaps most compelling, it featured "fast play excitement" in that a player could roll the nine balls in about 45 seconds and play an entire game in 68 seconds [2], providing the potential for rapid play and high earnings.

The alleys would be sold under a restricting agreement that was designed to enhance the value to prospective buyers. Alleys were sold and licensed to operate in a specific town or region. The agreement meant that the buyer would have the only Skee-Ball games in that town, giving them protection from local competition.

The first ad for Skee-Ball Bowling appeared on April 17, 1909, in The Billboard. [3] The Billboard magazine was (and still is) the major industry publication whose audience included trade people who worked in film, legitimate theater, amusement parks, swimming pools venues, carnivals, and circuses. With little money to spend, and difficulty in reaching a broad audience of potential customers in any other way, this was their best hope, and was the approach used by hundreds of vendors and suppliers of the day.

The ad copy read:

> *For pleasure resorts, parks and amusement parlors. New and the most popular game ever invented. A most profitable and easily*

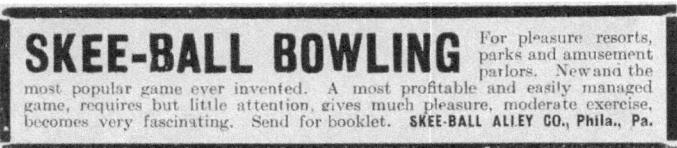

Advertisement April 17, 1909, The Billboard
(Author's Collection)

Joseph Fourestier Simpson posing with two Skee-Ball Alleys in Atlantic City, NJ near Young's Pier.
(Courtesy Vineland Historical and Antiquarian Society)

managed game, requires but little attention, gives much pleasure, moderate exercise, becomes very fascinating. Send for booklet.
SKEE-BALL ALLEY CO, Phila PA. [4]

It was touted confidently as "New, and the most popular game ever invented," in spite of the fact no alleys had actually made it onto the market.

More text ads appeared on May 8 and May 15. And on May 22, the same ad laid out with a line drawing of the game appeared. [5, 6, 7]

That was the launch of Skee-Ball. There was no fanfare, no band. There were no spectators waving pennants. They launched the ad as if into space, with full confidence that soon they would all be rich; just Harper, Simpson and Nice, waiting for the first response to come in from an ad in The Billboard.

They did not have to wait too long, because the alleys began to sell.

The first alley was sold to James T. Noell, of Roanoake, Virginia, on May 25, 1909, and he bought a second alley on September 7, becoming the first repeat customer as well as the very first customer for Skee-Ball alleys. [8]

Popular Mechanics was the classic magazine of popular technology launched in 1902. Do-it-yourselfers, and readers eager to discover the latest machine or mechanical devices for fun and potential profit made up that early audience. It was a great way to get some visibility in those early days, when they were exploring exactly who might be interested in buying Skee-Ball alleys.

In July, an article appeared in "Popular Mechanics" titled "Skee-Ball Bowling Game."

It read:

Skee-ball bowling, in which the ball is jumped or skeed into the pockets in the same manner as a skee-jumper rises from the bump in his flight, is a new and unique hand ball game that seems destined to great popularity. The alley is built in two sections, each 16 ft. long. At the end of the first section is the bump, and at the end of the second, which is enclosed at the sides and back with with netting, are pockets. These pockets are numbered from 10 to 50, and are arranged as shown in the illustration. The two pockets numbered 40 and 50 are cuplike and just large enough to receive the ball. The 30 pocket is the same shape but more than twice the size. The two small score pockets form the two outer rings of the circle. In playing the game, the ball, which is 3½ inches in diameter, is rolled along the alley. When it strikes the hump, it is sent

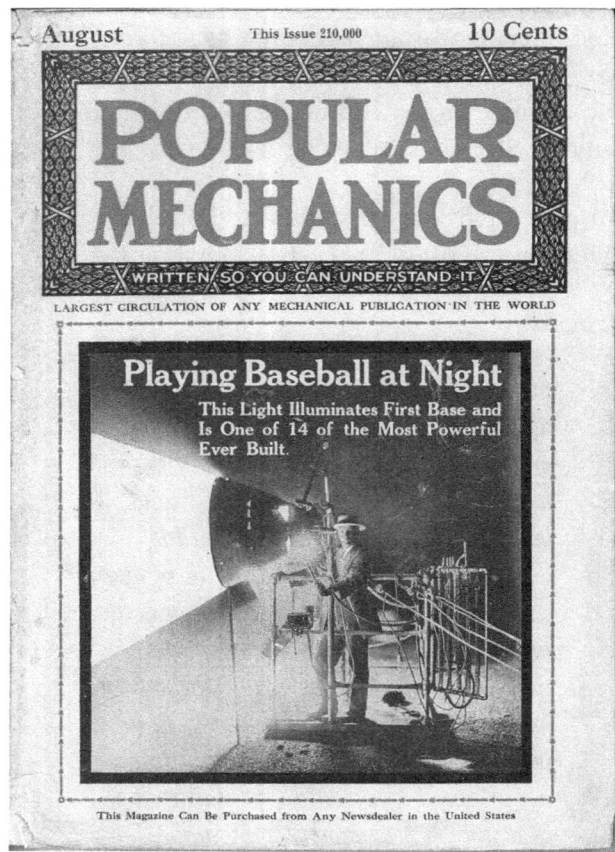

Popular Mechanics Magazine, August 1909.
(Author's collection)

into the air and if properly directed will hit its target dropping into one of the pockets. Great skill is required to consistently make a good score. The maximum score with nine balls, is 450 and after months of trials the alley score reached at the factory was 410. An electric device automatically adds up the score and shows it on the indicator. [9]

A new ad appeared in Popular Mechanics in August 1909, and ran again in September. The copy read:

SKEE-BALL

Very profitable. No attendants. A man's game. Length 32 feet. Balls 3½ inches. Stiffly bowled rise in air from the alley and make a range to the target. An absolutely new idea in the use of a ball. A very beautiful and spirited game intended for hotels and amusement resorts. Slot machine attachment taking coins eliminates attendants. Balls return by gravity. Send for booklet M. SKEE-BALL ALLEY CO., Philadelphia, Penn. [10]

On September 8, the third alley was sold to John Clifford Warren, a cigar store owner in Ukiah, California. [11]

Two months later, on November 20, Andrew F. Gustav, of Gloversville, New York, bought an alley. [12]

SKEE-BALL

Very profitable. No attendants. A man's game. Length 32 feet. Balls 3½ inches. Stiffly bowled rise in air from the alley and make a range to the target. An absolutely new idea in the use of a ball. A very beautiful and spirited game intended for hotels and amusement resorts. Slot machine attachment taking coins eliminates attendants. Balls return by gravity. Send for booklet M.

SKEE-BALL ALLEY CO., Philadelphia, Penn.

Advertisement for Skee-Ball in August 1909 Popular Mechanics.
(Author's collection)

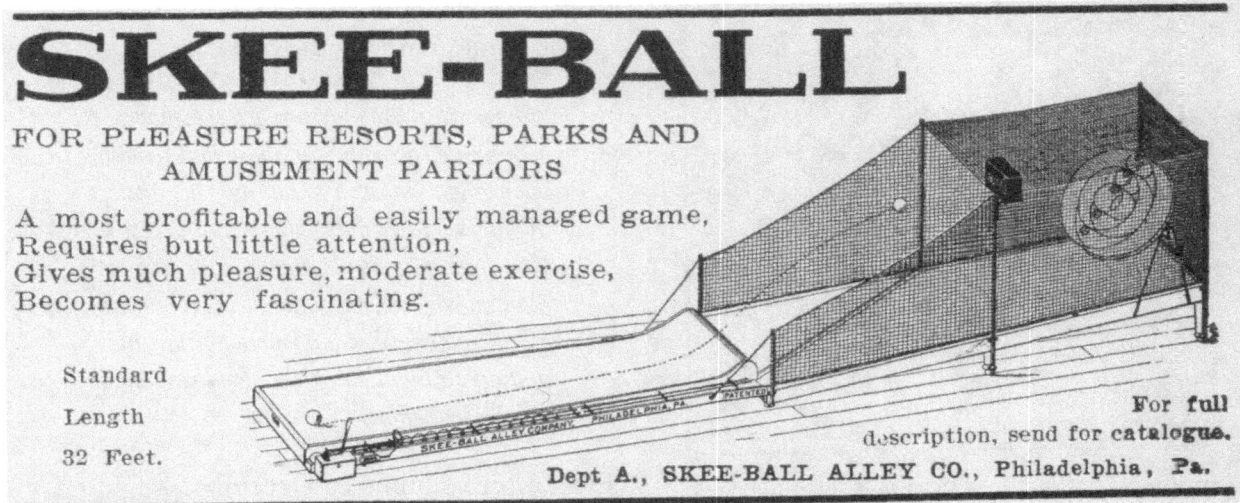

Advertisement with line drawing of Skee-ball alley from May 22, 1909.
(Author's collection)

The Beautiful Game of Skee-Ball, The Billboard, December 11, 1909
(Author's Collection)

Four days later, Mark Inman of Pana, Illinois, bought one. [13]

On December 14, F. J. Williamson, of Burlington, North Carolina, bought an alley, including the automatic scoring device, for $275. [14, 15]

On December 11, as the company continued to run ads in Billboard and Popular Mechanics, an article appeared in The Billboard titled "The Beautiful Game of Skee-Ball." [16] The article showed the same image of a man playing Skee-Ball as was being run in the ads in The Billboard since the 16th of October, and described the game in three paragraphs. This was the source of Simpson's remarkable insight about the elements of fascination that truly classic games have for the player:

> *"Games that are played when they have become old, are rare. Of those that remain, their origin is lost in antiquity. Our interest in games when analyzed is found to rest in three human elements, namely: the love of planning or cold calculation, the excitement of the imaginative and emotional faculties and the stimulation of the blood circulation by physical effort."*

Even more exciting, by December of 1909, there were two alleys running at the Steeplechase Pier in Atlantic City, a major tourist destination. [17] That was the most promising venue yet for the new game. In 1902, George C. Tilyou had purchased what was then called the Auditorium Pier. In 1904 he re-modeled it and renamed it after the amusement park he owned in Coney Island, New York: Steeplechase Pier. It sported dozens of games and attractions, including contracted performances by John Phillip Sousa's famous orchestra. [18]

The momentum was steadily building.

There were struggles in the background to be sure. William Nice wanted to keep the ads a little obscure, and he was suspicious of bringing in other people as collaborators and marketing partners, alienating potential support. He was also a difficult and sometimes nasty business partner. But as the orders continued to roll in, they finally breathed a sigh of relief. In December, William Nice Jr. and Foury filed for a Canadian patent for the game.

As the alleys sold, Harper and Simpson built at least one at their own expense, and installed it at Wildwood Crest Pier, which would be a great advertising opportunity at the very least, and perhaps begin to defray some costs. It was clear that Skee-Ball was going to be a big success.

The Panic of 1910

Just as the fledgling company was beginning to get a foothold, disaster struck.

In January of 1910, William Nice Jr. passed away unexpectedly of lobar pneumonia, contracted during the frigid Philadelphia winter. [19] He left no will. The implications for Foury and Harper would prove profound.

It was bad enough to lose the support of an enthusiastic investor. The fact that he left no will meant that his estate—controlled by relatives who had no interest in continuing to invest in Skee-Ball—now owned fifty percent interest in the Skee-Ball patent. After his father's death, Budd Nice continued to provide a trickle of money to the company, but nowhere near the investment required for success. Budd was now entirely responsible for the Pressed Steel Manufacturing Company, and focused on making the new ball bearing manufacturing concern successful. His half-sister Susan clearly had no interest in the game and looked forward to getting all the cash back in the Nice family's hands as quickly as possible.

On the other hand, William Nice Jr. had been somewhat of a problem. He had insisted on getting his fingers into every decision, having a say on how the game should be marketed, and perhaps worse, restricting the content

Steeplechase Pier, Atlantic City Boardwalk, NJ circa 1900-1915.
(Courtesy Library of Congress)

of the catalogs that described Skee-Ball to potential clients. He insisted that the play of the game not be described in any detail, fearing that, in spite of the patent, someone would steal the idea. The catalogs also contained no pricing. This made it difficult to convince many customers to buy alleys on first viewing the catalog, and requiring repeated contacts with them before being able to close the sale. He inserted himself into negotiations with potential clients and investors. He was also demanding with regard to money and terms of agreements, as were his heirs. This would prove extremely problematic to Harper and Foury as they tried to expand and sustain the business. In the meantime, progress continued as the Canadian patent for "alley, board and ball" was granted in February of 1910. [20] And Skee-Ball alleys continued to sell.

On March 3, 1910 an alley was sold to Allen and Sparks in Lincoln, California. [21]

Two weeks later, Fred J. Cossey in Benicia, California, bought a Skee-Ball alley. [22]

On April 10, Allen and Sparks bought four more alleys, and installed them at their pool hall in Lincoln, located in the foothills of the Sierras. They became the second repeat customer for Skee-Ball. [23]

At the end of April, Mrs. M. E. Lombard in Denver, Colorado, bought two alleys. [24]

Then, on June 1, 1910, J. E. Langford of Salt Lake City and Los Angeles bought four alleys, which were probably installed at the Saltair Park near Salt Lake City, Utah. [25] Saltair was the second major venue advertising Skee-Ball as a prime attraction. Saltair was a huge and elaborate resort, called a "Moorish Palace in Zion" built on the shore of the Great Salt Lake in Utah, 45 minutes by public transportation from the city center in Salt Lake City. The goal of Saltair was to create a Mormon "Coney Island of the West," intended to serve the Mormon community with a wholesome alternative to other amusement parks.

The alleys were selling. However, with half the profits going directly to the Nice estate there was little money to invest back into the company. William Nice Jr.'s money had been useful to launch the company, but it might have been too high a price to pay. In spite of the improving sales, there was not enough money to support the company's expenses, much less support its owners. It is not hard to imagine the intensity of their frustration, watching the Skee-Ball games pull in impressive amounts of money for their commercial customers, and yet, because of their business relationship with the Nice family, be unable to sustain the business.

By August 1910, the Skee-Ball Alley Company was unable to pay the shop rent, and had to move out of the manufacturing location in Philadelphia, into a smaller shop owned by a Mr. Edson in Vineland. The sorry state of the company and its owners was captured in a letter written from Harper to Simpson in August of 1910. As Harper notes, being rid of William Nice Jr.—who was in fact not nice at all, and an impediment to expanding the company— was a mixed blessing. Harper wrote:

PHILADELPHIA, PA. August 15th. 1910.

Dear Simpson,

I am in my new office - top floor of 533 Chestnut St. I got your letter this A.M. just after I sent you one. I enclose your two checks, and am much obliged for your effort. We have $1.61 still in bank according to my check book: I asked Budd for $50 a week ago but have not heard from him since. Mabe [sic] he is away. After I go home tonight I will make up a statement to date and send him and bill him again for $50. This account disgraces me at my bank, and I do not like it: this condition and my feeling in the matter would afford amusement for Wm. Nice, Jr, just so the account was not in his bank.

I think I had better do as you say and come down to Vineland Wednesday and put alley up, we can do it easily. I will go direct to our new shop and start right in. I sent nearly all the tools, and will bring some old clothes along and leave there in case I get a job cleaning out the stable for Edson.

As for my own funds I am entirely busted, and the only way to see our way out would be to force the Nice estate if it comes to that. His slopping over cut us out of an apparent proposition some time ago, and rather to be led along the same way as I was by Wm. Nice, I would drop all sentiment and use the law, it really may be necessary and I would not hesitate to do it: I should have so before, long ago. The old man liked to subject people and keep them in fear, but we know this does not pay, and we do not want to be bulldozed again by any other light weight scalawag.

If that memorandum was not entirely clear and satisfactory to you we can go over the books and show every item, but it would be for your own information. The amount you state ought to do much for the business; the worst is over and no more costly experiments are necessary. I'll try to make the 7.32 Wednesday, or one hour later for sure. I am certainly glad that alley is working in Wildwood. If we can't sell alleys we could

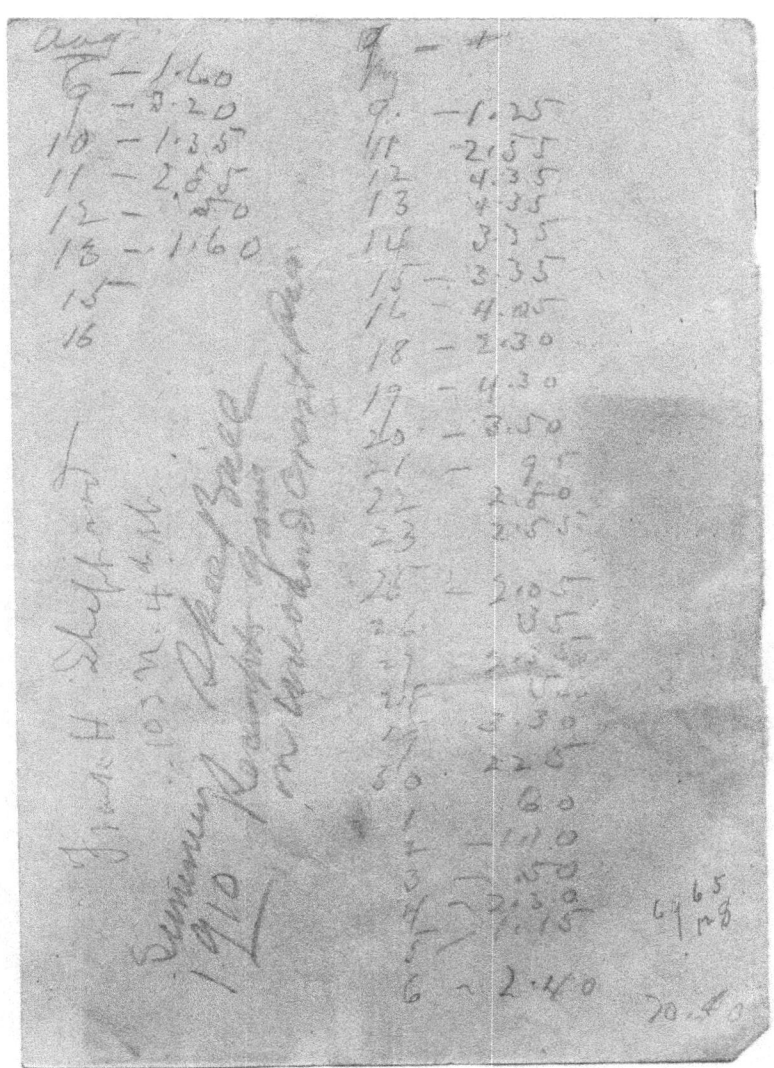

Skee-Ball receipts games on Wildwood Crest Pier, Summer 1910.
(Courtesy Vineland Historical and Antiquarian Society)

Seeking Redemption

Wildwood Crest Pier, Wildwood Crest, NJ.
(Courtesy Wildwood Crest Historical Society)

Saltair Amusement Park, Salt Lake City, Utah.
(Courtesy Library of Congress)

operate a dozen along the coast and make money, and the Nice estate could go to the D____

Yours truly, John [26]

Operating on a shoestring budget, and with Harper completely out of money himself, the company struggled to keep the doors open. They were unable to afford to more advertisements, and the sales began to dry up. At the same time, Harper was keen on finding a way to move the company forward. Without William Nice Jr. in the way, interfering and "slopping over," Harper began pursuing leads to find investors and sell stock in the company. But with the Nice family still holding legal claims and the purse strings, everything became more complicated.

August 25th. 1910.

Dear Simpson,

I imagine you have been to N.Y. and return; I trust the trip was profitable to you all.

About 6 months ago a friend of mine (I forget who it was) brought a friend of his in to see the game. Among other things this second party seemed to think we ought to sell stock for the SKEE-BALL ALLEY and I understood that was his business: I met this party later on the street and he seemed to be a very aggressive [sic] fellow. I have just found his card: Edmund Bury, 129 N. 20th. I have been thinking mabe [sic] he could work on our enterprise and dispose of stock for us.

I wrote to a friend for another party's address who has greatly interested in S-B, but have had no reply, and think the party to whom I wrote is away on a vacation.

I have a half notion to try to make the Nice estate put up their share of money, they would do so to me, and when people are not square they ought to be made so if there is any law for that purpose, altho it is a most difficult think to make most people on the level when it is beyond the general intelligence. I will be glad to do all I can for the game as I have done heretofore, but I must look out for a position as I have misappropriated so much money the last few years and now am at my end. Let me hear if there is anything new at your end.

Yours truly, John [27]

And a few days later, after Foury had suggested some more potential partners, Harper wrote:

I think without a question either of those N.Y. men you mention could make a lot

> *of money out of S-B. I guess those parks would be the greatest in the land for our game. I have the greatest confidence in the game and am positive that it ought to make good under the proper auspice.* [28]

Foury was not well-off, but at least he had his family to support him with a roof over his head. Harper, having lost his parents and living on his own was not as fortunate. His struggle with finances as a result of his involvement with Skee-Ball continued to worsen. He tried to get some of the money back from the Nice estate, having sunk more than $10,000 into the endeavor in the preceding three years himself, in addition to doing all the legwork and promotion. He was in dire straits himself with his property in jeopardy. In the same letter he wrote:

> *As for being short of money, I have to let the tax run over on my yard, some thing I have never done before since I owned it.... I have not been away owing to financial condition. I am now borrowing money to live.* [29]

But immediately, he returned to thinking about how they could make the business continue, and what they might do with Skee-Ball alleys that they still had stock for:

> *If the S-B alley could be operated for money in Vineland, give it to someone to operate on percentage; give them 40%; if it is operated in our shop give them 30%, or perhaps if the alley was moved to 1st floor, a person would be entitled to 50 to 60% if they paid rent. I mean if alley were moved further down town.* [30]

Harper wrote Simpson again on September 17, 1910, to report on the disappointing lack of progress in finding partners or investors, and still considering ways to make money from the alleys already built. [31]

As Harper struggled to make the Skee-Ball Alley Company solvent, Simpson remained in the background. Simpson was not a principal in the company, so it was not unreasonable from the perspective of their responsibilities. However, Simpson was increasingly pulled into the struggles of the Skee-Ball Alley Company, since his fortunes as the licensor were intimately tied up with the successful marketing and sales of the game. He continued to reach out to the business contacts he had made over the course of his career, and to potential investors they might suggest, as well as writing ad copy and material for the catalogs.

In the meantime, ever the inventor, Simpson continued to design related products, including a shorter alley, an outdoor version of the game, folding ten foot alleys and a "toy" sized tabletop version of the game. None of this,

I trust you do not let any of your friends read any of my letters. Destroy them promptly.

August 27th. 1910.

Dear Simpson,

Yours of yesterday is at hand. I think without a question either of those N.Y. men you mention could make a lot of money out of S-B. I guess those parks would be the greatest in the land for our game. I have the greatest confidence in the game and am positive that it ought to make good under the proper auspice. As my relation with the Nice estate, my account shows that I am credited with $840 more than they, and it is only right that I should have this money; if there is anything in my agreement with Wm. Nice to entitle me to this money I shall try to get; if not in an easy manner then by a little force. I do not consider Budd anyother than a rowdy and just about as safe a man to do business with as his father and I do not feel safe in my business connection with either of them. I find that W. M. Nice has balled up my Grandfather's estate in such a manner as to now cause the heirs much trouble and expense. As Curtis Baker has a Phila. office I should like to employ him to straighten out my affair with the Nice Estate should it be necessary, and would like to know from him just how far I can go. I have handed out $10000 and more during the past 2 years and I will now try to spend some of my time getting some of it back if it be possible.

Letter from John W. Harper to Joseph Fourestier Simpson, August 27, 1910
(Courtesy Vineland Historical and Antiquarian Society)

Give me firm name & address of Barrus Phila office.

I have been too easy a mark as you know and it may be too late to go to the other extreme but I shall try anyhow. Everything has gone the wrong way and left me without means except what I need to be very very careful. My opinion of men is that they are mostly dishonest rascals, and this opinion hurts me more than it improves to whom it is aimed. I would not want to tie up S-B and am doing all I can for it, but I do not want to be bamboozaled further by anyone by the name of Nice. If I assert myself a little more mabe Budd would lose a little of his self importance. Now don't think I am going to throw any cold wanter on SPEE-BALL, but I am going to try to collect, if it be possible, the amount of money due, long overdue from the Wm. Nice estate. I may not be entitled to it under our agreement, but I will employ Baker to find out.

I saw Ramsay yesterday and I expect he will look after the Lukens matter for me.

As for being short of money, I have to let the tax run over on my yard, some thing I have never done before since I owned it.

If the S-B alley could be operated for money in Vineland, give it to someone to operate on percentage; give them 40%; if it is operated in our shop give them 30%, or perhaps if the alley was moved to 1st floor, a person would be entitled to 50 or 60% if they paid rent, I mean if alley were moved further down town. I have not been away owing to financial condition. I am now borrowing money *to live.*

Letter from John W. Harper to Joseph Fourestier Simpson, August 27, 1910
(Courtesy Vineland Historical and Antiquarian Society)

however, was helping the endeavor become solvent. Harper reminded Simpson of that fact many times during these early years.

Dear Simpson,

Your letter was received yesterday morning just as I was starting out of the house to be out of town for the day or until too late to you see you. I trust you called on Nacke if you were here.

I received a letter from one of the parties I had in mind, with your yesterday: this party says, "the thing looks good but I am so tied up at present in other matters I cannot take it up."

There is a party at 5th. and Chestnut Sts. I think worth seeing, he has been in a dozen times and was more than taken with the game, and I understand he is associated with men of means.

There would be no difficulty in finding plenty places for the present game if it were well advertised: 'twould be better to get the old game started before taking up the new. The outdoor game might be a good thing: of course it would be cheaper to operate in the open, but we could talk about this later after we got the other started. I am sorry I did not see you yesterday, but when you intend to come to the city again, let me know a day or so before as I am jumping around now and want to look out for a position. I suppose of course you keep shop locked on account of tools. I trust you are well. Let me hear from you.

Yours truly, John. [32]

There was one man out of the entire amusement industry who was their best prospect for a partnering relationship, or who might be interested in investing in alleys: Henry B. Auchy.

Auchy owned the only amusement park in Philadelphia that was not operating at a loss. [33] Most of the amusement parks were "Trolley Parks" intended to make money for the trolley companies that owned them by the increased revenue produced by just ferrying customers out to the parks and back. Auchy was not a trolley line owner. He was a businessman.

Auchy's Chestnut Hill Park, also known as "White City" for the brilliant, clean white paint covering all of the buildings, was a different story. Auchy's primary investment when he first opened it, was Chestnut Hill Park. He was was determined to squeeze as much money out of that investment as possible. Even he admitted that "no attempt is made to cater to the high class trade." It was highly profitable because Auchy owned and operated not only the park, but all of the services, rides and games in the park, except for the popcorn concession. His park, however, appealed to a wide middle class audience who were eager to spend their weekends and their money at White City.

Auchy also owned the Philadelphia Toboggan Company that manufactured rides like coasters and carousels for his own park, as well as leasing them to other parks.

Auchy would be the perfect target for a proposition.

They had originally contacted him the year before, but the Nices had been controlling and less than enthusiastic about getting an agreement—another case of their "slopping over," in Harper's colorful language— so nothing had come of it. Harper, however, was ready to try again.

On September 19, he wrote to Foury:

> Dear Simpson,
>
> Your letter of the 17th. is here this A.M., the postal you wrote Wednesday afternoon, I received Friday morning. I guess you have received the letter I wrote you Saturday last.
>
> I am sorry we did not arrange with Auchey [sic] the last time we had the matter up with him: he could not have done any worse than we have and it might have been that the business would have been paving its way by this time. Didn't Budd say he would agree to sign bond such as Auchey [sic] wanted? I am under that impression. If so, mabe [sic] he would agree to do so again. Write to Auchey [sic] and say we have sold 18 alleys on very little advertising and received $3200.00 cash for them: tell him all the worst is over and he would only need to build a few alleys and put some money in advertising to do the business: that is, we are through experimenting and no more money is needed for this purpose. Say Mr. Nice died without a will and his estate or heirs do not want to furnish any more money owing to the estate being tied up, and I have no more. Tell him what you wish but do not say that we have been trying to get subscriptions - a good many things a fellow needs to keep to himself. Tell him each alley ought to net him $50.00 and if he did 1/10 the business the Box Ball people claim to do, he would make some money. Say we have sold 10 alleys since he was here with hardly any advertising. Say anything you desire but, "we have tried to interest others."
>
> Yours truly, J. [34]

He wrote a note at the bottom, "How about

Chestnut Hill Park
(Courtesy Philadelphia Toboggan Coasters, Inc. Archive)

Chestnut Hill Park
(Courtesy Springfield Township Historical Society)

writing the BoxBall people." Box Ball was the natural competitor to Skee-Ball, but a slower and less exciting game, and the American BoxBall Company was not interested.

Foury followed up and contacted Auchy directly. Unfortunately, the difficulty caused by the Nice family did not pass on with William Nice Jr. On October 10, 1910, Auchy wrote him a terse response:

My Dear Sir:

Your letter of October 8th is received and contents noted. After taking the matter up with my friends in reference to the Skee Ball business, they don't seem to be very much interested at this time.

After going to all the trouble we did last Spring and trying to make this a business proposition, it did not seem to interest you folks sufficiently to give us a satisfactory agreement and we do not feel now that you are in any position to do much difference, and therefore it would not interest us.

Very truly, H. B. Auchy [35]

Harper and Foury were disappointed. Harper was still intent to make things work although the stress was clearly wearing on him. On October 15, he wrote to Foury describing a different kind of business proposal, courtesy of one of his business mentors, C. J. Enochs:

Dear Simpson,

Yours of the 12th is at hand. It looks at [sic] if we would have to let Auchey [sic] slip. I had a long talk with Enochs yesterday. He suggested forming SKEE-BALL Exhibition Co. by trying to interest 25 people to the extent of $100 each, for the purpose of building and placing in one good location 5 complete alleys and operating them for money and exhibition. The above 25 people to be given $100 worth of common stock in a SKEE- BALL ALLEY Construction Co which would build and sell the alleys. He thinks he could interest 25 people under these circumstances in a short time and if the Exhibition Co. proved a success there would be no trouble in forming Exhibition Cos. in all large cities in the country and be able to sell many alleys. He has great confidence in starting the business this way and cannot see how it could fail.

Please hand enclosed check to Edson [the owner of the shop space they were renting]. It is my own as the company has not $10 in bank, and I am certainly tired of putting up the money, and if Budd does not soon do something, I will take the tools and give you

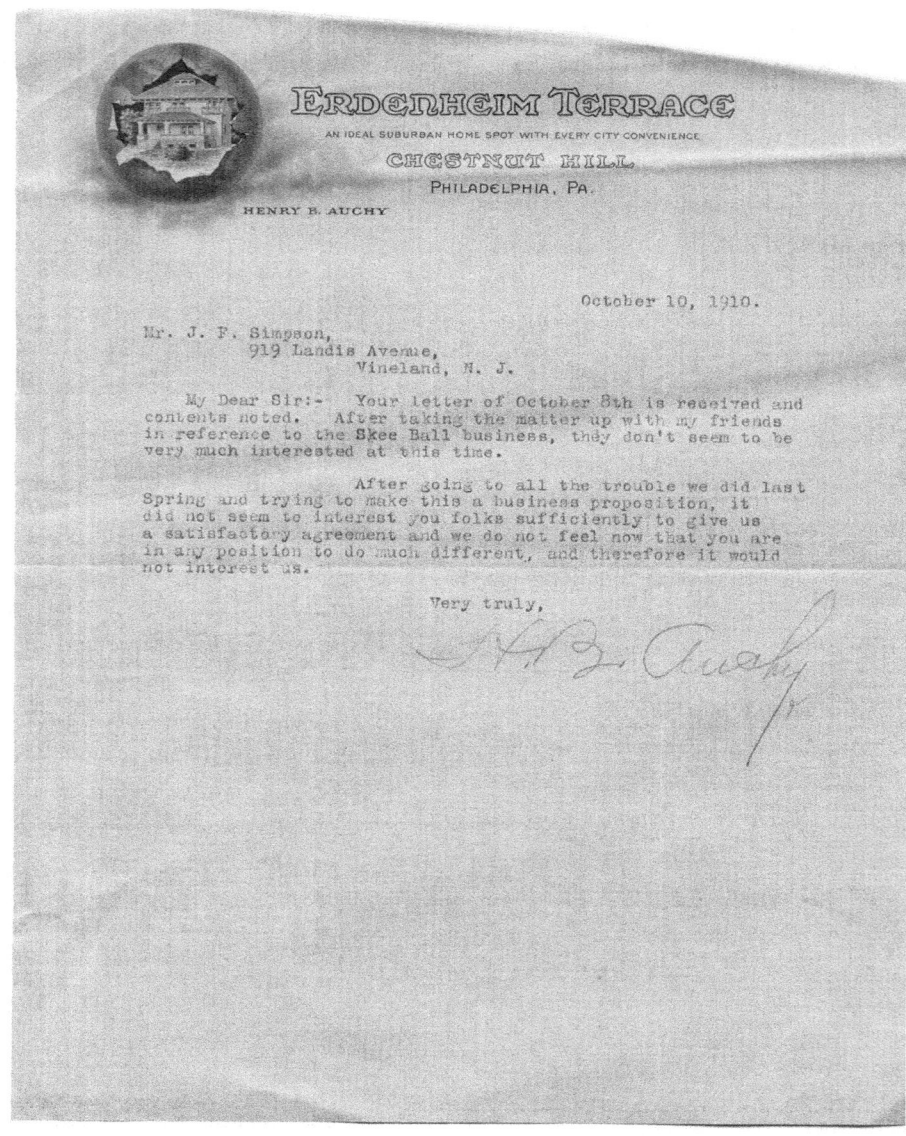

Letter from H. B. Auchy to Joseph Fourestier Simpson October 10, 1910
(Courtesy Vineland Historical and Antiquarian Society)

JOHN W. HARPER,
PHILA., PA.

October 15th. 1910.

Dear Simpson,

Yours of the 12th. is at hand. It looks as if we would have to let Auchey slip. I had a long talk with Enochs yesterday. He suggested forming SKEE-BALL Exhibition Co. by trying to interest 25 people to the extent of $100 each, for the purpose of building and placing in one good location 5 complete alleys and operating them for money and exhibition. The above 25 people to be given $100 worth of common stock in a SKEE-BALL ALLEY Construction Co which would build and sell alleys. He thinks he could interest 25 people under these circumstances in a short time and if the Exhibition Co. proved a success there would be no trouble in forming Exhibition Cos. in all large cities in the country and be able to sell many alleys. He has great confidence in starting the business this way and cannot see how it could fail.

Please hand the enclosed check to Edson. It is my own as the company has not $10 in bank, and I am certainly tired of putting up the money, and if Budd does not soon do something, I will take the tools and give you or burn the rest of the stuff. This business has nearly turned my head. Can't you give that alley to someone to run on shares, in someother part of the town?

Yours truly,

John.

Letter from John W. Harper to Joseph Fourestier Simpson, October 15, 1910
(Courtesy Vineland Historical and Antiquarian Society)

or burn the rest of the stuff. This business has nearly turned my head. Can't you give that alley to someone to run on shares, in someother [sic] part of the town?

Yours truly, John. [36]

At this point, C.J. Enochs contacted Foury directly to describe the new approach.

Dear friend Simpson:

Have been talking to Mr. Harper about getting Skee-Ball down on a more business like basis and suggest that you folks Organize a $50,000. corporation known as Skee-Ball Construction Co. to manufacture, and sell alleys, another another company Skee-Ball Exhibition Co to equip a parlor in a good location in Phila.

On this basis $2500.00 cash would buy five or six alleys from the Cons. Co, pay rent and and a salary to a young man attendant for one year which would cover the Exhibition Parlor, operating before the Public here.

To get investors to invest this $2500.00 to boost the game along, it would be advisable to allow them to participate also in the Construction Co. so that each investor of $100.00 in the Exhibition Co., would receive as a bonus an equal amt of stock in the Cons. Co.

The Cons. Co. could be divided up into a 51% control which control could be divided equally, or as agreed between yourself Nice and Harper. In addition Harper and Nice get stock in the Cons. co to equal the amt of money they have already invested. Then the 2500 Bonus to Exhibition Co. investors would leave about $15.000. Skee Ball Cons. Co. stock to be sold for the enrichment of that company and for Mfg of alleys.

With the Ex. Co. working and making new friends and customers for the alleys the whole scheme should work out for the benefit of the Cons. Co. and pave the way to get the business started on a large scale.

Was talking to a gentleman to day about the Exhibition scheme, and he seems quite interested, in fact desires to see one of the alleys, and I told him he would have to go all the way to Vineland N. J. which he seemed willing to do, he suggested sunday [sic] morning and while he has not said definitely, he is to let me know tomorrow, if he will be able to go sunday, as he wished to take a couple of friends along, so while I am not certain that we will be down sunday morning, yet I will just tell you so as to keep your eye peeled for us, and arrange your affairs so as to be able to show us the alley.

Don't know whether Harper said anything to you, but the above will give you a brief outline of what I have in mind, and if I had the time to devote to this scheme for a month or two, believe I could clean the whole business up, am however doing the best I can under the circumstances.

yours. C. J. Enochs [37]

Foury, patent holder and licensor, tried to wrap his head around the investment possibilities and how to pursue them, as he continued his refinements and elaboration of the game possibilities. In the meantime, Harper continued desperately trying to juggle all his responsibilities as the manager of the Skee-Ball Alley Company: promoting Skee-Ball; responding to enquiries from potential customers; maintaining the space and tools needed to build the alleys; scraping the money together for rent; and finding strategic partnerships and business propositions to save the company.

On October 22, he wrote:

Dear Simpson,

Your letter is just at hand, also one from Enochs. I read Enochs letter rather hurriedly and after reading it the second time I see he says he wrote you about his plan and intended visit to Vineland tomorrow Sunday, if possible.

His intention would be to work the business on a large scale, and merely form an exhibition company at the start so as to gain the confidence among the subscribers to such a company and prove the merit and popularity of the alleys. His idea is to interest any or all members of the exhibition company, in a construction company; and it would be working them in gradually.

It is raining very hard now and we can tell nothing about the weather tomorrow, but I will make an effort to see Enochs by noon today and learn what further information he has in regard to the party or parties who want to come to Vineland to the shop. This A.M. is the first I have heard from him or anyone coming to the shop or I would have advised you before. Enochs has been trying to plan out something for our good and I am very anxious that it will develop. More anon.

Hastily, Harper.

I would advise parties coming down afternoon & most likely I'll come along. I have had 5 enquiries within a week or ten days. [38]

Things seemed to be moving ahead, but the stickiness of their partnership with the Nice family, and Budd Nice in particular, was not making it easy.

In a letter on October 30, Harper wrote to Simpson about his progress:

> *Dear Simpson,*
>
> *I saw Budd yesterday. Relative to the plan Enochs advanced, he said we three ought to come to some idea of the proportion of stock we would be entitled each in a construction company, should an exhibition company be formed according to the idea and plan of Mr. Enochs. That is to say, we incorporate for an amount as a construction company, let Enochs form an exhibition company with 25 each subscribing $100 each or $2500 altogether (mabe [sic] less than 25 people would subscribe the above amount- say 10 or a dozen) and for each $100 GIVE them an equal amount of interest in the construction company. In other words suppose we would form a construction co. for $10000.00 we three keep $5100.00 worth of stock, give to the members of the exhibition company $2500.00 worth of stock and sell $2400.00 worth (the balance) (I simply mean this illustratin [sic] to form proportion - not amount) We might incorporate for 25 or $50000 Budd wants to know what amount of the 51% would you think you are entitled, what amount of the 51% is he entitled, and what amount of the 51% am I entitled. I trust you understand what I am trying to tell or ask you. [39]*

At this point, he was even looking for opportunities to market one of Simpson's more recently invented refinements on the game: a tiny, toy version of Skee-Ball.

> *Here is something else.*
>
> *If I can start a campaign on the toy game 4 feet and under, what royalty would you want from me on each game? I have a party in mind I would see on this matter. You may answer both matters as soon as convenient.*
>
> *Yours truly, John [40]*

Harper's last few letters of the year to Foury are telling and depressing. On November 16, he sent the last rent check and told Foury to give notice to Mr. Edson, the landlord of their manufacturing space. They would be moving out, and needed someplace to store tools and materials:

> *Dear Simpson,*
>
> *Please hand the enclosed check to Mr. Edson, and tell him at the end of our*

SKEE-BALL ALLEY CO.,
PHILADELPHIA, PA.

November 16th, 1910.

Dear Simpson,

Please hand the enclosed check to Mr. Edson, and tell him at the end of our 6 months we will have to make other arrangements: we would like to find storage room at a very low rent. I got what looks to be a live enquiry yesterday from a party in Mo. from whom we have heard a half dozen times before; he says he means business. I have had no word from Pudd about his idea of royalty on the toy game.

Yours truly,

J.W.H.

Letter from John W. Harper to Joseph Fourestier Simpson, November 16, 1910
(Courtesy Vineland Historical and Antiquarian Society)

6 months we will have to make other arrangements: we would like to find storage room at a very low rent. I got what looks to be a live enquiry yesterday from a party in Mo. from whom we have heard a half a dozen time before; he says he means business. I have had no word from Budd about his idea of royalty on the toy game.

Yours truly, J.W.H. [41]

Finally, on Dec 2, 1910, an exhausted John Harper wrote:

Dear Simpson,

Your letter duly recd.

The party I had in mind for the toy game thinks it splendid, but money is about the only thing that talks in such a matter, and I am not sure that he can do anything with it.

I have ventured just as far as possible and have had to borrow money to meet expenses and as for any more money for the S.B.A. Co., I must be excused. I have no money and on account of Bill Nice & Bill Lukens, I am just where I was 10 years ago, and would be glad to get a position at $10 a week.

Will you try to rent part of our space to the party who has the machine shop? Budd does not seem to want to give it up entirely and I cannot afford to subscribe another dollar. What I say to you I expect you to keep to yourself, my business is mine alone.

Yours truly, J.W.H. [42]

Harper and Foury focused on getting the tools and materials moved quickly so they owed no more rent, and looked for ways to eke out a little cash to keep them afloat.

Dear Simpson,

Your card was duly received. I trust the stuff can be moved by the 15th so we can escape the rent: if necessary I'll come to Vineland as you suggest on the day we move. I wish Edson, or any one who rents the space we now have could let our traps be piled along the wall. I wonder if Baker would buy that alley for $105. I don't suppose you would care to ask him. Is there a box that will hold all the tools except the drill press & punching machine? I'd put them in one box & send them to Budd he would like to have them. Mabe [sic] you could arrange to have someone operate alley in Wildwood & put up enough money to build a second or third alley: I think there are 2 new targets, 2 new nets, legs & everything but bodies & covering: if anyone put up $125, there would be 3 alleys. Would it be worth while *to mention this to Baker?*

Yours, J.W.H. [43]

And on December 29, it was clear they had given up on the grand business plan proposed by C. J. Enochs. As Harper raced to tie up loose ends, he also found himself desperate enough to reach out one more time to Henry Auchy with a new proposal, as he described in a letter to Foury. By this time, Foury had been pulled back into the physical work of constructing some of the alleys, and Harper had found it necessary to go to work for his brother's auto dealership, to keep body and soul together.

Dear Simpson,

Your card was received Tuesday evening, a day or two late; I think it was dated 12/23.

Budd sent rent to Edson yesterday. Will you please put all tools except drill press and belt punching machine in a box and I will send you shipping directions; I want to use some and Budd wants to use some. Will you arrange for and have things moved to that $2 place of Edson's you mentioned as soon as you can both of us desire at this time to move to the cheapest possible place. The rent Budd paid covers up to Jan. 15th. and we would like to be away before that time.

I think I will write to Auchey[sic] and offer to build him two or three alleys at cost; it would give us a chance to get rid of the stock we have on hand, and might be the means of getting the game started, that is Auchey[sic] could try it out and if it proves good he might become interested. Of course I do not count on using the slot or counting machines. If he agreed to do this it would give you something to do for a month and now would be the time. I am working for my brother, I leave home about 7 A.M. and get home not earlier than 7 P.M. 12 hours for $1.00 a day and it just serves me right. My success is like a crab walking backwards.

I will thank you to look after the above for me as soon as convenient. If Auchey [sic] replies to my letter and thinks favorably of proposition, I will let you know. I trust you are all well.

Yours truly, John [44]

Chapter 5

THE STRUGGLE FOR REDEMPTION
H. B. Auchy and White City

Henry B. Auchy was a self-made man. He wrote of his own background that he was raised on a farm, had little education and no capital. A short, stocky fellow, of German-American heritage, he was round-faced and jolly looking and cheerful. He was also a highly motivated and very clever businessman who understood exactly what it took to make money. In the 1890s, he had started with a small hotel in Montgomery County, which he expanded and then added a horse racing track, "combining outdoor public entertainment with recreation."

Soon after, he made the move to the big city, and bought a saloon in North Philadelphia, near the Northwest suburb of Chestnut Hill. A natural salesman, he developed partnerships with some landowners in the area and bought ten acres of land which would become the nucleus for Chestnut Hill Park. When all was said and done, Auchy, along with his partner Arnold Aiman, owned the land, the park, and all of the amusements in it, from carousels and organs, to the buildings, to the boats on the

Henry B. Auchy
(Courtesy Philadelphia Toboggan Coasters, Inc. Archive)

lake, to the game attractions. Although smaller than some of the more famous parks, it was easily accessible to the city, and overwhelmingly popular.

He also founded the Philadelphia Toboggan Company in 1902, which manufactured many of the attractions, including carousels and toboggan roller coaster cars for his own park, and the same equipment to be used in other amusement parks. He wound up a very successful and wealthy man. This was just the kind of opportunity the struggling Skee-Ball endeavor needed. [1]

Harper spent several weeks courting Mr. Auchy once again, with this new proposition. Suddenly, with no warning, on January 9, 1911, Auchy and his partner arrived in person at Harper's office in Philadelphia. They insisted on traveling to Vineland by train that very day to try to meet with Simpson in order to negotiate a deal. Unfortunately, Simpson was nowhere to be found. After visiting Simpson's home and checking the shop, they were forced to give up for the day. [2]

Harper agreed to develop a proposal to build out three alleys at cost in Auchy's shop, and give them to Auchy to run in Chestnut Hill Park as soon as the season opened. He submitted the proposal to Auchy's firm, the Philadelphia Toboggan Company, on January 11, 1911 along with the terms.

Dear Sirs:-

We think we could build nearly three complete alleys from the parts we have in VINELAND shop, except woodwork for bodies and cork carpet covering.

We think the alleys could be built in your shop complete for $150 to $160 each. That is what they cost us when building them at Chestnut Street, and we do not think they would cost any more to build in your shop altho it is much further away from any material we might need to complete the number alleys we decide to build. This does not include painting. We would not care to pay any storage for pieces, parts, or material left after completing alleys, and we do not include any rent during the building of the above alleys in your shop.

We would agree to see you the above for cost, and writer would agree to give his time to you without cost during the completion of the 3 or 4 alleys, but in lieu of this we would expect you to pay freight of parts from Vineland, which would cost about $11.00.

I have written the old carpenter who used to work for us, but have not heard from him yet.

I trust my suggestion gets the business started this time and the balls keep rolling for years.

We will write for quotation on 3 or 4 adding machines [i.e., scoring displays] Trusting this is clear and satisfactory, I remain

Very Truly Yours, [3]

Harper sent Foury the good news of the agreement January 15. Unfortunately, Foury, not realizing the good fortune that was about to fall in their laps, had mailed a registered letter to Harper, cancelling their agreement to market Skee-Ball.

Since running out of money the previous year, Harper had been picking up work with his older brother. D. Walter Harper had found his love in life as an early race car driver, piloting steam and then gas-driven automobiles on racing courses in Wildwood, New Jersey and other tracks in the region since the turn of the century. He had parleyed that daredevil career into a business, becoming a dealer in high end automobiles. His dealership, Cameron Auto Sales, was located at 2534 N. Broad St. in Philadelphia, and Harper juggled his Skee-Ball Alley Company activities with his responsibilities at the dealership. Harper was often left to tend the shop while his brother was away at auto shows. Because of the long hours Harper was obliged to spend there, Foury assumed that was the end of Harper's attention to the game. Their letters crossed in the mail. On January 19, Harper wrote back:

Dear Simpson,

Your registered letter dated yesterday was received by me tonight on my return from office. Cancelling the agreement is all right and I accept it in the same spirit as it is given, but your idea of me being finished with the game is away off, I am not finished yet by a long shot, and if you read the copy of the suggestion I made to Mr. Auchy, carefully, you will see that I am still anxious to try to get the game started without slopping over, that is to say I am trying to win Mr. Auchy's confidence in the game by giving him an unusual inducement. Our former talks with Mr. Auchy and Mr. Aiman were all SLUBBER, and if I can get his confidence in the business I am going to do so in the proper or what I think is the proper way or manner. The alleys tied up in VINELAND or anywhere else is hurting the business, and I have agreed to give up my job to help SKEE-BALL along. I have worked just as hard and earnestly as anybody connected with the game but have been jerked back every time I have tried to get next to someone with a halter. And don't

Philadelphia Toboggan Company Carousel, code named Excelfi.
(Courtesy Philadelphia Toboggan Coasters, Inc. Archive)

Henry Auchy, Arnold Aiman and others.
(Courtesy Philadelphia Toboggan Coasters, Inc. Archive)

Philadelphia Toboggan Company Duval St., Germantown, Philadelphia, Pa.
Courtesy Philadelphia Toboggan Coasters, Inc. Archive

Letter from Harper to Simpson February 2, 1911.
(Courtesy Vineland Historical and Antiquarian Society)

you make any mistake about the amount of money I have put into S-B; it was all mine earned in a hard honest manner. I was let into the game in a spongey manner, and you bet your life if I can get Skee-Ball started I will be very glad to do so for your benefit as well as mine. I simply do not watt want to pay rent in Vineland if the suggestion I made to Mr. A can do us some good; it may do us harm but the sooner we know the good or bad, the better. I do not misunderstand your letter; you misunderstand mine.

I got the enclosed enquiry tonight with your letter. Return it early for answer. I guess you know by this time S-B is no good in Vineland. Let me know if Edson got rent from Budd. My brother is in show at Broad and Callowhill; I keep the shop. Come up anytime but let me know beforehand.

Yours very truly, John. [4]

Heartened again, and anxious for one more chance at success, Foury agreed. On February 2, Harper again wrote to him that the deal was on.

Dear Simpson,

I just heard from Mr. Auchy who says,"You can send your goods to my factory Duval St.,Gtn. and the Park Company will pay for the completion of the three alleys, as you mentioned, and the balance we will pay you for the actual cost of the material shipped,however it is understood the alleys are not to exceed $160.00 each,complete, in cost to us.

I will say there will be no charges for rent for the storage of any material which you mention to complete alleys(?)

If this is satisfactory to you, you can make shipment at once".

Will you please [advise me of the] rate of freight via the P. R. R. from VINELAND to Chelten Ave. Frt. Sta. Germantown, and can you arrange this stock for shipment alone or shall I hunt up Joseph to help you? Look the situation over and let me know as soon as convenient if the alleys and parts are in such shape that you can handle them alone or will you need Joseph or get a man down there to help get in shipping ??? There is a small home made type writing desk that you might express to me here at this address. As long as I expect to go to Auchy's factory and work on alleys, the tools can be shipped wit the other stock. If this is not clear, let me know. You can use the stencils to mark crates and etc. I will send you definite name and address within a short time. I think Budd sent rent to Edson; you might this out from

Edson. I hope this means business.

J.W.H. [5]

After scrambling to pack and ship the tools and the alley parts, they ran into the next problem: Getting the score adding mechanisms made, without which the alleys would be crippled. Their normal supplier of the adding mechanisms, a fellow named Bradshaw, was suddenly too busy or too disinterested. A very frustrated and angry John W. Harper wrote:

> *…That fellow Bradshaw in my mind is a yellow pup, and has been ever since Nice wanted him to make the adding machines. My business relations with him during the entire time he was the building the machines was indeed HELL. Here we have a fair chance to see if the alleys will take well with the public, and that damn fool says he is filled with work until fall he also says he has no model or blue prints of the machines he built for us: now I supposed I am to have merry HELL again to have someone else build some other idea for a machine (trouble, delay, and expense). Skee-Ball has been a rotten proposition throughout owing to the most excellently ignorant yellow bull pups that have tried to do work for us on some of the parts. The fellows who have tried to make parts for us correspond to the most likely ability of about 90% of those who have encuired [sic] for alleys. Mankind is about the same throughout. I was just thinking you once took a rough drawing of the adding machine [sic] and with the model (your own) you might be able to build a machine equal to the one Bradshaw built. How about it? If you have the drawing. Mr. Auchy and Aiman want the alleys complete and this question of adding machine may knock us out again.*
>
> *My brother is somewhat short handed at the shop and most likely I will send Jos. down to help you. I trust you can so arrange the work that he will not have to stay over night. I expect he will call on me tomorrow Wednesday: I think he can come down any day. I will write you again tomorrow sometime.*
>
> *Yours very truly, John[6]*

Finally, with the adding mechanisms being produced by another vendor, all of the tools and materials shipped to Auchy's facility, and their carpenter, Joseph Oyen, finally available to start work, the plan was coming together. That day, Foury received news that his beloved aunt Sophia was gravely ill. Harper wrote a personal note in longhand, on the old stationary left over from his lumber company:

Dear Simpson

Your card received. I am so sorry to hear about your aunt; she is certainly a very dear old lady and more active and entertaining for her wonderful age than anyone I ever met: her mind was just as bright and clear as a person half her years. If this illness means her passing beyond, I certainly trust it is without pain, as I am sure her sweet character and disposition deserves a quiet and comfortable end.

If the earthly bond is canceled, let me know immediately.

We are getting along fairly well with the alleys. The day you came to Germantown, I was about 1 hour late or I would have seen you.

I trust your mother and sister are well as can be expected under their sorrow and care.

Yours very truly, John [7]

Foury's Aunt Sophia passed away at the end of March. While the alleys were being assembled in early April, what should have been an exciting and happy time, Foury was grieving and deeply depressed. And he, too, was out of money, and embarrassed as a grown man that he was depending on his family for room and board.

On June 6, what should have been a time of celebration and optimism, with Skee-Ball finally finding a home and a base of operations, it was a muted victory. Harper again wrote to Foury with a suggestion:

Dear Simpson,

Just been thinking you might care to operate the alleys at Chestnut Hill this season. The fellow there is tired his job and I SUPPOSE you could make a decent living there and the entire change of your condition might be a help to you and also to the business.

If this seems half satisfactory to you under your present condition I would be glad to take the matter up with Auchy for you, or you can do it yourself.

I do not know what the job would pay but I suppose whatever it would be would help you in more ways than one.

If there is anything in this suggestion let me know at once. Yours truly, J.W.H. [8]

In the meantime, Harper had been meeting with Budd Nice, trying to work out a way to sell out of the business, and find a less stressful way to contribute to moving the game forward.

JOHN W. HARPER
SUCCESSOR TO WM. NICE, JR.

..Lumber..

319 TO 327 MONTROSE STREET

TELEPHONE CONNECTION   PHILADELPHIA 3/31/ 1911

Dear Simpson,

Your card received. I am sorry to hear about your aunt; she is certainly a very dear old lady, and more active and entertaining for her wonderful age than any one I ever met: her mind was just as bright and clear as a person half her years. If this illness means her passing beyond, I certainly trust it is without pain, as I am sure her sweet character and disposition deserves a quick and comfortable end.

If the earthly bond is cassed, let me know immediately.

We are getting along fairly well with the alleys. The day you came to Germantown, I was about 1 hour late or I would have seen you.

I trust your mother and sisters are well as can be expected under their sorrow and care.

Yours very truly, John

Letter from John W. Harper to Joseph Fourestier Simpson,
March 31, 1911.
(Courtesy Vineland Historical and Antiquarian Society)

SKEE-BALL ALLEY CO.,
PHILADELPHIA, PA.

June 6,1911.

Dear Simpson,

    Just been thinking you might care to operate the alleys at Chestnut Hill this season. The fellow there is tired of his job and I SUPPOSE you could make a decent living there and the entire change of your condition might be a help to you and also to the business.

If this seems half satisfactory to you under your present condition I would be glad to take the matter up with Auchy for you, or you can do so yourself.

I do not know what the job would pay but I suppose whatever it would be would help you in more ways than one.

If there is anything in this suggestion let me know at once.

                    Yours truly,
                      J.W.H.

Letter from John W. Harper to Joseph Fourestier Simpson,
June 6, 1911.
(Courtesy Vineland Historical and Antiquarian Society)

SKEE-BALL ALLEY CO.,
PHILADELPHIA, PA.

June 14th, 1911.

Dear Simpson,

    Yours received. I saw Mr. Nice yesterday. Mr. Nice and I would agree to sell the portions of the interests we hold in the United States for ten thousand (10000) dollars cash and a royalty of $5 each on full sized alleys.

    You know I feel a great interest in the game and if this matter is carried out I would be glad to hold some position with the business if you could arrange it, as I understand the details thououghly and believe I would be of service.

    I enclose a letter from Sparks which Mr. Nice handed me. What do you think of this? I myself have not entire confidence in Sparks, but it is true he is in touch with the Park people.

Sincerely yours,

John.

Letter from John W. Harper to Joseph Fourestier Simpson,
June 14, 1911.
(Courtesy Vineland Historical and Antiquarian Society)

Dear Simpson,

Yours received. I saw Mr. Nice yesterday. Mr. Nice and I would agree to sell the portions of the interests we hold in the United States for ten thousand (10000) dollars cash and a royalty of $5 each on full sized alleys.

You know I feel a great interest in the game and if this matter is carried out I would be glad to hold some position with the business if you could arrange it, as I understand the details thoroughly and believe I would be of service.

I enclose a letter from Sparks which Mr. Nice handed me. What do you think of this? I myself have not entire confidence in Sparks, but it is true he is in touch with the Park people.

Sincerely yours, John. [9]

Simpson, also out of cash and out of energy, demurred for the time being. But he suddenly needed to take up a much more active role in the business if it was to survive or even transition. And the difficulties seemed to pile up.

The one alley that they had provided on speculation to Philip Baker, the owner of the Pier at Wildwood Crest, was still operating. Suddenly, in June, manager William F. Boogar abruptly informed Foury that due to business changes, he needed to remove it at once or he would have to dispose of it. [10]

In desperation, Simpson again contacted Holcomb and Hoke, the owners of the popular alley game Box Ball, Skee-Ball's closest competitor, to see if they would have an interest in buying out the Nice family interest in the game, or controlling the entire thing.

J. J. Holcomb was a former traveling salesman, and his partner Fred Hoke was a former hardware store employee. The two had met on one of Holcomb's trips to Indianapolis, and decided that if there were ever an opportunity, the two should start a company. Box Ball was the first of those opportunities, bought but not developed by their company. An early mechanized form of bowling, Box Ball was initially successful for a few years, but sales dropped off considerably after 1909. Having no particular experience in games, they were already withdrawing their support for that product, in favor of an entirely different business opportunity, but Simpson was apparently unaware of that fact when he wrote to them.

Simpson invited Mr. J. J. Holcombe, the Vice President of the American Box Ball Company

Box Ball alleys in operation circa 1908.
(Author's Collection)

in Indianapolis, Indiana out to Chestnut Hill Park to see the game in action, and how profitable it might be. Simpson wrote to them on June 24, 1911.

> Dear Sir
>
> You will remember the Skee Ball game and visiting Mr. Nice and me in Philadelphia nearly 3 years ago.
>
> After you saw me, I sold a small part of my interest in the game to a Mr. Harper and he and Mr. Nice formed a copartnership. Eighteen months ago, Mr. Nice died suddenly, just as the game was gotten into shape and a small amount of advertising began.
>
> Only $317 was spent in this way, mostly in the "Billboard" and a very little in "Popular Mechanics". This sold 18 games, $3450. -- cash in advance, and over 800 communications were received, without being followed up with literature, faster than sending a booklet and price list. All but one game went west & south.
>
> You will remember saying to us, to put the games in some favorable place and see what they would do. This has been done but a few weeks ago, at the Chestnut Hill Park, Philada, and the game is decidedly a success. Three weeks ago, 3 games at the Park played on a Sunday, from 2 P.M. until 11.30 P.M. without one moments cessation on any one game. This statement is exact. The two succeeding Sundays, about 3/4 of more of the time. As you know it depends on the weather and the crowd.
>
> I see that you now have a New York office and are likely East at any time, as the Nice Estate's interest might be had reasonably at this time as Mr. Harper informs me they do not know what the games are doing at Chestnut Hill.
>
> I told you when I saw you that I did not think Skee Ball stood in competition with the Box Ball, but would simply be an addition to your business if you controlled it. My observation of the crowd confirms this. It seems in many instances to interest people who do not usually play other games, as it did Mr. Nice and Mr. Harper.
>
> Both the Box Ball and the Skee Ball are playing at the Park, side by side. When your 4 games were full our [sic] were full, and when yours were partly going, ours was partly going, showing that the games each had their individual interest. If I could meet you at his Park on a Sunday P.M., when the games are most played we could make our observations together.

{No reply was ever received to the following letter} {copy}

Vineland, N.J.
June 24/11

Mr. J.J. Holcombe
V. Pres. Amer. Bay Ball Co.
Indianapolis, Ind.

Dear Sir

You will remember the I Kee Ball game and visiting Wm. Nice and me in Philada nearly 3 years ago.

After you saw me, I sold a small part of my interest in the game to a Mr. Harper and he and Mr. Nice formed a copartnership. Eighteen months ago, Mr. Nice died suddenly, just as the game was gotten into shape and a small amt. of advertising began.

Only $17. was spent in this way, mostly in the "Billboard" and a very little in "Popular Mechanics". This sold 18 games, $3 & 50. — cash in advance, and over 800 communications were received, without being followed up with literature, farther than sending a booklet and price list. All but one game went West & South.

You will remember saying to us,

Letter from Simpson to J. J. Holcombe June 24, 1911, p. 1
(Courtesy Vineland Historical and Antiquarian Society)

2. Copy to J. J. Holcombe.
continued.   June 24,

to put the games in some favorable place and see what they would do. This has been done but a few weeks ago, at the Chestnut Hill Park, Philada, and the game is decidedly a success. Three weeks ago, 3 games at the Park played on a Sunday, from 2 P.M. until 10:30 P.M. without one moment's cessation on any one game. This statement is exact. The two succeeding Sundays, about 3/4 or more of the time. As you know it depends on the weather and the crowd.

I see that you now have a New York Office and are likely East at any time, as the Nice Estate's interest might be had reasonably at this time as Mr. Harper informs me they do not know what the games are doing at Chestnut Hill.

I told you when I saw you, that I did not think the Skee Ball stood in competition with the Box Ball, but would simply be an addition to your business if you controlled it. My observation of the crowd confirms this. It seems in many instances to interest people, who do not

Letter from Simpson to J. J. Holcombe June 24, 1911, p. 2
(Courtesy Vineland Historical and Antiquarian Society)

3. Copy to J.J. Holcombe
Root X   June 24/11

usually play other games, as it did Mr. Nice and Mr. Harper.

Both the Box Ball and the Ska Ball are playing at the Park, side by side. When your 4 games were full, ours were full, and when yours were partly going, ours were partly going, showing that the games each had their individual interest. If I could meet you at the Park on a Sunday P.M., when the games are most played we could make our observations together.

Since I now see what the game will really do, I am beginning to make every effort to interest enough capital to push it properly. I feel sure that your Co. would best handle it and believe from every point of view it would be well for you to control it. This opinion may sound ulterior and seem gratuitous, but I am sincere in expressing it.

Hoping to hear from you I am, with regards.

Very truly yours,
S.A. Simpson

Letter from Simpson to J. J. Holcombe June 24, 1911, p. 3
(Courtesy Vineland Historical and Antiquarian Society)

Since I now see what the game will really do, I am beginning to make every effort to interest enough capital to push it properly. I feel sure that your Co. could(?)/would(?) best handle it and believe from every point of view it would be sell for you to control it. This opinion may sound alterior [sic] and gratuitous, but I am sincere in expressing it.

Hoping to hear from you I am, with regards,

Very truly yours

J. F. Simpson [11]

No reply was ever received to this letter.

The same day, Foury sent a similar letter to Mr. Brandt C. Downey, of the Continental National Bank of Indianapolis Indiana, trying to determine if a different company owned another alley game, Tenpinnet Co., so that he could make them the same offer. [12]

Desperate, he also contacted the Indianapolis News that same day, inquiring about taking out an advertisement for a Business Opportunity ad offering Skee-Ball for sale or investment, that the companies might see and respond to.

In early July, Foury got a dismissive response from Brandt Downey, with a double dose of bad news. Downey wrote:

Dear Sir

Replying to yours from of recent date regarding the American Box Ball and Tenpinnet Co., I beg to advise that these companies are one and the same.

As you know, they have been in business a number of years, and have been quite successful. The company advises me that the market for this product is being rapidly exhausted. They are not minded to take up any additional lines of a similar nature.

In fact, Mr. Hoke tells me, that he investigated your company some time ago, and decided it did not have sufficient merit to warrant therein taking it up. Mr. Hoke tells me they would not be interested in putting any capital in your business at this time.

Yours very truly,
B. C. Downey.
Cashier [13]

Showing shades of the undaunted man who went five rounds with the U.S. Patent Office over Skee-Ball, a defiant and somewhat prophetic Simpson wrote back:

> Copy of letter of Mr. Downey
> in reply to letter of J.F.S.
> of June 24/11 —
>
> Indianapolis
> July 3. 1911
> Continued on A4
>
> J.F. Simpson
> Vineland. N.J.
> Dear Sir
>
> Replying to yours from of recent date regarding to American Box Ball and Tenpinnet Co., I beg to advise that these companies are one and the same.
>
> As you know, they have been in business a number of years, and have been quite successful. The Company advises me that the market for this product is being rapidly exhausted. They are not minded to take up any additional lines of a similar nature.
>
> In fact, Mr. Hoke tells me, that he investigated your company some time ago, and decided that it did not have sufficient merit to warrant their in taking it up. Mr. Hoke tells me they would not be interested in putting any capital in your business at this time. — Yours very truly
>
> (Signed) B. C. Downey

Letter from Brandt C. Downey to Simpson July 3, 1911
Courtesy Vineland Historical and Antiquarian Society)

Copy

Vineland, N.J.
July 5, 1911

Mr. Brandt C. Downey
  Cashier
  Continental Nat Bk.
    Indp. Ind.

Dear Sir

Your favor of the 3rd inst. received and I beg to thank you for your kind attention.

Mr. Hoke is probably right in what he says regarding the Box Ball and Tea pinrok games. The avenues of sale becoming filled and the public tiring to a degree of the older devices, demand of course, new attractions.

The Skee Ball being in its infancy, I believe, has a very bright future.

I remain,
Very truly yours,

Letter from Simpson to Brandt C. Downey July 5, 1911
(Courtesy Vineland Historical and Antiquarian Society)

Dear Sir

Your favor of the 3rd inst received and I beg to thank you for your kind attention

Mr. Hoke is probably right in what he says regarding the Box Ball and Tenpinnet games. The avenues of sale becoming filled and the public tiring to a degree of the older devices, demand of course, new attractions.

The Skee Ball being in its infancy, I believe, has a very bright future I remain, Very truly yours J. F. Simpson [14]

A newly energized John Harper had been in Philadelphia frequenting Chestnut Hill Park, and on August 5, sent Simpson an update and copy of an ad to attract business capital. He wrote:

August 5th. 1911.

Dear Simpson,

Your card duly received. I am very well and trust you are also. The only thing new is new SkeeBall [sic] players most every day who seem to enjoy the game thoroughly, and the enclosed endorsement.

I put an ad in tomorrow's Record under Business Opportunities for capital. ….

Yours truly, John. [15]

Having the Skee-Ball games up and running in Chestnut Hill Park, right next to the Box Ball alleys, was a huge win for Harper and Simpson, and for the Skee-Ball Alley Company. They now had head-to-head revenue numbers, and proof of Skee-Ball's fascination for players. They had a place to show prospective investors and buyers the true market potential of the game, and to feel the excitement around it, watching the enthusiasm of the live players.

It was also beginning to be noteworthy of mention in its new venues. On August 12, a local paper reported on a gathering at the Santa Cruz Beach Boardwalk, home to at least one of the alleys. "At the International Typographical Union convention in Santa Cruz a redwood tree was named 'Jim Lynch' after the president of the Union and in the evening the party organized to capture every championship on the boardwalk including Skee-Ball." [16]

There was another advantage that came along with their presence at Auchy's operation. They had the full support of the manager of Chestnut Hill Park, Mr. John Merrill, who was marketing enthusiastically with Harper, visiting potential investors, clients and customers all over the northeast.

Both Harper and Simpson were ready to be done with the production and marketing end

SKEE-BALL ALLEY CO.,
PHILADELPHIA, PA.

August 5th. 1911.

Dear Simpson,

Your card duly received. I am very well and trust you are also. The only thing new is new SkeeBall players most every day who seem to enjoy the game thoroughly, and the enclosed endorsement.

I put an ad in tomorrow's Record under Business Opportunities for capital.

The alleys work fine especially the actuating device, it works better than I ever expected because I made it; I had one apart the other day and was surprised to see that it is about absolutely as good if not better than when I made it: the idea is Al. The only fault with the alleys is the Dutch brains that helped build them.

I thank you but I will come down and help celebrate the (51st) home week. Excuse me from a crowd every time.

Yours truly,

John.

Letter from Harper to Simpson August 5, 1911
(Courtesy Vineland Historical and Antiquarian Society)

of the business, and anxious to have someone take it over. In many ways, this was a classic start-up business case. They developed and launched the product, but had not enough cash to get through the initial market offering, and then to hand it over to normal business operations. The game was not quite strong enough in the market yet, and they were desperately low on funds. Building ten alleys at once would have been much more economical and efficient than building one at a time. That was the conundrum with orders just trickling in one or two at a time—a most frustrating situation.

They spent the rest of the year contacting potential investors and partners, and following up with inquiries about the game from clients and customers. They were getting used to rejection.

8-6-11

Mr. J. F. Simpson Vineland N.J.

Dear Sir

I received your letter a short time ago and related the contents to the Pitman Supply Co. but they have been very busy and decided it would impossible to take hold of the game just at this time. Wishing you success I remain

Yours Truly

H. W. Rainier Pitman N.J. [17]

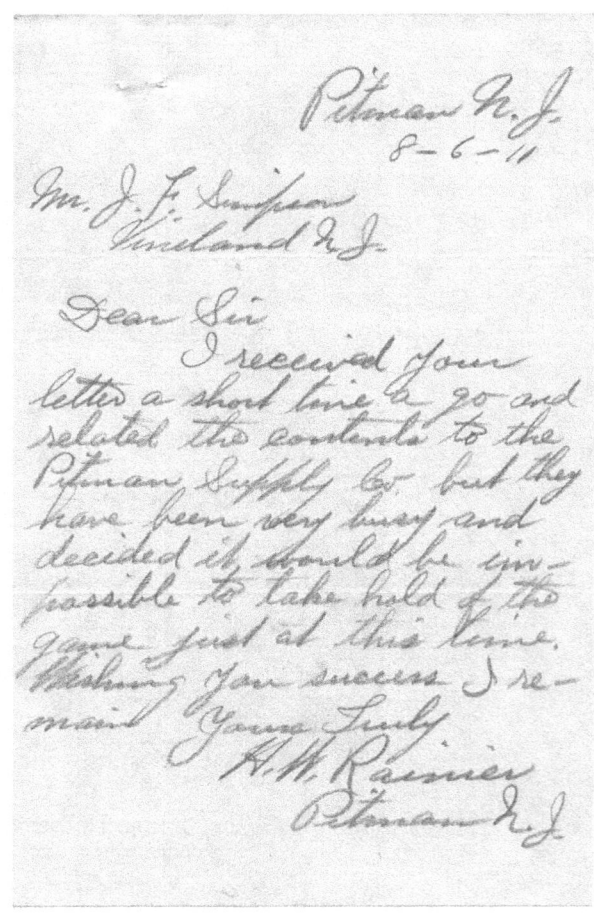

Letter from H. W. Rainier to Joseph Fourestier Simpson
August 6, 1911
(Courtesy Vineland Historical and Antiquarian Society)

From another potential customer:

> 8-14-11
>
> Dear Sir:-
>
> *We are in receipt of your letter of August 12th addressed to Mr. Bensinger, who instructs us to say to you in reply, that the skee-ball [sic] bowling device is one in which we would not care to interest ourselves. We have attempted on two or three occasions to put something similar on the market and have made a pronounced failure. Therefore, we have decided to confine ourselves strictly to our regular lines. Regretting our inability to give anything more encouraging, we are,*
>
> *Yours truly,*
>
> *The Brunswick Balke Collender Co.* [18]

Some potential buyers helpfully suggested the game be modified to their specifications and the price dropped.

> *Sept 3 1911*
> *To The Skee Ball Alley Co*
>
> *Dear Sirs*
>
> *sometime ago I wrote you re a Skee Ball Table, you sent a long catalogue. I want to you send me by return of mail full particular of rea the table I want one not to be over three hundred weight to be built in four sections each section to be 7&6 ft*

Letter from A. H. Bell September 22, 1911.
(Courtesy Vineland Historical and Antiquarian Society)

Seeking Redemption

full length 30 feet. I want it to be easily put together less bolts and screws as possible I want it for traveling the shows let me know the price F. O. B. I may state that I have four Base Ball tables travelling [sic] Australia and I want some thing new if I secure a table end every thing is satisfactory it is sure to lead to further Business

I remain:yours respectfully

J. Rath 9 Harold Street Newtown N. S. W. Sydney [19]

Saskatoon Sask. Sept. 22. 1911

Dear Sir

Will you let me know what length of a place you would require for your Skee Ball Bowling alley & your lowest price complete. There is 25% of duty and a long trip out here, so if you make the price right, I might invest.

Yours truly A. H. Bell 119-20th St. West Saskatoon . Sask. [20]

Some wanted more information, since the circulars printed under William Nice Jr.'s tenure were intentionally vague, and didn't contain a description of how the game was

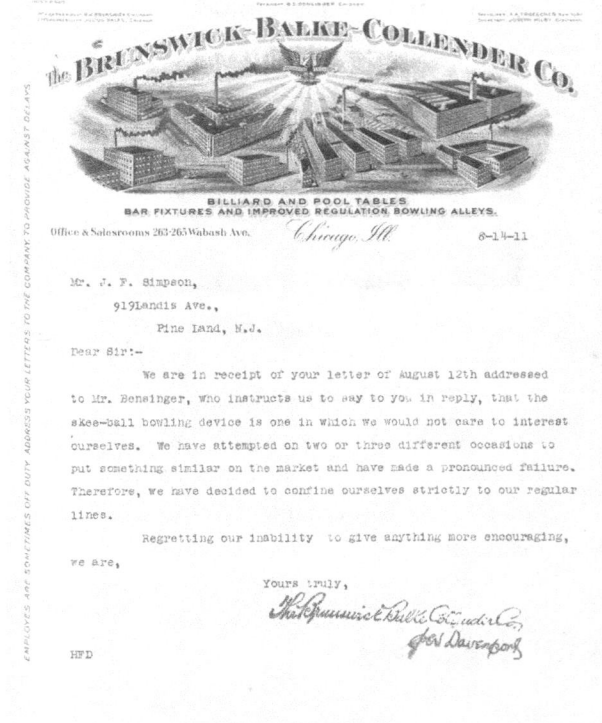

Letter from The Brunswick-Balke-Collender Co. to Joseph Fourestier Simpson, August 14, 1911.
(Courtesy Vineland Historical and Antiquarian Society)

played or the price of the alleys. This meant more hours of personal follow-up, with no guarantee of a sale at the end.

The potential customers were also a mixed bag. They wrote their correspondence on every scrap of paper one could imagine, including their own store receipts, like the following one.

9/11/1911 Skee-Ball Alley
Co Philadelphia, Pa

Gentlemen

I received a small circular today of your new Skee Ball Alley and would like you to give me full particulars of same in size price and terms and all there is to know about it if satisfactory will buy one at once

Hope to hear from you by return mail I remain yours truly WAGonder [21]

Harper set out the situation clearly in this letter, and somewhat prophetically, reminded Simpson that "these alleys are going to make money someday for somebody":

September 20th. 1911

3 P.M.

Dear Simpson,

I guess you have my several postals by this time. I saw Mr. Nice yesterday. If you can sell the patent outright do so I will be glad to sell for the amount you mention.

Just got a letter a few minutes ago from one of our first customers in California, who says among other things, "I am pleased to tell you I have made very good money since I purchased my alley from you: it is certainly a very quick money getter."

At noon today I shipped one of the alleys from the park to FULTON, N.Y. to a

Letter from W. A. Gonder to the Skee-Ball Alley Company, September 11, 1911.
(Courtesy Vineland Historical and Antiquarian Society)

Seeking Redemption

party who will try to sell alleys for us. He operated Box Ball for some time and made some money: he says this is greatly superior to Box Ball in every way.

Mr. Auchy and Mr. Merrill ARE very much impressed with these alleys, and it may be I can do something with Mr. A in a very short time.

Mr. Merrill and I intended operating alleys at ALLENTOWN FAIR, but we were a little too late. We'll get 'em going yet.

Sell out to the first person who come along with good money. You and I are almost worn out.

These alleys ARE GOING TO MAKE MONEY SOME DAY FOR SOMEBODY. I am going to do my best to get Mr. Auchy started on building 5 or 10 so he can tell just about what they will cost.

I think I CAN greatly improve the appearance of alleys.

A few Saturdays ago when I said I expected to go away for a day or so, we seemed to get extra busy at the park and I kept right on the job. I think I could enjoy a day or two right now at the shore.

I trust you are all better than when last I heard.

Yours very truly, John. [22]

Simpson began calling in favors from his social and professional network for recommendations, so he could be connected with people of means who might take over the business and buy them out. A judge who was a long-time colleague of Simpson wrote on his behalf to Mr. C. A. Birdsall, President of Johnson Farebox Company, which made fare boxes for trolleys and rail roads. Birdsall might well have been in the position to understand the value of Skee-Ball as an amusement in the trolley parks, and have money to invest in the venture. Judge Matthews wrote:

Wildwood Crest, N. J. Sept. 26, 1911.

My dear Birdsall:

This introduces you to Mr. J. F. Simpson of Vineland, N. J. who has in invention which, in my judgement, possesses great merit and it occurred to me that it might interest you to look into the matter with a view of taking an interest. Mr. Simpson is a gentleman of high character and standing in his community and I am quite satisfied that whether or not you fell disposed to take an interest that you will find his acquaintanceship very pleasant.

SKEE-BALL ALLEY CO.,
PHILADELPHIA, PA.

September 20th, 1911
5 P.M.

Dear Simpson,

I guess you have my several postals by this time. I saw Mr. Nice yesterday. If you can sell the patent outright do so I will be glad to sell for the amount you mention.

Just got a letter a few minutes ago from one of our first customers in California, who says among other things," I am pleased to tell you I have made very good money since I purchased my alley from you; it is certainly a very quick money getter."

At noon today I shipped one of the alleys from the park to FULTON, N.Y. to a party who will try to sell alleys for us. He operated Box ball for some time and made some money; he says this is greatly superior to Box ball in every way.

Mr. Auchy and Mr. Merrill aRe very much impressed with these alleys, and it may be I can do something with Mr. A in a very short time.

Mr. Merrill and I intended operating 2 alleys at ALLENTOWN FAIR, but we were a little too late. We'll get 'em going yet.

Sell out to the first person who come along with good money. You and I are both almost worn out.

These alleys ARE GOING TO MAKE MONEY SOME DAY FOR SOMEBODY. I am going to do my best to get Mr. Auchy started on building 5 or 10 so he can tell just about what they will cost.

I think I CAN greatly improve the appearance of alleys.

A few Saturdays ago when I said I expected to go away for a day or so, we seemed to get extra busy at the park and I kept right on the job. I think I could enjoy a day or two right now at the shore.

I trust you are all better than when last I heard.

Yours very truly,

John.

Letter from John W. Harper to Joseph Fourestier Simpson, September 20, 1911
(Courtesy Vineland Historical and Antiquarian Society)

With sentiments of high regard, I am, Very sincerely yours, [23]

Simpson followed up immediately with an offer:

C. A. Birdsall
1463 Irving St.
Wash. DC

Dear sir

I beg to enclose a letter of introduction to you from Judge Matthews. To go into my matter requires some considerable explanation and I may say briefly it is the manufacture and sale of a game of skill, for use in Public Parks, Piers, Clubs and private use. As the business was about established the sudden death of my advocate held the affair up. This summer 3 of these games established at the White City Park at Chest Hill Phila, have proved to a certainty the very great value of the game.

…

If this interests you I should be glad to go into particulars Very truly yours J. F. Simpson [24]

And Mr Birdsall replied:

Mr. J. F. Simpson Vineland, NJ

Dear Sir,

Yours of 27th inst received, and I am very sorry that other enterprises in which I am interested require so much time and capital that I cannot take up anything more at this time. Thanking you for the opportunity extended I am

Very truly yours CHBirdsall [25]

By the end of the season, there was no question that Skee-Ball was a very profitable game. Three Skee-Ball alleys had easily out-earned seven Box Ball alleys. It was clear that people preferred Skee-Ball, as Harper described in his letter to Simpson of Oct 3, 1911:

October 3rd. 1911.

Dear Simpson,

When I got home after leaving you today I received a letter from Merrill saying the 3 SKEE BALL ALLEYS had earned $$522.00 [sic] this season, and the 7 BOX BALL ALLEYS had earned $450.00 this season. They had 4 Box Ball Alleys only during 1910 and they earned $557.00 during 1910 season. Understand?

C. A. Birdsall
1463 Irving St
Wash. D.C.   Copy

Wildwood Crest, N. J., Sept. 26, 1911.

My dear Birdsall:

    This introduces to you Mr. J. F. Simpson of Vineland, N. J. who has an invention which, in my judgment, possesses great merit and it occurred to me that it might interest you to look into the matter with a view of taking an interest. Mr. Simpson is a gentleman of high character and standing in his community and I am quite satisfied that whether or not you feel disposed to take an interest that you will find his acquaintanceship very pleasant.

    With sentiments of high regard, I am,

                      Very sincerely yours,

Letter from Judge Matthews to C. A. Birdsall, September 26, 1911
(Courtesy Vineland Historical and Antiquarian Society)

Letter from Joseph Fourestier Simpson to C. A. Birdsall
(Courtesy Vineland Historical and Antiquarian Society)

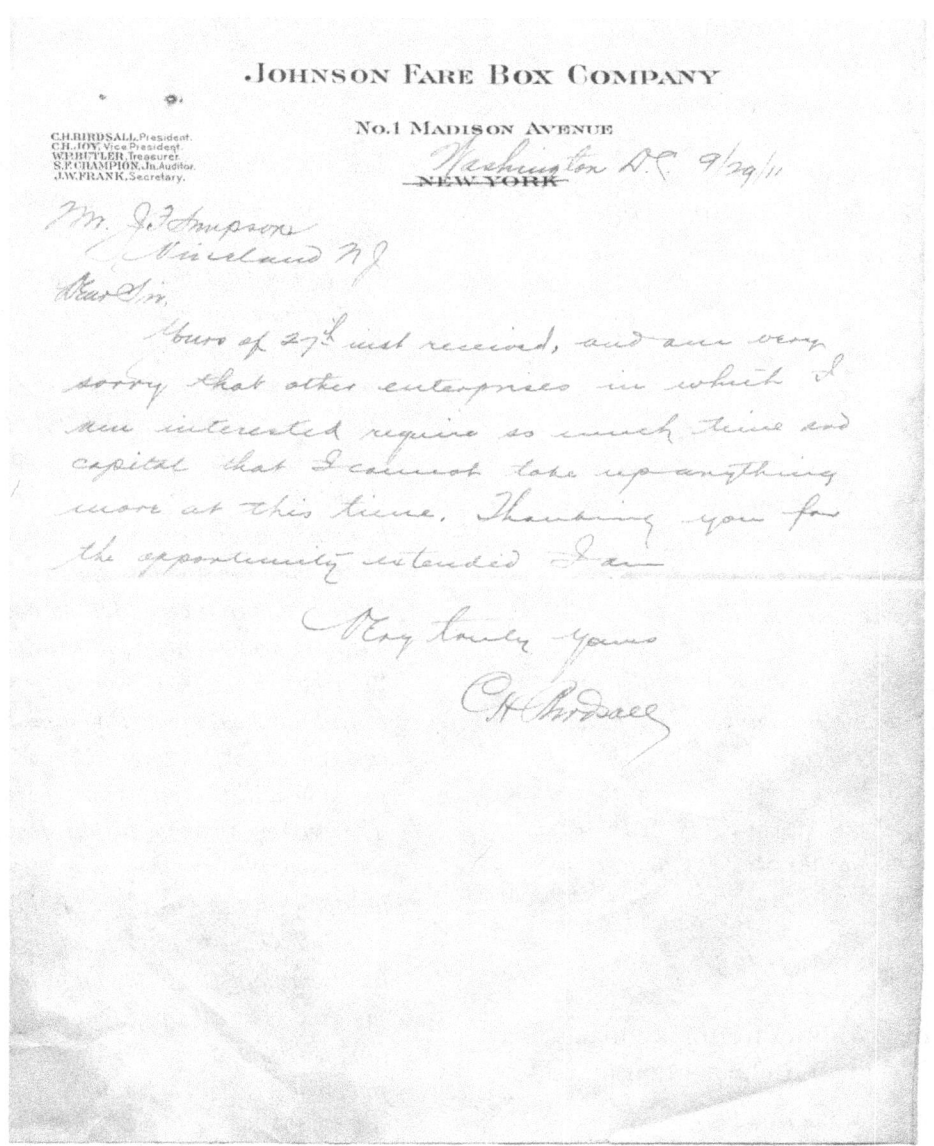

Letter from C. A. Birdsall to Joseph Fourestier Simpson, September 29, 1911.
(Courtesy Vineland Historical and Antiquarian Society)

If anything comes of our talk with Mr. Smith today, please let me alone to deal with Mr. Nice. I no know my reason and advise you for the best. I could turn over every bit of interest outside of your own, to a [sic] individual or company for $10000.00 on easy terms, and this is something you could not do.

If it comes to anything let me alone with Mr. Nice as it would be to your advantage, & do not tell ANYONE I would agree to get out of it altogether as it would weaken the case, then I would not mention it unless the matter or question is asked me. It weakens everything to see to much & talk too much before the proper time.

Mr. Smith seems like a very fine fellow and I trust he can interest someone whom he has in mind.

I have Mr. Merrill very much interested in this matter and he has Skee Ball at heart; he has 3 nibbles.

Very truly yours, J.W.H [26]

More and more inquiries from potential customers rolled in, and Harper continued to field them:

October 19-1911.

Dear Simpson,

Your several cards received. I am plugging away every day answering enquiries. I sent out 500 of the endorsements and have had about 10 enquiries this week. If our literature were a little more explicit it would save me a lot of work and might do some good. WHow [sic] in the Devil knows how to operate SKEE BALL from the catalogue; the explanation always was sloppy, Nice would not have it otherwise, he didn't want it explained to any body. Every day I am asked the question by mail "how is it operated send full particulars" I wish you would write a full discription [sic] "Playing SKEE BALL, or How S-B is Played" without saying too much. I enclose cuts spread [sic] on large sheet and think it would be well to describe the alley in detail. Tell meaning of name at start. It will cost some money to have these printed but we must do something as I cannot write the make up a thousand times on typewriter; I have something else to say when I answer enquiries. The enquiries I am receiving are from parties that we have already heard from and we ought to certainly get some of them started.

If you write a discription [sic] write a little

larger than usual: you may have to cut up a catalogue or two to place illustration where you need them and arrange them to suit yourself.

I am sorry Smith has done nothing altho it would surprise me if anyone does anything outside of ourselves, then you see my interest is so botched I could not move if I had money to put in the business. If it cost too much I will have discription [sic] of How to play S-B printed without cuts; I am afraid with cuts would cost $25.00 per M.

Yours truly, , J. W. H.

The enquiries I receive are alive., [sic] a number from those operating BOX BALL. [27]

Harper continued to work assiduously at getting the business sold to someone who could profitably take it forward.

November 1-1911.

Dear Simpson,

Your card was received yesterday. I had an engagement to meet Merrill yesterday A.M. in west Phila.aed [sic] tried to arrange to be at Glendennings by 12, but Merrill tnd [sic] I got so mixed in our efforts with SKEE I was with him until 8 P.M.last eve., we covered full 40 miles. We took a party from 62 and Market to Chestnut Hill and party seems enthused. We got back to Terminal at 6.15, met a party by appointment from Souderton, I had them to dinner at Broad St. Sta. and left them at 8.P.M. Merrill also talked a half hour with third party who seems very much interested.

Of course I would like to get away from the business but I CANNOT get going without sticking to it.

If Merrill and I can arrange to form a new SKEE BALL ALLEY COMPANY, would you take royalty for each alley sold in all other except the 5 states already arranged by you and myself? If so, how much royalty would you want per alley, that is for your share or interest alone. Party I saw yesterday asked me several questions I could not answer and I find it will be very hard to proceed if I cannot answer everything asked me relative to this matter. If they all find it complicated they will shy away, and I try to tell everyone it is absolutely clean and clear.

I have not seen Budd but want to take it up with him just as soon as I leave Merrill today.

Merrill and I were going to Souderton early this morning but he called me over phone just as I was leaving home and said he was side tracked by mail: we expect to leave Terminal today at noon. I do not know when I will get back, but you bet your life we are on the jump. Yesterday was a terror to me: it had my goat.

I was up to factory a short time ago, and I find I have been nearly stripped of everything I had, tools, hardware and etc. I am anxious to get away from that hole for ever. No more working in shop with some other fellows men.

When you come to town let me know the day before as you see I cannot always meet you.

Let me hear from you early. I am off on a 66 mile jaunt. Merrill is certainly more active and faithful than you can imagine- to take such an interest in us.

Yours very truly, (Hastily)

J.W.H [28]

However, as hard as they worked, with Merrill's help, the sticking point was always Budd Nice, like his father before him.

November 11-1911.2P.M [sic]

Dear Simpson,

Merrill and I have certainly been doing some heavy batting for about 3 weeks but all the balls have landed foul.

We thought we had certainly made a home run to SOUDERTON, P.A. but when I took up the matter with Nice he also wanted 3% royalty, and I get in the neck as usual. I feel like a damned fool in the matter-the goat. Everytime [sic] I get near someone with a halter there is some condition to yank the party away.

The latest thing is to have Merrill to try to interest the Box Ball People We sent them a letter dated Nov. 4th. and they certainly took notice of it, the letter was sent to Holcomb, N.Y.City from Indianapolis and Merrill got reply from both ends. Holcomb said among other things he would see Hoke within about a week and would take the matter up with him; he also said the past 3 months were the best in the history of their company. This does not seem to agree with that he told the cashier of the bank you communicated with: does it?

The party in FULTON, N.Y seems to think a great deal of SKEE BALL as you can see from enclosed endorsement: he is trying to interest some of his friends, and I will send him a list of enquiries from N.Y. state. I have already written 18 letters this month in regards to SKEE and a number of them have been long 4¢ ones.

After talking with Budd a little while I asked him where I was to come in if he wanted 5% and you wanted 5%, I would not think of asking anyone more than 10%: he then said he would take 4% if you would take 4% and 3% for me; I did not tell him but I would be very glad to take 2% if you and Budd would divide 8%, of course this is in case we can do something. I was sure I had two fellows who would invest $2500.00 between them, and I DO KNOW if we got the thing started and it looked good I COULD GET $10000.00 if needed without going over one half mile away; this was assured me.

That last reply you sent to the bank cashier at Inda. had more to the square inch than anything I have seen for some time; I have studied it by heart. When you write increase the size of it. Yours truly,

John. [29]

At this point, even the new orders for Skee-Ball that trickled in were more of a pain than a blessing. Harper was acutely feeling the stress. He had already lost his investment, his land, his home, and was living with friends in a humble row house, struggling to put food on the table. Each new request for a Skee-Ball alley put additional stress on him. He had to find a location to build them, invest in parts, and recover scattered tools as well as take the time to construct the alley, all while managing the business.

November 17-1911.

Dear Simpson,

Yours of yesterday with contents received. I have what looks like an order for a complete alley from N. Carolina, from a friend of the fellow in FULTON,N.Y. The Fulton man expects $30.00 Commission or 10%, as I agreed to give him on direct sales.

I have not the order absolutely, but if I had, how in the Devil could I fill it? I have no shop or anything else necessary, everything is scattered around and it would cost ME,ME,ME,Me, more to build one alley under the circumstances than I could get for it, and who would lose? ME,ME,ME,ME, of course as usual. I am certainly SICK of the rotten business and wish I had never heard of the Damned game. You stick pretty close to Smith, he may be able to do something, and do not forget to see him about the first of Dec. about the Canada patent. Give him half, he might be able to start something.

You could get rid of me easier than anyone

else: I'll sell on the easiest terms you ever heard of: the interest on $2500 would suit me. The sooner I am loose the better.

The damned rotten Nice Estate won't help me one bit, and NEVER did, it is a good thing the old man is dead or he would have ruined me entirely. If you can get Smith started I will try to make Nice's terms and mine very cheap. I am tired of huckstering the thing around; I'd rather dig ditches for a dollar a day.

The second part of the Popular Mechanics matter is almost identical with the Sporting Goods Dealer; if I were having of these printed, I would cut out the second part.

I am in a hell of a stew in case I get an order for one alley. I could take care of ten or more; but one at a time is too many. If we had the money and could afford a shop I would come to Vineland. I don't want any more Auchey [sic], either.

Write a decent ad for a $10 space in the Billboard. Another bill I have to pay.

J.W.H. [30]

On December 9, two ads appeared in The Billboard. The first one advertised the game itself. The image and width of the ad were the same as ads that appeared in 1910, however, the copy that accompanied the ad had been expanded to read:

An entirely new idea in BOWLING. Susceptible to the highest SKILL in play. Positively no bowling game so fascinating as SKEE BALL. For men and women. Size 32 ft. long, 3 ft. wide, net 8 ft. high. Nine balls, 3 1/2 inch diameter. Balls stiffly bowled midway of alley mount in the air and fly to target. SCORING: AUTOMATIC; progress of count seen by player and audience. This feature a winner. Balls return by gravity. Slot machine attends alley. ARE YOU SEEKING A PROFITABLE BUSINESS? LOOK INTO THIS! Do you want a valuable District Agency? If you do, and you are the right man, this is your chance.

For full description, send for catalogue.

Dept. A

SKEE BALL ALLEY CO., Philadelphia, Pa. [31]

The second ad, this one advertising the business opportunity, read:

Owing to Death

Will sell all or part interest of valuable amusement device. A number in successful

SKEE-BALL ALLEY CO.,
PHILADELPHIA, PA.

November 17-1911.

Dear Simpson,

Yours of yesterday with contents received.
I have what looks like an order for a complete alley from N.
Carolina, from a friend of the fellow in FULTON, N.Y. The Fulton
man expects $30.00 Commission or 10%, as I agreed to give him
on direct sales.
I have not the order absolutely, but if I had, how in the Devil
could I fill it? I have no shop or anything else necessary,
everything is scattered around and it would cost ME, ME, ME, Me,
more to build one alley under the circumstances than I could
get for it, and who would loose? ME, ME, ME, ME, of course as
usual. I am certainly SICK of the rotten business and wish
I had never heard of the Damned game. You stick pretty close
to Smith, he may be able to do something, and do not forget
to see him about the first of Dec. about the Canada patent.
Give him half, he might be able to start something.
You could get rid of me easier than anyone else: I'll sell on
the easiest terms you ever heard of: the interest on £9500
would suit me. The sooner I am loose the better.

The damned rotten Nice Estate won't help me one bit, and NEVER
did, it is a good thing the old man is dead or he would have
ruined me entirely. If you can get Smith started I will try
to make Nice's terms and mine very cheap. I am tired of
huckstering the thing around; I'd rather dig ditches for a
dollar a day.
The second part of the Popular Mechanics matter is almost
identical with the Sporting Goods Dealer; if I were having
of these printed, I would cut out the second part.
I am in a hell of a stew in case I get an order for one alley.
I could take care of ten or more; but one at a time is too
many. If we had the money and could afford a shop I would
come to Vineland. I don't want any more Auchey, either.
Write a decent ad for a $10 space in the Billboard. Another
bill I have to pay.

Letter from John W. Harper to Joseph Fourestier Simpson, November 17, 1911.
(Courtesy Vineland Historical and Antiquarian Society)

operation. New, high class, practical patented proposition.

Possibilities gigantic. Address

AMUSEMENT DEVICE,

Care The Billboard, Cincinnati, Ohio. [32]

They had several responses to these ads. Harper also contacted C.W. Parker, a wealthy manufacturing giant in Leavenworth, Kansas, with a huge factory and generous pocketbook. He would have been a great prospect to buy the business, but his response was disappointing. He was willing to manufacture them, but was not interested in taking over the business:

LEAVENWORTH, KANS. 12-19-11

John W. Harper 3262 N. Park Ave. Philadelphia, Pa.

Dear Sir:-

I am in receipt of your favor of the 8th and I believe you have a very good proposition, but at this time will not have the time to take this up as I am leaving for a two or three weeks vacation in the south. But I have the largest factory in the world devoted to the manufacture of amusement devices and no doubt I will be in position to build these devices for you.

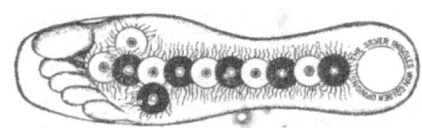

Classified advertisement that appeared in The Billboard, December 9, 1911
(Courtesy Vineland Historical and Antiquarian Society)

Early draft of an advertisement that appeared in The Billboard, December 9, 1911.
(Courtesy Vineland Historical and Antiquarian Society)

SKEE BALL — For Pleasure Resorts, Parks, and all year Amusement Parlors.

An entirely new idea in bowling. Susceptible to the highest skill in play. Positively no bowling game so fascinating as Skee Ball. For men and women. Size 32 feet long, 3 feet wide, net 8 feet high. Nine Skee Ball balls 3 1/2" diameter Balls stiffly bowled. Midway of the alley balls they mount in the air and fly to the target. Scoring, automatic; progress of count seen by player and audience. This feature a winner. Balls return by gravity. Slot machine attends the game.

ARE YOU SEEKING A BUSINESS? LOOK INTO THIS! Do you want a valuable district agency? If you do, and you are the right man, this is your chance.

SKEE-BALL ALLEY CO., PHILADELPHIA, PA.

Later draft of an advertisement that appeared in The Billboard, December 9, 1911.
(Courtesy Vineland Historical and Antiquarian Society)

Final ad that appeared in The Billboard, December 9, 1911.
(Author's Collection)

Yours very truly, CWParker [33]

Some were referrals to yet other potential buyers:

Dec. 21, 1911-- Mr. John W. Harper 3262 N. Park Ave. Phila. Pa.

Dear Sir

We are in receipt of your favor of the 18th inst., with enclosures & regret to advise you that we are not in a position to take up your proposition.

Griffith & Crane, Lippincott Bldg. Philada are A. 1. people in this line of business and we are sure that they would be good people to get in touch with.

yours very truly Diamond Novelty Co Stowell. [34]

In December, it became apparent to Simpson that John Harper was at the end of his rope. He had been working hard on getting another company interested in Skee-Ball, so far to no avail. William Sauter worked as a manager for the Edward K. Tryon Company in Philadelphia, described as "importers and manufacturers of firearms, fishing tackle, cutlery and athletic goods." Sauter managed the athletic goods operation.

Sympathetically, Simpson wrote:

Dec. 16. 1911 Vineland N J

Dear John I have yours of the 13th inst. I note what you say about Sauter.

Do you not think that an appointment with him on a Sunday, when the matter could be talked over quietly and considered would be well. It could not be done in Tryon's office on a week day. If you want to make an appointment with him for a Sunday and can do so, let me know and I will come to the City earlier on the Sunday and we can talk over the thing before we see him. Bring along the figures I sent you as I made no copy. You do not say in your present letter what you proposed to him. --

My letter was just an outline - in the way of suggestion to get at some definite conclusion - or as a basis to think on.

I do not wonder you are tired of the whole business and I sympathize with your efforts.

I am sorry that the adver in "Billboard" brought but two answers. It may be that if we so do so later and again it may be that it is the wrong time of year. I do not know and I am be damned if I do not begin to feel that I don't know anything anyway. _____

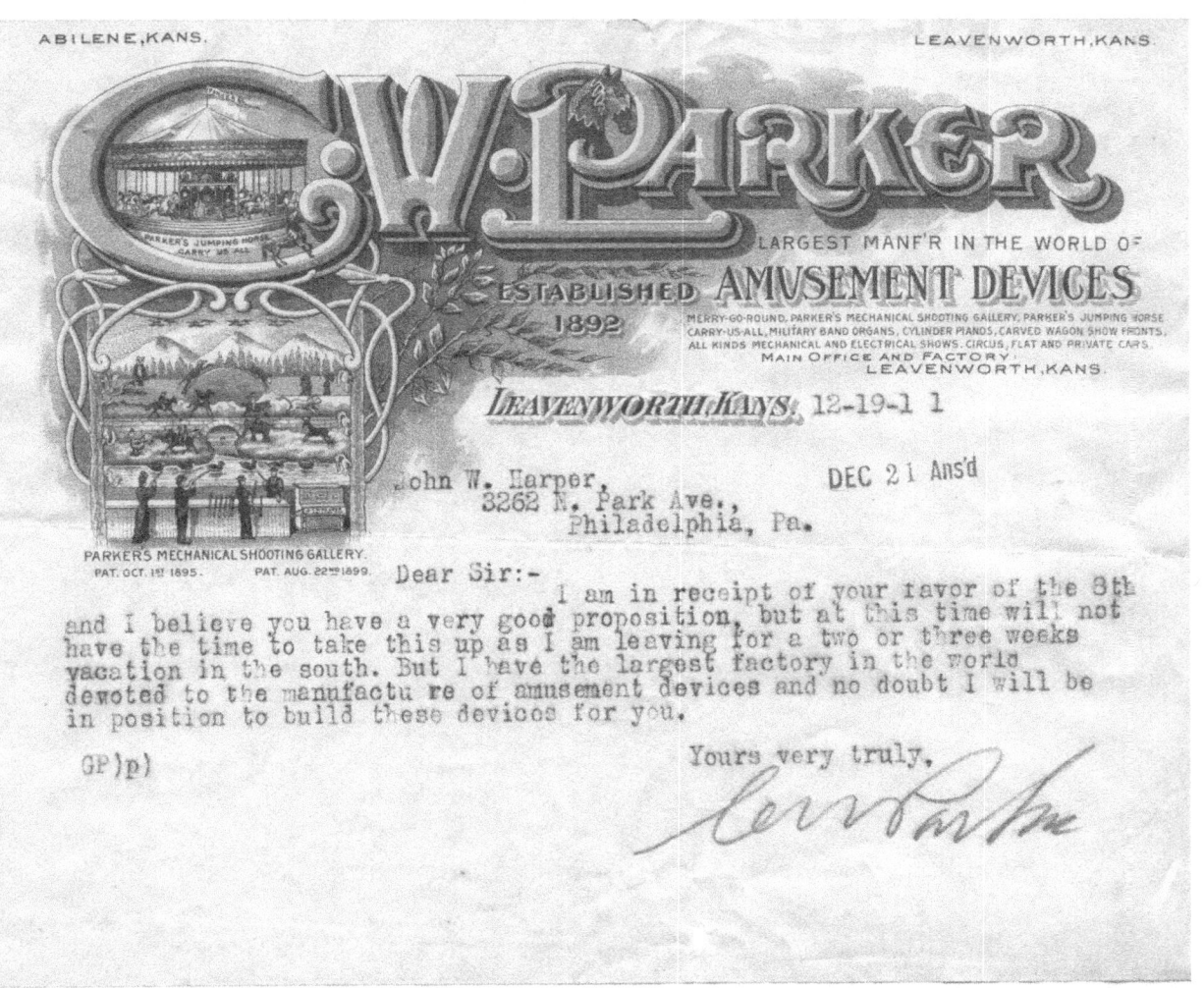

Letter from C. W. Parker to John W. Harper, December 19, 1911.
(Courtesy Vineland Historical and Antiquarian Society)

Letter from Diamond Novelty Company to John W. Harper, December 21, 1911.
(Courtesy Vineland Historical and Antiquarian Society)

Smith, I am at a loss to understand. --

I am very sorry you have been at the expense of the "Billboard" ad as I feel you put it in at my urging. I thought it might revive the thing.

You should have got that DuPont man to give you enough powder to blow the whole damn thing up. --

I have not bought a new ticket which costs about $27.00 - and have nothing to go to loan for, unless we can get Sauter on a Sunday. Praying for a change in our fortunes and with kind regards

Yours truly, Simpson [35]

By the end of the year, Harper was so desperate to sell out of the company, he instructed Simpson on how to present the offer and to outright lie about when the game was developed.

12/20/1911.
Dear Simpson,

Your card received. With all my heart let Millen the attorney you mention sell SKEE BALL.

Do not complicate it too much, that is do not tell just how much of the patent each one of us own: in other words you can have my interest by an understanding between you and myself to make your one have of the entire intact. If anyone would want to buy SKEE BALL all the care about is the price and do not care anything about how it is held between you, Nice and myself: we could adjust it among ourselves.

SKEE BALL WAS NOT completed until this spring (1911) no matter how long it has been in our head: it IS BRAN[sic] NEW, not known yet: it is just ready right now and never before to go ahead with- no matter how long we have been trying to develope [sic] it. Don't tell anyone else what we know: tell them the best of it: put plenty of guilt paint on your extolment; refer 'em to Merrill; he will tell anybody it is the real sugar coated article.

I enclose you some literature: I have NONE of the acrostic cards: I wish I had.

Give the attorney you mention (I am not sure of the name)(you write TOO small) anything to sell the game; and it IS certainly something that has value and ought to interest someone: damn it there is no doubt about that. Only talk to the fellows that might be interest interested; the others will laugh at you. Better read Timon of Athens Christmas.

Very truly yours. John. [36]

The year came to a close with no solid offers. Simpson and Harper, exhausted by their efforts were devoutly hopeful that the next year would bring a change in their fortunes.

They soon learned—be very careful what you wish for.

The first few months of 1912 were more of the same struggle. In addition to responding to multiple inquiries for purchase of alleys, they searched desperately for someone to buy out the company. Harper had been traveling, but the weather was miserable, freezing cold and snowing. Both men were working overtime, trying to get something, anything, to move forward.

On January 12, Simpson wrote a letter to Morris Edgar Smith in Philadelphia. Smith was an attorney whom Simpson knew rather well. He offered him a proposition about Skee-Ball and the Canadian patents he held on the game. [37] January 13, Smith responded to Simpson's letter telling Simpson that given his current financial condition, he could not take up the Canadian patents. Smith went on to say that he thought Simpson had something good going and with enough money he believed that the game would make considerable money. [38]

On Wednesday, January 31, Simpson wrote William Sauter a letter with the overarching goal of getting him to come to Vineland to see Skee-Ball in person, along with two smaller versions of the game that Simpson had developed: a twelve foot game that folded; and a three foot parlor version. Simpson wrote to Sauter that:

"this thing enterprise is of sufficient importance to be gone into very carefully and every point well considered, so that no mistakes can be made or misapprehensions entertained." [39]

Simpson approached him as "a businessman of intelligence and experience in this line of work" and impressed upon him that Simpson had thoroughly studied the game from a business perspective: "I think we could come to a just conclusion regarding it, and be able to properly present it to your house." [40] Simpson offered to reimburse Sauter for his ticket to Vineland and back and promised to entertain him while he was in Vineland if he was willing to come on Sunday, February 4. [41]

That meeting never happened. However, Harper went to see Sauter in person on Friday, February 23. He reported it was a pleasant meeting but Sauter said he was very busy and had not been able to consider Simpson's proposal. The letter was on his desk and he would consider it in a day or two. [42] This

SKEE-BALL ALLEY CO.,
PHILADELPHIA, PA.

12/20/1911.

Dear Simpson,

    Your card is received. With all my heart let Millen the attorney you mention sell SKEE BALL.
Do not complicate it too much, that is do not tell just how much of the patent each one of us own: in other words you can have my interest by an understanding between you and myself: we make your one half of the entire intact. If anyone would want to buy SKEE BALL all they care about is the price and do not care anything about how it is held between you, Ace and myself: we could adjust it among ourselves.
SKEE BALL WAS NOT completed until this spring (1911) no matter how long it has been in our head: it IS ITS NEW, not known yet: it is just ready right now and never before to go ahead with— no matter how long we have been trying to develope it. Don't tell anyone else what we know; tell them the best of it; put plenty of guilt paint on your statement; refer 'em to Merrill; he will tell anybody it is the real super coated article.
I enclose you some literature: I have NONE of the acrostic cards: I wish I had.
Give the attorney you mention (I am not sure of the name) (you write TOO small) anything to sell the game: and it IS certainly something that has value and ought to interest someone: damn it there is no doubt about that. Only talk to the fellows that might be ~~interest~~ interested; the others will laugh at you. Letter read Timon of Athens Christmas.

                                      Very truly yours,

                                            John.

Letter from John W. Harper to Joseph Fourestier Simpson, December 20, 1911.
(Courtesy Vineland Historical and Antiquarian Society)

turned into yet another polite dismissal of the game.

They were approaching everyone who might have any interest in the game, and had reached out to their entire network of social and professional connections to get help. A wealthy friend of John Harper's and of the late William Nice Jr.'s, Dr. E. L. Klopp, had a hand in putting many business deals together, including new propositions for Budd Nice, getting him started in the paper canister business. Dr. Klopp referred Simpson and Harper to a potential investor in Philadelphia, Mr. I. N. Levi, who was looking to get into some business, possibly Skee-Ball. He had the money to invest, but needed to be convinced of the potential profits. Harper developed an extensive and detailed cost analysis for Levi, with projections, and comparisons to similar games. [43]

Of the engagement with I. N. Levi, Harper wrote on Jan 17:

> "I wish we could interest Levi: it is pretty hard to show profit on paper; it is damned hard to show anything on paper. This rotten game is enough to set Hell on fire; it makes me sick everytime [sic] I hear or see the name. If I got more out of it than cost I'd feel like a robber." [44]

Wednesday, January 24, Harper wrote Simpson a letter at 10:00 A. M. He enclosed a card that he received earlier that morning from I. N. Levi and trusted he would get a nibble for his efforts and "it seems to me it is now or never." [45] That nibble never materialized.

There was suddenly some renewed interest from American Box Ball Company. On Saturday, January 20, Fred Hoke of the American Box Ball Company wrote to John Harper, saying that he was replying to Harper's letter of January 17 to lock box 133 in Indianapolis, Indiana, and that if Harper had a good thing they could put it on the market. [46]

The following Monday, Harper wrote back to Simpson, stating that he had not written that letter Hoke referred to, and that he "perceived carelessness" on Hoke's part at the American Box Ball Company. [47] He was probably right to be suspicious. Box Ball was not doing well in the market at all, and Hoke certainly might have been happy to destroy a competitor.

In a letter Harper wrote Simpson two days later, he finished with the following:

> *I do not know what to think of Box Ball Co., mabe [sic] they are not doing so much business with their own game, and do not think much of ours. Return this letter with instructions so I can answer it.* [48]

Skee-Ball alley cost analysis for Levi, p. 1.
(Courtesy Vineland Historical and Antiquarian Society)

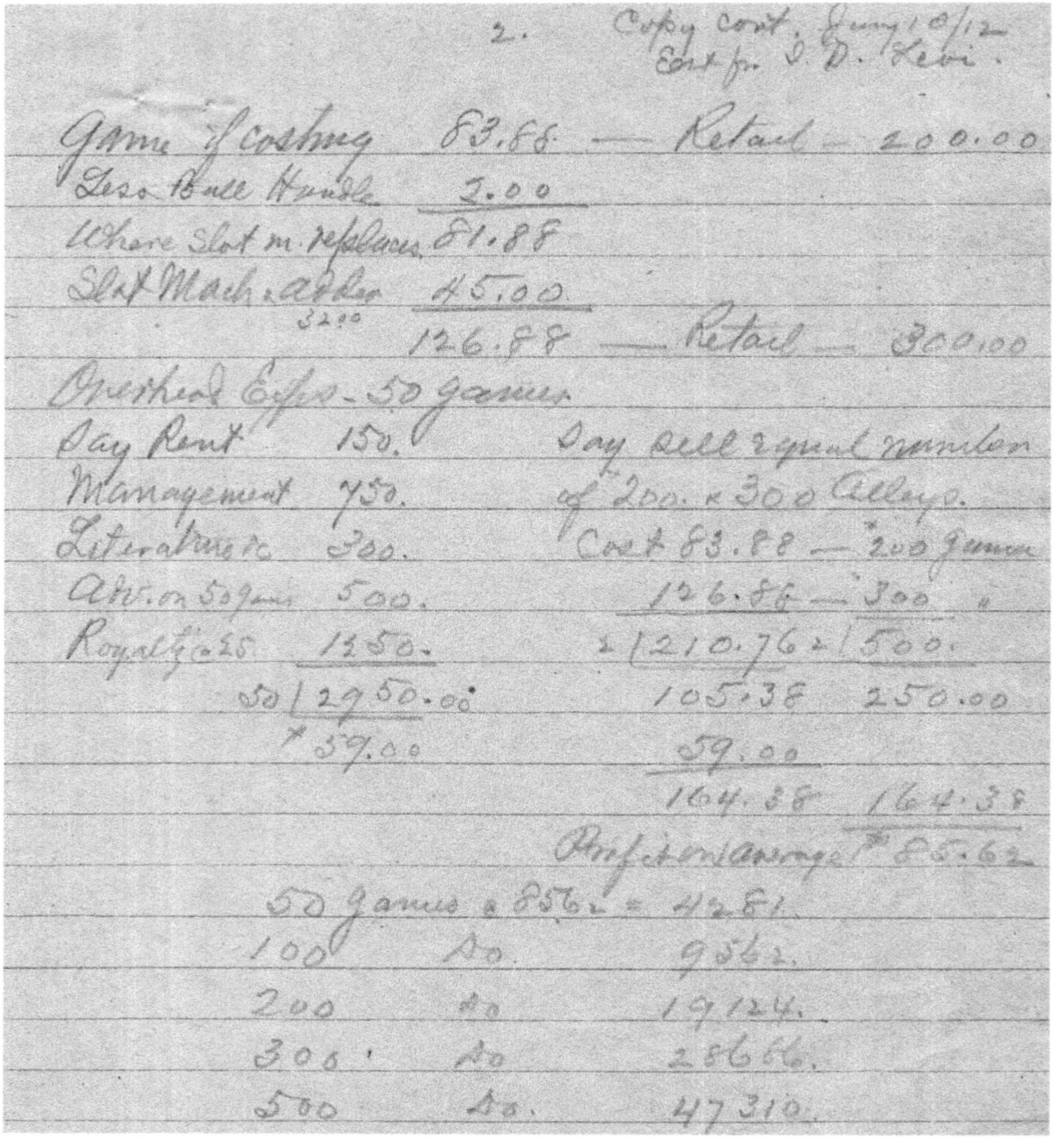

handwritten notes:

2.   Copy cost, Jany 10/12
     Sent for I. D. Levi.

Game of costing   83.88 — Retail — 200.00
Less Ball Handle   2.00
Where Slot m. replaces 81.88
Slot Mach. added   45.00
                3200
                     126.88 — Retail — 300.00

Overhead Exps - 50 games
Day Rent   150.   Say sell equal number
Management   750.   of 200 & 300 alleys.
Literature &c   350.   Cost 83.88 — 200 games
Adv. on 50 games 500.   126.88 — 300 "
Royalties 25   1250.   2)210.76 2)500.
            50)2950.00   105.38   250.00
              + 59.00   59.00
                             164.38   164.38
                            Profit on average 85.62

      50 games @ 85.62 = 4281.
     100   do   9562.
     200   do   19124.
     300   do   28686.
     500   do   47310.

Skee-Ball alley cost analysis for Levi, p. 2.
(Courtesy Vineland Historical and Antiquarian Society)

Skee-Ball alley cost analysis for Levi, p. 3.
(Courtesy Vineland Historical and Antiquarian Society)

On Sunday, January 28, Harper scanned through the Philadelphia Inquirer classified ads from investors, looking for patents to purchase or businesses to invest in. He cut out several that seemed most promising and sent them to Simpson so he might reply. Since Harper was still too broke to afford rent, he also told Simpson that he had been offered a job for $12 a week counting lumber, working out in the cold from 7 A. M. to 6 P. M. He had done that awful work before in his father's lumber yard, and lamented that he did not want to go back to such slavery. [49]

This was the measure of how far they had fallen. John W. Harper had started his career with that miserable job of counting lumber, in the heat and the rain and the snow, and finally worked his way up to owning the lumber yard. Falling into times so hard that he had to return the bottom again, in that brutal, low-paying position, was more than he could bear. It was clear that something needed to happen soon.

Harper wrote to Simpson on Wednesday, February 28, to tell him that he had a meeting with another potential investor, but the individual in question told Harper that the finances were too tangled. Harper told Simpson that he assured the person that he could give them a clean proposition. He made the following proposal to Simpson:

Would you agree to the $5 from me in the 5 states, and 1/3 of 10% in the other states: this would equal 6.67 for alleys selling for $200; $10 for alleys selling for $300. Budd said, today, he would agree to anything I say.

I would suggest if party put up $2500, and agree to spend $2500 within 3 years to make & advertise skee ball, we agree to give him control of skee for that length of time.

If this does not work as an individual, I might work two or three parties for $1500 each, including Sauter.

If someone wanted to buy patent within the 3 years; we would agree to take 1/2 of selling price providing it is $50000 or over (fifty thousand) [50]

He also informed Simpson that he expected a party from Cincinnati to come and see an alley in operation on Saturday. After he signed the letter he wrote in a box off to the side:

We might interest 5 people @ $1000. each.

Anything! [51]

There was yet one more piece of bad news, perhaps the worst of all.

On Wednesday, February 21, 1912, against the

sound of the pounding rain, Harper mailed Simpson a letter updating him on his struggles to find work. Harper wrote that every day or so he had answered advertisements for jobs and had not received any replies to them. He had hoped to get a job at Chestnut Hill Amusement Park for the season and parlay that position to interest someone into investing in Skee-Ball. [52]

And then he dropped the bombshell.

Chestnut Hill Park was to be sold to a syndicate of wealthy homeowners in the Chestnut Hill area of Philadelphia, who planned to close the park and develop it as residential real estate. [53]

A desperate Harper was still pinning his hopes on William Sauter at Tryon, and the closing of the park was a real blow, as he was hoping to show him the alleys in operation at the park. He told Simpson that he would go to see Sauter the following day anyway.

He finished the letter by saying:

> *If all else fails, can't we start stock company, or if Tryon would sell product we could get Auchy to build alleys: he said he would like to build them.*
>
> *The papers say, today, C. H. Park sold to syndicate.* [54]

The Fall—The Closing of White City.

Surely having Skee-Ball alleys at Chestnut Hill Park, a profitable and prosperous amusement park, could be the one solid, reliable anchor in the midst of the instability and disappointment that was the Skee-Ball business. But even this was destined to be a part of the chaos. Why would one of the most popular amusement parks in the region, and the most profitable, suddenly close?

Chestnut Hill Park was actually located in Erdenheim, adjacent to the suburb of Wyndmoor, in Springfield Township, Montgomery County. It was located just outside of the wealthy suburb of Chestnut Hill, which the last neighborhood at the very edge of northwest Philadelphia before crossing into Montgomery County. Chestnut Hill proper was a well-to-do suburban Philadelphia neighborhood. It had originally been a vacation destination where wealthy people would leave the city for their large homes with wide verandas to spend the summer. With the arrival of trolley lines, it became a year-around residential neighborhood with a distinct environment, open and undeveloped, genteel and surrounded by nature. Several trolley lines served the neighborhood: Union Traction from Center City, Lehigh Valley from Allentown, and Schuykill Valley from Pottstown and Reading.

Wyndmoor and Erdenheim were just beginning to transform from farm villages into neighborhoods of estates for the wealthy that made them a natural extension of Chestnut Hill. But this location just outside the city had also made it an ideal location for Chestnut Hill Park, which had opened in 1898. The park was designed to attract working, middle-class people looking to spend their spare cash on weekend leisure activities. In this Victorian era, no liquor was allowed on the grounds of the park, and people were expected to dress up in their Sunday best to be allowed on the grounds. Although Auchy himself lived in Erdenheim, and required formal dress and behavior standards for people entering the park, it was still seen by the neighborhood as an ingression of lower class people into their idyllic surroundings.

On the other hand, there was a rather notorious tavern, The Wheel Pump Inn, across Bethlehem Pike from the park. The inn's proprietress and Auchy had a running battle. She sold alcoholic beverages, and allegedly had gambling and other dubious activities on the premises, resulting regularly in fights and arrests. Of course, this was anathema to the tone Auchy was trying to set with the park. It was too easy for people to cross the Pike, have a snort of liquor, and return somewhat inebriated. Predictably, there were police raids and arrests at the Wheel Pump Inn on a

Philadelphia Inquirer article announcing the sale of Chestnut Hill Park in early 1912.
(Author's Collection)

fairly regular basis, and rightly or wrongly, she thought Auchy was the instigator of the raids.

She retaliated. At this time, there were a number of "blue laws" in effect regarding what you were prohibited from doing on the Sabbath, including playing music and creating excessive noise. The laws were enforced pretty rigorously during much of the 19th century, but only sporadically in the late 19th and early 20th century throughout the state. Enforcement came either during periods of political reform or when districts needed to raise some revenue. In spite of her obvious infractions at the Wheel Pump Inn, she turned around and used the Blue Laws as an excuse to call police (who were likely making some extra cash from the proprietress) to Chestnut Hill Park. They arrested people for offenses like playing music on the Sabbath. Although it was just a form of petty harassment, it was quite annoying to Auchy, since he would have to go down and bail out his employees and musicians every time this happened. [55]

At the beginning of 1912, a syndicate of four wealthy landowners, George C. Thomas Jr. Charles N. Welsh, Wilson Potter, and Jay Cooke III offered Auchy $500,000 to buy the park. Their stated intention was to develop the open real estate into a neighborhood of genteel homes. From Auchy's perspective, the park was becoming a nuisance. He owned the Philadelphia Toboggan Company, which manufactured the carousels and toboggan coaster cars and park furniture. He profitably leased these rides and amusements to other parks under a master shell company, the Maple Company. He used a separate shell company for each project to protect his assets from lawsuits, should he be sued for accidents with the rides. [56] A savvy businessman focused on maximizing his profits, and minimizing his liabilities, he was probably tired of the day to day difficulties associated with running Chestnut Hill Park. He sold the park and never looked back.

In the end, the syndicate prevailed. They bought out the park with the nominal intention of doing real estate development, but really, it was to relieve the neighborhood of an undesirable attraction. The neighborhood of high-end homes was never constructed. Thus ended the saga of Chestnut Hill Park.

Simpson, Harper and the Skee-Ball Alley company were just collateral damage. But in spite of the numbingly bad news, they persevered.

On Saturday, March 2, Harper waited for that interested party from Cincinnati to come meet with him. He never showed up. [57]

Two days later, Harper asked Simpson to make

him a proposition so he had the licensing terms of a business agreement to offer a prospective buyer for manufacturing the alleys. He told Simpson that it might be easier to interest two people instead of one, each paying for half the investment they were trying to get. He reported that the individual he was hoping would come see him did not make the meeting, making the observation: "Amusement people are thoroughly unreliable: all of them are N[o]. G[ood]." [58]

Desperate, Harper attempted to persuade Arnold Aiman, the co-owner of Chestnut Hill Park, and Sauter to invest in Skee-Ball. They declined his offer. Harper then went to another prospect, a Mr. Rosatto, and tried to get him to invest. Again, no interest. Finally in a last ditch effort he wrote a letter to the E. T. Burrowes Company in Portland, Maine. They declined his proposal as well. [59]

On Saturday, March 16, a large display ad appeared in The Billboard. Chestnut Hill Park, Philadelphia, was selling off the entire contents of the park because the property had been sold for real estate development. Among the items listed for sale were two Skee-Ball Alleys. [60]

By the following Monday, a deeply depressed Harper wrote Joseph Fourestier Simpson a letter.

Dear Simpson,

I can see nothing but defeat for Skee; I am all out.

I tried to coax 2 into the fold and last week I got their final report -- I cannot interest them, altho they both think Skee O.K. -- Aiman and Sauter were the parties. Then I tried Rosatto. I could not interest him a little bit. Then I wrote Burrowes Co., Portland, Me nothing doing. Now I am through.

I am sorry I have tools & parts scattered around Aucheys[sic] shop & Chest. Hill, but I have no place to keep them, and suppose I will loose[sic] them. I can do nothing.

I am trying for a job in lumber yard.

Yours, J. W. H. [61]

That was the last communication they had that year. Although the balls continued to roll down the alleys and fly toward the targets in dozens of locations across the country, the Skee-Ball Alley Company was effectively dead.

SKEE-BALL ALLEY CO.,
PHILADELPHIA, PA.

3/4/12

Dear Simpson

Expected to hear from you not later than this morning. Make a proposition to me alone that I may make a proposition to anyone whom I can interest in manufacturing the alleys. It might be easier to interest two persons for ½ an amount than interest one person for the whole amount.

I expected party on Saturday last from Cincinnati; but he came not. Amusement people are thoroughly unreliable: all of them are N. G.

Let me hear from you by return mail. I have a funeral Wednesday next.

11 A.M.

Yours truly,
J.

Letter from John W. Harper to Joseph Fourestier Simpson, March 4, 1912.
(Courtesy Vineland Historical and Antiquarian Society)

The Wheel Pump Inn across from Chestnut Hill Park
(Courtesy Springfield Township Historical Society)

Chestnut Hill Park, Philadelphia, Sold for Real Estate Development, hence these

UP-TO-DATE PARK AMUSEMENTS & PERSONAL PROPERTY TO BE SOLD AT A SACRIFICE

Owing to the rapidly increasing values of real estate, this most popular Philadelphia Park has been sold, which throws their entire possessions on the market for immediate disposal. As there was no intention of selling the park until within the last few months, everything is in first-class condition. Ten thousand dollars worth of the personal property was purchased new in season of 1911. This is a rare chance for amusement men to purchase devices and goods at unheard-of prices. Following are but a few of the thousands of articles for sale:

One Coaster Ride, 2,100 ft. runway, with machinery and cars, can be moved.
One Carousel, 47 ft. diameter, 3 row abreast, 2 rows jumpers, 1 row stationary—all nearly new.
One Carousel, 47 ft. diameter, 3 row abreast, all stationary, good condition.
Two large Carousel Buildings, can easily be moved.
One Scenic Railway Structure, cars and machinery.
Yellowstone Park Scenery, machinery and cars for panoramic ride.
Ladies' Cottage Building, including plumbing.
Four large Refreshment Stands, up-to-date architecture.
Fifteen Ticket Booths, various designs.
Teddy-in-Africa Amusement Device, will sell machinery and plans.
Miniature Railway Outfit, including engine, tender, 3 up-to-date cars and 1,200 ft. trackage.
300 Theatre Chairs, good condition.
Two up-to-date Moving Picture Machines.
Two Pianos, also one Nickel-in-Slot Piano, nearly new.

One large Grand Stand, seating 600 people.
One large Public Speakers' Stand.
Picnic Pavilions.
Red Mill Outfit, with boats, chain and machinery; has incline and chutes, and will sell with plans for re-erection.
New Mirror Puzzle Device, 40 plain mirrors, 30x72 and 15 comic mirrors. Will sell mirrors and plans. Good paying amusement.
Third Degree Amusement. Will sell machinery and plans.
Two Soda Fountains, 12 syrup innovations, copper tanks, ice cream cabinets.
One Roulette Wheel Outfit.
1,800 ft. 2-Rail Iron Fence & 50 Arc Lamp Posts.
Five Patent Lawn Swings and Frame.
Seven Box Ball Alleys.
Two Skee Ball Alleys.
Twenty new Steel Row Boats.
Twenty-five Wooden Row Boats.
One Racine Naphtha Launch, 18 ft. long, good condition.
One new Naphtha Launch, 16 ft. long.
One 87-key Gavioli Organ, cardboard endless system, with 400 yards music.

One 48-key German Brueder Organ, with 250 yards music, endless cardboard system.
One 92-key Marenghi Organ, 250 yards music, endless cardboard system.
One 66-key German Military Organ, 300 yards music, endless cardboard system.
2,900 4 C. P., 4,000 8 C. P. and 5,000 16 C. P. Incandescent Edison Base Lamps, in good condition. Will sell for $5.00 per 100 lamps.
11,000 Edison Base Lamp Sockets, made in streamers, good condition.
120 Helios Arc Lamps.
Twenty-five Motors, 550 volts, from ¼ to 50 h. p. Will sell at half price.
Eight Ceiling Fans.
One Two-oven Kitchen Range, Clads make, good condition.
One large Gas Stove, new.
Two large Water Heaters, new.
Six complete Bedroom Suites and Rugs, used only one season.
Lot of Bed Linens and Table Linens.
Large lot of Kitchen Utensils, Dishes, etc.
500 Park Benches, good condition.
70 large Picnic Tables, with benches attached.

175 Square Top Diningroom Tables, 30x48.
650 high back Diningroom Chairs.
429 round back Chairs.
Fifty High Stools for Lunch Counter.
275 Rocking Chairs for carousel buildings.
Lot Cashier's Chairs.
Lot Carpenters and Machinists Tools.
Lot Electric Wire and Supplies.
Lot Bunting and Decorations.
Lot Stepladders, Rope, etc.
Lot Piping, Hardware, Wire, etc.
Five Refrigerators, Water Coolers, etc.
Two Bathroom Outfits, lot of plumbing, etc.
Deep-well Pump and Fire Pump.
Lot Awnings.
Lot Fire Hose.
Eleven National Cash Registers.
Six Coffee Urns.
Lot Showcases.
Lot Popcorn Machinery, Marble Slabs, etc.
About 1,600 ft. ¾-inch Garden Hose.
One large U. S. Flag—the largest in the world—65x135 feet, made of the best Government bunting. Will sell at cost.

Prices Quoted on Grounds—No Mail Inquiries Answered

The Billboard advertisement announcing the sale of goods of Chestnut Hill Amusement Park.
(Author's Collection)

150   Chapter 5 • The Struggle For Redemption

SKEE-BALL ALLEY CO.,
PHILADELPHIA, PA.

3/18/12

Dear Simpson,

I can see nothing but defeat for Skee; I am all out. I tried to coax 2 into the fold and last week I got their final report — I cannot interest them, altho they both think Skee OK — Aiman and Sautter were the parties. Then I tried Rosatto. I could not interest him a little bit. Then I wrote Burrowes Co., Portland, Me. Nothing doing. Now I am through. I am sorry I have tools & parts scattered around Auchey's shop & Chest. Hill, but I have no place to keep them, and suppose I will loose them. I can do nothing.

I am trying for a job in lumber yard.

Yours, JWH

Letter from John W. Harper to Joseph Fourestier Simpson, March 18, 1912.
(Courtesy Vineland Historical and Antiquarian Society)

Chapter 6

THE RESURRECTION
J. D. Este

The Skee-Ball Alley Company, it turned out, was not dead, but perhaps in a lengthy coma.

Lumber industry players seem to play an inordinately large role in the early history of Skee-Ball. Simpson's first business was running a lumber planing mill. John W. Harper owned a lumber yard he bought from former owner and later business partner William Nice Jr. And the eventual savior and heir to the Skee-Ball business was the son of a major lumber merchant in Philadelphia: Jonathan Dickinson (J. D.) Este.

The Este family residence was located only a few blocks from Simpson's childhood home in Philadelphia. Unlike the middle class Simpson family, the Estes were fairly wealthy, part of the Philadelphia elite, with several of them being members of the prestigious Union League. The Estes were also descendants of the founder of Princeton University. Naturally, Charles Este, owner of the Charles Este Lumber Company, sent his son J. D. Este to Princeton when he was of age, to earn his degree and then take his place in the family business. The network of contacts J. D. Este developed while at Princeton was to prove crucial to his success, and to the success of Skee-Ball.

When J. D. Este returned to Philadelphia after graduation in 1909, he made a pass-time of playing Skee-Ball at one of the local venues starting in 1910. He joined his father's lumber company as a clerk, and by 1912, he was promoted to the office of company Treasurer. A man of medium height and slender build, he was restless and adventurous, and not cut out to stay in the lumber business. From the day he returned to Philadelphia, he was searching for an opportunity to spread his wings.

While Este was playing Skee-Ball, and rising in the company ranks at Charles Este Lumber, Simpson continued to tinker and invent things while trying to keep himself and his endeavors afloat. On May 21, 1913, Joseph F. Simpson returned to his merchant roots and filed a patent application for a "Shipping Package" to ship fragile items like eggs safely over the road and the rails. His patent stated:

> "My invention relates to improvements in packages and more particularly improvements in packages for shipping eggs, fruit and similar articles that are of a fragile nature and liable to be broken or bruised in ordinary shipping packages, and the object of my invention is to furnish a package for this purpose that will be inexpensive and efficient and all the parts of which may be separated and laid out flat for the purpose of taking up a minimum space for storage or in shipment to the point where they are to be assembled for use." [1]

In late 1913, J. D. Este became interested enough to explore the possibilities of Skee-Ball as a business. It appears that he helped the struggling Skee-Ball Alley Company by getting them into a new manufacturing facility at 20th and Cumberland Streets [2], a location just behind the Charles Este Lumber Company where he was the Treasurer.

After more than a year's hiatus, a quarter page ad for Skee-Ball appeared in the November 29, 1913 issue of The Billboard from the Skee-Ball Alley Company, showing the new address, and a drawing of a man playing the game.

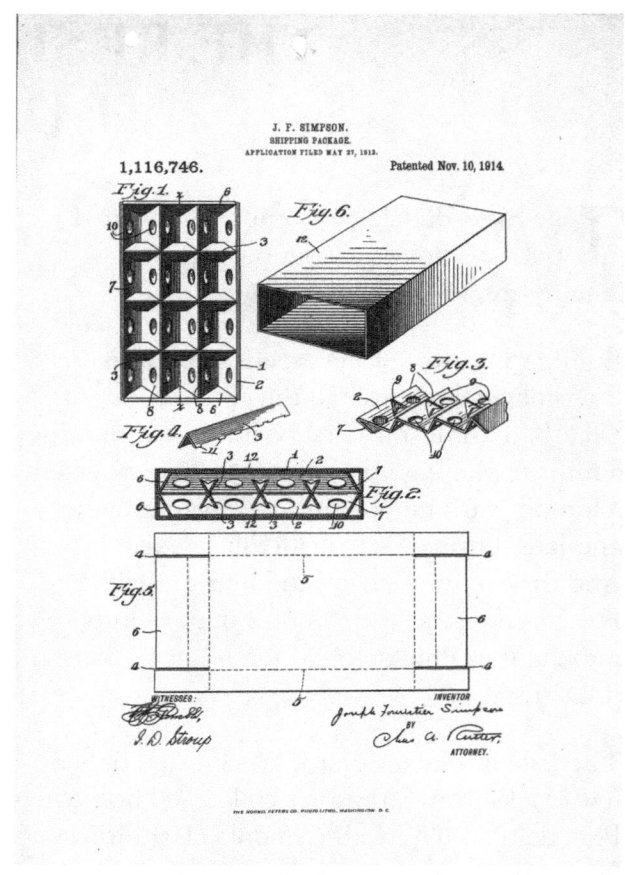

US Patent No. 1,116,746, Shipping Package.
(Courtesy National Archives and Records Administration, Kansas City)

SKEE BALL

Most Fascinating And Skillful

Game Of The Century

LARGE RETURNS ====
INVESTMENT MODERATE *For Pleasure Resorts,*

Parks and Amusement Parlors Write today for full particulars

SKEE BALL ALLEY CO.

20th and Cumberland St., Philadelphia, Pa. [3]

Although Este had no venue for the alleys himself, he arranged for a popular billiard room near the Princeton University campus to install two Skee-Ball alleys, and furnished them at his own expense. January 24, 1914, an ad from the Skee-Ball Alley Company appeared in the Daily Princetonian inviting undergraduates to see the introduction of Skee-Ball in Princeton at C. Von Voigt's Pool Parlor on Nassau Street.[4]

Unfortunately, the game was popular for a few weeks and then the enthusiasm for it fizzled. [5]

Este was undeterred. Borrowing money on his own account, he rented a location in Atlantic City, opposite the Million Dollar Pier at a cost of $3,000 a year, installed electric signs, and set up several Skee-Ball alleys. In a letter to his cousin Edward, Simpson described how he watched Este with concern. He let Este know he thought he was "taking a great risk," with his money, to which Este replied, "Mr. Simpson, this cannot be made to succeed any other way." [6] Truer words were never spoken. The performance of the alleys in Atlantic City must have met all of Este's expectations, and those of his investors, because within a few months, he made his decision to buy the company.

Another advertisement ran in The Billboard on March 21, 1914. The text of the ad copy read:

SKEE-BALL

For Pleasure Resorts, Parks, and All-Year Amusement Parlors.

An entirely new idea in BOWLING. Susceptible to the highest SKILL in play. Positively no bowling game so fascinating as SKEE BALL. [sic] For men and women. Size 32 and 36 ft. long, 4 ft. wide, 9 ft. high. Balls stiffly bowled; midway of alley mount in the air and fly to the target. SCORING: AUTOMATIC: progress of count seen by player and audience. This feature a winner. Balls return by

SKEE--BALL

UNDERGRADUATES! You are invited to assemble to-night at the pool parlors of one C. Von Voigt, in Nassau Street, to see the introduction of SKEE-BALL, a bowling game with a different thrill.

SKEE-BALL is brand new. It is a con test of skill, easy to play but hard enough to master, shot through with a fresh variety of excitement. Come to-night! Spin the ball down the middle of the alley and watch it leap high and dart into the targe SKEE-BALL will get you if you do.

THE SKEE-BALL ALLEY CO.

Skee-Ball Alley advertisement from the Janyary 24, 1914 Daily Princetonian
(Courtesy Princeton University)

gravity. Slot machine attends alley. ARE YOU SEEKING A PROFITABLE BUSINESS? LOOK INTO THIS! Two alleys just installed earned $72.00 in one week.

For full description send for catalogue.

Dept. A.

SKEE BALL ALLEY CO.,

20th and Cumberland Streets, Philadelphia, Pa. [7]

While waiting for his patent for the egg crate to be granted, Simpson finally succumbed to financial pressures. He'd had no income from Skee-Ball for over a year, and no prospects for other work. His own business plan had been to continue as the patent owner and licensor, so that he would have an income stream on which to retire. Harper was clearly desperate to sell, the Nice family dearly wanted their money back, and Simpson was exhausted. When J. D. Este was finally convinced he had the evidence that Skee-Ball could be successful, he was ready to make the investment that Harper and Simpson had been waiting for. They were about to sell the Skee-Ball Alley Company, and all plans and patents, to J. D. Este.

On April 22, Este went to Delaware and filed incorporation papers on the same day for two new corporations: The J. D. Este Company and the Skee-Ball Alley Company. By May 1914, Este had completed the purchase. He paid $15,000 to John W. Harper, and hired him on the spot to join his new company. He also bought all rights to the U.S. Skee-Ball patents from Simpson and the Nice estate for $25,000.00. [8] Simpson retained ownership of the Canadian patent, licensing Este to sell into Canada for a royalty of $50 per alley. [9] Despite any misgivings Simpson may have felt, it was still an incredible relief.

Este wasted no time in getting things moving again. He made John W. Harper the general manager, and moved all of the game sales under his new company, The J. D. Este Company. Este also procured new offices, and a new place to live, and the company offices officially moved to 1534 Sansom Street in Philadelphia shortly after the purchase. [10]

Este's money and his experience in the family business served both him and the game well. Positioning the shop in the new location near the lumber yard did two things for him immediately. First, he had a nearly infinite supply of lumber at very reasonable cost. Instead of having to order the lumber and get it shipped to his manufacturing operation, he could literally walk across the street for the lumber that he needed. The second advantage to placing his manufacturing operation there was the direct access to the adjacent rail lines, thereby making it cost effective to get his products from the manufacturing location onto trains without additional transportation charges.

After purchasing the company, Este immediately put "experts" to work fixing some problems that had plagued the game for the four years that Simpson had manufactured it, including the scoring device. On May 30, Joseph M. Doebrich, one of Este's engineers, was awarded patent 1,185,071 Scoring Mechanism For Game Apparatus, assignor to The J. D. Este Co. This badly needed improvement was one of the stumbling blocks for Simpson's version of the game. [11] Having access to equipment and better tools allowed him to refine other aspects of the game as well, and the alleys now sported a metal plate on each alley with The J. D. Este Company name prominently displayed.

Este's changes may have been a key part of Skee-Ball's rising success. When he released his new version of the game, sales took off. According to letters from Simpson to H. H. Russell of The E. T. Burrowes Company, Louis Berni, and David Tim, Esq., he stated that J. D. Este may have made $40,000 selling Skee-Ball Alleys in his first year, an astounding amount of money for the times. [12, 13, 14]

John T. Byrne was one of those early buyers of Skee-Ball alleys. In 1913, he had purchased property on the boardwalk in Wildwood, New Jersey. He outfitted his operation with four Skee-Ball alleys. Byrne hoped that the Skee-Ball alleys would attract a crowd and thereby form a new amusement center at his establishment on the boardwalk. By the end of his first summer, the alleys Byrne had purchased netted an average of $52.15 per day over the course of the summer. [16] That was an astounding average of 1043 games played per day. This would be a powerful marketing message of which Este would later take full advantage.

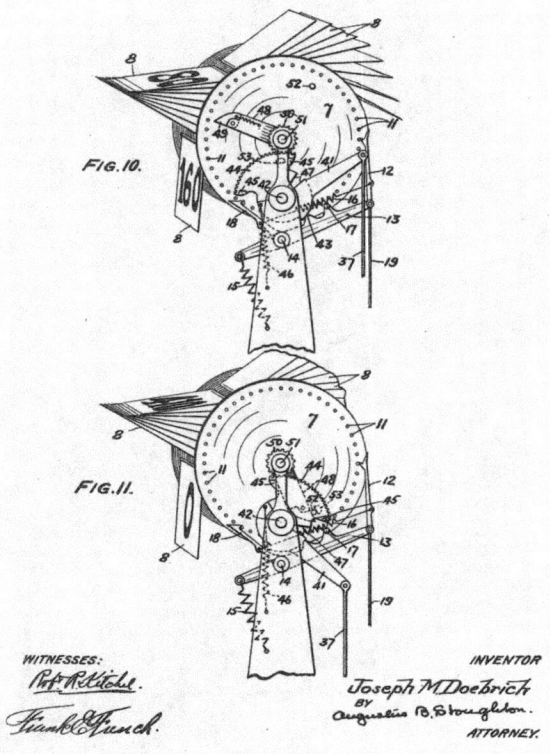

Doebrich Patent for Skee-Ball Scoring Device.
(Courtesy National Archives and Records Administration, Kansas City)

Mechanical Skee-Ball Scoring Device
(Courtesy Philadelphia Toboggan Coasters, Inc. Archive)

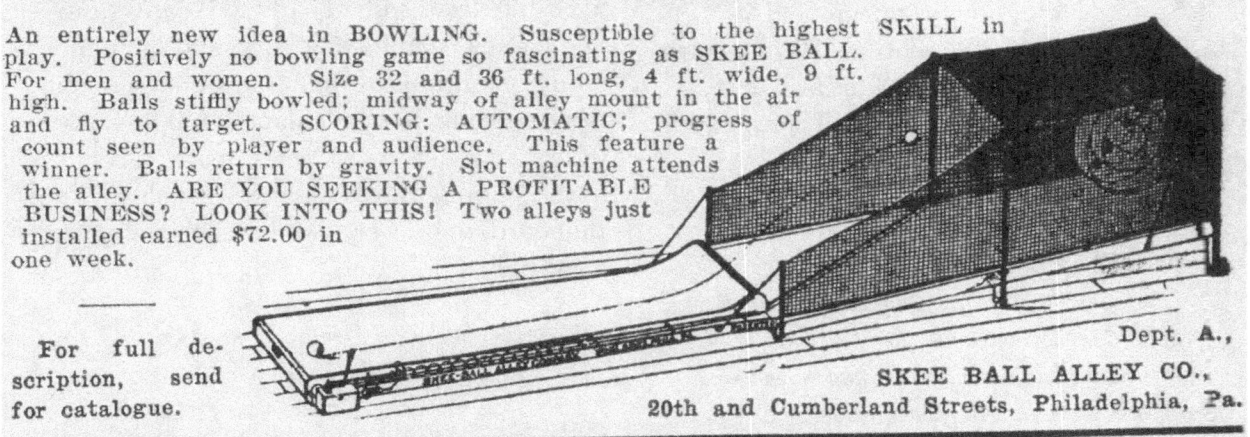

Skee-Ball Alley Company advertisement, March 21, 1914.
(Author's Collection)

Also during the month of April that year, Charles "Chief" Bender, a well-known pitcher for the Philadelphia Athletics, became enamored of the game. When not pitching for the Philadelphia A's, Charles Bender ran his sporting goods store at 1309 Arch Street in Philadelphia. Bender installed and operated three Skee-Ball alleys at his store. [17]

On May 6, an article appeared in The Springfield Union, in Springfield, Massachusetts about Bender having been part of a Skee-Ball competition. This article may be the first documented Skee-Ball competition event.

> *"Not content with honors attained in baseball and trapshooting, [Charles] Chief Bender of the Athletics, Monday attempted to land the Philadelphia skee-ball [sic] title. His natural keen-sightedness and sureness of arm stood him in good stead but the greater experience of his opponent proved too much to overcome."* [18]

The momentum of the game continued. A small article appeared in Variety on June 5.

> *"Skee-ball is a new amusement enterprise in which three members of the Philadelphia Stock Exchange have invested some money. They have secured the skee-ball concession at the Panama-Pacific Exposition and plan to operate a hundred alleys. Skee-ball is on the order of bowling."* [19]

With the beginnings of success for the alleys, the local governments began to take notice as well. In the compilation of ordinances for Atlantic City, Skee-Ball was listed as one of the businesses that had to pay a yearly licensing tax. The tax for Skee-Ball was $5 per alley. [20]

Skee-Ball fever spread early to Atlantic City and Coney Island, New York, and the major industry journals as well as local news media were noticing. In particular, The Billboard thought Skee-Ball was newsworthy. On July 4, in the "Coney Island Chatter" article in The Billboard, there were two line items about Skee-Ball:

> *"The Skee Ball Game is doing good business."*

and

> *"Skee Ball is doing well under the management of Mr. Hartman."* [21]

And on July 11, in the "Coney Island Chatter" article in The Billboard, there was mention of two new Skee-Ball Alleys being installed at Coney Island. One of the Skee-Ball Alleys was installed on the boardwalk between Brighton and Coney; the other was installed at Jones' Walk and the Bowery. [22]

Charles Bender
(Courtesy Library of Congress)

The momentum propelled the game forward, from media attention featuring even more articles, to the founding of sales companies devoted entirely to selling the game. Pacific Coast Skee-Ball Company incorporated in July as a Delaware corporation with a capitalization of $2,000,000. The incorporators were F. R. Hansell, Philadelphia; G. H. B. Martin and E. T. Vanell, Camden, New Jersey. [23, 24]

On both July 25 and August 1, a wanted advertisement appeared in The Billboard. The writer was looking to trade several items for Skee-Ball alleys. The alleys were beginning to outstrip their competitors at the American Box Ball Company, just as Simpson had predicted. The text of the advertisement read:

> WANTED--*Skee-Ball Alleys; will trade one concession tent, 10x10 like new; three automatic ten-pin pool tables, complete with cues and cue balls, or will sell several boxball alleys cheap. Also two 4x8 Brunswick pool tables. Address* SKEEBALL, *care Billboard, Cleveland, Ohio.* [25, 26]

Looking forward to expanding into the overseas business, on August 12, 1914, John W. Harper and J. Dickinson Este applied for a foreign patent for Skee-Ball under the title "Improvements in game apparatus" in Australia. [27]

Articles continued to appear in the industry and the local press.

An article titled "Skee-Ball." appeared in The Billboard on September 5, which correctly credited Joseph Fourestier Simpson of Vineland, New Jersey as the inventor of Skee-Ball, and noted that the J. D. Este Company of Philadelphia had purchased all patents and rights to the game. The article suggested that the reason for lackluster sales by Simpson's company was the unreliability of the automatic features, noting that J. D. Este took up Skee-Ball, "when it was in a very crude form."

It also announced that Arthur L. Wheeler, previously an All American of Princeton Football fame, resigned from a New York Stock Exchange house to become vice-president and secretary of the J. D. Este Company. [28]

By now it was obvious that Este, with his family connections and his university experience, was able to bring real business-people to the table. Arthur L. Wheeler must have seen major potential in the game to leave Wall Street and join the company, anxious to realize its potential for both popularity and business profitability. Arthur's brother Herbert, also a former athlete from Princeton University, soon joined him as one of The J. D. Este Company officers.

In the same issue of The Billboard in which the "Skee-Ball" article appeared, the J. D. Este Company's very first advertisement also appeared. It was a radical departure from previous advertisements and included a photograph of the game being played, not just the line drawings of the previous advertisements.

Este's company would use this general format over the next several years. The text of the advertisement read:

SKEE-BALL.

The success of Skee-Ball at the various seashore resorts this summer has been noteworthy. The game was invented in 1908 by J. F. Simpson, of Vineland, N. J., and had a desultory existence, due to the unreliability of the automatic features, until last spring, when in May the J. D. Este Company, a corporation with ample capital, purchased all patents and rights to the game and immediately put trained experts at work in perfecting the automatic scoring device and coin machine, with entirely satisfactory results.

only after a nickel has been inserted in the slot. This does away with the need of an attendant and makes it possible to play the game at any time of the day or night.

To the confidence and courage of Mr. Este, the president of the J. D. Este Company, belongs the credit of developing and perfecting the game. Mr. Este, who is a member of the firm of the Charles Este Lumber Company, of Philadelphia, took up Skee-Ball four years ago, when it was in a very crude form, and his persistent efforts have resulted in the present success.

Arthur L. Wheeler, who resigned from the firm of a New York Stock Exchange house, to become vice-president and secretary of the J. D. Este Company, is prominent in many branches of sport, but is probably best known as a football player at Princeton, where he had the unusual honor of being chosen for the all-American team for three consecutive years. The company maintains an attractive office at 1534 Sansom street, Philadelphia, and extend a cordial welcome to all who wish to try their hand at the game.

Skee-Ball article from The Billboard,
September 5, 1914.
(Author's Collection)

Clubs! Pool Rooms! Bowling Alleys!

Get your orders in now if you wish to enjoy the amazing financial returns that were the season's sensation at Atlantic City, Coney Island and other prominent resorts on the Atlantic and Pacific coasts.

The automatic coin device eliminates the expense of an operator. The automatic scoring device attracts the crowd. And the fascination of the game holds them. It is easy to play but hard to beat.

Write for booklet.

THE J. D. ESTE CO. Owners and Distributors 1534 Sansom Street, - Philadelphia, Pa. [29]

By now the game of Skee-Ball had begun to get serious attention in the area of West Philadelphia, so much so, that a lengthy article appeared in the Evening Ledger in Philadelphia describing the game and its phenomenal success in the region. Along with the text of the article was a box drawing showing players and spectators, and advancing and possible theories as to the origin of the game. This game in particular had an odd habit of attracting unfounded theories about its origin, and it would only get more pronounced over time.

War news and world's baseball series have been entirely forgotten these days by West Philadelphia storekeepers, life insurance agents, mechanics and salesmen. Veteran German pinochle players, Hungarians who play "klabias" and Italians who are experts in "trieste" have turned their minds to another game. West Philadelphia has gone mad over "skeeball," [sic] and even Hungarian goulash is forgotten.

Any resident in the vicinity of 52d and Market streets will tell you that you are not a real West Philadelphian if you have never heard of "skeeball." [sic] Red letters printed on a large white canvas sign, which is nailed over the front part of 5143 Market street, informs new residents of West Philadelphia that "skeeball" [sic] is the game of games. True West Philadelphians already understand all the scientific points about the game.

A well-known amusement promoter, who visited the West Philadelphia skeeball [sic] court, was so impressed with the game that he decided to establish skeeball [sic] alleys or courts in all parts of the city. The man believes that the people are in receptive mood for some new kind of amusement, and that they have been obliged to tolerate too much of one thing. Skeeball [sic] he predicts will solve the problem as it gives the player something to thing about and exercise at the same time. As a result of plans made by the promoter, skeeball [sic] promises to be not only a West Philadelphia fad, but equally popular all over the city. [30]

The article went on to very briefly describe the construction of the game and how it was played.

Continuing to aggressively market the game, Este arranged for Skee-Ball alleys to be installed at the Aquarium Court of the American Electric Railway Association's 1914 convention in Atlantic City, one of the trolley companies' major industry meetings. [31] In addition to having an exhibit to sell them, prizes were given for players scoring the highest number of points. A notice about the installation of the alleys was part of the writeup, "The Week's Entertainments." On the same page, the first day of scores were listed along with the person's name. And it was clearly no longer only "A Man's Game." The players and their scores were as follows [32]:

Mrs. W. E. Bryan	*180*	*D. H. Ackerson*	*240*
Mrs. George Allison	*150*	*J. R. Ong*	*240*
Mrs. C. Chamberlain	*150*	*A. K. McCarthy*	*240*

October 14, the best scores for Tuesday's players were published. The high scores for Tuesday were as follows:

Mrs. T. W. E. Connette	*220*
Mr. C. G. Chamberlain	*310*
Mrs. W. E. Bryan	*180*
Mr. T. M. Cluley	*290*
Mrs. R. M. Kerschner	*180*

The information about the Tuesday's scores also included the fact that The J. D. Este Company was supplying prizes for the highest scores each day, boxes of candy and cigars, and grand prizes for the highest scores of the week. [33]

This was the beginning of Skee-Ball's role as one of the great "Redemption Games" in history: Bowling for money and prizes. Since it was a game of skill, the desire for prizes and recognition was added incentive to play as often as possible, both for fun and a chance for the reward.

Este had photographs taken of the Skee-Ball installation at the convention that would later appear as part of the marketing campaign for Skee-Ball.

Another article appeared on November 2, this time in the Miami Herald, about the popularity of the Skee-Ball alleys recently installed at Bob Hill's new billiards parlor.

Theories as to the origin of the Skee-Ball game from the Evening Ledger, Philadelphia, Pa, 1914.
(Courtesy Library of Congress)

Continuing with their marketing effort, The J. D. Este Company prepared a folder of information about Skee-Ball. The company announced the availability of the literature in the November 7 issue of the Electric Railway Journal. [34]

Skee-Ball was having a lot of "firsts" in addition to its tournaments and prizes. On November 9, 1914, the first recorded skirmish related to Skee-Ball took place at John T. Byrne's poolroom at 4501 Lancaster Ave. in Philadelphia. While playing Skee-Ball a fight broke out involving the son of John Murray, a constable in Philadelphia. The young man was arrested and held on a $300 bond. [35]

With the robust investment of time and money, thanks to J. D. Este, along with his business connections and knowledge, Skee-Ball was not only revived, but successfully launched. And not a moment too soon for Este.

On the evening of January 3, 1915, just after the new year got off to a rousing start, a train on the New York division of the Pennsylvania Railroad came around a turn of an elevated section near the Charles Este Lumber Company. As the train made its way around the turn, sparks flew from the wheels and fell on the lumber yard below, causing the lumber to ignite. The fire spread quickly, and with a huge amount of lumber for fuel, the blaze rapidly became intense.

> **THE FIRE RECORD**
>
> **$900,000 Fire in Philadelphia Lumber Yards—200 Firemen Injured, 27 of Them in Hospitals**
>
> Philadelphia, Jan. 4. — The fire, which raged all day yesterday in the lumber yards of the Charles Este Company here, was still smouldering early today. Conservative estimate places the loss at $900,000. The entire stock of the corporation, its offices, sheds and stables, and 17 dwelling houses were destroyed. Twenty-seven firemen are in hospitals in critical conditions and nearly 200 other firemen suffered minor injuries.

Article about the fire at the Charles Este lumber yard.
(Courtesy Library of Congress)

With another large fire burning in Camden, firefighters were spread thin. A decision was made to bring one of the Philadelphia departments back to Philadelphia to try and fight the Charles Este Lumber blaze. More than 50 firemen were overcome by smoke and heat and were transported to local hospitals. The rail line was shut down for more than ninety minutes.

In addition to the lumber yard being a total loss, seventeen structures on Glenwood Avenue also burned to the ground. The next day, the lumber yard continued smoldering, sending the stench of burning wood into the chilly air. [36, 37]

With the lumber yard uninsured and the amount of damage astronomical, Charles Este decided to close the doors on the lumber business for good. At this juncture, J. D. Este, of necessity, made the Skee-Ball business his full-time focus.

In the February 6, 1915 issue of the Electric Railway Journal, an ad appeared for "Skee-Ball A Profitable and Fascinating Trolley Park Attraction" by The J. D. Este Co. There was a photograph of the J. D. Este Company booth at the 1914 AER Convention in October 1914 and was one of the pictures that Este had taken for publicity during the convention. [38]

Este's family connections benefitted Skee-Ball in multiple ways in those early years. The Union League was a prestigious Philadelphia club founded in 1862 to support the Union and the policies of President Lincoln. Like many other well-to-do gentlemen in Philadelphia, both Charles Este Sr., and Charles Este Jr. were members. On February 8, the League authorized an expenditure of "no more than $375" to purchase and install the game of Skee-Ball. [39]

Beginning February 13, and over the next few weeks, Wheeling Park in West Virginia ran advertisements for concession leases. In each of the advertisements they specifically called Skee-Ball one of the concessions that they were trying to lease. [40, 41, 42, 43] In the February 13 issue of The Billboard, an article about the San Diego Exposition listed the operators and managers of the concessions on the isthmus at the exposition, prominently featuring Skee-Ball. [44]

Three more items appeared in The Billboard for The J. D. Este Company in the March 27 issue. The first was the listing of the company in the Billboard's Directory under "Skee-Ball." [45] The second was an advertisement showing photographs of the boardwalk installation and Charles Bender's final tournament photograph. The advertisement read:

SKEE-BALL

FOR RESORTS, PARKS, CLUBS, BOWLING ALLEYS

THE NEWEST, CLEVEREST AND MOST PROFITABLE ATTRACTION

IN THIS MODEST LOOKING ESTABLISHMENT AT WILDWOOD, N. J., FOUR SKEE-BALL ALLEYS EARNED AN AVERAGE OF FIFTY-

TWO DOLLARS AND FIFTEEN CENTS ($52.15) EVERY DAY LAST SUMMER.

FINALS OF TOURNAMENT ON CHIEF BENDERS ALLEYS. THE BIG INDIAN TWIRLER CAN BE SEEN SITTING IN THE CENTER OF THE MIDDLE ALLEY.

The Automatic Scoring Device attracts the crowd;

The Automatic Slot Machine collects the money;

The skill and fascination of the games holds the players;

And the attendant looks pleasant and makes change.

Place orders NOW for early deliveries.

THE J. D. ESTE COMPANY

1534 Sansom Street, - - - - - -
PHILADELPHIA [46]

Finally, in that same issue, an article appeared titled, "Skee-Ball Draws Crowds" that appears to have been written by The J. D. Este Company as part of its marketing campaign. The article discussed how the game was not only drawing crowds, but how it kept them coming back—just to play Skee-Ball. It described the game very briefly and then went on to discuss the winter season for Skee-Ball. It listed a number of venues that had Skee-Ball installations including the Chevy Chase Club of Washington, Baltimore Country Club, Union League of Philadelphia, and the Philadelphia Racquet Club. It also listed companies that were involved with Skee-Ball including The Neptune Operating Company, Chief Bender's Sporting Goods Store, and the Pacific Coast Skee-Ball Company. The article also boasted:

> *"Preparations are now being made to meet the spring demand for skee-ball [sic] in the parks and The J. D. Este Company has been obliged to organize its own factory and is putting out an excellent alley."* [47]

The J. D. Este Company was looking for new ways to make Skee-Ball even more enticing to existing amusement owners. On April 3, they placed their standard listing in The Billboard's Directory, but in the April 3 issue of the Electric Railway Journal they tried a new tactic. They showed two Skee-Ball alleys installed over bowling alleys and stated:

> *"A Skee-Ball Alley can be placed over a bowling alley without injury to either..."* [48]

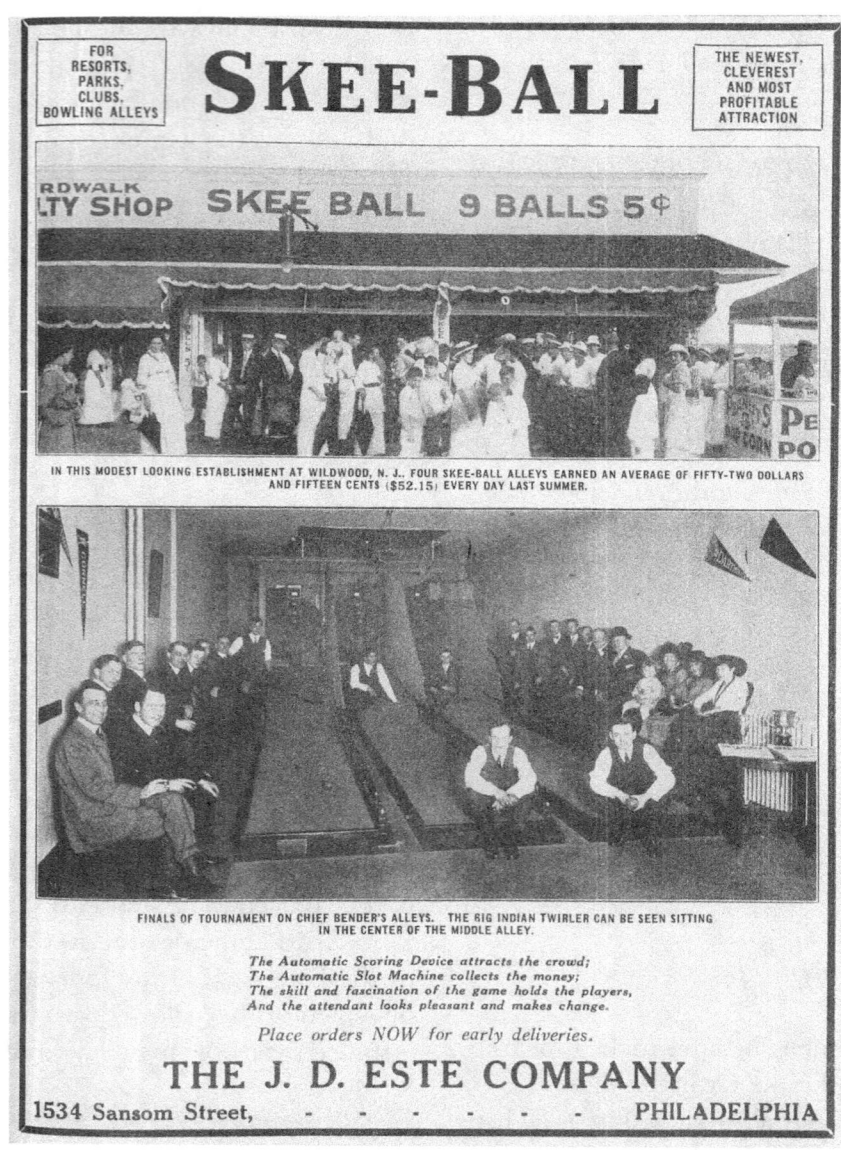

The J. D. Este Company advertisement, March 27, 1915.
(Author's Collection)

Attendant outside Playland in San Francisco, California.
(Courtesy James R. Smith Collection)

In what appeared to be an overnight success, Skee-Ball was suddenly the game to own and the game to play. A plethora of parks announced that they would be opening the 1915 season with new Skee-Ball alleys. The parks included Whalom Park, in Lunenburg, Massachusetts [49] Glen Echo Park, just outside Washington DC [50] Marshall Hall, in Washington DC [51] and Chesapeake Beach, Virginia. [52, 53, 54] Skee-Ball alleys were also being installed in more venues in Coney Island. [55]

Of the alleys in Coney Island, the New York Sun said that you needed blueprints to describe Skee-Ball — but the point was to play it: "yuh [sic] gotta see it. See?" [56]

An article in the June 1 issue of the Washington Herald reported that Marshall Hall started its season "with a gala crowd which thoroughly enjoyed the new amusements..." "...the skee ball [sic] alleys afforded new and intensely interesting amusement." [57] That same day Glen Echo Park reported that they were offering prizes for the highest scores at Skee-Ball. [58] Both Glen Echo Park and Marshall Hall ran numerous articles and advertisements in the papers about their new attractions, which included Skee-Ball. [59, 60, 61, 62, 63, 64, 65, 66, 67, 68]

Outside of the Virginia and Washington, D.C. area, Riverview Park in Springfield, Massachusetts, also installed Skee-Ball alleys as one of their new attractions. [69]

With their empire ever expanding, The J. D. Este Company took out an ad that appeared in the July 3 issue of The Billboard. The ad copy read:

SKEE-BALL

Is this fascinating and profitable bowling game in your park? If not, why not?

EUCLID BEACH PARK, Cleveland, *carries the banner with twenty-three alleys--some of the other parks and public resorts where SKEE-BALL can be seen are--*

Panama-Pacific Fair.
San Diego Fair.
Coney Island, N. Y.
Brighton Beach, N. Y.
Sheepshead Bay, N. Y.
Rockaway Beach, N. Y.
Rye Beach, N. Y.
Classon Point, N. Y.
Rorick's Glen Park, Emira, N. Y.
Times Square, N. Y.
Atlantic City, N. J.
Cape May, N. J.
Wildwood, N. J.
Ocean City, N. J.

Skee-Ball advertisement showing Skee-Ball alleys installed on top of bowling alleys.
(Author's Collection)

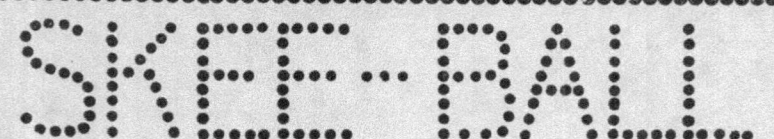

The J. D. Este Company advertisement from The Billboard, July 3, 1915.
(Author's Collection)

Stone Harbor, N. J.
Riverview Beach, Pennsville, N. J.
Glen Echo Park, Va.
Ocean Park, Va.
Petersburg, Va.
Marshall Hall, Md.
Chesapeake Beach, Md. [sic]
Pen Mar Park, Md.
Riverside Park, Springfield, Mass.
Whalom Park, Fitchburg, Mass.
Canobie Lake, N. H.
Rocky Point, R. I.
Crescent Park, R. I.
Woodside Park, Phila.
Pt. Breeze Park, Phila.
Four-Mile Creek Park, Erie, Pa.
Harvey's Lake, Wilkesbarre, Pa.
York, Pa.
Marlin Park, Pottsville, Pa.
Luna Park, Cleveland
Meyers Lake Park, Canton, Ohio
Springfield Lake, East Akron, Ohio.
Riverview Park, Chicago, Ill.
Electric Park, Kansas City, Mo.
Charlotte, N.C.
Corpus Christi, Texas.
Miami, Florida.
Venice Park, Calif.
Ocean Park, Calif.
Long Beach, Calif.
Redondo Beach, Calif.

Besides in many private clubs, country clubs, billiard rooms, bowling alleys, welfare associations and foreign countries.

THE J. D. ESTE COMPANY

1534 Sansom Street, PHILADELPHIA, PA. [70]

Their ambitions to spread Skee-Ball beyond the continent were moving forward, as John W. Harper and J. Dickinson Este were granted patent number 14.173/14 for Skee-Ball on July 6 by the Commonwealth of Australia. [71]

On July 16, an article appeared in the Corpus Christi Caller and Daily Herald titled "Skeeball [sic] The Latest Sport Craze Is Here."

SKEEBALL [sic] THE LATEST SPORT CRAZE IS HERE

Patrons of Beach Bowling Alleys Like the New Game Which is Easy to Learn.

Hear hear you failures at bowling, billiards and pinochle!

Your chance to be in the action, the firing line of sport is here. There's a new game in

Corpus Christi. Start now and you won't be laughed at for your bungles for nobody is up on the fine points of this brand new skill tester and nickel taker yet.

It's Skeeball [sic]. Maybe you have heard of it. Everybody's doin' it in Philadelphia and other watering places in the East. That is sufficient to excuse to make it the rage here or anywhere else--"it's the rage in the East."

Skeeball [sic] isn't in the dictionary. Just what the origin of the game is nobody seems to know. The Philadelphia Ledger cartoonist thinks that the caterpillar siege gun, so popular in Europe just now gave the idea for the action of the ball--you toss it--is similar to that of the shell hurled from the caterpillar gun over the walls and fortifications of a besieged city.

The Skeeball [sic] outfit that has just been installed at the Beach Bowling alleys resembles somewhat vaguely the regulation alley. A woman viewing the arrangement yesterday was heard to remark that it resembled a wash-tub or series of washtubs into which the ball from one's hand is catapulted from a ridge in the alley--if one has thrown the said ball properly, and thereby hangs the game.

The little tub and the furthest away from the is the goal usually being that which entitles him to the higher number in the total score. He throws, or rolls, nine balls (five cents) down the alley. Some fifteen feet away from him is a ridge that raises the ball into the air and into the tubs. There is a large net to save the grace of a bum marksman.

One point in favor of Skeeball [sic] is that it is absolutely neutral. There is no "English" to be used as in billiards. It is believed from the interest the game has already attracted that Skeeball [sic] has come to stay. Women have the same chance for proficiency that man has. [72]

Over the course of the month of August, Skee-Ball was mentioned in articles in Washington, DC, and New York City. [73, 74, 75] Events where Skee-Ball was one of the main activities had become prevalent enough that Skee-Ball started showing up regularly in the news. On August 31, both The Washington Times and The Washington Herald reported that the Washington Plate Printers Union Local 2 had an outing that featured a Skee-Ball tournament for both men and women. [76, 77]

On November 13, 1916, John T. Byrne, a Skee-Ball operator on the boardwalk in Wildwood, New Jersey, reported that he had his most successful day ever with six Skee-Ball alleys. The six alleys earned an amazing $262 in one day or $43.65 per alley average. [78] At a nickel a game, that came to 5,240 games played in one day.

The J. D. Este Company ran a unique advertisement in Life Magazine on October 21. The ad showed well-to-do men playing Skee-Ball dressed in tuxedos while equally well-dressed spectators watched. This was part of a concerted effort to elevate the game to appeal to the well-to-do patrons as well as the general public.

SKEE-BALL

For the Clubman

SKEE-BALL *alleys have been added to the equipment of the most exclusive clubs in the East. The fascination of this best of bowling games--a combination of skill and sporting changes--makes it tremendously popular. When the links and courts are in bad shape--when the liveliest city club is dull, Skee-Ball invariably draws the crowd that wants action. Skee-Ball alleys are conveniently built to fill odd space, they are handsome in appearance and require no attendants.*

Women play Skee-Ball too--it is splendid for the home.

WRITE FOR OUR ILLUSTRATED CATALOGUE

THE J. D. ESTE COMPANY

Skee-Ball Alleys

1534 SANSOM STREET ::: PHILADELPHIA, PA. [79]

The following day, Herbert Wheeler, Celeste Captell, Richard Walford and Jonathan Dickinson Este incorporated another company. Celeste Captell, was a former organ dealer, and by 1916, would be the President of the Canarsie Coaster Co. Inc., in New York. The four men formed the Skee-Ball Operating Company, solely to operate Skee-Ball Alleys in a building across the street from the New York Times offices in Times Square. [80, 81] Skee-Ball Operating Company, Inc. filed its Certificate of Incorporation with New York State on October 28, 1915. [82] Este and his friends had been working on installing a Skee-Ball parlor in Manhattan in Times Square for some time.

The space was described as being furnished attractively with basket chairs and a huge window that commanded a view of Times Square. It was reported that Skee-Ball alleys "burst into bloom on the Great White Way" in New York. There were a number of notable

The J. D. Este Company advertisement in Life Managzine, October 21, 1915.
(Author's collection)

sports figures in attendance at the opening including: Beef (Arthur) and Bert (Herbert) Wheeler (Princeton); Fred Crolius (Dartmouth Halfback of 1900); Big Bill Edwards and Bummy Booth (Princeton); J. C. Anderson (Yale); and Jack Munn (Princeton Halfback). Also in attendance was Lester Wilson who had the distinction of being able to make a high percentage of perfect scores at the game. [83]

Two more newspaper articles about Skee-Ball appeared toward the end of November. On November 13, 1915, a snippet appeared in The New York Clipper about "Tacks" Neuer, who was raving about Skee-Ball at the Hurtig & Seamons Apollo Theater on 129th Street. A picture of the lobby appeared in the ad, in what was fast becoming the sophisticated "Este Company style." [84]

On November 27, an article appeared in the New Rochelle Pioneer stating that D. J. Kennedy had installed Skee-Ball alleys at his bowling alley located at 238 Huguenot Street. The article went on to say that from one to twelve cigars or one to eight packages of cigarettes were being given away on scores made, making Skee-Ball a premier "redemption game," with prizes for scores. This was to become an enormously popular way to encourage and reward more and more plays, and higher proficiency and dedication to the game. [85]

Another ad appeared in The Billboard on December 18, 1915, for The J. D. Este Company's Skee-Ball alleys. The ad touted the revenue generating ability of the alleys stating that "Their owner advises us that they average $55.00 per day." [86]

Skee-Ball had arrived.

The following year was at least as eventful.

With the game's success and expansion across the United States, The J. D. Este Company looked next to expand across the Atlantic. The company filed a patent application in Great Britain for "Improvements in or relating to Game Apparatus." [87] The abstract for the patent read:

> *103,532. Wade, H., (Este Co., J. D.).*
>
> *Feb. 2, 1916. Scoring and marking apparatus; outdoor games.-In a game apparatus wherein balls are rolled along an alley 23, Fig. 1, and are caused to rise into the air by a hump 16, balls falling into the compartments of a target 17 are led down channels 1 - - 5, Fig. 2, to a runway 15. In passing down the channels, the balls tilt weighted levers 18, which actuate to varying extents a rod 20 connected to a known scoring mechanism 6 displaying numbered cards hinged on a rotating cage. The balls*

The J. D. Este Company advertisement for Skee-Ball alleys at Hurtig & Seaman's Apollo Theatre.
(Author's Collection)

are arrested in the runway by a gate 13, but nine of the balls are allowed to pass and fill the lower part of the runway by actuating a coin-freed hand-lever 9, which at the same time operates a counter 12, temporarily places a guard 14 over the leading balls, zeroizes the scorer 6 by means of linkage 10, and withdraws the guard 14 to permit the removal of the balls.

That February 26, 1916, two items appeared in The Billboard relating to Skee-Ball. The first was a small ad listing six Skee-Ball alleys for sale. [88] The second was a large display ad for Seal Beach in Los Angeles, California, for concessionaires that Seal Beach was interested in having at their venue, including Skee-Ball. [89]

Another ad appeared in The Billboard on March 18, this one showing a line drawing of a man playing Skee-Ball, and emphasizing the profits to be made. [90] The ad copy reads:

SKEE BALL

HERE'S THE GAME THAT ATTRACTS THE CROWD AND EARNS THE MONEY

Each alley can take in $3.00 per hour and in many cases a single alley has earned $25.00 to $30.00 in a day.

The Automatic Scoring Device invariably draws the interest of the crowd, and the Slot Machine, by collecting the nickels and checking them up, reduces the operating expenses to a minimum.

No amusement park can afford to omit

SKEE-BALL

from its attractions.

Place order now to insure early delivery for coming season.

WRITE FOR ILLUSTRATED CATALOGUE

THE J. D. ESTE COMPANY 1530 SANSOM STREET, PHILADELPHIA.

The Electric Railway Journal, a premier publication for the trolley industry and trolley parks, carried an announcement on Friday, February 23, in the Trade Notes column that:

"J. D. Este Company, Philadelphia, Pa., has issued a catalog describing the game of "skee-ball" which is being used as a drawing card by a number of amusement parks operated by electric railways, and which is also adapted for use by employees' welfare associations." [91]

Skee-Ball had made huge inroads into all kinds of amusement parks, but Este was not leaving that situation to chance. He repeatedly made a point that the game was not only fun for customers who happened to be there, but it actually drew them to the park.

On March 13, 1916 there was an announcement that the city was in the planning stages for a bowling tournament that would take place in Philadelphia on April 3. As part of the event they promised there would be dancing each night, and eight Skee-Ball alleys to provide plenty of play opportunities. [92]

Emphasizing Skee-Ball's fit with trolley parks, he put a half-page informational ad into the April issue of Electric Traction, a leading trolley industry journal. The ad showed a picture of a man playing Skee-Ball and the alley and described how the game was played. It also described the scoring mechanism, the space requirements, and made a point that the game was self-operating, requiring no attendant. The ad also pointed to the popularity of the game with the following snippet:

> "The popularity of this game is shown by the fact that the Skee-Ball Company of Illinois, on November 1, 1915 had 39 alleys in use, and has orders in for 150 new alleys." [93]

The J. D. Este Company advertisement from
The Billboard, March 18, 1916
(Author's Collection)

In the same journal, another article appeared titled, "Trap-Shooting As A Park Attraction" which used Skee-Ball as the metric for popularity of other games:

> "In other words, the outdoor sports are the alluring ones to park patrons, as the primary purpose of their visit is to be out in the open with nature. Consequently such exhilarating attractions as roller coasters, carrousels, bowling or skee-ball alleys, athletic fields, etc., are almost indispensable." [94]

The rapid adoption of Skee-Ball into amusement parks and outdoor recreation markets was stunning. Skee-Ball was becoming such a staple for parks that references to it were showing up routinely every time amusement park games were mentioned. The market penetration continued, and continued to be news. On April 6, The Rochester Democrat And Chronicle announced that Skee-Ball would be installed at Manitou Beach sometime in the summer. In the meantime there were Skee-Ball alleys at the Grand Central Academy that people could try out. [95]

By now, Skee-Ball had also officially evolved beyond being a Man's Game. Now its draw was that it attracted everybody: Men and women, the mature and the young, the wealthy and the ordinary folks. It was a healthy, wholesome game that everyone enjoyed, maximizing both the draw and the profits.

A full-page ad appeared from The J. D. Este Company in the May 6, 1916 issue of the Electric Traction Journal. The text of the ad read:

> *They All Enjoy SKEE BALL*
>
> *Here's the game that attracts everybody. It affords clean, wholesome fun and healthful exercise. Lively enough for the young--yet not too strenuous for the older folks.*
>
> *It's a money-getter. No amusement park can afford to omit these Skee Ball Alleys from its attractions.*
>
> *A single park in Cleveland has 23 alleys; another in Chicago has the same number; a man in Coney Island has 21; another in Atlantic City 19, etc. Wherever once installed they prove so popular that more alleys have to be ordered to meet the demand of the fun-loving crowds.*
>
> *The amusement park season soon opens-- place your orders now and clean up a big profit on a small investment.*
>
> *Write today for our illustrated catalogue.*
>
> *The J. D. ESTE COMPANY*
> *1534 Sansom St., Philadelphia, Pa.*
> *Dept. E [96]*

Several articles appeared in newspapers around the country announcing that they would have Skee-Ball alleys at venues in their towns. On May 20, The Des Moines News reported that Riverview Park in Des Moines, Iowa, would open with new concessions including Skee-Ball. [97] On May 28, Marshall Hall announced that its grand opening for the season would take place on May 30, and would include Skee-Ball alleys. [98]

Additionally, an advertisement appears on May 29, 31, June 2, 3, 6, 8, and 9, in the Evening Public Ledger which read:

> *"AMUSEMENT CASINO being built on new boardwalk in a fast-growing seashore town. concessions for amusements will be rented: bowling alley, shooting gallery, skeeball[sic], dancing pavilion, soft drinks, ice cream and so forth will be popular. rentals low for first season. Apply South Jersey Realty Co., 3d and Walnut sts."*
> *[99, 100, 101, 102, 103, 104, 105]*

Skee-Ball ads no longer appeared every month in The Billboard. They didn't need to. The orders kept rolling in. While the orders were rolling in, the players kept rolling too.

In spite of the wholesomeness and popularity of the Tournaments, the Blue Laws that had helped close Chestnut Hill Park were also threatening Skee-Ball and other popular attractions in Atlantic City.

After being pressured by the "Church Element" of Atlantic City, July 6, 1916 William F. Sooy, Director of Safety, Atlantic City, New Jersey, gave police orders effective Sunday, July 9 to see that all noisy amusements were to be closed on Sundays. The order included: bowling alleys; pool rooms; Skee-Ball stands; Japanese ping pong parlors; shooting galleries; mechanical waltz rides; and all other places where music was played. [106] The order did not affect any of the piers except for Alamac Pier which had Skee-Ball alleys, a mechanical horse and auto races. Chief of Police Miller said that the order was directed at eliminating noises on Sundays without interfering with the entertainment of visitors. A similar ban had been in effect the previous year. [107]

On August 6, 1916, the original complainants, believing that the authorities had been too lenient, caused the police to arrest nine amusement proprietors and managers including: E. P. Dentzell, agent of the L. A. Thompson Scenic Railway Corporation; Julius Goldman, manager of the Magic Waltz; Thomas Ireland, Henry Larken, J. Kawamath, George M. Saldein, T. Wooster Grookert and Charles Mangold operators of Skee-Ball alley concessions; and William H. Dentzel, the Philadelphia carousel manufacturer who had been operating his carousel at the time of the raid. In addition to the proprietors and managers, the police also arrested seventeen employees. All were incarcerated and later released under cash bails ranging from $5.00 to $200.00, except for William H. Dentzel who spent the night in jail because his real estate security was declined.

Dentzel refused cash bail from friends. His stated objective was to bring action against the city for refusing his real estate security. Of the 26 individuals incarcerated, they represented about 30% of the amusement men that the authorities had intended to arrest as part of their raid.

On August 7, Dentzel was released and immediately held an indignation meeting on part of the harassed amusement proprietors of Atlantic City. A protective organization of twenty-five representatives was created as the result of the meeting and each person in the newly formed organization put up $100 for the purpose of engaging the best talent in the state of New Jersey to battle the allegedly unequal, discriminatory treatment. August 12, a meeting between the city authorities and the amusement men was held and a compromised reached. The amusement men could again operate on Sunday's but could not open before 2:00 PM. August 13, with the new agreement in place, the amusement men opened at 2:00 PM and were not bothered by the city authorities. [108]

So in addition to catching the fancy of all manner of people to play Skee-Ball at their varied and favored venues, Skee-Ball also played an important role in liberating Atlantic City from the most repressive of their Blue Laws.

Chapter 7

THE TOURNAMENTS
Skee-Ball as a Sport

The years 1915 and 1916 were newsworthy in general.

The U.S. had successfully avoided being drawn into World War I at this point, thanks to Woodrow Wilson, who was later re-elected on that basis. Women were making inroads into the government, even before they achieved the right to vote nationwide, and thirty-six year old Jeanette Rankin from Montana was about to become the first woman elected to the U.S. Congress. And Albert Einstein completed his mathematical formulation of a general theory of relativity, including the theory of gravity.

Skee-Ball was without serious competitors to this point, having so far avoided the war being lost by traditional Box Ball and Tenpinnet. Women were proving that Skee-Ball was not just a man's game, and established themselves as a force to be reckoned with, based on their tournament performance. And gravity was at least temporarily defied as the game of Skee-Ball continued to rise in popularity and profitability.

Tournaments were one big reason why. With the tournament craze that began in 1914 and was soon in full swing in Philadelphia, Skee-Ball was being treated like any other sport. Regular write-ups in the local papers included player names, teams and scores. They started almost immediately after Este incorporated his companies, and the first was held at Charles "Chief" Bender's Sporting Goods store. But it was far from the last. Bender's regular play-offs gave way to permanent teams and an enthusiastic tournament culture.

On Saturday, December 19, two Skee-Ball teams faced off in a competition at Charles Bender's Skee-Ball alleys: The Revere Rubber Company; and the U. S. S. Tire Company. [1] Each team had five players and were competing for the S. S. Poor Cup. Rolling for the Revere Rubber Company were: Fuller; Clements; Jackson; Link; and Stone. Rolling for the U. S. S. Tire Company Team were: Poor; Whidden; Ritter; Kates; and List. Fuller rolled the highest score overall, 1580 and led the winning team. At the end of the competition the scores were as follows:

Skee-Ball alleys and players at Harvey's Lake in Luzerne County, Pennsylvania, circa 1915.
(Courtesy Luzerne County Historical Society)

Revere Rubber vs. U. S. S. Tire scores			
December 19, 1914			
Revere Rubber		U. S. S. Tire	
Fuller	1580	Poor	1410
Clements	1420	Whidden	1320
Jackson	1470	Ritter	1150
Link	1220	Kates	930
Stone	1460	List	1120
	7150		**5930**

Following the success and enthusiasm that multiple Skee-Ball contests had created, Charles Bender announced in the Philadelphia's Evening Public Ledger his interest in forming a Skee-Ball league in Philadelphia. [2]

Charles Bender had been holding ad-hoc Skee-Ball competitions at his store at 1309 Arch Street in Philadelphia ever since the alleys were installed. Bender announced a Skee-Ball competition to take place over the 1915 New Years celebration, at his store. The winner would receive the "Este Cup" from Bender and get a chance to meet Andy Carty of the Philadelphia Racquet Club. The ten high scorers from the qualifying round on December 31 would compete on January 1. [3]

The Skee-Ball tournament craze was in full swing. Several hundred men and women competed on August 3, 1915 at Young's Old Pier in Atlantic City. Women's participation in Skee-Ball tournaments was celebrated in the Washington Post sports section. "Miss Hilda M. Kolar of Washington, D.C. today won the ladies' skee ball [sic] tournament on Youngs old pier. Miss Kolar totaled 170 at the novel game to take the award in topping several hundred players." [4]

Not to be outdone, the Manhattan Skee-Ball Alleys ran a tournament on August 11. Four men competed in the tournament: Herbert W. Stewart; George Meeker; W. McBride; and F. P. Hughes. Herbert W. Stewart won the tournament with a score of 1850. [5]

Manhattan Skee-Ball Alley Tournament	
August 11, 1915	
Herbert W. Stewart	1850
George Meeker	1830
W. McBride	1790
F. P. Hughes	1730

By this time, Skee-Ball had taken hold enough in the Philadelphia area as a bona fide sport. Not only were there regular Skee-Ball contests, but things had become organized enough that there were now standing teams with official names. May 18, 1916, an article appeared in the Lebanon Daily News announcing that a Skee-Ball contest would take place at Paul B. McKinney's Market Square Billiard Parlors on May 19 at 8 o'clock. McKinney made "a special invitation to ladies to attend and learn how the game is played." [6]

Paul B. McKinney's - Big 5 Scores May 19, 1916						
Beam	130	130	190	130	200	780
Bachman	210	130	220	240	150	950
Hallman	130	150	160	170	210	850
Marley	230	130	180	200	230	970
Stuhley	200	150	230	210	190	1010
Totals	**900**	**750**	**980**	**950**	**980**	**4560**

Paul B. McKinney's - Skee-Ball Six Scores May 19, 1916						
Fox	210	250	140	180	170	950
Bollinger	160	160	120	140	180	750
Burlholder	200	170	230	150	160	910
Fittery	130	180	170	140	210	830
Jackson	140	230	90	270	250	980
Totals	**810**	**980**	**750**	**880**	**970**	**4420**

The results of the contest were revealed on May 20. Two teams played five games each. The teams were the Big 5 and the Skee Ball Six. [7]

These games were described in the papers the same way they would have described live professional baseball or football games.

"After the contest John A. Jackson rolled individually and totaled 860 points, which was the highest score of the season so far. For his high score he was awarded a prize of $2.50." [8]

May 26, there was an announcement that there would be two "interesting" games of Skee-Ball at McKinney's Market Square Billiard Parlors in which the Hotel Weimar Girls were going to play the Lebanon Skee-Girls. Following the first game the Big 5 would clash with the Stohler's Slide Easies. [9]

The Hotel Weimar Girls won their contest 1710 to 1400 while Stohler's Slide Easies "trimmed the sails" of the Big 5 in a close contest 4640 to 4630. [10]

Stohler's Slide Easies vs. Big 5 May 26, 1916			
Stohler's Slide Easies		Big 5	
C. Bachman	960	Haulman	830
Stine	1070	Heverling	1970
Woltemate	820	Beamesderfer	810
Smith	920	H. Fox	880
Fox	870	Stahley	1040
Totals	**4640**		**4630**

June 2 brought an announcement that the Big 5 and Lebanon teams would be competing at Paul McKinney's Market Square Billiard Parlors at eight o'clock. [11]

The results of that contest were announced: The Skee Ball Six beat the Big Five Rollers 4030 to 3590.

Skee-Ball Six Scores						
June 2, 1916						
Jackson	290	150	290	250	250	**1230**
Bollinger	200	180	290	170	170	**1010**
Fitterer (Capt.)	220	200	120	190	170	**900**
Harkins	200	160	200	150	180	**890**
Totals	**910**	**690**	**900**	**760**	**770**	**4030**

Big 5 Scores						
June 2, 1916						
Stahley	200	150	170	350	130	**1000**
Macgley (Capt.)	220	220	210	220	210	**1080**
Stohler	210	170	140	180	140	**840**
Lichty	190	160	130	90	100	**670**
Totals	**820**	**700**	**650**	**850**	**580**	**3590**

After the team contest, individual games for prizes were rolled. Jackson broke his record of 360 points in one game by 20 points for an all time high of 380, which was reported to be the parlor high score. [12] Paul B. McKinney announced on June 10 that he was making arrangements to open a branch parlor at Spruce and Mifflin streets. The alleys for the new venue were due in on the 10th or early the following week. [13] June 15, Paul B. McKinney had a grand opening of his new Skee-Ball parlor at Spruce and Lehman streets in Lebanon, Pennsylvania. [14]

Some vendors were interested in milking Skee-Ball alleys for all they were worth, the enthusiasm for the game and practice for the tournaments having reached a fevered peak. On June 14, the Surprise Vaudeville Company ran an ad in The Billboard for a bright active man to take care of Skee-Ball alleys. The salary was $15 for 12 hour days and a seven day work week. [15]

On July 27, the Lebanon Big Six team defeated Mt. Gretna at Mt. Gretna by more than 500 points. [16]

The tournaments continued, and on August 3, there was an announcement that the Big Six and Mt. Gretna Skee-Ball teams would once again compete, this time at Paul McKinney's Billiard Parlor at 12 Ninth Street. An item of note about the July 27 game was that a lady on the Mt. Gretna team rolled against a man on the Big Six team. In that week's game she would be "...matched against her own sex" after getting a higher score than any of the men. [17] Shortly thereafter, separate women's and men's teams became the norm. The next day, in the second game of their series, the Mt. Gretna team defeated the Big Six at Paul McKinney's Billiard Parlors on South Ninth Street, 6640 to 6550. Stahley had the highest individual score, 270 points in a single game, Harbaugh of Mt. Gretna rolled 260. Miss E. Waltz of Mt. Gretna defeated her opponent, Miss S. Huber, with a score of 940 to 710. [18]

On August 10, in the third game of their series, Mt. Gretna was defeated by the Big Six by a score of 6840 to 6560. The Big Six won the first game, only to be outrolled by Mt. Gretna in the next two games. The high scorer of the evening was Margut with 1280. Schreiber and Hoffman, who substituted for Margut, together totaled 1220. Jackson of the Big Six had the highest individual score of 290. [19] On August 18, Mt. Gretna and the Lebanon Big Six began a new series of three games at the Palace Skee Ball Parlors on South Ninth Street. [20]

Mt. Gretna vs. Big Six August 4, 1916			
Mt. Gretna		Big Six	
Harbaugh	1140	Stahley	1100
Schreiber	1120	Margut	1160
Miss E. Waltz	940	Miss S. Huber	710
Mays	1160	Heverling	1140
Gates	1120	Bollinger	1240
Hoy	1160	Ringler	1200
Totals	**6640**		**6550**

On August 24, the Mt. Gretna team was beaten by the Big Six, 7390 to 7010. Heverling was the high scorer for the Big Six with 270 points for one game, and his total of 1430 was the high score for all six games combined. [21]

Mt. Gretna vs. Big Six August 24, 1916			
Mt. Gretna		Big Six	
Harbaugh	1360	Heverling	1430
Schreiber	1280	Ringler	1130
Miss E. Waltz	1100	Miss Varholy	1030
Mays	1180	Bollinger	1270
Gates	1150	Margut	1300
Hoy	940	Stahley	1230
Totals	**7010**		**7390**

Informal tournaments were popular too. On September 9, three thousand members of Local No. 2 of the Plate Printers' Union and their families attended their annual excursion to Chesapeake Beach, Virginia, and one of the highlights was a Skee-Ball tournament. [22, 23] Another source reports that on September 19, a truckload of Skee-Ball enthusiasts from Lebanon, Pennsylvania went to Palmyra, Pennsylvania, to Paul McKinney's new Skee-Ball parlor to play several contests in front of the large crowd. [24]

By the end, Skee-Ball was prominent and popular enough to command a loyal following, both in popular play and in the tournaments.

Just when Skee-Ball was cresting as the game to beat, the first whisper of new competition emerged, from an unexpected source.

Chapter 8

A CHALLENGER
Simpson Re-Appears

After selling his U.S. patents for Skee-Ball to Este and watching the game take off, Simpson may have had second thoughts about the decision to sell his interests outright. Simpson continued to invent, and to try to patent and make money from his inventions. Unable to sell or license his egg crate patent successfully, he had turned to starting his own business, the American "Flexible" Egg Crate Carrier Company (J. F. Simpson, proprietor).

But Simpson was at heart an inventor, not a businessman. By 1916, it was clear that the egg crate business was not going to support him. He was anxious to focus on a moneymaker because, as he wrote to his friend Evelyn Parker, *"I have given up on my egg box, as there is no real profit in it and it is a lot of bother."* [1]

He was looking forward to turning his game creativity into cash once again, and this time more expeditiously. The success of Skee-Ball with the right management bolstered his belief in himself and his ingenuity. Harper had been right when he wrote, "These alleys are going to

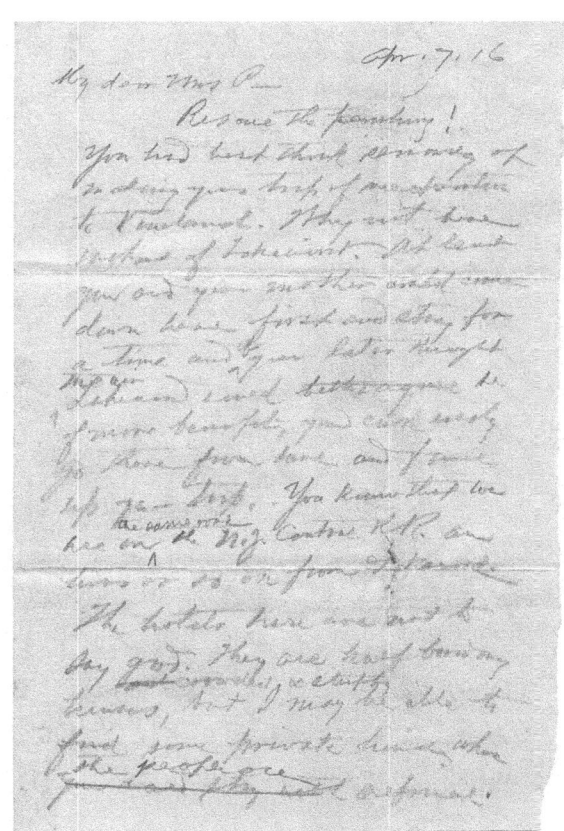

Letter from Joseph Fourestier Simpson to Evelyn Parker, April 7, 1916, p. 1.
(Courtesy Vineland Historical and Antiquarian Society)

Letter from Joseph Fourestier Simpson to Evelyn Parker, April 7, 1916, p. 2.
(Courtesy Vineland Historical and Antiquarian Society)

make money some day for somebody."

Simpson was still keen on becoming one of those "somebodies" for more than the amount Este had paid him for the patent rights. As he was marketing his egg crate, living off the proceeds of the sale of the Skee-Ball patent, he had invented another game using Skee-Ball as a jumping off point. That game that would be known as Bridge Ball. Late in January of 1915, Simpson had filed a patent application for "Game." The patent application stated:

> "My invention relates to an improved bowling game and the object of my invention is to furnish an inexpensive and interesting game which may be played by one or more persons. My invention comprises an alley of a suitable length and width, a perforated target placed some distance to the rear of the alley, a narrow bridge connecting the rear end of the alley and the target, a ball or balls adapted to be rolled along the alley and bridge, an automatic recording device for indicating the score of a number of rolled balls, and a means for automatically returning a rolled ball to the playing end of the alley." [2]

In October 1915, U.S. Patent 1,156,438 was granted to Joseph Simpson for this new "Game." An alley game similar to Skee-Ball but without the "skee-jump" in the middle of the alley, it instead had a narrow "bridge" that players needed to roll the ball up squarely in order to get the balls into the scoring pocket. [3]

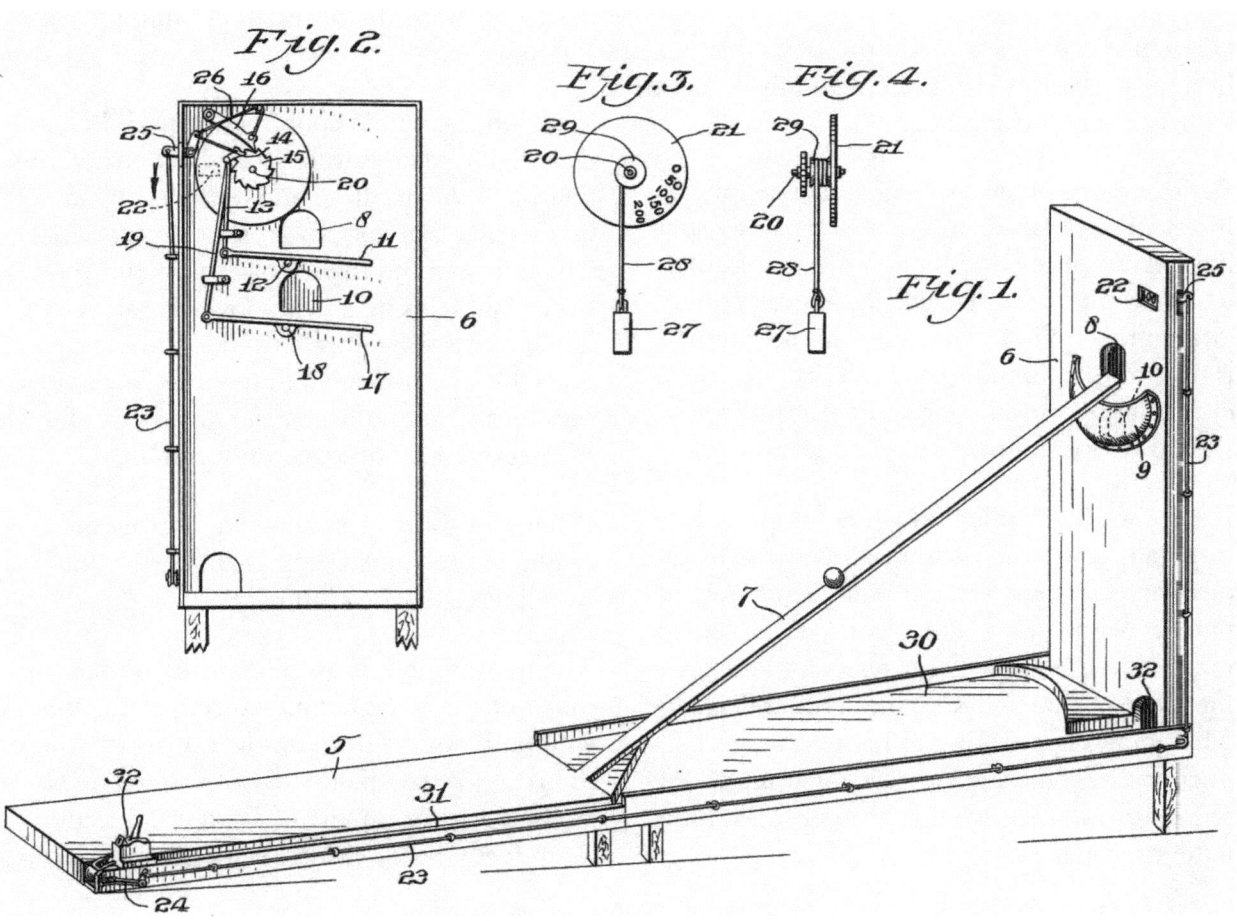

U.S. Patent No. 1,156,438, Game.
(Courtesy National Archives and Records Administration, Kansas, City)

Seeking Redemption

Covering all his bases, on October 7, Joseph F. Simpson also filed for a Canadian Patent for Bridge-Ball. [4]

When he finally gave up on the Egg Crate business in early 1916, there was only one path left to pursue: Bridge Ball.

But there was an additional challenge for him with this game, over and above the usual business issues of finding a buyer or an investor who had the means to launch, manufacture and market. When Simpson sold the patent rights for Skee-Ball to J. D. Este, Este made it clear that he would tolerate no infringement should Simpson invent another game.

It is somewhat ironic that while Simpson originally sought to patent many of the features of Skee-Ball, he wound up only being able to patent two of them: The obstruction (skee-jump) in the middle of the alley; and the lever mechanism that actuated the scoring device. That ended up working to his advantage. Technically, if he steered clear of using those two features, there would be no grounds for a patent infringement suit.

That didn't mean that Este might not still file suit, though. Simpson still had a working relationship with Este, since he retained the rights to the Canadian patent on Skee-Ball, and received $50 in royalties per game sold there. He initially offered Bridge Ball to Este, as he thought it might round out his company with another winning game, but Este declined, on the grounds that it might cut into the Skee-Ball market.

Simpson, being Simspon, persevered. Being the original patentor for Skee-Ball earned him considerable attention and openness when he contacted people about the new game, which he assured them was even better than Skee-Ball. Closing a deal, however, proved much more difficult. He tried to sell the patent outright, and to work a number of alternative remuneration and licensing agreements, but the negotiations dragged on for months.

When Simpson approached a number of manufacturers, including H. B. Auchy, they were initially quite enthusiastic.

The new game was given consideration by many of the large manufacturers of the time, who had initially turned down the opportunity to invest in Skee-Ball. This included The E. T. Burrowes Company of Portland, Maine, manufacturers of rustless screens. They wrote:

> *Dear Sir:*
>
> *Replying to yours of the 16th,- we have thousands of games offered to us. We do not say that we would not be interested in a good one.*

The writer would be glad to call on you the next time he is in New York, or perhaps you would be willing to send one of these games down and explain it to us and let us look into it.

We would not wish to state to you that were not interested until we had a chance to see what your proposition is, but we will state that we have hundreds of games put up to us every year that are not, in our opinion, available for our business.

Yours respectfully, THE E.T. BURROWES CO. [5]

The Brunswick-Balke-Collender Co., makers of carom and pocket-billiard tables and "improved regulation bowling alleys," also responded with interest on March 23, 1915:

The BRUNSWICK-BALKE-COLLENDER CO.

CAROM AND POCKET-BILLIARD TABLES AND IMPROVED REGULATION BOWLING ALLEYS

Dear Sir:

We have your favor of the 20th inst. regarding a new game, which you recently invented, and in reply to same, wish to advise, we have referred your communication to our New York Office, with instructions that they investigate your proposition, and if same should prove interesting to them, to arrange to send it on to us for inspection. You can, therefore, accordingly expect to hear from our New York manager in short order.

Yours truly, The Brunswick Balk Collender Co. By P. L. Deutsch [6]

H. B. Auchy of the Philadelphia Toboggan Company, suddenly showed interest as well, perhaps regretting that he hadn't jumped on the Skee-Ball opportunity when it was available. On March 26, 1915 he wrote:

My Dear Mr. Simpson:- Yours of the 23rd instant received and noted about your new patent, - Bridge Ball.

I would be very glad indeed to come over and see this, but it is utterly impossible for me to get away just now from my business- this is always the very busiest time of year for me, but this year we are exceptionally busy- strange to say considering the general complaint.

If you have a good thing, no doubt I can help it along considerable and do you some good. I am really anxious to see the device. Could you mail me some sketch, or literature so I can get an idea of what it is- I get all

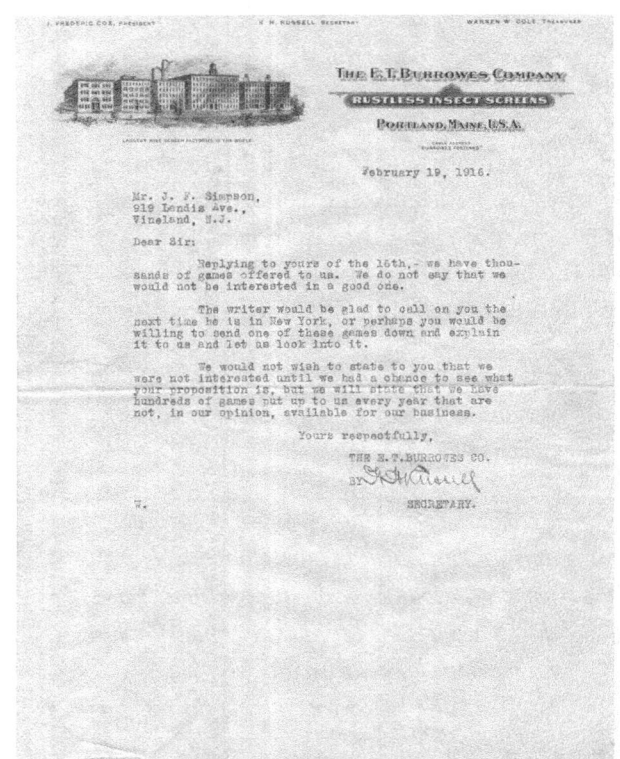
Letter from The E. T. Burrowes Company to
Joseph Fourestier Simpson, February 19, 1916.
(Courtesy Vineland Historical and Antiquarian Society)

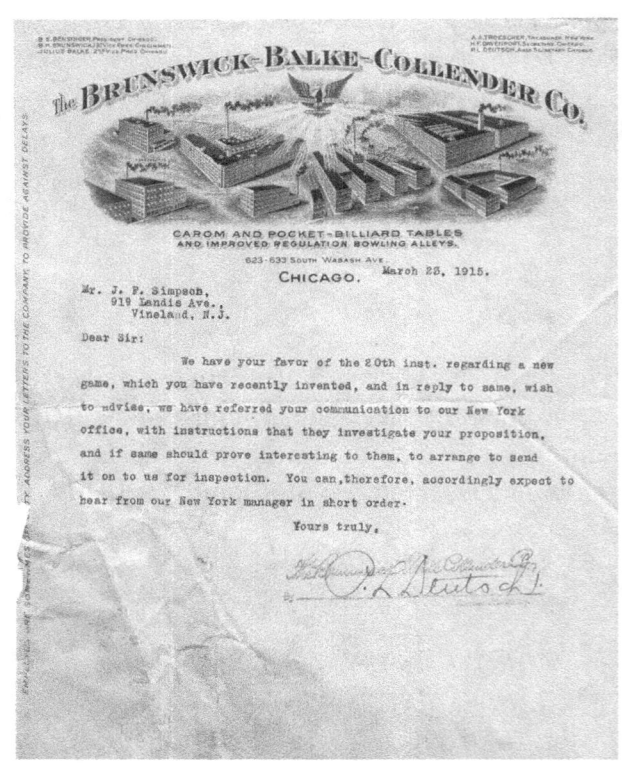
Letter from The Brunswicke-Balke-Collender Co. to
Joseph Fourestier Simpson, March 23, 1915.
(Courtesy Vineland Historical and Antiquarian Society)

over the country these days and should be glad to introduce it or speak of it among amusementmen. [sic]

With best wishes and hoping to hear from you further, I remain, Yours very truly, HB.Auchy President. [7]

Hearing of this opportunity through a friend, Louis Berni of Berni Organs (Builders and Importers Mechanical Band Organs) showed an interest. On September 28, 1915 he wrote:

Dear Sir:-

I have heard that you were the inventor of the Skeeball game, througha [sic] friend of mine, Mr. Snaden. He tells me you have a new patent out similar to the Skeeball. I am interested in this thing, so if you come to New York, at my expense, we can talk this thing over.

Trusting to see you soon, I am Yours very truly, Lous Berni LB/MF. [8]

Even Simpson's cousin Edward Browning, and Browning's partner, Mr. Newlin Trainer, were giving it significant consideration, and continued to explore it for months.

One letter that Simpson wrote to The Brunswick-Balke-Collender Company, a potential manufacturer, provided some trenchant insights. First, he articulated the difficulty of introducing a new game, fundamentally different in its appeal to players, to potential business investors, who were conservative by nature. Second he shared a key insight into the nature of the appeal of Skee-Ball-like games, and why they were "fascinating" to people who were the "temperamentally nervous and imaginative types" because of its fast rate of play, unlike the traditional tenpinnet games.

That letter dated April 5, 1915, read:

Gentlemen:-

I beg to acknowledge your favor of the 2nd instant, and to thank you for meeting my view in having someone to look over the new game.

This game I have named Bridge Ball, and would direct your attention to its being in the same class with the Skee Ball game.

I would speak to you of the peculiarity of the Skee Ball game, as it is now an admitted success and the facts regarding it can be guaged [sic]

When I first showed the Skee Ball, the most of my level headed friends pronounced it "no good;" and the rest were doubtful. I had

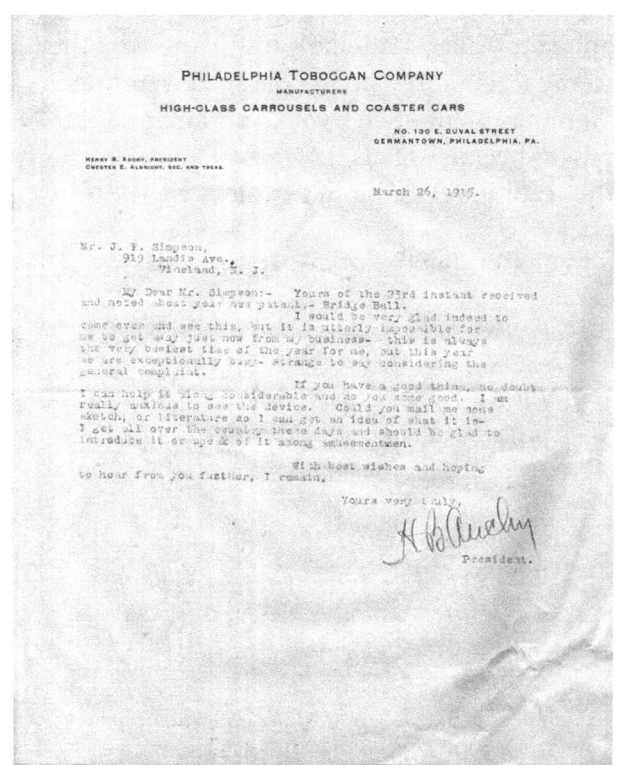

Letter from H. B. Auchy to Joseph Fourestier Simpson, March 26, 1915.
(Courtesy Vineland Historical and Antiquarian Society)

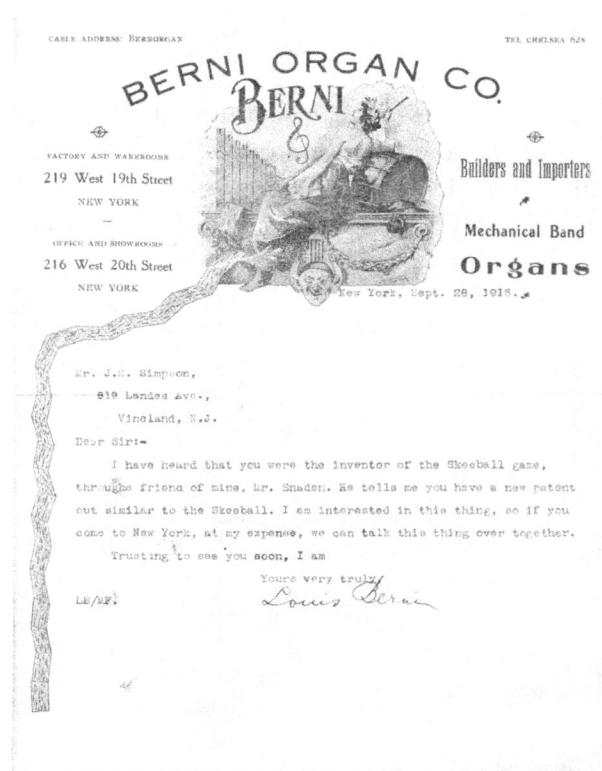

Letter from Louis Berni to Joseph Fourestier Simpson, September 28, 1915.
(Courtesy Vineland Historical and Antiquarian Society)

to accept the fact that the usually successful business man is not given to depart from his accepted conceptions. He is apt to compare the newer things unfavorably with the things that are familiar. He is generally not a man of marked imagination. It thus took 7 years to rightly get the game before the public. The men who combine conservatism with imagination become our big business men. Evidenced by the magnitude of your corporation, its heads must be men of this kind, and to whom I speak.

It is necessary to an understanding of the matter to bring this class of games under psychological analysis.

The first question frequently asked, was whether the Skee Ball was better than ordinary bowling, and whether it would supplant it. I did not understand, then, that this had absolutely nothing to do with it, but simply different people liked different games.

What I, with the rest, did not apprehend, but which time evidenced was that the game appealed to imaginative people, which was the key to its success. I observed, at least in its first or early reception, that it was not much cared for by the Tenpin bowlers. It seemed to be to the temperamentally nervous and imaginative type. There are very many of these people. There are very many of these people to whom regular bowling does not appeal, who immediately on public display like this game. A quite spontaneous and universal expression applied to the game has been that it is fascinating. I think the work has been applied to any other game and the expression likely defines the kind of people who first took to it. The others to some degree, now naturally follow.

The practical point is this—that it offered to a class of people, and that a very large one, a bowling game adapted to their fancy, thus discovering a greatly enlarged field from with to derive profit. I have naturally been a very close observer of the game's effect and believe this reading is correct.

The Skee Ball has 9 balls. It takes 45 seconds to cast them and an average of 68 seconds in actual play. The revenue is about $2.40 an hour, as against, as I am informed, about 60¢ on a bowling alley. Thus 5 alleys will equal in revenue 20 bowling alleys, with ¾ of the rented space in addition, and reduced attendance. The charge in the Skee Ball is restricted to 5¢ for 9 balls.

My new game of BRIDGE BALL, will I believe at least equal the Skee Ball in popularity.

I cannot of course yet know of the impression the game will make on Mr. Lyons, but in event of its being unfavorable I have thought it best to state to you now the views herein given, rather than after his visit, which I might then find necessary but nevertheless embarrassing.

I remain, Very truly yours, [9]

However, many of the potential partners, investors and buyers balked at the threats Este made around the patents. Simpson furnished copies of patents for both games, showing that there would be no possibility of infringement, but it was to no avail. Even if Este could not win a suit against them, just defending against one might be too expensive and distasteful.

In spite of their interest in the game, and Simpson's extensive evidence from independent patent attorneys that no patent infringement actually existed, Brunswick, like many other potential buyers, declined to invest, saying "It appears to us rather clearly, however, that this game would be a very close infringement upon the rights of the previous one, and as we are not looking for any kind of litigations, we think we had better not consider it any further." [10]

In his August 16 letter to his cousin Edward Browning, who was still considering investing in Bridge Ball, he laid out the issues thoroughly, honestly and in meticulous detail. This letter provided fascinating detail into the financial issues of getting a game launched, as well as the possible consequences of a meritless infringement suit, if Este should choose to launch one.

Vineland, N.J. August 16, 1915

Dear Cousin Edward:-

Since our conversation on the phone this morning by which I believe you and Mr. Trainer are serious into looking into the matter of the Bridge Ball game I have been thinking over the matter of any arrangement that could be made, more seriously. I would not want to put you to a lot of trouble under an impression that I have doubtless given you, as to my proposition that all I needed was protection against suit. It will therefore be best that I define my situation what what it is possible for me to do under it.

In the early summer I could have placed four games in Wildwood on a 40 o/o of the gross receipts to me. (The 4 Skee Ball games at Wildwood took in $3800. last summer) I could also have placed 4 games at Coney Island on the same terms. Both men entirely responsible. At that time I was about to consumate [sic] the arrangements, *when the Este people came down to look at the game. I had put it up to show them and their delay in coming had afforded others the opportunity of seeing it. The offers to me were entirely unsolicited. The Wildwood man went up to see the Skee Ball and spent over $1.00 in trying it out in Chief Bender's place and told me the Bridge Ball had it skinned a thousand miles. He arranged an option on a place, on a store in Wildwood which I had to have him call off as the Este people came and the next day wrote me saying they regarded the new game an infringement. Now at that time it was in my mind that if some one would put up the money for a suit in case they brought one that I would then go ahead, as I believed I would likely get $2.000 or $2..000out of the operation. When I first spoke to you in June this impression was still in my mind as it has been since and so remained when I spoke to you on the phone this morning.*

As it stands now I see that I would be unable to make the proposition in this way as I have not the means to do so and again my health is not was 1 could wish it and I might make promises that I could not carry out without a great deal of worry which I am now unfit for. I see that I could not supply the capital which the business would take to conduct it properly. For instance, another year I might have anyone willing and ready to put games in as I had this year and would then have to rent a place myself and put them in.

When Mr. Este took hold of the Skee Ball, he put two games at Princeton at his own expense. These went for about two weeks and then the novelty was worn off. He did not stop there, but rented a place at Atlantic City at $3.000 a year and built 5 [simpson slashed the 5 out] games and put them in also at his own expense. Este had a fine courage which made the business succeed These games began to bring orders from other parts of the country.

Este raised $25.000 in actual cash simply in payment for the patent and then formed the J. D. Este Company. He put a game in the Raquet Club and it took in over $100. a week, the fourth week it took in $119. The receipts kept up and a few months ago the company put in a second game and Mr. Wheeler shortly after told me that the two games were making $120. a week

The J. D.Este Company was capitalized at $100.000 and Mr. Wheeler got twenty thousand of this stock for $10.000. Este kept $35.000 for himself and Harper got $15.000. The balance was sold at par or at the rate of $100.000 for the game.

In my agreement of sale of my portion I retained Canada, and they afterward arranged with me to pay $50. a game royalty for games sold in Canada. About the time I was at your home they had paid me $100.00 for two games just sold and told me at the time that they had to enlarge their floor space three times and had 40 men then turning out games on orders. I have not seen them since, but about a week ago I received from them another $100. for two more games sold in Canada. In acknowledging the remittance I spoke to then [sic] of considering the taking out of the foreign patents and offered them a one half interest to do so and to subsequently keep the patents alive under the various requirements of the countries in which patented. I told them I would call on them in relation to the proposition when in Philadelphia. I have not as yet called on them.

I may say to you that besides the games mention as at Atl. City and Wildwood, there were also placed 2 in the New Cape May Hotel and in that exclusive situation they took in $618. in 34 days. Ten games at Coney Island cleared $4500. 100 games were sold to the Carstairs people at $375 atgame [sic] with the control of the Pacific Coast states for one year. They were overloaded, but 41 games were placed and I think they let on them in a manner by still requiring the full payment of $37.500, but arranged to give them some of the middle west states to control.

The games this year have gone all over the United States. I imagine that they have not put out less than 300 games in all and the profit is about 189 dollars a game. The cost of the games they told me being $186. The Bridge Ball I think would cost in quantity about $75. a game.

When I saw Este last I spoke to him again about taking the new game up. He said he could not do so at least now as it would hurt the Skee Ball. He said that they might consider it next year. Mr. Wheeler later said the same thing to me.

Mr. Kaler whom I mentioned to you on the phone as having spoken to me about taking the matter up is away on vacation. I do not know if it meant anything but he said "If I take it up I shall put it through." He is very able and I beliebe [sic] could do it if he wished to.

Mr. Wheeler told me that there would be 25 games in Coney Island this year. You probably know that the games are in New York, about 44th and Broadway I believe.

I am sending you a catalogue of the Este

Co. but do no care to have you show it as coming from me, nor would I have you mention outside the information I have given you regarding their company. They are the people who should own this game in their own interest. While I do not think their attitude to me is a right one, I can sympathise [sic] with their situation and certain admire the work they have done. But I have tried to give them every opportunity to control this game before making any attempt to have others do so.

I am telling you all this because the thing is not a small thing and should be handled in an ample way. If it should go successfully in bowling parlors it would greatly exceed the Skee Ball in value.

Eighteen people who have seen the Skee Ball have said to me without my asking the question that the new game is better.

I see that in putting the new game forward that I must secure sufficient capital to launch it as it deserves and the backing to fight any law suit that might come up. Such a suit might never be brought and some tell me that it might not prove very expensive if it was brought, and that defending it is not as expensive as bringing the suit Howard Okie thought that he could conduct it through the local court and the Curcuit [sic] Court if appealed for about $250. for both and that if the suit went against me that I would have the court expenses to pay which would be about $250. more. Total $500. An Atty. here, not a patent lawyer thinks about $750. in all and that carrying it through the Supreme Court woul [sic] fall with 1500. Mr. Rutter who does not wish to conduct a case in court would give me no opinion as to what the cost would be. Mr. Rutter insists that it is no infringement, and he is a good atty. with a clear and unexcitable head on his shoulders.

I can give you copies of both patents if you should wish to submit them to anyone.

Their [sic] are several propositions that could be made for an arrangement if you should wish to go into the affair after looking it over.

I have thought it best to write you as I have to avoid any misconception. With my kind regards, believe me,

Very sincerely, [11]

He again sought help and counsel from his cousin Edward as he began to look in earnest for someone to buy the patent or invest in taking the game to market. In another revealing letter to Edward on September

Seeking Redemption 207

21, 1915, it was clear that he now understood just what it would take to make this new game successful. He firmly credited Este with having been willing to do what was necessary to make Skee-Ball a success:

Dear Edward:-

To your letter of yesterday I sent you two additional postals today; one to Devon and one to Camden. Yesterday afternoon Layman stopped in at the place and said he had been over in New york [sic] for several weeks. He is looking around for a business. He asked me if I wold [sic] send a game to New york [sic] if he would run it there. He is financially responsible but somewhat unsettled in his mind about things I think. He is able to take care of a place as he as on the N. Y. Police force for seven years. He remarked to me that he [liked?] the Bridge Ball Skee Ball much better than the Skee Ball.

I would impress you that in anything I say to you there is no grain of exaggeration. The game as a game is out of season and therefore difficult to tey [sic] out properly at the moment. It is well that you go to Atlantic City to see the Skee Ball, but it would be best seen on a Sunday or in the evening. It is of course late in the year to see it at its best.

It occurs to me that as the Skee Ball games are sold under restrictions and only one set to a town, that there are doubtless other people in such towns who would like to have Skee Ball games, and as they cannot get them they would like to have this game, which would make the introduction easy. If a small few line advertisement were put in all the Sunday papers of the U.S. that it might bring very man replies. I think about $25. would do this. That is one idea simply.

At the Crest this summer the man who has the bowling alleys on the Pier was very desirous of having an alley there, but as you know I was not in a position to send it on account of starting a suit. It has often occurred to me that a couple of alleys would go at Anglesea which is the upper end of Wildwood. A great many people I believe go there very early, and late in the season to fish.

I should have said that the man who has the alleys at the Crest Pier every season is also the manager of the largest bowling parlors in Trenton and an alley might be put in there. I do not remember his name. A visit to Trenton would get at this.

A plumber stopped in at the place today to cover the water pipe with asbestos and said to me that he had recently been playing

Skee Ball at Atlantic City but thought this Bridge Ball the better game. More skillful he thought. A little boy dropped in today and played the game a few minutes. He handled the balls beautifully and put many of them in the center. I remarked on it and he said he had worked in a bowling alley parlor. I took his address and can get him when you come down again. I asked him if he could get some boys to come with him and he said he could. I think a better judgement can be made on the game when it is seen in play by a number of people. Koering has bowling alleys here and came to see me three times when I first put the alleys up wantin [sic] an alley in his place. He wanted a slot machine on it so that he would not have to trust his customers on the play. It might not be a bad place to try it. No final judgement however, should be made on s c trials. Someone recently told me that Koering said to them that if he had have had B.B. at the Carnival here that he could have cleared $50.-I think he would have cleared very much more in the week.

It may be that at the Country Fairs which will be held from now on through the fall that the game could be favorably tried out. I think that when the game is once seen and known that there will be plenty of people to buy it.

Senator Baker, head of Baker Bros. owners of Wildwood and Pres. of one of our banks here and also Pres. of the Vineland Feeble Minded Institution here, recently joined me on the street and said that every one who had spoken to him, said the new game was better than the S.B. Mr. Kaler, his son-in-law was the one whom I told you played it one evening and put in six balls out of ten. Kaler said he would like to take the matter up with me and said if he did he would carry it through. I have not seen him for several weeks. He started with his wife on his vacation in a car and was laid up in Providence, R.I. with an operation his nose and throat, and on his return had to go to the Jefferson for another and since that is laid up in Wildwood expecting now to return in a week if all right.

It strikes me that if we come to an arrangement, it might be well to rent some inexpensive room in Phila., put up a game and put an adver. in the papers announcing it. This is all I think of at the moment in the connection you ask me about.

It is well to keep in mind that Este entered no half measures, He spent his own money to put the games at Princeton. They failed. If I recollect rightly he went to Atlantic next and at his own expense on bo [sic] borrowed money rented a play opposite the

Million Dollar Pier at $3000. a year and built his own alleys. He put up electric signs also. I said to him at Atlantic that I thought he was taking great risk. He said to me, "Mr. Simpson, this cannot be made to succeed in any other way." They have certainly spared no expense to put the Skee Ball out right and have played with courage. Of course what I say about Este borrowing money is a confidential statement and in fact I would not want you to refer in any way to the affairs of the Skee Ball Co.

In conclusion I would say to you that the best way for you to judge the Bridge Ball would be to come down here and stay several days and we would get people into play it. You can form the best and I believe the only true judgement in this way. I have thus formed mine and it is confirmed in my own mind.

Tired out. Good Night.

Sincerely, [12]

He continued to contact potential investors and manufacturers, diligently following up to get them to see the game, and negotiate terms. In the end, he wanted more money than they were willing to agree to, they were too busy to run the traps, they were scared off by the threat of a patent infringement suit, or they simply could not invest the time, energy and money required.

After months of discussion, Holcomb & Hoke, owners of the American Boxball Company, finally decided that they, also, had no interest in the game. They directed one of their managers, Briant Sando, to write to Simpson and inform him they of this fact. Sando initially minced no words. He wrote to Simpson:

Dear Mr. Simpson

Your letter of the 24th was waiting for me when I arrived home last evening. Mrs Sando informed me that she had just mailed a little note to your sister, so I will trust to that to take care of the social end side you friendship and proceed to business. It is with considerable regret that I inform you that Holcomb and Hoke cannot "see" Bridge Ball. My own position here has a vital relationship to the profits I am able to make the business show -- and it seemed to me that the good margin of profit in your device much help us along. They think your proposition of $15.00 per alley royalty or one third of the profits is utterly preposterous. The most they seemed consider is less than half that say $20.00 or $25.00 per alley. From the way you talked when I was in Vineland I don't suppose *you would lower your figures that much, although I told Holcomb and Hoke you had indicated a willingness to accept somewhat less if necessary. On top of all this, W arises the possibility of an unfortunate mix up on your patents. Of course if you have anything further to suggest along these lines, I will be glad to hear from you and try to get the most favorable action possible for all parties concerned --*

Faithfully yours Briant Sando [13]

However, as he referenced in the letter, Simpson's sister Alice knew Briant Sando's mother socially, and arranged for Simpson to get in touch with Briant Sando directly. Sando, it turned out, was a dissatisfied employee of Holcomb & Hoke. As General Manager of the American Box Ball Company, he was in charge of managing their Tenpinnet and Box-Ball games which, according to Sando, the owners were neglecting in favor of their new Butter Kist Popcorn machine.

Anxious to get out from under their employ and strike out on his own, Sando suggested that while he didn't personally have the money to invest, he had a banker who might invest in the enterprise. That social connection, along with his personal dissatisfaction, was enough to get him to take a new tack. The next day he wrote:

Dear Mr. Simpson

When I dictated yesterday's letter to you from the office, I realized that I was most certainly writing the final chapter in negotiations between yourself and Messers Holcomb & Hoke. The differences between your viewpoint and theirs are so utterly irreconcilable that I don't believe anyone but myself could even have gotten them to consider Bridge Ball in conferes(?) as we did, but I confess not very seriously on account of what they considered your exorbinate [sic] demands. Perhaps one consideration is the fact that H.&H. are just now making another fortune. This time from their Butter Kist pop corn machine and are not much interested in anything else. I am let alone entirely in the management of Box Ball and Ten Pinnet enterprises -- as my fortune is still to be carved out, it is only natural that my experience and knowledge of the business tell me they should capitalized in exploitation of a business that I owned a good share in -- and it is on this basis that I wait(?) to hear from you in regard to Bridge Ball. I don't have money myself but I hav [sic] a Banker friend who is one of the squarest and cleanest fellows in the world and who would go in with me on a venture of this kind, providing we can come to terms with you. This of course would necessitate my leaving my present

Letter No. 1.   Indianapolis – Ind.
April 27th 1916

Dear Mr. Simpson

Your letter of the 24th was waiting for me when I reached home last evening. Mrs. Sando informed me that she had just mailed a little note to your sister, so I will trust to that to take care of the social end side of our friendship and proceed to business. It is with considerable regret that I inform you that Holcomb and Hoke cannot "see" Bridge Ball. My own position here has a vital relationship to the profits I am able to make the business show —

Letter from Briant Sando to Joseph Fourestier Simpson, April 27, 1916, p. 1.
(Courtesy Vineland Historical and Antiquarian Society)

patents. Of course, if you have anything further to suggest along these lines, I will be glad to hear from you and try to get the most favorable action possible for all parties concerned—

Faithfully yours,
Briant Sando—

Copy—

and it seemed to me that the good margin of profit in your device would help us along. They think your proposition of $75.00 per alley royalty or one third of profits is utterly preposterous. The most they would consider is less than half that—say, $20.00 or $25.00 per alley. From the way you talked when I was in Vineland I don't suppose you would lower your figures that much, although I told Holcombe and Hoke you had indicated a willingness to accept somewhat less if necessary. On top of all this M. raises the possibility of an unfortunate mix-up on your

Letter from Briant Sando to Joseph Fourestier Simpson, April 27, 1916, pp. 2-3.
(Courtesy Vineland Historical and Antiquarian Society)

connection which is good but I believe I would be safe in doing this from what I know about sale possibilities for the new game. It is not any purpose to go into details in this letter which is only introductory in this phase of the thing, but I'd like to know at an early date just how you feel as the whole proposition.

Faithfully yours Sando [14]

The rest, as they say, was history.

Soon after, Briant Sando resigned as the General Manager of American Box Ball Company to become the Vice President and General Manager of Briant Manufacturing Company, which was organized to manufacture and sell "games and specialties." [15] The company began its operation from the second floor of the Industrial Building at 416 W 10th St (at the corner of 10th and the canal) in Indianapolis. [16] George A. Bittler, also Vice President of Merchants National Bank in Indianapolis, was the President; Isaac A. Lewis, another Vice President, listed his occupation as Investor, located in the Merchants National Bank Building; and Mark E. Archer was Secretary/Treasurer. [17]

So began the saga of the Briant Manufacturing Company, (later renamed Briant Specialty Company) launched by Briant Sando and his partners. In 1917, the City directory listed the company as a manufacturer of "bridge ball games" and equipment.

For Simpson, this was the ultimate solution for the manufacture and marketing of Bridge Ball. Sando agreed to begin with Bridge Ball, in part to understand and get a foothold in the alley market. He had his own designs under development, and this would give his company a leg up when they were ready to take their product to market. With Simpson's experience in marketing, and seeing how Este successfully marketed Skee-Ball, selling the benefits of this new game was easy.

On October 14, 1916, the Briant Manufacturing Co. ran the first large display ad for Bridge Ball in The Billboard. The ad copy read:

BIG MONEY   YEAR-'ROUND

In Newest Bowling Game

Bridge-Ball, the newest bowling game, fascinates old and young, women and children--holds steady patronage--even professional bowlers, because they can use all their skill and science. It is a big profit-maker wherever there is a listed waste space--in pool and billiard rooms, clubs, regular bowling alleys, confectioneries,

Letter number 2 —

2427 Pierson ave—
Indianapolis Ind.
April 28th 1916

I put that number up there — he did not

Dear Mr. Simpson

When I dictated yesterday's letter to you from the office, I realized that I was most certainly writing the final chapter in negotiations between yourself and Messrs Holcomb & Hoke. The differences between your viewpoint and theirs are so utterly irreconcilable that I don't believe anyone but myself could even have gotten them to consider Bridge Ball in conference — as we did. But I confess not very seriously on account of what they considered

Letter from Briant Sando to Joseph Fourestier Simpson, April 28, 1916, p. 1.
(Courtesy Vineland Historical and Antiquarian Society)

Letter from Briant Sando to Joseph Fourestier Simpson, April 28, 1916, pp. 2-3.
(Courtesy Vineland Historical and Antiquarian Society)

etc.--just the thing for winter resorts and all concessionaires.

Draws Big Trade

As Side-Line of Exclusive Business

Each game will take in $2.50 per hour--you can afford a choice location. You can install several games in two hours in an ordinary room or tent--they are only 3x32 feet each. No attendant necessary, no score sheets or upkeep expense. It is ALL clear profit!

Entirely Automatic!

Drop a nickel in the slot, pull lever and ten balls are released for play. The idea is to roll the ball up the bridge--some do and some don't! Straight shots go into target box at back end of bridge and work the automatic scorer. That gets the crowd--you get the nickels--just scoop them out of money-box at closing time. Each game attractive in appearance and well made--everything fully guaranteed.

FOR A BIG PROFIT-MAKER THIS WINTER (NEXT SUMMER, TOO) WRITE OR WIRE US AT ONCE FOR SPECIAL INTRODUCTORY PRICES AND TERMS. FIRST CUSTOMER IN EACH TERRITORY GETS EXCLUSIVE RIGHTS. HERE'S YOUR OPPORTUNITY--ACT TODAY!

"Just leave it alone, and the nickels come home."

BRIANT MFG. CO., 422 West 10th Street, Indianapolis, Ind. [18]

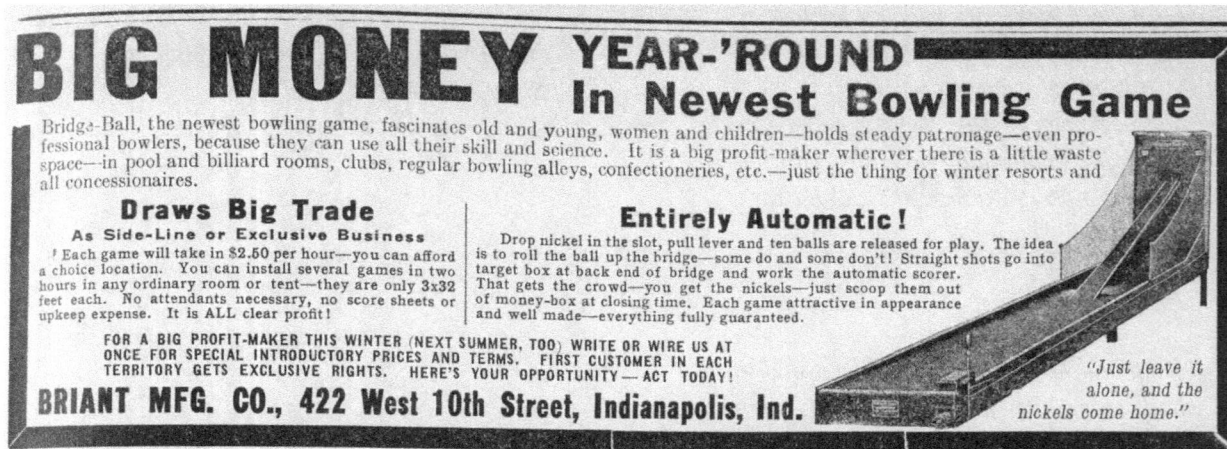

Briant Manufacturing Bridge Ball advertisement from The Billboard, October 14, 1916.
(Author's Collection)

Chapter 9

THE COMPETITION
Engaging the Enemy

Around the turn of the year between 1916 and 1917, the Great War raged on in Europe, the Middle East, and Africa as Europe carved up the African continent. Grand rulers and power players passed away and were replaced. Franz Joseph I, Emperor of Austria and King of Hungary, died and Charles I took the reins. In Great Britain, Prime Minister H. H. Asquith resigned and was succeeded by David Lloyd George. Robert Nivelle replaced Joseph Joffre as Commander-in-Chief of the French Army. Some powerful figures were simply destroyed: Grigori Rasputin, Russia's éminence grise, was assassinated on December 29. In a bold move in January of 1917, the Germans attempted to bring the war directly to the New World, proposing an alliance with Mexico against the United States.

In the U.S., a different and somewhat less violent war seethed as well: The battle between Skee-Ball and Bridge Ball.

Briant Manufacturing Company continued to fire shots across the bow at The J. D. Este Company, as Briant used Bridge Ball to establish a beachhead for the new business. Simpson fought his corner of the war by filing more patents. The J. D. Este Company played enthusiastic offense and rudimentary defense, as it continued to dominate the field. Unlike the Great War, this was a war of documents, threats of infringement suits and legal action, and a sometimes colorful war of words as they each attempted to conquer the amusement markets.

This new entry into the market, heralded by the October 14 Bridge Ball ad, appeared to have caught Este's attention. On October 21, The J. D. Este Co. placed its first display ad in The Billboard since March 18, 1916, and they continued to run weekly. The ad copy read:

SKEE BALL ALLEYS

Fully Protected by Domestic and Foreign Patents.

Get Ready for the Winter Season

SKEE-BALL IS SURELY COMING TO YOUR TOWN

Why don't YOU be the one to introduce this wonderful money making device and own an independent and successful business?

Write for Illustrated Catalogue.

The J. D. Este Co.

1534 Sansom St.,

PHILADELPHIA [1]

On October 28, a nearly identical ad ran in The Billboard. The ad ended with the rather ominous statement:

> *Users of infringing games will be prosecuted and are liable for to injunction and for all profits and triple damages.* [2]

The text at the bottom of the advertisement regarding "infringing games" appears to be an indirect threat to the Briant Manufacturing Company which was now manufacturing Simpson's Bridge-Ball game. Este had not been able to intimidate Briant with threats of patent infringement against his company, since there were no features that infringed on the original Skee-Ball patents, Este modified the attack. This time, it focused on warning potential buyers of the Bridge Ball alleys that they, as users and purchasers, might be liable "for injunction and all profits and triple damages." It was an empty threat, but part of the psychological warfare endemic to both international and commercial conflict.

Este also continued to run ads to emphasize the unique and expansive value of Skee-Ball. The J. D. Este Company ran a full-page display ad in The Billboard on December 16 with a glowing endorsement from John T. Byrne, in Wildwood, New Jersey who had been one of the game's earliest customers back in 1913. The ad copy read:

SKEEBALL ALLEYS

The Bowling Game with a Punch that a thrill for player and spectator alike. The leaping balls give a life to the game that no crowd can resist. A smashing big success for three years and daily growing stronger. A real honest-to-goodness day in and day out money-coiner for the owner. Read the following:

Wildwood, N. J.

November 13, 1916.

The J. D. Este Company

Philadelphia, Pa.

The J. D. Este Company advertisement from
The Billboard, October 28, 1916.
(Author's collection)

Gentleman:

At your request to hear from me as to my success with your game of Skee-Ball, would say:

Three years ago I purchased from you four Skee-Ball Alleys. At that time I had just acquired a property on the Boardwalk at Wildwood, New Jersey. My object in buying the Skee-Ball Alleys was to attract a crowd and thereby form an amusement center; In this I have been amazingly successful, due entirely to Skee-Ball.

Not only has Skee-Ball increased the value of my property, but it has been very profitable for me to operate. The first year my four alleys earned an average of $52.15 (or $13.04 each) daily throughout the summer. The second year I purchased two more alleys and my earnings were increased. Last year was by far the most successful of the three. On the 3rd of last September my six alleys earned $262.00, and average of $43.66 per alley, per day.

I attribute my success partly to the fact that I use the greatest care in keeping my alleys clean and in good condition. The balls are sandpapered, the carpet scrubbed, the woodwork rubbed down and the brasswork polished daily, so that after three years of the hardest kind of pounding they look practically as good as new.

With best wishes for your continued success and with kind personal regards, I am Very sincerely yours,

(Signed) JOHN T. BYRNE

This is just one experience out of hundreds in towns and cities ranging in population from 500 to 5,000,000--genuine, actual experiences, not guess-work or estimates.

Our books show that 42% of our alleys have been sold on repeat orders; in other words, nearly one-half of our alleys were sold to customers who had already tried out the game to their entire satisfaction. Can you beat that?

We have again been obliged to enlarge the size of our factory to meet the steadily increasing demand; it is now 500% larger than it was in 1914.

Get your order in now, even if you do not want immediate delivery, as materials and labor are advancing so rapidly that cannot maintain the present price after February 15th, 1917.

Skee-Ball is fully covered by domestic

and foreign patents. Users of infringing games will be prosecuted. They are liable to injunction and for all profits and triple damages.

WRITE FOR ILLUSTRATED CATALOGUE

THE J. D. ESTE COMPANY

OWNERS - PATENTEES - DISTRIBUTORS

1530 SANSOM STREET, PHILADELPHIA [3]

The J. D. Este Company ran another full-page ad in the January 6, 1917 issue of the Electric Railway Journal. [4]

In the meantime, Simpson pushed his new game ahead. He was granted Canadian Patent 174,409 on January 9, 1917 for his game of Bridge Ball. [5]

Bolstering Este's efforts to keep as much control over the game of Skee-Ball and its unique features as possible, on February 1, the company patented its improvements to overseas markets as well, and was granted Great Britain Patent 103,532, "Improvements in or relating to Game Apparatus" for their scoring mechanism. [6]

The war between Skee-Ball and Bridge Ball continued to play out in The Billboard, the battlefield for mindshare and market share in the amusement industry.

On February 3, The J. D. Este Co. ran a large display ad for Skee-Ball in The Billboard:

SKEEBALLALLEYS

Fully Protected by Domestic and Foreign Patents.

The ONE BIG HIT

Of the Atlantic City Boardwalk

For the past three years. Winter or Summer, the crowds gather just the same. Ask anyone who has been there. Is Skee-Ball in your town? If not, why don't YOU be the one to make the big killing?

Write for Illustrated Catalogue.

The J. D. Este Co.

1530 Sansom St.

PHILADELPHIA

Users of infringing games will be prosecuted and are liable to injunction and for all profits and triple damages. [7]

The Briant Manufacturing Company returned fire a week later with their ad for Bridge Ball, including their war of words defense, **ABSOLUTELY PROTECTED BY PATENTS** to reassure potential buyers that they would be protected from the Este Skee-Ball infringement threat. The new ad read:

START THE SEASON RIGHT WITH BRIDGE BALL

"CLEAN UP"--$3.00 OR MORE ON EACH GAME--ENTIRELY AUTOMATIC

MODERATE INVESTMENT STARTS YOU IN THIS BIG MONEY-MAKING BUSINESS

Bridge Ball draws steady trade from men, women and children. Not a game of chance--but a game of skill. Anyone can play. Its fascination keeps crowds playing--and coming back again. Just the thing for all resorts and concessionaires.

Drop Nickel In Slot--10 Balls for 5 Cents!

To score, the player must roll the ball up the bridge (see illustration). Watch the automatic scorer. It gets crowds--you get the nickels--just scoop them out of the money box at closing time. Each game attractive in appearance and well made. Parts are simple--everything guaranteed.

Automatic Scoring Device and Coin Collector--No Attendant Needed

Rapid earning capacity enables you to afford the choicest location. Games can be installed in an hour an any ordinary room or tent--they are only 3x32 feet each.

Write or wire us at once for prices and terms. Orders booked now insure prompt Spring Delivery and first chance at choice location. Send now for free descriptive matter.

ABSOLUTELY PROTECTED BY PATENTS

BRIANT MFG. CO., 426 West 10th Street, Indianapolis, Ind. [8]

Este's strategy was not limited to the battleground at The Billboard. He also continued to pursue the trolley park venues more directly. The company placed a half-page ad in the February 17 issue of the Electric Railway Journal, proclaiming "Skee Ball Alleys Prove a Great Drawing-Card at Trolley Parks." showing a man playing Skee-Ball while a fairly large crowd watched.

SKEE BALL ALLEYS

Prove a Great Drawing-Card at Trolley Parks

If you haven't one in your park, better get ready for the spring and summer.

Daily we receive letters from owners telling of the popularity of this game, and of its remarkable earning capacity. Six alleys in Wildwood, N. J. earned as high as $262.00 in one day. Have you any other amusement that can claim as much?

Skee Ball alleys are operated by the player and require no attendants.

They will pack your cars to full capacity.

Write for illustrated catalog.

THE J. D. ESTE COMPANY (OWNERS PATENTEES DISTRIBUTORS) 1534 SANSOM ST., PHILA. [9]

Skee-Ball was being used to draw people not only to amusement parks, but to all other kinds of amusement venues as well. In the February 22 issue of the Chicago Daily Tribune, an ad appeared listing a Shooting Gallery and Skee Ball alleys for sale, which were "[d]oing good business." [10] Skee-Ball was a key to selling the entire establishment to interested buyers, in part because of the location specific charter of the original sale of the alleys. Owners of Skee-Ball alleys could be sure that their neighbors would not be competing with them for the Skee-Ball attraction.

Although the Briant Manufacturing Company seemed to be using the same "location restricted" sales policy, they were not using that ammunition yet. If someone already held the Skee-Ball rights to operate in a town, others could still corner the market on Bridge Ball, with the same guarantee of protection. On February 24, they ran another traditional large display ad for Bridge Ball in The Billboard:

"$10 TO $25 Per Day on One Game"

YOU CAN INSTALL 2 TO 12 GAMES IN ANY ORDINARY ROOM OR TENT

"My receipts have been running $10 to $25 per day on one Bridge Ball Game. It's the quickest and easiest way of making money I have ever seen," write M. P. Dyer of Tennessee, in ordering two more games.

BRIDGE BALL *draws steady trade from men, women and children. Roll the balls up the bridge. A game of pure skill that anyone can play, but competition for*

The J. D. Este Company advertisement for Skee-Ball alleys, February 17, 1917.
(Author's Collection)

high score sustains interest. Bridge Ball fascinates crowds and makes bigger profits than any similar amusement. Especially fine for Parks, Beaches, Resorts and all Concessionaires

Fully Automatic

No attendants or up-keep expense. Score is registered automatically. The player can simply

Drop Nickel in Slot

10 Balls for 5¢

$3 an Hour Per Game

Bridge Ball earns money so fast and occupies so little space, you can afford the choicest location. Each game 3x32 feet. Can be installed anywhere in one hour.

Moderate investment starts you. Wire or write quick for prices and terms. Do this today--NOW--to insure prompt Spring delivery and first change at choice location.

Absolutely Protected By Patents.

Briant Mfg. Co., 432 W. 10th St., Indianapolis, Ind. [11]

Briant Manufacturing Company continued to push the same advertising approach to the same market, while Este spent some time strategically consolidating his business and tapping into his allies. When Este originally bought the patents from Simpson, Harper, and the Nice family, he incorporated the Skee-Ball Alley Company at the same time he filed incorporation papers for The J. D. Este Company. On March 31, the Skee-Ball Alley company officially went void. [12]

On March 3, an announcement appeared in The Editor & Publisher that The Fletcher Company Advertising Service would be placing newspaper copy in selected sections for The J. D. Este Company of Philadelphia. [13] Charles Este Jr., J. D. Este's brother, was the treasurer for the company. Este was able not only to bring business savvy and investment to Skee-Ball, but also to exploit his family ties in the promotion of the company. It was a big advantage.

Este also may have been circling the wagons because had other concerns on his mind. There was a war going on. Although he was too old to be drafted, Este had plans to contribute to the war effort in particularly personal ways. In 1916, he had quietly enrolled in The Philadelphia School of Aviation along with his friend from Princeton, Edwin V Dougherty, another Skee-Ball investor. [14] Este had a plan to fly fighter planes against the Germans.

Seeking Redemption

In the meantime, the war of the amusements continued, with help from Este's newfound allies.

That day, a half-page ad appeared in the Electric Railway Journal with a distinctively different look than their other previous ads. It stated: "Skee-Ball is always in the limelight of popularity." [15]

The alliance with the ad agency employing Este's brother produced some interesting new approaches in the war for market share. A few days later, on March 8, an ad appeared in the El Paso Herald for The J. D. Este Company. It was similar to other ads that had appeared in the Electric Railway Journal, but the extra copy at the bottom focused on introducing Skee-Ball as a financial opportunity to exploit languishing capital:

> "If you have real estate or small capital that is not working -- install Skee Ball Alleys and cash in on the fastest turn-over the amusement business has ever known. Experience in amusements is not necessary. The alleys virtually take care of themselves -- at low cost -- and the above letter shows how well they wear and how fast the profits roll in."

> "We do not want agents -- we want to sell direct to the man who is looking for a side-

Briant Manufacturing Company advertisement for Bridge Ball on February 24, 1917.
(Author's Collection)

line investment or a permanent, substantial business. Live wires everywhere are investigating this fast money-maker." [16]

Briant Manufacturing Company continued to batter the traditional venues. On March 10, the Briant Manufacturing Co. ran a large display ad for Bridge Ball in The Billboard, again touting:

"$10 TO $25 Per Day on One Game" [17]

A week later, their lack of clear market strategy showed, when the key change to the next full page display ad for Bridge Ball in The Billboard read identically, except for the implication that you could earn more by running more Bridge Ball alleys:

"$50 TO $100 Per Day on Four Games" [18]

The J. D. Este Company continued to use the John T. Byrne endorsement letter ad in the trolley journals. The full-page ad in the March 17 issue of the Electric Railway Journal repeated the advertising pitch for the thrill and excitement of the game, with language and stories evoking the sense of sustained success. Below the endorsement letter itself, the ad boasted of repeat buyers, expansion of the manufacturing capacity to meet the demand, and a subtle hint to buy before they were forced to raise prices. [19] The J. D.

The J. D. Este Company advertisement for Skee-Ball from the Electric Railway Journal, March 3, 1917.
(Author's Collection)

Este Company continued to raise the bar and harness a new, impressive weapon in his arsenal: Professional advertising language that spoke to the heart as well as the head, created the story, and tinged it with fear of losing an opportunity that just might not come again.

While The J. D. Este Company was selling Skee-Ball, they were not content with just one game in their amusement portfolio. Their emerging strategy called for diversification, but nothing that would cannibalize the Skee-Ball market. They had for some time been developing a new game smaller than, but similar to, Skee-Ball that they called Score-Ball. Simpson had done exactly the same thing, but never managed to bring those smaller games to market. By the time The J. D. Este Company started advertising the game in The Billboard on March 24, they had already placed the Score-Ball game into two high-visibility, popular venues: Atlantic City; and the Crystal Arcade, 14th Street, New York.

Their inaugural advertisement for Score-Ball read:

> *First Announcement of a New Game of Real Merit and Skill*
>
> *SCORE-BALL*
>
> *PATENT APPLED FOR*

> *A ROLL DOWN GAME WITH AN AUTOMATIC SCORER*
>
> *TEN BALLS--TEN CENTS--NO BLANKS*
>
> *SCORE-BALL IS A KID COUSIN OF SKEE-BALL AND A REAL WINNER FOR PARKS, ARCADES, RESORTS, CARNIVALS and CONCESSIONAIRES*
>
> *Score-Ball Is Earning Big Money at Atlantic City and the Crystal Arcade, 14th Street, New York.*
>
> *Our output this spring will be limited to five hundred Score-Ball Games, over a hundred of which are already sold. The dimensions of the game are two ft. eight inches wide and seven ft. ten inches long. The small space requirement to install a battery of Score-Ball Games enable you to obtain a choice location at a low rent. The games are well made, handsomely finished and low in price.*
>
> *WRITE AT ONCE FOR FURTHER INFORMATION. THE J. D. ESTE CO., 1530 Sansom St., Philadelphia, Pa. AGENTS WANTED EVERYWHERE.* [20]

The same issue of The Billboard featured

an article that described Score-Ball as "a kid cousin to Skee-Ball." Following the advertising psychology of the not too subtle message of "don't miss this limited opportunity," they announced a limited run of "500 games of which 100 have already been manufactured and sold." [21]

Briant Manufacturing Company responded in the only way that they could, since they had no immediate expansion strategy. Instead of just defending against the "infringement" threat, they began making infringement threats of their own. On March 24, the Briant Manufacturing Co. ran a large display ad for Bridge Ball identical to the "four games" ad, but with the following language at the end:

> *Bridge Ball is fully covered by patents. Infringers will be prosecuted and are liable for all profits and triple damages.* [22]

If Este expected Briant Manufacturing Company to be influenced to withdraw the game of Bridge Ball based on legal threats, he was to be sadly disappointed. On the other hand, if Briant Manufacturing Company couldn't up their game to match Este's command of the market, it might not matter. The war of words wore on.

On March 24, The J. D. Este Co. ran their large "Always In The Limelight Of Popularity" display ad, this time in The Billboard. [23]

The following week, the Briant Manufacturing Co. ran another large display ad for Bridge Ball. The ad copy was similar to the ad that ran on March 24, but they tightened their ad copy slightly:

> *$50 TO $100 Per Day on Four Games*
>
> *2 to 12 Games Go In Any Ordinary Room or Tent.*
>
> *"My receipts have been running $10 to $25 per day on one Bridge Ball Game. It's the quickest and easiest way of making money I have ever seen." writes M. P. Dyer of Tennessee, in ordering two more games.*
>
> *Bridge Ball draws steady trade from men, women and children. "Bowl the balls up the bridge." Thrilling sport--fascinates crowds. A game of pure skill that one can play--the real winner for parks, resorts and concessionaires.*
>
> *$3 an Hour per Game Everything Automatic*
>
> *Bridge Ball earns money so fast and occupies so little space, you can afford the choicest location. Each game 3x32 feet; weights 900 lbs. Can be installed anywhere in one hour.*

Briant Manufacturing Company advertisement for Bridge Ball, March 17, 1917.
(Author's Collection)

Moderate Investment starts you. Wire or write for prices and terms. Do this today--NOW--to Insure prompt Spring delivery and first chance at choice location.

Coin Device collects and records every game played. Score is registered automatically. No attendants or upkeep expense. The player can

Drop Nickel in Slot

10 Balls for 5¢

Watch the Automatic Scorer!

Briant Mfg. Co.

440 W. 10th St.

Indianapolis, Ind.

Bridge Ball is fully covered by patents. Infringers will be prosecuted and are liable for all profits and triple damages. [24]

That same day, The J. D. Este Co. ran a large display ad for Skee-Ball in The Billboard. Their ad was short and sweet, again using savvy ad language: "Why shouldn't YOU be making the big killing?"

SKEEBALL ALLEYS

Fully Protected by Domestic and Foreign Patents.

The ONE BIG HIT

Of the Atlantic City Boardwalk

For the past three years. Winter or Summer, the crowds gather just the same. Ask anyone who has been there. Is Skee-Ball in your town? If not, why don't YOU be the one to make the big killing?

Write for Illustrated Catalogue.

The J. D. Este Co.

1530 Sansom St.

PHILADELPHIA

Users of infringing games will be prosecuted and are liable to injunction and for all profits and triple damages. [25]

In the April issue of the Electric Traction Journal an article about Skee-Ball Alleys started this way:

> *"A crowd of spectators which makes no effort to hurry on their way marks a spot of excitement or interest, or both. This may*

be applied to the street fakir, the automobile accident, or an amusement attraction." [26]

In fact, Skee-Ball alleys were having this kind of crowd attraction. A friend of Simpson's, Evelyn Parker, wrote to him that she'd observed exactly that: A crowd on the boardwalk at Atlantic City, during the off-season, excitedly gathered around the Skee-Ball alleys. She bemoaned the fact that Simpson was not getting the recognition or the money due him for this phenomenal invention. [27]

A second large display ad for Score-Ball appeared on April 14:

HERE IS A NEW GAME OF REAL MERIT AND SKILL

SCORE-BALL

PATENT APPLIED FOR

A ROLL DOWN GAME WITH AN AUTOMATIC SCORING DEVICE

TEN BALLS--TEN CENTS--NO BLANKS

Score-Ball is a kid cousin of Skee Ball and a real winner for Parks, Fairs, Resorts, Carnivals and Concessionaires.

The boards are two feet wide (including ball rack), seven feet ten inches long and weigh about 150 pounds. They are easily transported and quickly set up. The small space required to install a battery of Score Ball Games makes it possible to secure a choice location at low rental. The games are handsome, well made and low in price. The scoring device is very accurate and lends a great fascination to the game. The way orders are coming in from the most experienced amusement men, convinces us that we have a winner.

Write at once for further information.

THE J. D. ESTE CO.
1530 Sansom Street,
PHILADELPHIA [28]

In the April 28, 1917 issue of The Billboard, an article about Score-Ball described how The J. D. Este Co. had been looking for a smaller game since the introduction of Skee-Ball and had found it in Score-Ball. [29]

At the end of the year 1917 there was a major internal shift for The J. D. Este Company, though it was likely that their customers hardly noticed. Arthur Wheeler, Vice President of The J. D. Este Company passed away unexpectedly. He was 44 years old. His obituary appeared in the December 29 issue of the Electric Railway Journal. [30] His brother,

The J. D. Este Company advertisement for Score-Ball in The Billboard, March 24, 1917.
(Author's Collection)

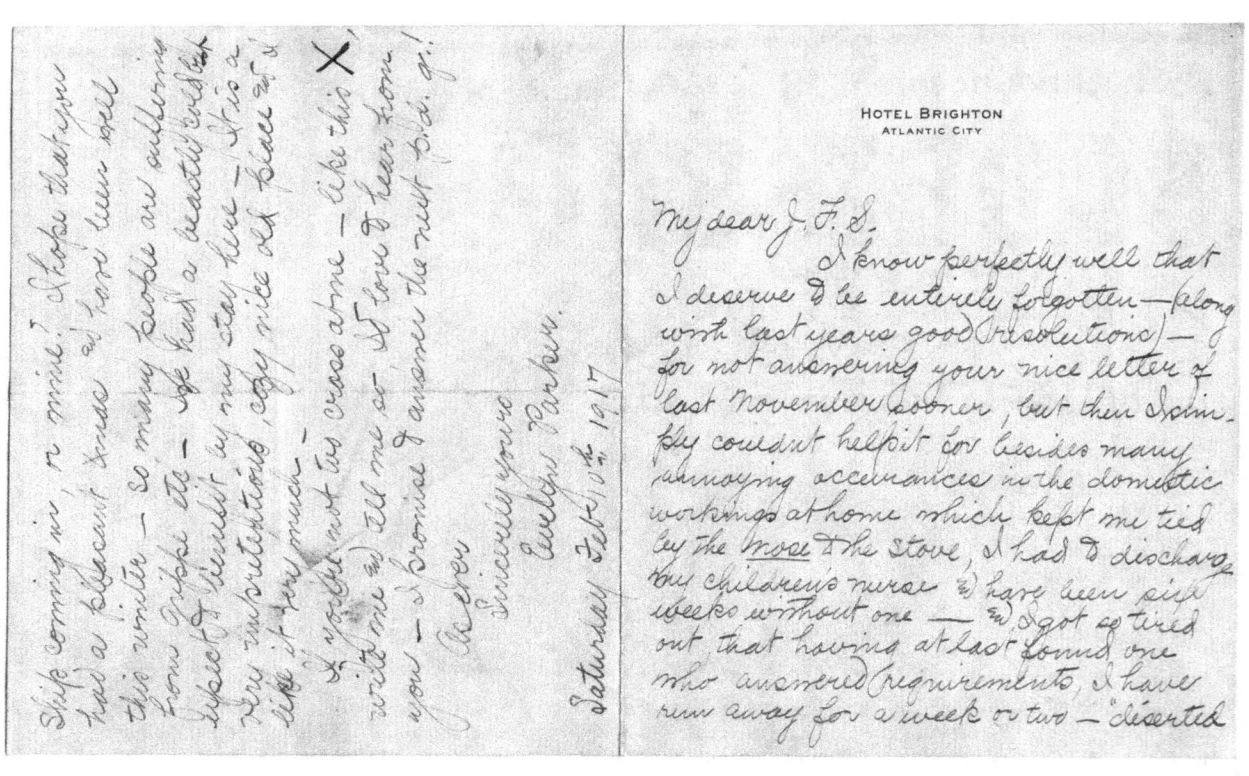

Letter from Evelyn Parker to Joseph Fourestier Simpson, February 10, 1917, pp. 1, 3.
(Courtesy Vineland Historical and Antiquarian Society)

the ship" literally — I'm as lonesome as a fish out of water (as I am alone). Otherwise I am enjoying the change & rest from running a lot of servants who won't be "run" — Of Course Mother is running things for me while I am away. I feel terribly cold & bad being off on a lark all by my lone! Something is missing though — oh I know what it is — no one to run up behind me calling "Mother"! Still, I shall try hard not to forget that I am married — (You see my being off on a lark is taking affect all ready!)

While rolling along in my "push-mobile" on the boardwalk this A.M. I noticed a large crowd all intently watching a game — The only game running through the winter season — yes you've guessed right! it was the Skee-ball! & it just made me feel all rubbed the wrong way when I saw it because of their mean dog-in-the-manger attitude with you! How have they been behaving lately about the Bridge ball? & have you been able to place it satisfactorily — you certainly ought to have made a fortune from these two &

I want to thank you for your very pretty Xmas card — was it a picture of your

Letter from Evelyn Parker to Joseph Fourestier Simpson, February 10, 1917, p. 2.
(Courtesy Vineland Historical and Antiquarian Society)

Seeking Redemption 237

Herbert Wheeler, would assume his position as Vice President.

This was particularly important, since the other big news that year was that Jonathan Dickinson Este had enlisted in the Army in April, and was about to go to war. [31]

As 1918 began, the war effort clearly dominated everyone's consciousness. With Este off to fly Liberty bombers and later fighter planes, the task of running the company fell to Herbert Wheeler, Arthur's brother. Now many ads for Skee-Ball began to appear featuring the game as a favorite of our troops.

January 12, 1918, a display ad began to appear in The Billboard:

SKEEBALL ALLEYS

NOW THE GREATEST ATTRACTION FOR CANTONMENTS

A big money maker for Indoor and outdoor places of amusement all year. Write for illustrated catalogue.

THE J. D. ESTE COMPANY

1530 Sansom St. Also Manufacturers of Score Ball Philadelphia, Pa. [32]

Another ad spelled it out even more clearly:

SKEEBALL

THE SOLDIERS' GREATEST PASTIME AND AMUSEMENT Now used at Cantonments. A highly moral game and exercise. Write for Illustrated Catalogue. Dept. B.,

THE J. D. ESTE CO. - - 1534 Sansom Street, Philadelphia, Pa.

ALSO MANUFACTURERS AND DISTRIBUTORS OF SCORE BALL GAME. [33]

There is little evidence that Skee-Ball sales suffered as a result of the new entry of Bridge-Ball into the market, and no evidence that Este ever made good on the threats to litigate. But this was only the first of many "me-too" games that featured advantages introduced by Skee-Ball.

Another significant challenger to Skee-Ball appeared that year as a brand new game came to market: Whirl-O-Ball.

Briant Manufacturing, now renamed Briant Specialty Company, brought its very own game to market, and it had now completely eclipsed Bridge Ball in the company's focus. This was a big reason that they initially had gotten started

The J. D. Este Company advertisement for Score-Ball, April 14, 1917.
(Author's Collection)

with Bridge Ball, to get a foot into the industry. They were marketing hard for their own product as the key competitor to Skee-Ball, and now they had an even more potent weapon in their arsenal. Whirl-O-Ball was not retreating from the market anytime soon.

Their ad touted Whirl-O-Ball's ability to generate $5 to $10 in revenue per hour for each game. The game, when assembled, was 20 feet long, 3 feet wide, 7½ feet high at the loop and weighed in at 600 pounds. It was shipped in three sections and each game could be set up in 30 minutes.

To play, the player rolled the ball briskly up the alley, which curved all the way up and back around toward the player before landing in one of the target openings. In describing the benefits of the game for amusement venue owners, they minced no words.

> *"Make BIG MONEY with Whirl-o-ball*
> *The new automatic Loop-the-loop game."* [34]

The J. D. Este Company continued to aggressively market Skee-Ball. In ad copy in The Billboard, trolley journals, and in regional and local publications, Skee-Ball continued to be prominently featured, reflecting the penetration of the game into everyday life. On March 16, a full-page ad appeared in the Electric Railway Journal for The J. D. Este Company, with the heading "Skee Ball For Trolley Parks." The ad featured a testimonial letter from A. Cohen stating how happy they were with their Skee-Ball alleys, and touting the fact that the Willow Grove Park in Pennsylvania had five alleys installed. [35]

In the April issue of Electric Traction, the electric trolley industry journal, featured an article titled "Fascinating Game of 'Skee-Ball.'" The article referenced the Atlantic City convention where the members of the trolley industry organizations may have played the game. The article discussed game-play, the automatic scoring system, the nickel-in-the-slot feature, and the dimensions and weight of an alley. [36]

On May 4, another article appeared in The Billboard, this time about the popularity of the "Este Games." It reported that Willow Grove Park, Philadelphia, Pennsylvania would add another ten alleys to the five that they first installed for the 1917 season. Coney Island would also add another ten alleys. [37] That same day, Woodside Park in Philadelphia would open to large crowds, with H. Deering running the Skee-Ball Alley concession at the park. [38]

Not all news about Skee-Ball was good news. On May 10, a fire swept through Coney Island in Cincinnati Ohio. Practically the entire Joy

The J. D. Este Company advertisement for Skee-Ball, January 12, 1918.
(Author's Collection)

The J. D. Este Company advertisement for Skee-Ball, June 29, 1918.
(Author's Collection)

City was wiped out on the midway. Overall, fourteen buildings were destroyed including the Skee-Ball concession. Damage to the park was estimated to be between $80,000 and $90,000. [39]

Skee-Ball was constantly in the press. July 2, Summit Park ran a display ad for July 4th in the Utica Herald-Dispatch. Among the attractions listed was Skee-Ball. [40]

On August 17, the New Process Gear Company and the Durston Gear Company both of Syracuse, New York held picnics at Lakeside. During the afternoon many athletic events were held, including Skee-Ball. [41]

The next day, an article appeared in The Brooklyn Daily Eagle about the arrivals at the Equinox House in Manchester, Vermont. Among the attractions featured in the article were the Skee-Ball alleys and the dance parlor at the Equinox. [42]

By the end of 1918, Skee-Ball stood head and shoulders above the rest in its class of amusements, and had become an integral part of the American amusement culture. Increasingly, and for decades following its introduction, Whirl-O-Ball found a place beside Skee-Ball in arcades and boardwalks and amusement parks across the country. But Whirl-O-Ball never overtook or outshone Skee-

Briant Specialty Company advertisement for Whirl-O-Ball, March 16, 1918.
(Author's Collection)

Ball in the businesses or the hearts and minds of customers. Although skirmishes would continue, it was clear who had won the war.

Briant Specialty Co. advertisement for Whirl-O-Ball March 21, 1931 in The Billboard.
(Author's Collection)

Skee-Ball at Playland in San Francisco, Ca.
(Courtesy James R. Smith Collection)

SKEE BALL

THE FASCINATING BOWLING GAME
GET NICKELS FROM OPERATOR.

WHITNEY BROS.

PLA...
INSTR...
Place Nick...
Pull han...
HOLD until ra...
Score device w...
will register to...

Skee-Ball and Whirl-O-Ball at Playland in San Francisco, Ca.
(Courtesy James R. Smith Collection)

Chapter 10

INTERLUDE
Mr. Este Goes To War

J. D. Este easily could have gone down in history as the founder of the Skee-Ball empire, if not the game's inventor, and could have pursued the life of a reasonably well-to-do businessman. However, the restlessness that had caused him to turn his back on the easy and prosperous job as Treasurer in the family lumber company, propelling him to take on the challenge of a start-up game business, would not let him rest on his laurels. A daredevil at heart, he had enrolled in a pilot training course at The Philadelphia School of Aviation in the spring of 1916. [1] Finally, in April of 1917, he was ready to do his part, flying missions against the Germans.

On April 15, 1917, Jonathan Dickinson Este enlisted in the Army at Fortress Monroe, Virginia, in the Aviation Section Signal Corps, and was given the rank of Sergeant. [2] He was assigned to the Newport News flying school in Newport News, Virginia, completing his course on June 1. [3] By June 20, he was in transit to Camp Kelly in Texas, and promoted to the rank of 1st Lieutenant in the Signal Officers Reserve Corps. [4]

It was wartime, and his military career moved rapidly. Este was given command of the 32nd Aero Squadron on July 20. [5] While Este was at Camp Kelly, his father, Charles Este, Sr., died, on August 10. [6] Este resolutely soldiered on.

Two weeks later, on August 23, Jonathan Dickinson Este embarked from New York, on the S. S. Baltic to begin a tour of duty in France, commanding the 32nd Aero Squadron. [7]

In September, Este was ordered to Brôn (near Lyons), France, to take command of the 5th Aviation Instruction Center, where he remained until December 20. [8] The day before Christmas in 1917, he was ordered to Headquarters, Air Service in Paris, France for staff duty. [9]

For a man of action like Este, it must have been frustrating to serve those months on Staff duty in Paris. It certainly was not the reason he

Aviation officers just prior to their decoration with Distinguished Service Cross, by Lieut. Gen. Hunter Liggett. Left to right: Capt. Jonathan Dickinson Este; Capt. "Eddie" Rickenbacker; Capt. Sollers; Lieut. Hugh Brewster; Lt. Charles R. D'Oliver; Lt. Bradley J. Gaylord; Lt. James Knowles, Jr; Lt. Howard G. Rath; Lt. L. C Somon. Rembercourt, Meurthe et Mosselle, France.
(Courtesy National Archives and Records Administration)

joined the Army. However, this was likely the place he met a very special nurse who would soon play a much larger role in his life.

Finally, on March 12, 1918, Jonathan Dickinson Este was ordered to the 3rd Aviation Instruction Center, Issoudun, for advanced flying instruction, which was followed in April with instruction in Aerial gunnery at Arcachon. [10, 11] Things were about to get much more exciting.

On April 20, Este was ordered to Production Center No. 2 at Romorantin. He was assigned as a test pilot to fly the first Liberty bomber, and his job was to make official test flights for the American-built DH4 planes. [12] On June 22, Jonathan Dickinson Este flew the first American-built plane from Paris to London. [13]

Finally, on July 1, Este joined the 13th Aero Squadron, 2nd Pursuit Group, 1st Army at the front as a pilot operating out of Toul, France. [14] Soon, he was flying two missions a day, morning and afternoon, engaging the enemy Fokkers in air combat, the World War I aerial "dog-fights." This is what he had dreamed of when he started flight school in Philadelphia, now worlds away.

His exploits over the next several months are recorded in the After Action Reports filed with the Army, but one in particular stands out. On September 13, Jonathan Dickinson Este shot down his first German plane.

The After Action Report read:

NUMBER OF E. A. ENCOUNTERED 7

ALTITUDE : 2400 meters

TYPE : Bi-Place [sic] Fokkers

COMBATS : 5

REGION : Chambley

CONFIRMATIONS REQUESTED : 3

PLANES SEEN TO HAVE GONE DOWN OUT OF CONTROL : 3 E. A.

Left Toul at 17:45 and followed the following route at 3500 meters. Flirey, Vigneulles, Joinville, [sic] Puxieux, Pagny, Solgne. Then went down to 2400 meters under the clouds that were banking up very thick. At Chambley were attacked by seven Fokkers which came out of the sun. Turned toward them, all climbing. The fight became a regular "Dog fight", my motor failed me for a moment and two Huns got on my tail. Lieut. Hays came down on one and shot him off. My motor then took and I was then able to attack two other Huns before the fight ended. I saw one plane, which I believe to be a Fokker going straight down

First pilots of Liberty Plane in France. Left to right: Lt. Jonathan Dickinson Este and Lt. H. C. Boricon, Aviation Supply Field, Romorantin, France, June 8, 1918.
(Courtesy National Archives and Records Administration)

in a nose dive. The patrol became separated largely due to the mist and clouds but during the larger part of the fight kept well together. The fight ended north of Chambray at 3500 meters at 18:55 o'clock. Lieut. Converse has not returned at time of making report. Three Fokkers were dark colored with streak of white lightening on side and black tails with white crosses also had white crosses on wings.

J. DICKINSON ESTE.
1ST. LIEUT. A. S. U. S.A. [sic] [15]

He continued to fly missions for the next two months. After the war ended on November 11, 1918, his heroism was recognized. On November 11, Jonathan Dickinson Este was awarded the Distinguished Service Cross.

> *J. Dickinson Este, first lieutenant, 13th Aero Squadron Air Service. For extraordinary heroism in action near Chambray, France, September 13th 1918. He was leading an Offensive patrol of five machines when a formation of seven enemy single-seaters approached the patrol from above. Although outnumbered and in a very disadvantageous position, he did not hesitate to lead his patrol to the attack. Through the combat that followed he was himself attacked by two enemy planes, which fired at him at point-blank range from the rear and above. By his skill and courage he was able to keep his formation together and they succeeded in shooting down three of the enemy planes of which he himself destroyed one and drove down another out of control. [16]*

On December 12, Jonathan Dickinson Este was honorably discharged from the military in Washington DC, having been promoted to the rank of Captain for his heroism. [17] The following week, he returned home to Philadelphia. On February 3, 1919, Este returned to Washington to be married to the nurse, Lydia Richmond Taber, of the Princeton Tabers, whom he met when he was serving in France during the war. [18]

Este returned from World War I a decorated hero, and a changed man, with new priorities. As he opened a new chapter of his life, focused on building his new family, he sold his shares in The J. D. Este Company to his partners.

On June 17, a meeting of the stockholders of the company was held at 1534 Sansom Street in Philadelphia, and the Certificate of Amendment of Certificate of Incorporation was created:

> *THE J. D. ESTE COMPANY, a corporation of Delaware, doth hereby certify that it has changed its corporate name to SKEE BALL COMPANY, said change*

having been declared by resolution of the Board of Directors of said corporation (above recited) to be advisable, and having been duly and regularly assented to by vote of a majority in interest of all the stockholders having voting powers, at a meeting duly called by the Board of Directors for that purpose; and the Judges' Certificate is hereby appended.

IN WITNESS WHEREOF, said corporation has caused this certificate to be signed by its President and Secretary, and the corporate seal to be hereto affixed, this 17th day of June A. D. 1919.

Signed:

Edwin V. Dougherty (President) Edward H. LeBoutillier (Secretary) [19]

After Jonathan Dickinson Este sold the Skee-Ball business to his partners, including Princeton friend and fellow pilot, Edwin V. Dougherty, John W. Harper stayed with the endeavor, now as an officer of the company. The new company was named the Skee-Ball Company. The officers of the company were:

Edwin V. Dougherty Jr. President

John W. Harper Vice President

E. H. LeBoutillier Secretary/Treasurer [20]

Skee-Ball, however, continued it's inexorable pace of expansion and success without a pause.

The balls rolled on.

Chapter 11

FLYING HIGH
Skee-Ball in the Roaring Twenties

For as successful as Skee-Ball was during the dark period of the Great War, it was poised to explode with the cultural dynamism and excitement of the Roaring Twenties. The 1920s was a period of sustained economic prosperity in the US, Canada and Western Europe, accompanied by a social and cultural awakening, and an era of giddy prosperity. Jazz music blossomed, and there was suddenly large-scale use of technology, and consumer demand for joy and excitement. Celebrity was the word of the day, and the new heroes were sports figures as well as musicians and movie stars.

Along with heady economic growth came a dance between the moral and the profane.

The moral was represented most powerfully by Prohibition, the law passed in 1920 with the idea of restraining drunkenness and the evils that accompanied that indulgence. However, the prohibition against alcohol did not abolish the desire for it, which led to opportunities for corruption of all kinds, from Al Capone and other mobsters, to speakeasies in every major city, playing out in a grand morality backlash. These forces drove the heady expansion of amusements of all kinds, including new palatial cinemas, and gigantic sports stadiums, as well as huge amusement venues and recreation opportunities, some moral and some less so, in all the major cities in the country.

Although there were big changes in the name and composition of the Skee-Ball Company, Skee-Ball itself was unchanged, and continued to dominate its market space as reflected in announcements and articles in The Billboard. It was constantly expanding the market into more amusement parks, more local venues, and into boardwalks and arcades across the United States and into Europe and England.

Whirl-O-Ball continued to market aggressively, making its own inroads, but failed to dent the progress of Skee-Ball. Businesses now advertised Bridge-Ball alleys "only used for two summers" for sale—cheap. [1] More and more stories about the success of Skee-Ball continued to appear in the news. [2]

With the death of Bridge Ball, Simpson seemed to retreat from the game industry for the last time. After the death of his mother, Josephine, in 1918, Simpson continued to live with his sister, Alice, and brother, Henry, at the house on Landis Avenue in Vineland. He listed his occupation as "inventor." [3] He spent most of his days experimenting with new ideas, and writing the family genealogy, a labor of love in memory of his aunt Sophia. Simpson quietly passed away in 1930 in Vineland at the age of 78. [4]

On January 24, 1920 the Skee-Ball Company again expanded its offerings, emphasizing Score-Ball, and a new, though short-lived, game called BaseBallLite, an attempt to capitalize on the new craze for all things sports-related. Their large display ad in The Billboard read:

SKEE BALL

SCORE BALL

More Popular Than Ever. Alleys Greatly Improved.

Games

Mechanically Perfect. A Great Money Maker

BASEBALLLITE

The Newest and Most Interesting Game. Highly Endorsed by the Greatest 2nd Baseman, EDDIE COLLINS.

SKEE BALL COMPANY,

Manufacturers and Distributors. 1015 N. Bodine St., PHILADELPHIA, PA. [5]

On May 1, in the Coney Island Chatter column of The Billboard, there was news that

Morris Goldberg was putting in a kiddie park and a ten-alley Skee-Ball game next to the Prospect Hotel in Coney Island, New York. [6] Goldberg had started as a manager for The J. D. Este Company and stayed on with the Skee-Ball Company until he launched his own venture in 1922, as an agent to sell Skee-Ball alleys: The Skee-Ball Sales and Security Company.

As Skee-Ball continued to grow, so did competitors, real and fraudulent.

Another copycat game, Jazz-Ball, was being marketed as similar to Skee-Ball, except this one was a fraud. The gentleman running the ad bilked his innocent partner out of the start-up money, collected payment for the non-existent game, and ran.

On June 5, the Animated Game And Toy Company of New York City ran a display ad in The Billboard for Jazz-Ball. The ad copy read:

PARKS, FAIRS, ETC. GET IN ON THE NEW INTERESTING SENSATIONAL GAME, "JAZZ-BALL"

Telephone, telegraph, or call for choice territory and Concessions, for Seashore, Mountain Resorts, Carnivals and Parks.

THIS DEVICE PAYS LARGE PROFITS

Is more fascinating, simple and entertaining than JAPANESE BALL, SKEE BALL, POOL, BILLIARDS, DERBY RACES, Etc.

Don't overlook this opportunity! Communicate at once.

ANIMATED GAME AND TOY COMPANY, 366 5th Ave.

Near 34th Street, Suite 706, Phone: Greeley 3749, Greeley 367, NEW YORK CITY [7]

Amusement companies were big business, so it's not surprising that swindlers appeared. The Kingston Daily Freeman, the local newspaper in Kingston, New York, reported that on Saturday evening, August 20, 1921, police had captured this "Master Swindler," Edward Arden Noblett. He had swindled his partner, a war veteran typical of the mark this particular swindler preyed on, out of his life savings of $30,000 to set up two bogus companies. One of them was the Animated Game And Toy Company. He was arrested and held without bail. There was no game of Jazzball, and never would be. [8]

Unfortunately, crime appeared to pay and pay well, apparently well enough to persuade a jury to acquit this career criminal with a history of fraud going back to 1893.

In 1921, the Skee-Ball Company, now managed by Morris Goldberg, relocated from Philadelphia to Coney Island, New York. [9] Although there was a huge amusement industry presence in Atlantic City and along the Jersey Shore, Coney Island became a major focal point for the amusement industry in the 1920s. It had been a resort since the mid-1800s. When the Brooklyn Rapid Transit connected Brooklyn to Manhattan in the early 1900s, Coney Island quickly became the recreation destination for thousands of New Yorkers seeking to escape the heat of the summer in the city tenements. With the opening of the new West End Terminal in 1919, Coney Island became busier than ever. Zoned exclusively for recreation and amusements, it rapidly became the mecca for the amusement industry. [10]

Skee-Ball continued to be prominently and regularly mentioned in The Billboard. On June 12, in the Coney Island Chatter column, Sam Crespie, who ran a Skee-Ball alley concession at Henderson's Walk and the Bowery, was identified as a "comer" in Coney Island. [11] The next week, the Rocky Glen Amusement Resort ran a display ad in The Billboard listing attractions that were being built for the park including a large roller coaster and carousel, and soliciting for concessions including Skee-Ball. [12] The Coney Island Chatter column on June 19 reported that K. Goldberg, assisted by Charlie Palmer and Manny, were running ten Skee-Ball alleys on Surf Avenue in Culver Depot. [13]

October 9, 1920, Morris Taxier ran a large display ad in The Billboard seeking shows, rides and Skee-Ball alleys for a park opening in Havana, Cuba, on November 1. [14]

Two announcements appeared on November 1, which ran in several issues that month, and heralded another step toward the redemption aspect of Skee-Ball: bowling for prizes.

> *"The one throwing the highest score at the Skee Ball Alley during this week will get a $7.50 shirt Saturday night."* [15]

> *"Prize will be given away at the Skee Ball Alley next Saturday night. The Smoke House."* [16]

Skee-Ball was generally found on the side of the moral and wholesome attractions. So was the Young Men's Christian Association.

The Young Men's Christian Association (YMCA) was founded in London in 1844, in response to unhealthy social conditions arising in the big cities at the end of the Industrial Revolution. As young men flocked to the cities to take their lowly jobs in the industrial revolution, they found themselves poor, without roots, often sleeping on the floor of their shops or in crowded rooms above the businesses in which they labored. Worse, they might find themselves on the streets of open sewers, beset by pickpockets, thugs, beggars, drunks and prostitutes. [17]

In the 1920s and 1930s, the YMCA provided the same kind of haven for young men flocking to the cities for work. The YMCA was founded in part on the conviction that a healthy moral spirit must be maintained by a healthy body. It is not surprising then, that Skee-Ball would be a perfect addition to the recreational opportunities at the YMCA.

In February of 1921, an ad appeared in the magazine, "Association Men," showing a picture of men playing Skee-Ball at the YMCA, and a letter of appreciation addressed to the manager, Mr. Morris Goldberg. Goldberg would remain a major player in Skee-Ball and Skee-Ball marketing and sales for many years to come.

This was the first ad of many that appeared for Skee-Ball at the YMCA. The organization was so thrilled with the Skee-Ball alleys installed in its first venue, it was recommended that the game be included in all YMCA Social Department equipment inventories. [18]

On April 2, 1921 there was a meeting of the directors of the Skee-Ball Operating Company at 365 Broadway, Manhattan Borough, New York. This company was originally incorporated by Este, Wheeler, Captell and Harper in 1915 solely to operate Skee-Ball Alleys in a building across from the New York Times building in Manhattan, in an effort to "elevate" the game and its appeal. Skee-Ball had come to dominate the amusement park

Seeking Redemption   259

Coney Island circa 1910.
(Courtesy Library of Congress)

market, and this venue, key to the introduction and popularization of Skee-Ball, was no longer key to its success. Skee-Ball Operating Company, Inc. voluntarily, and with none of the fanfare that marked its opening, dissolved on June 2, 1921. [19]

By this time, Skee-Ball was making its mark abroad as well. On December 6, an announcement appeared in The Edinburgh Gazette relating to the Great Britain Patent 103,521 which expired on February 2, 1921. The announcement was a notice that Harold Wade had made application for the restoration of the patent. [20]

The British premiere of Skee-Ball occurred at the prestigious London Olympia Christmas Carnival later in 1921, presented by George V. Tonner, of Blackpool and the Isle of Man. Harry E. Tudor, who represented many prominent American and European amusement devices, was highly enthusiastic about Skee-Ball, and said as much in The Billboard in their Dec. 10, 1921 issue. According to Tudor the introduction of Skee-Ball would "result in a wide demand for that popular game in England, in that bowling in every form is distinctly a British idea of skillful sport." [21]

Less than two months later, on February 4, 1922, an article about Arnold Neble, President of the Kentucky Derby Company in New York, noted that he was traveling in England, looking after the business of his Skee-Ball alleys. While he was there, he wrote an article for the "World's Fair," an English outdoor amusement publication.

"Olympia," London Jan. 5, 1922

To the Editor "World's Fair."
Oldham: Dear Editor--This is my first trip on business to England, and altho it is difficult for me to be away from my many enterprises thruout[sic] the States and Canada, I am glad I have come over.

I have found the same brotherhood exists between showmen in this country as on the American continent, and I want to thank all the fellows I have met at the "Olympia Christmas Fair" for the kindness and courtesy they have shown a stranger.

"It is the right spirit" and the only one and I hope sincerely that I can reciprocate if any of the boys should come to the States.

As to business. I wrote an article in the spring issue of The Billboard titled "They Haven't Got the Money," and this is about the same way I would judge the conditions in England today. The public are always good fellows and will spend fi they have it, this being the same condition all over the world.

We showmen should not expect too much this year, but we will get it again as soon as our friends, the working and middle classes and the general public, get it.

I am greatly impressed with the way the portable devices are built in this country and I consider myself lucky in having brought over a device in which G. V. Tonner of Blackpool has half interest in for Europe, i.e., the "Skee Ball Alleys," [sic] these also being very much along the lines of good portable devices.

I only ask our future customers to find out from the boys who were at the Olympia Christmas Fair whether the "Skee Ball Alleys" [sic] are o.k.

The climate in America offers better opportunities for outdoor amusements than this country. I am, however, firm in my belief that England and America can do very wonderful by "take and give" novelties from each other along the lines of outdoor amusements.

I shall at times be glad to give you some further news concerning our American amusements. Wishing you a Happy New Year.

Y. M. C. A. advertisement that appeared in Association Men in February 1921.
(Author's Collection)

Very faithfully yours,

Arnold Neble President Kentucky Derby Co., New York [22]

Ads for used Skee-Ball alleys began to appear as well. [23] There was no lack of interested parties to buy Skee-Ball alleys, though. For every offer of sale for used alleys, there were multiple announcements for new Skee-Ball venues. This resale market would make for some interesting legal issues about regions and location of operations agreed to by the initial owners, however. Would the terms restricting alleys to regions and specific venues be binding on subsequent owners? Skee-Ball would make legal history within a few years as well, dealing with this very issue.

An article in the February 25 issue of The Billboard about the Mid-City Park discussed improvements being made to the park for the 1922 season, including a new building to house the Skee-Ball concession to be run by George A. Appleton. Appleton was also the owner of the Skee Ball Company of Albany, an authorized sales agent for Skee-Ball alleys. [24]

Another article appeared in The Billboard on March 4, this time about White City Park in Little Rock, Arkansas, reporting that Skee-Ball would be a featured attraction. [25]

There was no question about why Skee-Ball Alleys were selling like hot cakes. On March 18, the Skee-Ball Company of Coney Island ran a half-page display ad in The Billboard. Skee-Ball was a sure thing, a proven success, and a guaranteed money maker.

GAMES MAY COME AND GAMES MAY GO BUT

SKEE-BALL

WILL GO ON FOREVER

A REAL ATTRACTION! A REAL GAME OF SKILL!

ELEVEN HUNDRED SKEE-BALL ALLEYS IN OPERATION DURING THE SEASON OF 1921 NETTED OVER

$1,000,000

(ONE MILLION DOLLARS)

Always New Always Popular

Always REAL Money-Getters!

SKEE-BALL ALLEYS HAVE ALWAYS OPERATED PERFECTLY!

The 1922 Model Represents the Height of

Mechanical Perfection

THE AUTOMATIC COIN ATTACHMENT PROTECTS THE OWNER AND INSURES HIS "GETTING IT ALL"

SKEE-BALL CO., CONEY ISLAND, N.Y. [26]

On March 25, the Skee-Ball Company of Coney Island, New York ran a large display ad in The Billboard, which was more succinct yet. Skee-Ball makes assured profits worry-free!

BEST IN 1914 SEASONABLE ADVICE!

INSTALL SKEE-BALL ALLEYS AND

DON'T WORRY

ABOUT

WHAT KIND OF

A SEASON

WE'RE GOING TO HAVE AND

YOU WILL GET YOURS

THE BEST TODAY

SKEE-BALL CO., Coney Island, N.Y. [27]

An article appeared in the March 25 issue of The Billboard about a new Skee-Ball factory and the story of the success behind it. By then, former manager Morris Goldberg had become an officer in the Skee-Ball Company.

NEW SKEE-BALL FACTORY RUNNING TO FULL CAPACITY

New York, March 14.--Morris Goldberg, secretary, treasurer and motive spirit of the Skee-Ball Company and its extensive Coney Island manufacturing plant, reports his being fully satisfied as to the outlook for outdoor show business of the coming summer season and that the demand for Skee-Ball equipment both thruout the United States and in Europe testifies to the enduring qualities of the public's taste for that clever and highly patronized device.

In transferring the manufacturing of alleys to the new factory buildings located at Neptune avenue and West 20th street, Coney Island, N. Y., the Skee-Ball Company has been able to provide for a large output, but already find their equipment and floor space little enough to cope with the ante-season orders that have been augmented by a spirited demand from the Western States and the Pacific Coast resorts.

> *The outstanding success that attended the innovation of Skee-Ball at the Christmas-New Year Olympian Carnival at London. Eng., assures the now-forming British Skee-Ball Company a repetition of the success of the original exploitation of the device in this country.* [28]

The Skee-Ball Company ran a large display ad in The Billboard for Skee-Ball in April, emphasizing how the game was an economic savior in times of trouble.

> *IT WAS IN The City of Bridgeport (Connecticut) that the aftermath of War struck with its Fullest Force. Industry was paralyzed and almost the entire Working Population was out of Employment. No business suffered so much as that of Bridgeport's New Park, Pleasure Beach, where every Concession shared the overwhelming Depression--and yet*
>
> *SKEE-BALL WON OUT!*
>
> *SKEE-BALL ALLEYS*
>
> *Pleasure Beach, Bridgeport, Conn. R. WEISBERGER, Owner*
>
> *September 21, 1921 SKEE-BALL COMPANY.* [29]

More Skee-Ball success stories appeared regularly. On April 8, the Skee-Ball Co. of Coney Island, New York ran a half page display ad in The Billboard that read:

> *Out in Sunny California!*
>
> *A MAN FROM MICHIGAN*
>
> *on a motoring trip with his wife and family to the Pacific Coast liked the looks of Venice and decided to locate there and thereabouts. He had operated 14 Skee-Ball Alleys at Park Island, Michigan and which perhaps, accounts for the following:*
>
> *Telegram No. 1*
>
> *Venice, Cal. October 21, 1921*
>
> *SKEE BALL CO., Coney Island, N. Y.:*
>
> *Please express 5 Skee Ball Alleys to Venice, California. Am mailing check. Thomas M. Reid.* [30]

Skee-Ball reached Chester Park and Coney Island in Cincinnati. Chester Park listed Skee-Ball among its attractions, which "[was] being run by a real trouper, Frank Roush." [31]

Ads for new amusement parks and venues continued to feature Skee-Ball as a major attraction. On June 10, Mid-City Park, located at 144th St. between 7th and Lenox Avenues in New York, ran a large display ad announcing its grand opening June 3, 1922 and soliciting concessionaires, pointedly mentioning Skee-Ball. [32]

The same issue featured an article about the "Playground of the Coal Fields," Schuykill Park, outside of Pottsville, Pennsylvania, which had just spent $100,000 to renovate the park for the new owner, the Eastern Pennsylvania Railways Company. It included changing the course of a river, and featuring exciting new attractions including the Skee-Ball alleys. [33]

Paradise Park Amusement Company of Rye Beach, New York, ran a want ad for concessionaires including Skee-Ball alleys [34] and an ad for Faulkner's Novelty Store in Cape May, New Jersey, ran that month listing Skee-Ball as a key attraction. [35]

People were willing to trade for Skee-Ball Alleys as well. On November 11, Grover Kortonic of 4353 Warner Rd., Cleveland, Ohio, ran a want ad in the classified section of The Billboard. His ad stated that he would trade a 1920 Maxwell Roadster in first-class shape (value: $400) for Skee-Ball alleys. [36]

On November 16, 1921, Morris Goldberg, the former officer in the Skee-Ball Company, founded the Skee Ball Sales And Security Company, Inc. and signed a certificate of incorporation in New York State. The three directors of the corporation were Morris Goldberg, his wife Minnie Goldberg, and Frank Montsko, listing their address at Neptune Ave and West 20th Street, Coney Island, New York, adjacent to the Skee-Ball factory. He apparently realized the huge opportunity that was emerging to supply Skee-Ball alleys to an increasingly enthusiastic world. [37]

The following year, the expansion of Skee-Ball fever continued unabated. White City Park in Little Rock, Arkansas, featured Skee-Ball alleys as they sought to expand [38] Flint Park & Amusement Company, Flint, Michigan solicited Skee-Ball concessions that year as well. [39]

Ads in the local press designed to attract customers to popular parks prominently featured Skee-Ball. In an advertisement for Ontario Lake Park, the Oswego Daily Palladium announced the opening of the park the following day on May 19, with a list of attractions and amusements that included Skee-Ball. [40] The Monticello Amusement Park in Monticello, New York, ran a full page display ad in the May 25 issue of the Republican Watchman listing Skee-Ball as a key attraction. [41]

On September 1, an article appeared in the Gloverville, New York, Morning Herald describing the State Coalmen's convention that was to start on September 10. Skee-Ball was among the attractions that the conventioneers could enjoy. [42]

As part of the Long Beach, California Amusement Zone full page display ad on December 15, the Silver Spray Pleasure Pier in Long Beach, California listed Skee-Ball as one of the amusements already in the park. [43]

Two weeks later, the Skee-Ball Company ran a display ad in The Billboard. Skee-Ball ads were simply reminders at this point, of the game that made everybody money.

> SKEE BALL
>
> *A safe investment for both Indoor and Outdoor Amusement Centers. Played by everybody--everywhere. Standard since 1914, with many imitators.*
>
> Write for Catalog.
>
> SKEE BALL COMPANY, Coney Island, New York [44]

A game which is considered "a safe investment" is surely the sign that your product has a solid and mature market.

Now longevity, not novelty, was the selling point for Skee-Ball. It was touted as a safe investment, immune to economic downturns, a game for everybody. Having Skee-Ball at your amusement park was the standard, and people would be disappointed if you didn't. This was the reassuring sign of a successful product.

Morris Goldberg became ever more prominent in the Amusement industry. On November 12, The Billboard featured an article titled "Morris Goldberg in Florida." The article reported that Morris Goldberg was in Florida on business and that many of his games were in the numerous towns and cities of Florida. [45]

He was covered in the local press as well, in connection with new amusement parks development. November 16, an article appeared in The Daily Argus of Mount Vernon, New York, titled "Great Progress Made In Preparing Rye Beach As a County Park." The article detailed the changes that were being made after the 1927 season closing of the park, as well as Playland, which included Skee-Ball. [46] Three days later, another article appeared in The Billboard titled "Morris Goldberg Home From Florida," reporting that Morris Goldberg was seriously interested in a promising location for a park in that state. [47]

Somewhat notably, confusion about the origins of Skee-Ball began to emerge in the advertising for the game. On March 22, 1924, The Skee-Ball Company ran an ad in The Billboard with the first known falsehood about the history of Skee-Ball—dropping the first five years of its existence, and fueling confusion over the origins of the game.

"Skee-Ball was first introduced in the summer of 1914 at Atlantic City and at Coney Island. It met with instantaneous success and has made Skee-Ball fans in all parts of the civilized world." [48]

On March 17, 1928, the Skee-Ball Company of Coney Island ran an ad in The Billboard that was the first of its kind. Instead of running ads for individual Skee-Ball alleys, this one focused on what was to be a new marketing theme: Entire banks of alleys. This was the first step in making Skee-Ball not only ubiquitous and an expected part of a park's amusement offering, but an entire investment strategy in a major amusement feature. It also emphasized how hundreds of amusement centers were investing profitably in entire banks of Skee-Ball alleys.

Amusement Centers Are Now Running

Skee-Ball

In Units of 6 to 18 Alleys

There's a Reason Free Catalog

SKEE-BALL COMPANY Coney Island, New York [49]

Skee-Ball reached San Francisco in the 1920s as well, as a concession at "Chutes at the Beach," later renamed "Playland." It started as a trolley park at Ocean Beach, near the famous Cliff House, and by the mid 1920s sported a battery of 8 Skee-Ball alleys, along with advice on how to play, the point scores and prize points for men and women, and cabinets full of prizes.

It is probably not a coincidence that concurrent with this leap in marketing scale, on March 23, 1928, Herman Bergoffen, Hugo H. Piesen and Maurice Piesen were drafting the Certificate of Incorporation of the National Skee Ball Company, Inc. [50] Skee-Ball was being prepared to move up to the next level of professional Amusement Industry management.

On March 24, the Skee-Ball Company, Inc., ran a large display ad in The Billboard, with even more detail on this new business strategy they would be promoting.

762 AMUSEMENT CENTERS NOW OPERATING SKEE-BALL

IN UNITS OF 4 TO 19 ALLEYS

CONTRARY to accepted business practices we published in our 1928 Catalogue a detailed list of installations for 1927. The smallest unit was 4 ALLEYS, the largest 16 ALLEYS. On June 14th 1927, Mr. John C. Boice of Revere Beach, Mass. installed 8 SKEE-BALL ALLEYS. About the 1st day of July Mr. Boice found it worth while to buy of the adjoining restaurant concession, fixtures, lease and all, and converted this space for SKEE-BALL purposes. On July 20th he added 8 ALLEYS to his original, making a total of 16 ALLEYS in one unit.

STRIKING FACTS

10 Skee-Ball Alleys located in a New Jersey summer resort grossed more than $21,000 during the season of 1927 . . . This place does operate Sundays . . .

18 Skee-Ball Alleys located on the Bowery, Coney Island, grossed more than $33,000 during the season of 1927 . . . An "off-season", as you'll recall . . .

15 Skee-Ball Alleys located on the Boardwalk, Coney Island, grossed more than $28,000 during the season of 1927 . . .

Write for Free Illustrated Catalog

SKEE-BALL COMPANY INCORPORATED

CONEY ISLAND NEW YORK [51]

The already wildly popular game was about to take a great leap forward in business marketing strategy under exciting new ownership.

Skee-Ball Company advertisement from March 17, 1928 in The Billboard.
(Author's Collection)

Skee-Ball Company advertisement from March 24, 1928 in The Billboard.
(Author's Collection)

Battery of 8 Skee-Ball alleys at Playland San Francisco, California
(Courtesy James R. Smith Collection)

Playland San Francisco, California
(Courtesy James R. Smith Collection)

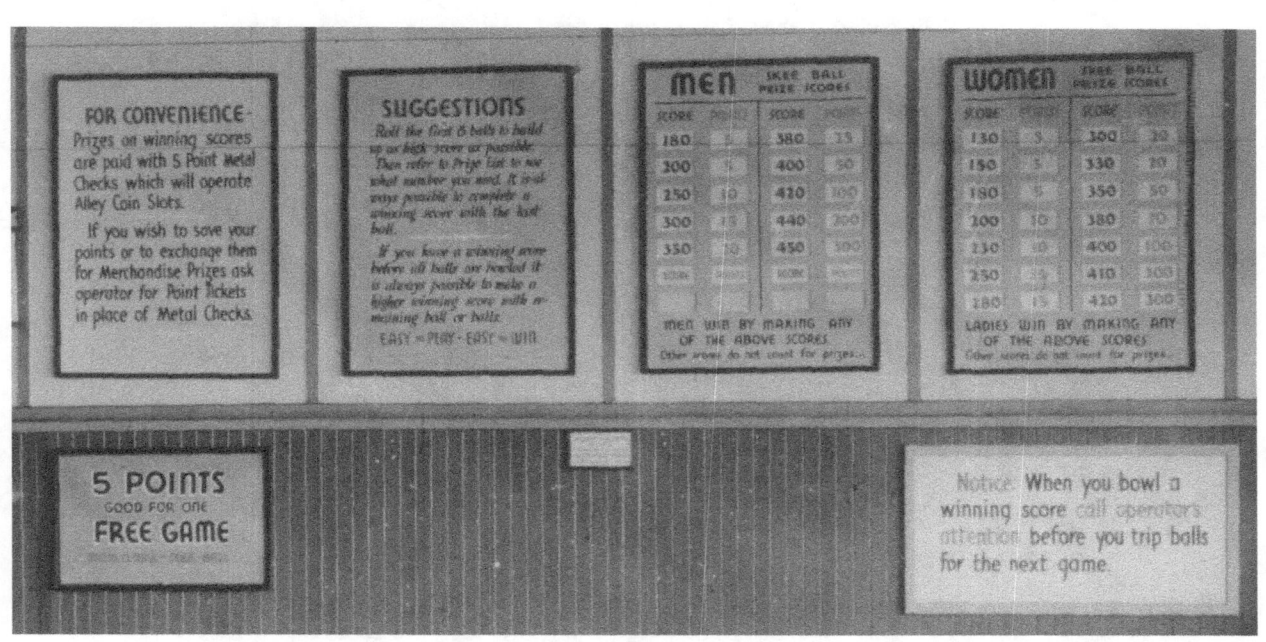

Close-up of Skee-Ball signs at Playland San Francisco, California
(Courtesy James R. Smith Collection)

Close-up of Skee-Ball prize cabinet at Playland San Francisco, California
(Courtesy James R. Smith Collection)

Chapter 12

STEALTH TRANSITION
Weathering the Great Depression

Unbenownst to the principals of either the Skee-Ball Company, Inc., or the National Skee-Ball Company, Inc., the soaring, carefree trajectory of the Roaring Twenties was about to meet with that abrupt stop at the bottom. This was commonly known as the Great Depression which began in October 1929 with the stock market crash. At its nadir in 1933, between 13 and 15 million Americans were unemployed and nearly half of the country's banks had failed.

The transition of the Skee-Ball business into the hands of seasoned amusement industry professionals was almost certainly a key survival factor for Skee-Ball. One of the reasons Skee-Ball was able to weather the storm was the deep pockets and professional resources of its new management. Holding massive Skee-Ball tournaments in 1932, with huge cash prizes, generated even more excitement. It also made the game even more attractive to strapped contestants, who were motivated to practice their skills in order to have a shot at big money, as well as smaller prizes.

The National Skee Ball Company, Inc. filed its certificate of incorporation with the New York Department of State on March 30, 1928. Each of the directors was issued ten shares of stock. [1] This marked the sale of the Skee-Ball Company to Herman Bergoffen, Hugo Piesen and his son, Maurice Piesen.

This was a significant step for Skee-Ball. To understand just how significant, it's necessary to look at the directors, particularly Herman Bergoffen.

Herman Bergoffen was born on October 12, 1879 in Neumarkt, Austria. [2] He emigrated to the United States with his family around 1886, and became a naturalized American citizen in 1903. [3] Strongly community minded for his entire life, he began his career as a teacher, and was deeply involved in education. He also spearheaded fundraising efforts for organizations like the Young Men's and Women's Hebrew Associations, Scouting and other community endeavors. [4, 5, 6, 7, 8, 9, 10] Legal-minded as well, on June 7, 1912,

Herman Bergoffen received his Bachelor of Law Degree from Brooklyn Law School. [11] He continued teaching while practicing law from 1916 into the early 1920s with his firm Bergoffen and Michaels. [12, 13, 14, 15, 16]

In May, 1921, there was a movement to unite the work of the 10,000 members of the Young Men's and Women's Hebrew Associations in the United States. Twenty-two delegates representing eleven communal associations approved plans to move things forward. Among the delegates in attendance were Herman Bergoffen and Hugo H. Piesen, who later became trusted business partners. [17]

In 1923, Bergoffen finally left his teaching position to become the Vice President and General Manager for the newly created Coast Holding Company in Coney Island, New York. [18] On January 12, 1925, Herman Bergoffen was elected one of the Vice Presidents of the Coney Island Chamber of Commerce. [19] In March, when plans for a $2,000,000 hotel on Coney Island were announced, Herman Bergoffen was one of the key people working on the project. The hotel was considered the first step in making Coney Island a resort that would be second to none in the country. [20]

In 1926, the Coast Holding Company changed hands. Herman Bergoffen stayed on for six months, then left to start his own real estate business. [21] By December 1927, he was President of the Hershbeck Building Corporation which would erect five two-story, four-family houses on the west side of E. 94th St. north of Avenue B. [22]

He remained very active in both Jewish and public charitable activities, as did Morris Goldberg of the Skee-Ball Company and the Skee-Ball Sales and Securities Company, and both men were active members of the Coney Island Chamber of Commerce. [23, 24, 25, 26, 27, 28, 29]

Late in 1927, Herman Bergoffen was listed as one of the public-spirited citizens of Coney Island in a full page advertisement promoting the resort. [30] He continued to invest in and broker real estate deals on Coney Island, served as a member of the Board of Directors for the Coney Island Chamber of Commerce, and protected the welfare of the area through political and legal action and social activities such as the Coney Island Emergency Relief Committee. [31]

It would be difficult to find a more well-respected and powerful member of the Coney Island community. When Bergoffen, Hugo Piesen, and his son Maurice bought the Skee-Ball Company, renaming it the National Skee-Ball Company, the game could not have been placed in better hands. Morris Goldberg,

Coney Island circa 1911.
(Courtesy Library of Congress)

Seeking Redemption

who was substantially running the Skee-Ball Alley Company by that time, wanted to get out of the manufacturing of Skee-Ball, concentrate on just selling the alleys through his own Skee-Ball Sales and Security Company, and expand his other real estate interests. Bergoffen, Hugo Piesen and Maurice Piesen, a law clerk in Bergoffen's office, bought the rights from Goldberg's Skee-Ball Company, Inc. for $100,000.

Maurice took on the manufacturing responsibilities. It was a small operation, run by Piesen, with a crew of six people who built the alleys by hand. [32]

These were powerful men in business, real estate and the amusement industry, well-positioned with extensive business networks and industry contacts, and perfectly positioned to take the game to the next level. Bergoffen already owned and managed multiple amusement venues and properties in Coney Island, New York, and on March 31, he ran an ad in The Billboard that he had spaces available for shows and amusements of various sizes both indoor and outdoor. [33] This was his core business, and Skee-Ball was about to play a very big part. They all became officers, and movers and shakers associated with the National Association of Amusement Parks (N.A.A.P.), later known as the National Association of Amusement Parks, Pools and Beaches (N.A.A.P.P.B.).

On March 31, the Skee-Ball Company of Coney Island, New York, ran their final ad in The Billboard. [34]

And on September 22, the National Skee-Ball Co., Inc. of Coney Island, New York, ran their first of many ads in The Billboard. The ad copy read:

> SKEE-BALL
>
> *Is Now Standard Equipment in Every Modern Amusement Park.*
>
> *NATIONAL SKEE-BALL CO. INC.*
>
> *CONEY ISLAND*
>
> *NEW YORK* [35]

As Whirl-o-Ball continued to run full page ads hyping their alley, Skee-Ball simply settled into a comfortable, steady pattern of success born of deep market penetration and 15 years of increasing sales.

Morris Goldberg, owner of the Skee-Ball Sales and Security Company, continued to do major sales of Skee-Ball as the National Skee-Ball Company took over manufacturing and marketing. Goldberg had become quite wealthy and had become a major player in the amusement industry as well. In March of that year, he had already purchased the Silver Baths and intended to build a hotel in 1929. [36]

Then disaster struck. In the wake of the great stock market crash known as, Black Tuesday, on October 29, 1929, Goldberg remained optimistic. On November 30, 1929, an article titled "All Set for Greatest Outdoor Conventions" ran in The Billboard. The article reported:

> *"Also our fellow member, Morris Goldberg, is the donor of the Goldberg Award of $50 in cash to be given to that individual participating in the program, whether from platform or floor, who makes the best constructive talk for the general good of the industry having to do with getting business."* [37]

The Goldberg Award was bestowed on December 13, at 3:20 PM. [38]

The ensuing economic depression had a decidedly negative impact on the amusement industry. Coney Island itself, however, still attracted New Yorkers to the beach, which was free, and only a nickel ride on public transportation. Probably due in great part to the deep pockets of its owners, Skee-Ball rolled on. Not everyone was poor, even during the Great Depression, and Skee-Ball was

an inexpensive amusement. Bergoffen also remained a stalwart optimist, and continued to invest in Skee-Ball and foster new venues.

In 1930, another challenger game appeared on the horizon, this one bearing a huge resemblance to Skee-Ball. On April 19, the Washington Bowling Billiard Co., of 1120 Tower Building in Washington, D.C. ran an ad for a game named "Skill-Ball." The ad copy of the display ad was reminiscent of both Whirl-O-Ball and Skee-Ball ads. [39] This would be the first of the "Clone" games since the original patents on the "skee-jump" feature expired in the late 1920s.

Skee-Ball, however, continued to expand its reach. On January 24, 1931, the National Skee-Ball Company, Inc., ran a series of display ads in The Billboard, similar to the last ad from the Skee-Ball Company, touting the expanded number of installations in the US and Canada. The ad copy read:

> *SKEE-BALL THE MOST POPULAR AMUSEMENT DEVICE IN THE WORLD*
>
> *856 INSTALLATIONS IN THE UNITED STATES AND CANADA ALONG 507 SKEE-BALL ALLEYS are earning profits in the New York play area*

> **SKEE-BALL** FOR 1931—A GAME THE PUBLIC WANTS
>
> The Bowling Game of precision. Earning profits for 856 owners in the United States and Canada alone.
>
> Booklet on request.
>
> **NATIONAL SKEE-BALL CO., Inc.,** - - Coney Island, New York City

National Skee-Ball Co., Inc. advertisement March 21, 1931 in The Billboard.
(Author's Collection)

NATIONAL SKEE-BALL CO., INC.
CONEY ISLAND, NEW YORK
CITY [40]

On March 14, the National Skee-Ball Co., Inc. ran a display ad in The Billboard.

> *SKEE-BALL FOR 1931--A GAME THE PUBLIC WANTS*
>
> *The Bowling Game of precision. Earning profits for 856 owners in the United States and Canada alone.*
>
> *Booklet on request. NATIONAL SKEE-BALL CO., Inc. - - Coney Island, New York City [41]*

Two weeks later, the National Skee-Ball Co., Inc. of Coney Island, New York ran a large display ad with a photograph in The Billboard.

NATIONAL SKEE-BALL CO., INC.

A TYPICAL BATTERY OF SKEE-BALL ALLEYS MEN, WOMEN AND CHILDREN EVERYWHERE PLAY SKEE-BALL

Because it is a clean game of skill. Because it furnishes exercise and excitement of competition. And because they can watch their scores and judge their improvement from week to week and season to season.

AMUSEMENT OPERATORS BUY SKEE-BALL ALLEYS

Because the [sic] work with a minimum payroll, being coin-controlled and automatic. Because they consistently earn good profits from year to year. Because honest materials and skillful workmanship makes them staunch and durable.

NATIONAL SKEE-BALL CO., Inc.,
Coney Island, New York [42]

Marketing batteries of Skee-Ball alleys seemed to have been successful. On March 28, 1931, The Billboard reported that Crystal Beach in Buffalo, New York spent approximately $65,000 for improvements to the venue. Among the items added was a battery of eleven Skee-Ball Alleys. [43]

Skee-Ball Stadium

Now that Skee-Ball was under the direction of some of the major players in the National Association of Amusement Parks (N.A.A.P.) and big names in the amusement industry, the game gained even more prominence and industry prestige. In 1932, another leap forward for the game occurred: A major venue completely dedicated to Skee-Ball, Skee-Ball Stadium, would be built and operated by Layman M. Sternbergh in Atlantic City, New Jersey. [44]

Sternbergh, born in 1887, was an inventor and a businessman. [45] He started his career managing a confectionery and stationery store belonging to his father, David H. Sternbergh, in Paterson, New Jersey. [46] By 1924, he had gone into the Amusement business, [47] and by 1926 had two Skee-Ball alley arcades in Asbury Park, New Jersey, one at 207 Lake Ave. and the other at 37 Surf Avenue. [48, 49]

In 1929 he filed a patent for an improvement to Skee-Ball alleys, to make changing the rubber buffers on the target quicker and easier for unskilled labor to perform, minimizing the alley down-time. [50] By 1931, he had done so well in the business that he broke ground for the the Skee-Ball Stadium, the first major amusement venue dedicated to Skee-Ball alleys.

August 22, the National Skee-Ball Co., Inc. of Coney Island, New York ran a large display ad in The Billboard:

> *TO THE MEMBERS OF THE N.A.A.P.*
>
> *Permit Us To Announce*
>
> *A NATIONAL INSTITUTION*
>
> *On October 1 of this year ground will be broken in Atlantic City, New Jersey, less than one block from the new Convention Hall, for the finest building ever designed specially for SKEE-BALL operation.*
>
> *A fire-proof building embodying many new and unique features, which will be fully described in a later announcement, will house twenty-one specially constructed, De Luxe SKEE-BALL ALLEYS, the largest battery in the world.*
>
> *This National Institution will be operated under the ownership-management of*

National Skee-Ball Company, Inc. advertisement March 28, 1931 in The Billboard showing a battery of Skee-Ball alleys.
(Author's Collection)

Layman M. Sternbergh on the same plane of good taste that has characterized his ten years of highly successful SKEE-BALL operation on the Boardwalk in Ocean Grove, New Jersey, home of the Methodist Camp Meeting.

The formal opening is scheduled for Christmas week, 1931, and you are cordially invited to attend.

Mr. Sternbergh's method and style of operation will be a revelation to you.

While you are in New Jersey, a visit to Asbury Park and Ocean Grove will be of special interest to you if you inspect the SKEE-BALL ALLEYS at the North End Pavilion, Ocean Grove, Boardwalk.

MR. STERNBERGH WILL WELCOME YOUR VISIT

NATIONAL SKEE-BALL CO., INC. CONEY ISLAND - - - - - NEW YORK [51]

That August 29, The Billboard reported that among many individuals, Maurice Piesen and Herman Bergoffen of the National Skee-Ball Co., Inc. attended the dinner of the Manufacturers' Division at the Half Moon Hotel. [52]

Laying Claim to the Name

The National Skee-Ball Company, Inc., was the first to legally protect the name Skee-Ball. As the game gained dominance and visibility, they became aware of the value of trademarking the name, which could be at least as valuable as the patents on key features, some of which had by then expired. Skill-Ball may have just been the wake-up call they needed.

TO ALL WHOM IT MAY CONCERN:

Be it known that National Skee-Ball Company, Inc., a corporation duly organized under the laws of the State of New York, located at Coney Island, County of Kings, City and State of New York, doing business at Neptune Avenue and West 20th Street, Coney Island, N. Y., has adopted for its use the trade-mark shown in the accompanying drawing.

The trade mark has been continuously used in its business in interstate commerce since December 8th, 1908.

The particular description of goods to which the trade mark is appropriated is a game in the nature of a bowling game and parts thereof comprised in Class 22, *Games, Toys, and Sporting Goods.*

The trade mark is usually displayed by printing the same on labels which are attached to packages containing the goods. The word "ball" is disclaimed from the mark shown in the drawing.

National Skee-Ball Company, Inc.

Herman Bergoffen (President) (Signed) [53]

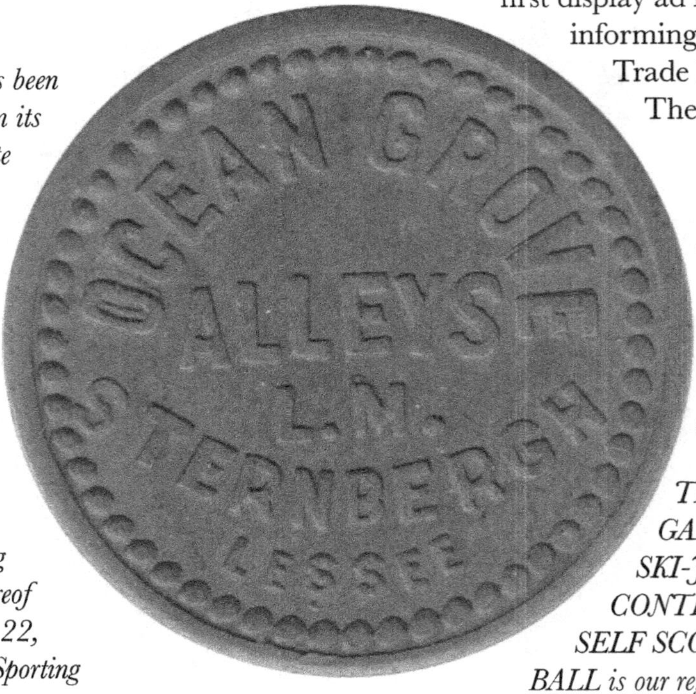

December 5, 1931 the National Skee-Ball Co., Inc. of Coney Island, New York ran the first display ad in The Billboard informing the public of the Trade Mark Registration. The ad read:

SKEE-BALL

(Trade Mark Registered United States Patent Office.)

THE BOWLING GAME WITH A SKI-JUMP, COIN CONTROLLED AND SELF SCORING. SKEE-BALL is our registered trade mark and can only be used on bowling games manufactured buy the NATIONAL SKEE-BALL COMPANY, INC., Coney Island, New York City. [54]

But with stunning success comes competition. Skill-Ball was not to be the only competitor, and in 1931, another patent was filed by an unknown inventor, that might also chip away at the dominance of Skee-Ball.

On December 1, a patent 1,834,317 was issued to a Dominick Peccerillo for "Game" [55] which was for a pin-ball version of a Skee-Ball-like game. A "clone" game would appear a few years later that looked remarkably similar. Patenting new features and trade-marking the name would be critical actions to take as the Clone Wars heated up over the next few years.

In the meantime, Skee-Ball continued to thrive. The December 12, 1931 issue of The Billboard listed the National Skee-Ball Company prominently among the exhibitors at the sixth annual Manufacturers Division meeting of NAAP. [56]

The First National Skee-Ball Tournament

Skee-Ball tournaments had always been about money and prizes. Now, in 1932, Skee-Ball tournaments were about to become very big money for the players as well as the Skee-Ball operators. On March 5, the National Skee-Ball Co., Inc. of Coney Island, New York ran a display ad in The Billboard.

> *VISIT THE NEW*
> *SKEE-BALL STADIUM*
> *Boardwalk, at Florida Ave., Atlantic City, N. J.*
>
> *Featuring 21 Specially Built SKEE-BALL ALLEYS DE LUXE Write for Booklet NATIONAL SKEE-BALL CO., Inc., Coney Island, N. Y.* [57]

One key feature of the "DeLuxe" alleys was that they were much shorter than the original 36 foot alleys, and these were manufactured to fit seamlessly together in a bank. This shorter alley was the brainchild of Maurice Piesen, and would become the standard from 1932 forward, allowing them to fit into smaller spaces, and have more games and earning opportunities in smaller spaces with lower rent, a key success factor for survival during the Great Depression. [58]

The stakes for winning a Skee-Ball Tournament increased an order of magnitude overnight. On March 12, 1932, an article appeared in The Billboard announcing a national Skee-Ball tournament to be held October 1 and 2 in Atlantic City, New Jersey at the Atlantic City Skee Ball [sic] Stadium.

> *"The prizes will be five popular makes of automobiles."* [59]

Edgar A. Storms of Great Neck, Long Island who operated 36 Skee-Ball alleys at Revere

MOCK & BLUM
113 WEST 42ND STREET
NEW YORK

19

STATEMENT

TO ALL WHOM IT MAY CONCERN:

Be it known that National Skee-Ball Company, Inc., a corporation duly organized under the laws of the State of New York, located at Coney Island, County of Kings, City and State of New York, doing business at Neptune Avenue and West 20th Street, Coney Island, N.Y., has adopted for its use the trade-mark shown in the accompanying drawing.

The trade mark has been continuously used in its business in interstate commerce since December 8th, 1908.

The particular description of goods to which the trade mark is appropriated is a Games and parts thereof, in the nature of a bowling game, comprised in Class 22, Games, Toys, and Sporting Goods.

The trade mark is usually displayed by printing same on labels which are attached to packages containing the goods. The word "Ball" disclaimed apart from the mark shown in the drawing.

NATIONAL SKEE-BALL COMPANY, INC.,

By _Herman Bergoffen_
President

Herman Bergoffen

276901-3

National Skee-Ball Company, Inc. application for trademark for Skee-Ball.

Beach, Massachusetts was elected temporary chairman of the tournament comittee. The executive committee members were:

>Fred Fansher, Fansher Amusement Company, New York
>
>Paul E. Moses, Danerch, Pennsylvania
>
>Layman M. Sterbergh, Skee-Ball Stadium, Atlantic City
>
>Frank S. Terrell, President Frank Wilcox Company, Savin Rock, West Haven, Connecticut
>
>Walter Haenie, Long Branch, New Jersey
>
>Edward Goldsmith, Bradley Beach and Belmar, New Jersey
>
>J. Shields, Long Beach, Long Island
>
>Edgar Storms, President Storms & Boice, Inc., Revere Beach, Massachusetts
>
>Will L. White, newly appointed manager Grand View Park, Singac, New Jersey
>
>Nathan Faber, Rockaway Beach
>
>Kenneth Campion, Ocean City, New Jersey
>
>Herman Bergoffen, National Skee-Ball Co., Inc.

Their recommendation was that the finalists be picked by an elimination contest, with operators to cover transportation and all expenses for the local winners. Morris Goldberg would donate one of the autos as a prize. In the end, the actual prizes awarded were monetary, starting at $1000 for the top prize, which was a huge amount of money in the wake of the stock market crash and the midst of the Great Depression. [60]

And new Skee-Ball installations continued to open.

On June 18, The Billboard reported that Rock Springs Park in Chester, West Virginia had installed a new Skee-Ball alley in one of the concession buildings. [61] and that H. C. Humphreys opened a Skee-Ball game in a new building at Arnolds Park, Iowa. [62]

In the same issue, The Billboard noted that the Skee Ball [sic] Operators Association announced a change of date for the National Skee-Ball Tournament. The tournament was originally schedule for October 1 and 2 at the Skee-Ball Stadium in Atlantic City. The dates were changed to September 24 and 25 because it was belatedly discovered that the Jewish High Holidays that year fell on October 1 and 2. In addition the article listed batteries at parks and resorts that were enrolled in the tournament. They included:

New Jersey
Palisades Amusement Park, Palisade
Columbia Park, North Bergen
Woodlawn Park, Trenton
Ocean Grove

Atlantic City
Wildwood
Sea Isle City
Long Branch
Beach Haven
Cape May
Seaside Heights
Bradley Beach
Ocean City
Belmar
Schroon Lake

New York
South Beach, Staten Island
Rockaway Park
Long Beach
Coney Island
Playland, Rye Beach
Edgemere, Rockaway
Sheepshead Bay
Rockaway Beach
Arverne
Midland Beach, Staten Island

Massachusetts
Revere Beach
Norumbega Park, Auburndale

Pennsylvania
Kenneywood Park, Pittsburgh
Central Park, Allentown
Elm Beach Park, Manchester
Lianerch Swimming Pool, Lianerch
Woodside Park, Philadelphia

Connecticut
Savin Rock Park, West Haven

West Virginia
Rock Springs, Chester

Ohio
Euclid Beach, Cleveland [63]

Tournament fever was ramping up. On June 18, an article appeared in The Billboard announcing that on September 12-16 at Playland in Rye, New York there would be a

Skee-Roll advertisement from 1933.
(Author's Collection)

Skee-Ball Tournament. The winner would be sent to the National Skee-Ball Tournament in Atlantic City, New Jersey. [64]

The economy may have been bad, but at least some amusement parks and Skee-Ball continued to survive. On June 25 in The Billboard, Herman Bergoffen, realtor and President of the National Skee-Ball Co., Inc. opined:

> "...Coney's reputation as a refuge for amusement-hungry denizens, whether they are out of work or not, will always keep the island in a class by itself. 'They will stall the baker and the butcher in order to satisfy their craving for amusements,' and he predicts the season will be good when the weatherman redeems himself." [65]

Meanwhile, across the pond on August 20, The Billboard reported that Rogers & Four of Paris, France, were installing an amusement resort in the basement of the new Palais Berlitz. Among the games listed to be installed were Skee-Ball alleys. [66]

On August 27, the National Skee-Ball Co., Inc., ran an ad in The Billboard as the company contemplated expanding its games offerings.

SKEE-BALL MARCHES ON!

The two greatest batteries in the history of SKEE-BALL were installed in 1932 Atlantic City Stadium--21 de luxe alleys. Euclid Beach, Cleveland--19 alleys

Write for particulars on our perfected Table Game EL DORADO A game that will bring large revenue from small space.

NATIONAL SKEE-BALL COMPANY, 2002 Neptune Avenue, Coney Island, New York [67]

Finally, on September 24 and September 25, after all the fanfare, a national tournament was conducted at Layman Sternbergh's Skee-Ball Stadium in Atlantic City. Over one hundred finalists qualified, coming from over forty towns reaching from the Atlantic Seaboard to Cleveland, Ohio. Each contestant played one game on each of the twenty-one alleys at Skee-Ball Stadium and the combined score was used to determine the overall winner of the event. On Sunday evening $2,400 in prizes were given to the winners, and all of the contestants received medals for their participation.

The winners of the Men's Championship were:

First Prize $1000.00 Rolland K. Strong, Greenville, Pennsylvania representing Central

Park, Allentown, Pennsylvania operated by R. Sukerman

> Score: 5240
> Average: 249.5

Second Prize $500.00 Laurence Lipkin, Cedarhurst, Long Island, New York representing Edgemere, Long Island, alleys, operated by Morris Cohen

> Score: 5070
> Average: 241.4

Third Prize $200.00, Al Schoenfeld, Far Rockaway, Long Island, New York, representing Edgemere alleys

> Score: 4950
> Average: 235.7

Fourth Prize $100.00, Harry M. Gardner, Atlantic City, representing Skee-Ball Stadium

> Score: 4860
> Average: 231.4

The Winner of the Women's National Championship, $300.00 was:

Mrs. R. G. Phelps, Fieldston Gardens, Riverdale, New York representing Skee-Ball Stadium, Atlantic City, New Jersey

> Score: 4480
> Average: 213.3

In addition to the cash prizes fifteen prizes of $20.00 gold pieces were awarded to the remaining 16 highest scorers.

There were several unique players including:

J. H. Gloniger of Pittsburgh, aged 73 who rolled 4410, average 200

Robert Marshall Jr., Millburn, the youngest entrant, scored 4040, average better than 192

George Compton, aged 13, Trenton, New Jersey scored 4050, average 192.5 [68]

Skee-Ball was truly a game for everyone.

In an important, but little-heralded move, on October 4, 1932, Herman Bergoffen filed for a new patent for a game that looked like modern day Skee-Ball. [69]

November 28, at the meeting of the N.A.A.P. Manufacturers and Dealers' Division Fred Fansher was elected president. Among those in attendance were those familiar names, Herman Bergoffen and Briant Sando. [70] Sando's Briant Specialty Company would continue to be a thorn in the side of Skee-Ball for at least the next few years, as it continued to promote new offerings.

At the same time, Skee-Roll, a shorter version of Skee-Ball, began to gain prominence. Even

First National Skee-Ball Tournament at Skee-Ball Stadium in Atlantic City, NJ
(Courtesy Philadelphia Toboggan Coasters, Inc. Archive)

Simpson had produced small and miniature versions of Skee-Ball, understanding that the "fascination" factor was in the concept, not the size of the alley. They were just as functional and fun to play as the larger version, they made the same amount of money, and they fit in smaller spaces. As a result, this was a huge win for the Skee-Ball market.

On December 10, The Billboard reported that the National Skee-Ball Co., Inc. was at the annual N.A.A.P. Convention to show its new offering, Skee-Roll. Representing the company were Herman Bergoffen, Maurice Piesen, and Paul E. Moses. [71]

Skee-Ball Makes Legal History

One other notable development occurred in 1932, a legal case that is still cited regarding chattel law. Remember that one of the early advantages to any amusement operator buying Skee-Ball alleys was the assurance that they would have the only alleys in town, securing them an extra measure of advantage over potential competitors in the local amusement market. When the alleys were sold new, the purchase agreement had to specify a location where they were to be operated, and set up a restriction that they could not be set up in an area or locale where other Skee-Ball alleys were already installed, in the same borough or town, for instance.

With the advent of a secondary market, buying and selling used Skee-Ball alleys, a problem arose. Was the purchaser of the used alleys subject to the restriction, or could they set them up wherever they liked? This was a sticky question, because if they could, then National Skee-Ball Alley Company could not make good on their promise that purchasers of new Skee-Ball alleys would have their sole rights to the region protected. In 1932, the courts finally answered that question.

The suit was brought by the National Skee-Ball Company against Mr. Seyfried, and is described in the court filing National Skee-Ball Company, Inc. v Seyfried.

Mr. Seyfried legally purchased three used Skee-Ball alleys

> *"and removed them to Manasquan, New Jersey, where he set them up in operation. There was no other skee-ball[sic] game in Manasquan at the time, and there is no allegation of a violation of the agreement so far as Manasquan is concerned. But the defendant moved the alleys to the borough of Seaside Park, Ocean county, New Jersey, and began business there a few days after he had been informed that the complainant [The National Skee-Ball Alley Company, Inc.] had sold six alleys to the Shore Amusement Company, Incorporated, under*

an agreement by which the complainant gave that company the exclusive right to operate in that borough. This bill was then filed."

The court found that: "A prime objection to the enforcibility [sic] of such a system of restraint upon sales and prices is that they offend against the ordinary and usual freedom of traffic in chattels or articles which pass by mere delivery." As such, the restriction that was enforceable on the original purchase, which also protected the original purchaser, could not be extended to the purchaser of used alleys. [72]

Thus the court found that purchasers of used Skee-Ball alleys were not bound by the original purchase agreement signed by the seller. The protection for original purchasers could no longer be guaranteed. This decision had major repercussions in a variety of industries for decades.

Apparently, Skee-Ball had made sufficient inroads that the loss of this provision did not create a significant problem in the market. There were other issues that continued to challenge Skee-Ball, including the economy still in the grip of the Great Depression, and the rise of cheaper alternatives to Skee-Ball, often using that previously unique feature, the skee-jump: The rise of the clones.

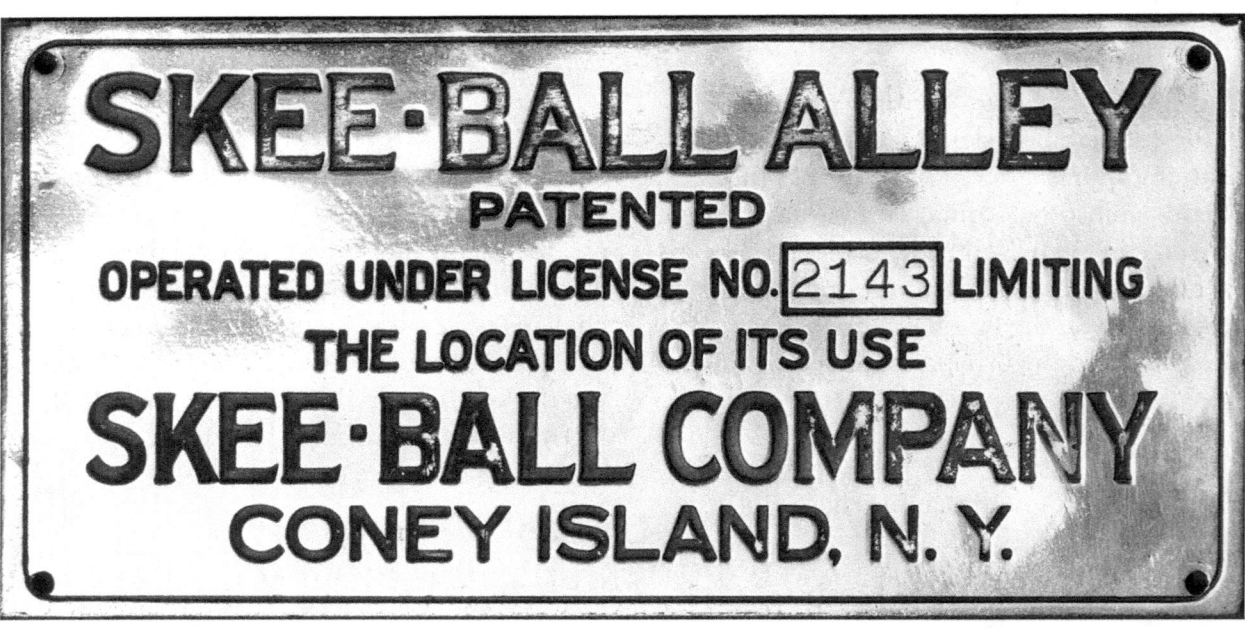

Skee-Ball Alley placard that showed the license number that the alley was operating under. This license was used to limit where the alley could be operated.
(From author's Collection • Photo by Argun Tekant)

Chapter 13

THE CLONE WARS
Chasing Zero

Skee-Ball had faced competition from other alley games from the time it started to become popular in 1916. Briant Manufacturing, later Briant Specialty Company, was a recurrent competitor. Simpson's new game and the first Briant Manufacturing offering, Bridge Ball, had a narrow bridge that the player had roll the ball up the incline precisely or the ball would fall into the pit and not reach the target at all.

Briant Manufacturing then rapidly brought Whirl-O-Ball to market, with the first ad appearing in the January of 1918. [1] Whirl-O-Ball was designed so the ball would run up at the end of the alley and curl back on itself before landing in the target. It also contained many of the unpatented but characteristic features of Simpson's original Skee-Ball alley and Bridge Ball: The Automatic Ball Release, Automatic Coin Collector, Automatic Ball Return, and Automatic Scorer. Bringing this set of features together was part of Simpson's design and business genius, and though not patentable, was widely copied and embraced.

On January 13, 1918, the four-story Industrial Building in Indianapolis, Indiana, housing dozens of firms, burned down. Briant Manufacturing was one of them. The company suffered losses of approximately $8,000. [2] But the devastating fire at the company gave the firm an opportunity to rethink their strategy and scope of products. The company relocated to 108 S Capitol Ave, and incorporated as Briant Specialty Manufacturing Co. "to manufacture metal specialties." [3]

A new game called Bank Ball appeared in 1932 under the Briant Specialty Company, which continued to market Whirl-o-Ball. Now, the City Directory described the company as "[Manufacturers of] Amusement Devices and Automobile Accessories."

On April 23, the Briant Specialty Company of Indianapolis ran its first display ad in The Billboard for Bank Ball. The ad copy reads:

BANK BALL NEW--FOR ALL AMUSEMENT CENTERS

Everybody plays--men, women, children--9 balls for 5¢. Automatic Coin Collector and Scoring Device. Each Bank Ball Game is 3x20 ft., and has an earning capacity of $4 an hour. You can place 2 to 12 Games in any ordinary room; take in $15 to $75 per day. Price $600 Each. Terms to responsible parties. Write for Catalog. [4]

The New Challengers

The unique Skee hump had been protected by patent until the mid-1920s. After the original patent had expired, there were some alley game challengers, but no real clone "skee-type" games. However, in the 1930s, clones and knock-off games featuring the skee-jump or the characteristic target cups or both appeared from every major manufacturer inside of a few years. The question was: Would they displace Skee-Ball?

There were suddenly multiple games out that made use of the previously patented skee-jump features. Several appear to be replicas of Skee-Ball and Skee-Roll. Many of these claimed patents that didn't exist, or were completely unrelated to the games, and owned by someone else.

Typically, when "Clone Wars" of "me-too" products break out, there is no defining feature that establishes one as significantly more valuable than the other, and the only truly distinguishing feature is the ever dropping price. "Chasing zero" refers to the brutal price competition when cutthroat competition occurs, followed by a decline in quality, until the price can no longer be dropped, and the participating companies simply go out of business or discontinue the product.

In addition to Bank-Ball, there were many other clone competitors.

SKILL-BALL

Skill-Ball, manufactured and marketed by the Stirling Novelty Company, Skill-Ball was a direct clone of Skee-Ball, copying the following features of Skee-Ball:

- method of play
- the skee-jump
- the concentric target
- the length of 14 feet.

In addition to being "electric" and having modernistic curved features, it had a handful of enhancements.

SKILL-BALL does not just offer one single game--extra replacement fronts at small cost can be had so as to change to Baseball, Football and other popular games. These replacement fronts are animated and *illuminated and fit right onto present game. Each one is a light-up backboard panel that easily slides into place. REMEMBER--you actually get a dozen different games when you buy SKILL-BALL! It's PORTABLE--can be assembled by operator on location in 5 minutes. SKILL-BALL on location since January 10, 1936, shows consistent net earning of from $30.00 to $40.00 per week. SKILL-BALL remains on location for a long period of time, not just a day or a week. SKILL-BALL takes advantage of the bowling craze that is sweeping the country!* [5]

BANK-ROLL

Bank-Roll manufactured by Genco, and distributed by the George Ponser Company. was clearly a clone of Skee-Ball copying the following features:

- the skee-jump at the end of the alley
- the concentric targets.

An additional feature that Genco added was the game would automatically shut down if more than nine balls were played. [6]

ROLL-A-BALL

Roll-A-Ball, from George Ponser, Co. Roll-A-Ball advertised no new features, and claimed even before it ever appeared in venues that it was "already a proven sensational profit earner." [7]

PAMCO TANGO

Tango, manufactured by the Pacific Amusement Manufacturing Company (PAMCO) copied several features from Skee-Ball:

- an alley length of 14 feet
- the skee-jump
- 9 balls for 5¢

The game offered a slightly different arrangement of holes in the target. The advertising copy touted "No attendant required." Simpson had set the stage for all the alley games with some or all of these features and they all followed his lead in the marketing of the game. [8]

BALLY-ROLL

Bally-Roll from Bally Manufacturing Company of Chicago, again used almost all the features developed by Simpson, most obviously the smooth alley and hump at the end, and the identical target configuration, with a slightly modified profile and finish. It followed Skill-Ball in being "portable," easily separated into sections so it can be moved. Otherwise, it was a virtual replica of Skee-Ball. [9]

HURDLE HOP

Mutoscope's HURDLE HOP was a small Skee-Ball clone in what resembled a pin-ball cabinet. [10] This strongly resembled the mechanism that Dominick Peccerillo had patented several years before. [11]

Hurdle Hop also made the rather outrageous claim that it had the same target configuration as Skee-Ball and had permission from the National Skee-Ball Company to use it.

Another advertisement from Mutoscope shows that Mutoscope also made a full size "Skeel Game" called Bowl-A-Game. [12]

BOWL-A-GAME

Bowl-A-Game was another Skee-Ball near clone, marketed through the Automatic Games Company of St. Paul, Minnesota. This game was slightly smaller than the competitors at twelve feet long and two feet wide, standing on legs, but otherwise had the same features. The one differentiating feature was the different target array. [13]

ROCK-O-BALL

Rock-O-Ball from Rock-Ola was another clone competitor. In fact, distributors of Rock-O-Ball made no secret of their intentions, advertising it subtly as a way to cash in on the Skee-Ball craze cheaply. One of the distributors of Rock-O-Ball, The Electro-Ball Company of Dallas, Texas ran an ad in The Billboard on August 29, 1936. They offered an opportunity to trade in other games for credit toward Rock-O-Ball. The advertisement also stated: "This is especially important if you are in a closed territory, for Rock-O-Ball is legal everywhere." The reference to being "in a closed territory" was likely a reference to the limitations on selling Skee-Ball alleys to only one client per town or region. Rock-O-Ball was a way to get the Skee-Ball experience regardless of who had the Skee-Ball concession in the region.

A golden opportunity to convert idle equipment in Rock-O-Balls. We will accept as part payment--Slots, Pay Tables and Counter Games. Send us a list of what you have and get our offer. This is especially important if you are in closed territory for Rock-O-Ball is legal everywhere. Don't sit and hold idle equipment--trade for Rock-O-Ball! [14]

GYRO

Gyro, a table-top version of Skee-Ball, was available from Star Manufacturing. Gyro was all steel and a pin-ball type plunger version of the game, similar to Hurdle Hop. [15]

BOWLETTE

Bowlette was the clone offering from J. H. Keeney and Co. This Skee-Ball clone, was 14 feet long, with an identical target, and a typical "portable" three section design. [16]

The brutal competition was not limited to companies in the United States. The Billboard featured another article describing clones appearing in England:

> *"Bowling tables with coin release for balls are topping the bill at seaside resorts. Strongest numerically is Skee Roll, which originates in America and handled here by Delaney. Competing with it are Ski-ball made in London and Skee Shot made in Belgium."* [17]

Another article described even more competitors:

> *February 25, 1936, the second annual London Coin-Operated Machine Exhibition opened at the Royal Hotel, Woburn Place. Among the exhibitors were: Amusement Equipment Company Ltd., Wembley, showing Skee-Roll (under license from National Skee-Ball Co., Inc.); and C. Ahrens showing Skee Ball bowling table of his own manufacture.* [18]

The clone games were typically 12-14 feet long, if not outright tabletop sized, and fit in more places, occupied less real estate, paid the same, and offered customers the same "fascination" and fast play. This fact was not lost on the National Skee-Ball Company, and they began pushing the shorter Skee-Roll as hard as they had been marketing Skee-Ball.

CHIME BALL

Some of the clones made impressive inroads. Chime Ball was a much more refined, art-deco design, but still fundamentally a Skee-Ball clone, with the skee-jump, and a slightly different target arrangement. Like Skee-Ball, it featured automatic scoring, coin operated ball delivery, and provided nine balls for a nickel. Banks of Chime Ball alleys were featured at Asbury Park, New Jersey, and Chime Ball was featured along with Skee-Ball at the 1939 World's Fair in New York City. [19] The classic design of Chime Ball would have looked equally at home in the high-end art deco penthouses of New York as it did in the boardwalk pavilion arcades at the Jersey Shore.

Skee-Ball Strikes Back

In a succession of ads, the strategy for defense against the clones emerged, with tactic after tactic to hang onto the market.

June 11, 1932 the National Skee-Ball Co., Inc. of Coney Island, New York ran an ad in The Billboard emphasizing a long history of customers so satisfied that they are replacing the old ones with the newest models, not some other game.

The ad copy read:

Chime Ball at Asbury Park, New Jersey.
(Courtesy Philadelphia Toboggan Coasters, Inc. Archive)

---> *proof of solid merit*

After 18 years of profitable operation of

19 SKEE-BALL ALLEYS

HUMPHREY'S EUCLID BEACH, CLEVELAND, O., *has just replaced them with*

19 NEW SKEE-BALL ALLEYS, 1932 Model

NATIONAL SKEE-BALL CO., Inc. Coney Island, N. Y.

GEORGE P. SMITH, Jr.,

SPECIAL

REPRESENTATIVE 1678 EAST 93rd ST., CLEVELAND, O. [20]

country and the world.

Orders have been received from South Africa, Belgium, Canada, California, Arkansas, Indiana, New Jersey and elsewhere.

Better rush your for timely shipment Write for Catalogue NATIONAL SKEE-BALL COMPANY Coney Island New York [21]

SKEE ROLL
From COAST to COAST-- and OVERSEAS--

NEW SKEE-ROLL ALLEYS Will Be Earning Big Profits This Season Rush Your Orders For Prompt Shipment [22]

And for the first time, it went on to encourage the buyer to pay attention to the aesthetics, envision the quality, the beauty of manufacture, the durability, countering the image of the cheap, "me-too" opportunities to save money by diminishing quality.

Co-marketing Skee-Ball and Skee-Roll

On April 27, 1935, the National Skee-Ball Company, Inc. of Coney Island, New York ran an ad in The Billboard for Skee-Roll making the point that Skee-Roll is already all over the

YOU KNOW WHAT SKEE ROLL IS--AND WHAT IT WILL MEAN TO YOU.

IF YOU HAVE NOT SEEN SKEE ROLL ON DISPLAY OR IN OPERATION -- WRITE FOR INFORMATION.

SKEE ROLL ALLEYS are each equipped with individual light brackets designed effectively to illuminate target and score register, regardless of location lighting defects.

The woodwork is cypress and birch thoroughly dried and seasoned to prevent warping. It is finished in a natural light color with a waterproof varnish surface.

The mechanical parts are of phosphor bronze or cadmium-plated steel. They are designed to stand up for at least ten years under hard usage.

The bowling surface is heavily lacquered green cork carpet, easily cleaned to remove dirt and ball marks.

The target is made of the same carpet with seven-ply machine belting used for the target circles.

SIZE: 14 FEET X 2½ FEET.

WEIGHT 355 LBS. NATIONAL SKEE BALL CO. CONEY ISLAND NEW YORK [23]

On April 11, the National Skee-Ball Company, Inc. ran an ad in The Billboard for Skee-Roll. The other element emphasized in many ads was "legitimacy" and "the original," in other words, no cheap imitations: The Real Thing. The message was, your customer WANTS the real thing. The brand recognition factor was important to your customers. Accept no substitutes.

An International Institution

IN AMUSEMENT PARKS THE WORLD OVER

The Perfect Set-Up for Fairs and Carnivals

The Three Dimensional Bowling Game everybody can play and enjoy.

Entirely automatic--the player does everything himself. SKEE ROLL requires no ballyhoo. The set-up and the players furnish the flash that draws the crowds.

Legitimate in every way--9 balls for 5¢ gives every play his money's worth. Wherever people play--There SKEE ROLL pays.

Size of Alley: 14x2½ wt. 355 lbs.

SKEE-ROLL

Amusement Parks that have installed SKEE ROLL testify to its drawing power, its player-appeal, its earning capacity. Patrons look for SKEE ROLL when they come into your park.

Send for Latest Catalogue

ORDER NOW FOR EARLY DELIVERY NATIONAL SKEE-BALL CO.

CONEY ISLAND, NEW YORK [24]

The following week, the National Skee-Ball Company ran an ad in The Billboard for Skee-Roll, in case anyone believed the "licensing" claims made by Mutoscope's ads. The ad copy read:

THERE IS ONLY ONE SKEE-ROLL

.... AND IT IS SOLD DIRECTLY TO OPERATORS ON TERRITORIAL ARRANGEMENTS. NO ONE IS LICENSED BY US TO MANUFACTURE OR DISTRIBUTE OUR GAME OR ANY SIMILAR BOWLING DEVICE

Size of Alley: 14'x2½' wt. 355 lbs. [25]

This lengthy ad from the June 27 issue of The Billboard for Skee-Roll hit most of the tactical selling points and differentiators from the clones in the "Five Outstanding Features."

There's Long Life and Consistent Earning Power in SKEE ROLL [sic]

Skee Roll [sic] is the result of 20 years' experience in the amusement device business. It has been improved according to operators' recommendation and adopted for heavy duty under all kinds of operating conditions. Skee Roll [sic] has been tested on every type of location with uniformly successful results. Skee Roll [sic] is entirely mechanical in operation with no electrical experiments to cause trouble. You need a game that will really do the job. Place your order for Skee Roll at once.

Get the original 3 dimensional bowling game that everyone can play and enjoy. Entirely automatic--the player does everything himself. SKEE ROLL [sic] requires no ballyhoo.

The set-up and the players furnish the flash that draws the crowds. Legitimate in every way. 9 balls for 5¢ gives every player his money's worth. The competitive value is great. Players can easily watch one another's scores and will vie with each

other sometimes for hours, thereby inducing the greatest repeat play ever known in an amusement device. If you want a game that will REALLY do a job, place orders for SKEE ROLL [sic] at once.

FIVE OUTSTANDING FEATURES

1. SKEE ROLL [sic] is a real piece of furniture. Its modern design with chromium fittings attracts the crowds.

2. SKEE ROLL [sic] opens up new locations unheard of with other coin operated machines. It is NOT a gambling device. Churches and organizations have approved it because it provides clean, wholesome amusement.

3. Perfect mechanical construction. Needs no servicing except to take your profits.

4. Young and old alike get equal thrills playing SKEE ROLL. [sic] No strength is needed. It is purely a game of skill.

5. THERE IS ONLY ONE SKEE ROLL [sic] ALLEY.

Dimensions:

Length, 14 ft.

Width, 29 in.

Height at Rear, 6 ft. 2 in. Weight 355 lbs.

Weight crated, 525 lbs.

Send Now for Descriptive Literature and Prices.

*NATIONAL SKEE-BALL CO.
CONEY ISLAND, NEW YORK.* [26]

The Last Straw

The Clone Wars took some toll on the business of Skee-Ball because we know they sold into venues that might have gone to Skee-Ball instead. But more important, the clone wars indicated the direction that the game ought to go to survive and thrive: shortened alleys, to fit the current venue opportunities; and emphasis on high quality and sterling reputation, to stay out of the "chasing zero" scenarios.

To do that, at least one additional patent would be necessary, to secure the uniqueness of the distinctive Skee-Ball alley of the future. Herman Bergoffen had already submitted a U.S. patent claim for the newest feature of the game, a mechanism that released a predetermined number of balls for play by rocking a gate, integrated into what looks like a modern Skee-Ball alley. [27]

In May 25, 1935, The Billboard excitedly reported:

> *"Herman Bergoffen, barrister, teacher, amusement realtor and Skee-Ball Company front man is in the throes of one of the most important legal assignments he has had in years. You'll read about it in the Brooklyn newspapers."* [28]

But tragically and unexpectedly, Bergoffen succumbed to a heart attack at age 55, before he could complete that assignment. This was a huge blow to the National Skee-Ball Company, as well as to the friends and beneficiaries who knew and loved him.

The Billboard reported:

> *Friends and associates were in deep mourning for Herman Bergoffen, prominent realtor and Skee-Ball projector, who died in Atlantic City. It was only last week, in these very columns that Mr. Bergoffen furnished a brief history of the Herman Popper Building, where Syd Kahn has installed his Fascination game. The last time I saw Mr. Bergoffen was in his Coney office where he was telling me of the work has was assigned to by the Supreme Court in Brooklyn, which always called upon his legal wisdom in deciding cases affecting property. His wife had been urging him to go with her and a party of friends to visit her favorite fortune teller's den in Manhattan, but Herman had to forego it due to the pressure of work. I mention this last bit merely to bring in the prophesy angle and am just wondering if his friends who did attend the ouija board conclave, brought back something in their minds to predict his unexpected passing. I don't happen to be a devotee of the supernatural art, but I believe its advocates often claim tremendous prophecies for it. Were I an ardent follow of ouijas and its off-shoots and I had been told that Herman Bergoffen was scheduled to depart from the scene, the first thing I would have done was punch the [fortune] teller in the nose. Herman Bergoffen was one swell guy.* [29]

On June 15, in "The Final Curtain" column of The Billboard, the following obituary ran for Herman Bergoffen:

> *BERGOFFEN -- Herman, 55, whose death in Atlantic City June 1 was reported briefly in the last issue, was real estate and office manager of the Coast Holding Company, which built Coney Island's (N. Y.) Boardwalk in 1923. He joined the company after a number of years as instructor in English in Brooklyn Technical High School, Brooklyn, where he lived. Shortly afterward he became vice-president and general manager and in 1926 established his own realty office. Two years later he organized the National Skee-Ball*

Company in Coney Island with Maurice Piesen, now at the Brussels (Belgium) Exposition with the company's devices. His realty firm, headquartered in the resort's Loew Theater Building has negotiated 400 amusement leases, the majority in Coney where he was a member of the Chamber of Commerce and an energetic civic worker. As a lawyer he had appeared as expert in several Supreme Court proceeding affecting show properties. He as active in the National Association of Amusement Parks Pools and Beaches and of that organization's affiliate Manufacturers and Dealers Section, now called the American Recreational Equipment Association and about a year ago served on the Coney advisory committee to the boro president of Brooklyn. He was a native of Austria, coming here at an early age. Burial in Lebanon Cemetery, Brooklyn, June 2. Widow, two daughters and a brother survive. [30]

On July 8, the National Skee Ball Company, Inc. went ahead and filed for the same patent in England for Bergoffen's new ball release, titled, "Improvements in or relating to Apparatus for Playing a Game." to patent a mechanism that releases a predetermined number of balls into play. The abstract read:

459,521. Games apparatus. DEHN, F. B., 103, Kingsway, London.-(National Skee Ball Co., Inc. ; 2002, Neptune Avenue, Brooklyn, New York, U.S.A.) July 8, 1935, No. 19527. [Class 132 (ii)] In games apparatus in which balls are rolled along a platform to strike a hump and jump into receptacles, a predetermined number of balls is released for play by rocking a gate 41, Fig. 2, about its pivot 42<1>, into the position shown in Fig. 3, where it is latched by a latch 56 until the first ball returning from the receptacles rocks a lever 65 connected to the latch by a wire 67. The gate is locked in its initial position by a latch 52 which is withdrawn by a wire 48, the wire also rocking the gate. The wire 48 is operated by a knob 60 (which may be coin-freed) connected by a universal joint 62 to a crank 64 to which the wire 48 is attached. [31]

U.S. Patent 2,010,213 was granted posthumously on August 6, to Herman Bergoffen for his "game," the modern version of Skee-Ball. [32] This was Bergoffen's final gift to the beautiful game of Skee-Ball. After Bergoffen's untimely death, Piesen soldiered on.

On November 2, 1935, the National Skee-Ball Company, Inc. of Coney Island, New York, announced it would exhibit at the upcoming N.A.A.P.P.B. (National Association of Amusement Parks, Pools and Beaches) convention, [33] and that Maurice Piesen would give a presentation about the Brussels Exposition at the N.A.A.P.P.B. Convention in Chicago, Illinois on Friday, December 6, at 4:45 PM. [34]

The National Skee-Ball Company ran an ad in the November 30 issue of The Billboard for Skee-Roll. The ad copy read:

> SKEE ROLL
>
> *COIN CONTROLLED Play it at the A. A. P. P. & B. Convention*
>
> *The Perfect Setup for Indoor and Outdoor Locations Write for Catalogue*
>
> *National Skee-Ball Company Coney Island New York [35]*

Two weeks later, on December 14, The Billboard published the list of exhibitors, and their representatives who attended the N.A.A.P.P.B. Convention in Chicago. The National Skee-Ball Co., Inc. was represented by Maurice Piesen, showing their Skee-Roll game. [36]

Discussions about where the company would go may have been in the works for some time, and the National Skee-Ball Company was looking for a rescuer. On December 16, Morris Goldberg's Skee Ball Sales And Security Co., Inc., which appears to have been the sales organization for the National Skee-Ball Company manufacturer, was dissolved by proclamation by the State of New York. [37]

After Herman Bergoffen's death, the entire burden of running the company fell to Maurice Piesen. He was effectively owner, operator, manufacturer, distributor and promoter, in addition to running the small manufacturing crew. But the popularity of Skee-Ball continued to grow. The shorter alleys made the game much more accessible to people of all ages, and were achieving huge popularity in the US and overseas. In Copenhagen, Tivoli Gardens ordered a bank of Skee-Ball alleys for the arcades. Skee-Ball was successfully launched into Europe with the Brussels Exposition in 1935. [38]

When 1936 arrived, Maurice Piesen carried on for several more months, advertising Skee-Roll and attending various functions. On January 25, there were candid shots from the Coin Machine Exposition. One of the photographs of Maurice Piesen included a caption that read:

> *Morris [sic] Piesen, of National Skee-Ball Co., writing another order. [39]*

But a change was in the works.

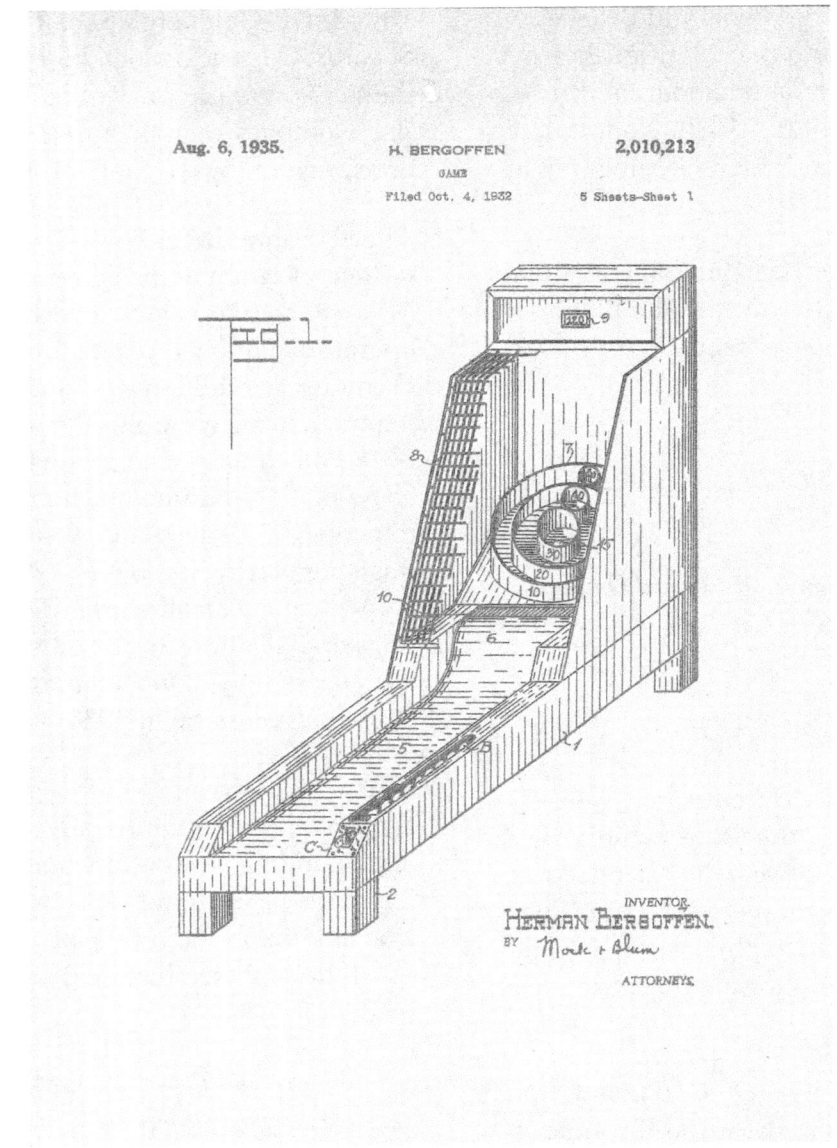

United States Patent No. 2,010,213.
(Courtesy National Archives and Records Administration, Kansas City)

United States Patent No. 2,010,213
(Courtesy Philadelphia Toboggan Coasters, Inc. Archive)

With Herman Bergoffen having passed on, Goldberg's Skee-Ball Sales and Security Company out of the picture, and more than a half-dozen direct competitors using the skee-jump feature from Skee-Ball, the weight of the company fell heavily on Piesen's shoulders. Although he could produce a reasonable quality product, and was well positioned in the industry, he apparently felt the burden of the sudden competition. It was a very smart move on the part of the National Skee-Ball company to trademark the name when the original patents ran out. But it wasn't enough.

With the European market beginning to open, and the increased demand for the shorter alleys, Piesen was faced with either expanding operations in an uncertain economy, or selling. In this financially challenging time, with clones nipping at their heels, perhaps it was time for more sophisticated advertising, manufacture and prestige to maintain the game's viability. Or perhaps it was time for someone with more facilities and deeper pockets to take some of the risk. In any case, the members of the National Skee-Ball Company, Inc. decided it was time to move on and turn Skee-Ball over to a company that would be able to take the game to the next level.

That company would be The Rudolf Wurlitzer Manufacturing Company.

Chapter 14

MANUFACTURING ELEGANCE
Wurlitzer Takes Charge

In 1936, the nation was still in the aftermath of the depression. The economy was still sluggish. Amusement venues were stagnant, and many had closed. The loss of Herman Bergoffen was stunning. Hugo and Maurice Piesen weren't alone in this endeavor. Herman's nephew Julian I. Bergoffen had become the secretary of the corporation and served as the corporate attorney. While Herman had a fascination with the amusement business and the community, and the game itself—enough to have redesigned some of its functionality and patented it—Julian had more love for business law than for the game and the amusement industry. That interest would serve him and the Piesen family well.

Having the new patent, and owning the trademarks for Skee-Ball and Skee-Roll meant that the National Skee-Ball Company had something of value to negotiate with beyond the game itself. That year, The National Skee-Ball Company sold the Skee-Ball concern to The Rudolph Wurlitzer Manufacturing Company. This marked Wurlitzer's expansion from musical products like the military band organs, theatre organs, other musical instruments, and juke boxes, into amusement games. Hugo and Maurice Piesen, and Herman Bergoffen's nephew, Julian Bergoffen, sold all rights, patents and trademarks for Skee-Ball to Wurlitzer, but not before assuring themselves of a secure financial future. [1] While in the beginning of Skee-Ball's history, lumbermen dominated the management of the companies, in this period, attorneys dominated.

Wurlitzer Corporation had apparently watched Skee-Ball alleys earn as much as four times what their jukeboxes did in taverns and saloons. Assuming that the profits for game owners would be translated into broad market demand for the game itself, they bought all of the rights to Skee-Ball and Skee-Roll from the National Skee-Ball Company and prepared to ramp up production of the alleys on their very capable manufacturing assembly lines. [2] They had an enthusiastic sponsor in Wurlitzer Vice President Homer Capehart. Paul Bennett, formerly of Rock-Ola, the manufacturer of the

Skee-Ball clone "Rock-O-Ball," was brought in to head the new games division, which was supervised by Capehart. The Billboard ran an article entitled "Wurlitzer in Game Field; Buys National Skee-Ball Co." on June 18, 1936. The article detailed the purchase of the rights to Skee-Ball and the creation of a new games division. [3]

Reminiscent of the hard bargain driven by William Nice Jr. and his half ownership of the original Skee-Ball patent, Julian Bergoffen drove a hard bargain with Wurlitzer. The contract read, in part:

> *the Seller has covenanted and agreed to sell and the Purchaser has covenanted to purchase, all tools, dies, jigs, plans, drawings. designs, patterns. and fixtures heretofore used or for use by Seller in the manufacture of National skee balls [sic] and/or skee rolls [sic] or alleys (excluding machines, machinery, office furniture and office equipment, large skee ball [sic] alleys previously manufactured and skee roll [sic] alleys which may be repossessed, accounts, bills, notes and contracts receivable and cash on hand) together with all unfinished inventory of material on hand when Seller ceases such manufacture as hereinafter provided and also all patents, trademarks, trade names, and copyrights and applications therefor,*
>
> *whether in the United States or in a foreign country, relating to the manufacture and/or sale of National skee balls[sic] and/or skee rolls [sic] or alleys heretofore owned or used by the Seller in such manufacture or sale together with the advertising material and testimonials and good will of said skee ball [sic], skee roll [sic] or alley business heretofore conducted by the Seller, also the right to use the word National in connection with said alleys and games all for the sum of Five thousand dollars ($5000.00) cash plus the royalties hereinafter agreed to be paid, by the Purchaser as follows: Purchaser agrees to pay the Seller a royalty in the amounts hereinafter set forth on each skee roll [sic] or alley (hereinafter called a unit) sold or disposed of and invoiced by it to-wit:* <u>*Ten dollars ($10.00) each on the first three thousand (3000) units, Seven Dollars ($7.00) each on the next succeeding seven thousand (7000) units, and Five dollars ($5.00) each on all succeeding units above the first ten thousand (10,000) but payment by the Purchaser of all royalties shall cease and determine when and if a total sum of Two hundred thousand dollars ($200,000.00) in royalties shall have been paid*</u>*, and Purchaser shall then be under no liability to pay any further royalties or sums of money under this agreement, and nothing contained in this agreement shall be*

THIS AGREEMENT

MADE AND ENTERED INTO this 19 day of June, 1936 by and between NATIONAL SKEE BALL COMPANY INC., a New York corporation with principal place of business at Coney Island, New York, hereinafter called the Seller, MAURICE PIESEN, HUGO H. PIESEN, and JULIAN I. BERGHOFFEN, individually, and THE RUDOLPH WURLITZER MANUFACTURING COMPANY, a New York corporation with principal place of business at North Tonawanda, New York, hereinafter called the Purchaser.

WITNESSETH:

That for and in consideration of the sum of One dollar ($1.00) and the covenants and agreements hereinafter contained, and other good and valuable consideration, the Seller has covenanted and agreed to sell and the Purchaser has covenanted to purchase, all tools, dies, jigs, plans, drawings, designs, patterns, and fixtures heretofore used or for use by Seller in the manufacture of National skee balls and/or skee rolls or alleys (excluding machines, machinery, office furniture and office equipment, large skee ball alleys previously manufactured and skee roll alleys which may be repossessed, accounts, bills, notes and contracts receivable and cash on hand) together with all unfinished inventory of material on hand when Seller ceased such manufacture as hereinafter provided and also all patents, trademarks, trade names, and copyrights and applications therefor, whether in the United States or in a foreign country, relating to the manufacture and/or sale of National skee balls and/or skee rolls or alleys heretofore owned or used by the Seller in such manufacture or sale together with the advertising material and testimonials and good will of said skee ball, skee roll or alley business heretofore conducted by the Seller, also the right to use the word "National" in connection with said alleys

Agreement between National Skee-Ball Company Inc. and Rudolph Wurlitzer Manufacturing Company, June 19, 1936, p. 1.
(Courtesy Philadelphia Toboggan Coasters, Inc. Archive)

and games, all for the sum of Five thousand dollars ($5000.00) cash plus the royalties hereinafter agreed to be paid, by the Purchaser as follows: Purchaser agrees to pay the Seller a royalty in the amounts hereinafter set forth on each skee roll or alley (hereinafter called a unit) sold ~~or disposed of~~ *and invoiced* by it to-wit: Ten dollars ($10.00) each on the first three thousand (3000) units, Seven dollars ($7.00) each on the next succeeding seven thousand (7000) units, and Five dollars ($5.00) each on all succeeding units above the first ten thousand (10,000) but payment by the Purchaser of all royalties shall cease and determine when and if a total sum of Two hundred thousand dollars ($200,000.00) in royalties shall have been paid, and Purchaser shall then be under no liability to pay any further royalties or sums of money under this agreement, and nothing contained in this agreement shall be or be construed to be an agreement on the part of the Purchaser to manufacture, sell, dispose of or pay royalties on any specific or minimum number of units whatsoever.

The aforesaid sale and purchase is made in consideration of and subject to the following additional covenants and agreements, to-wit:

FIRST: The Seller, Maurice Piesen, Hugo H. Piesen, and Julian I. Berkhoffen represent, warrant and agree:

(a) That all the property and effects sold are the sole and exclusive property of the Seller as of the date hereof and are subject to no liens or encumbrances.

(b) That attached hereto and marked Schedule A is a full true and complete statement of the names, addresses, and amounts of all creditors of the Seller; that the Seller has no other creditors or obligations of any sort.

Agreement between National Skee-Ball Company Inc. and Rudolph Wurlitzer Manufacturing Company, June 19, 1936, p. 2.
(Courtesy Philadelphia Toboggan Coasters, Inc. Archive)

(c) There is no litigation threatened or existing against the Seller and there is no litigation existing or threatened involving the capital stock of the Seller or in any way affecting the right of the Seller to sell the property and effects in accordance with the terms of this agreement.

(d) That the Seller will take proper and legal corporate action to evidence the Seller's right to make this agreement and the sale herein provided for.

(e) That the Seller has not entered into any contracts, agreements, or other committments, granting any territorial or sales rights relating to skee rolls or alleys which are presently in force, except as set forth on the annexed rider marked "Rider A".

(f) That when the sale is closed and the property and effects conveyed to the Purchaser as hereinafter provided the situation as regards the matters hereinabove mentioned in (a), (b), (c), and (e) shall be unchanged except for such committments and changes as shall have been made in the ordinary and normal conduct of the business of the Seller and the Seller shall then be in as good position to convey to the Purchaser good and valid title to the property and effects herein described as at the date hereof.

SECOND: The Seller, Maurice Piesen, Hugo H. Piesen and Julian I. Berghoffen further agree:

(a) That the representations, warranties and agreements contained herein or in any other paragraph hereof shall not be discharged or dissolved by the delivery of the said property and effects to the Purchaser or the payment therefor by the Purchaser.

-3-

Agreement between National Skee-Ball Company Inc. and Rudolph Wurlitzer Manufacturing Company, June 19, 1936, p. 3.
(Courtesy Philadelphia Toboggan Coasters, Inc. Archive)

RIDER A

The following are the contracts, agreements and other commitments excepted from the provisions of paragraph first in (e)

1. Agreement dated 8th day of May 1935 by and between NATIONAL SKEE BALL COMPANY, Inc. as first party and THE QUEEN CITY AMUSEMENT CO. of 421 Park Avenue, Plainfield, New Jersey, as second party

2. Agreement dated September 30, 1935 by and between NATIONAL SKEE BALL COMPANY, Inc. as first party and MOREY KUTZEN of 3345 Cortland Avenue, Detroit, Michigan, as second party

3. Agreement dated June 26, 1935 by and between NATIONAL SKEE BALL COMPANY, Inc. as first party and the AMUSEMENT EQUIPMENT CO. LTD. of Hong Kong Works, Wembley, Middlesex, England, as the second party.

Agreement between National Skee-Ball Company Inc. and Rudolph Wurlitzer Manufacturing Company, June 19, 1936, Rider A.
(Courtesy Philadelphia Toboggan Coasters, Inc. Archive)

(b) That from and after the time the physical property and unfilled orders are turned over to the Purchaser as provided in paragraph Third hereof, all enquiries or orders from old or new customers relating to the business sold shall be promptly turned over to the Purchaser and that the Purchaser shall have the right to advertise the fact that it has purchased the business of the Seller, but not, however, until ~~August~~ July 1st, 1936.

(c) That the Seller will at least ten (10) days before the closing of the sale, make and deliver to the Purchaser a full and detailed inventory showing the quantity and so far as possible with the exercise of reasonable diligence, the cost price to the Seller of each article to be included in the sale and shall furnish the Purchaser at least fourteen (14) days prior to such closing a written list of the names and addresses of the creditors of the Seller with the amount of the indebtedness due or owing to each and certified by the Seller under oath to be a full, accurate and complete list of such creditors, and of Seller's indebtedness, which said inventory and list shall be certified under oath by the Seller.

THIRD: That the sale provided for herein shall be closed at Purchaser's office or such other place as may be mutually agreed on fourteen (14) days after the receipt by the Purchaser of the inventory and list of creditors last above mentioned and the Seller shall then deliver to the Purchaser good and sufficient assignments of all patents, copyrights, trade marks and/or trade names hereinbefore agreed to be sold, a bill or bills of sale covering all personal property agreed

—4—

Agreement between National Skee-Ball Company Inc. and Rudolph Wurlitzer Manufacturing Company, June 19, 1936, p. 4.
(Courtesy Philadelphia Toboggan Coasters, Inc. Archive)

to be sold; drawn up and executed in due form of law so as to be filed or recorded in proper offices if desired. The Purchaser shall then pay the Seller the sum of Five thousand dollars ($5000.00) hereinbefore mentioned but the Seller may retain the physical property sold and use the same for a period of *eight* (8) days from date hereof, during which time it may use the same and use up so much of the inventory of raw material and if necessary add to same at its own expense, as to manufacture *forty five* units of skee rolls or alleys which units shall be the property of the Seller to be retained or disposed of by it as it shall see fit. At the end of the *eight* day period the Seller shall turn over to the Purchaser all unfilled orders on hand and load the physical property included in this sale, together with the then remaining inventory of unfinished or raw materials all properly prepared, packed and crated at Seller's expense and ship the same by freight to the Purchaser at its North Tonawanda plant and said Purchaser shall pay the freight.

FOURTH: The Seller, Maurice Piesen, Hugo H. Piesen, and Julian I. Berghoffen, do further in consideration of the premises and as an incident to the sale and transfer of the said property and business and the good will covenant that neither the Seller nor said individuals during the period that the Purchaser shall be engaged in the manufacture of skee balls, skee rolls or alleys (except during the *eight* day period) from date hereof to the extent hereinabove expressly outlined) directly or indirectly as owner, owners, officer, officers, stockholder, stockholders, manager, managers, partner, partners, financial backer or backers, endorser, endorsers, lender or lenders, salesman, salesmen, solicitor, solicitors, agent, agents, manufacturer, manufacturers, employee, employees, pro-

Agreement between National Skee-Ball Company Inc. and Rudolph Wurlitzer Manufacturing Company, June 19, 1936, p. 5.
(Courtesy Philadelphia Toboggan Coasters, Inc. Archive)

with the business to be sold and that the Seller shall after said ~~eight~~ *eight* day period at once discontinue the use of its corporate name either by change thereof, dissolution or discontinuance of operations, excepting that the Seller shall have the right to use its corporate name until January 1, 1937 for the purpose of disposing of large skee ball alleys repossessed, skee rolls and skee rolls manufactured by it as provided in paragraph Third hereof, for collecting outstanding accounts, and also in connection with legal and governmental requirements until the said corporation is legally dissolved or its name changed, it being expressly understood and covananted that the Purchaser shall acquire the full and exclusive use of the words National Skee Ball, Skee Roll, Skee Ball Alley and combinations and/or variations thereof to which any of the parties hereto other than Purchaser are now entitled, and the right to manufacture, use, sell or dispose of devices known as National Skee Balls, Skee Rolls, and Skee Ball Alleys without any interference or competition either as to names or similar names, devices or similar devices.

FIFTH: The Seller, Maurice Piesen, Hugo H. Piesen and Julian I. Berghoffen, shall at their own cost and expense defend all of the patents, ~~patent rights, applications therefor and~~ copyrights, and defend and hold the Purchaser harmless from any and all loss, claims, demands, damages, charges and suits based on claim or assertions that the same are or constitute interference with or infringements of other ~~patents, patent rights, applications for patents, or articles,~~ names, and/copyrights, ~~or devices;~~ and Purchaser shall have the right to withhold payment of royalties, pending final and favorable disposition of any claims, suits, or proceedings involving interference/ with or infringements,/of such copyrights real, claimed or alleged, unless the seller shall furnish a bond or undertaking in a reasonable amount, in which event the royalty shall be continued to be paid.

- 6 -

Agreement between National Skee-Ball Company Inc. and Rudolph Wurlitzer Manufacturing Company, June 19, 1936, p. 6.
(Courtesy Philadelphia Toboggan Coasters, Inc. Archive)

SIXTH: It is agreed that the provision as to the payment of royalties shall apply only to the sale or disposal by Purchaser of units embodying one or more of the features of the patent or patents to be assigned to Purchaser or sold or disposed of under the trade name or names skee ball, skee roll, skee ball alley, with or without the word National or any combination of said words, and/or any similar bowling device. However, the expiration by statute law of a patent, patents, copyright, copyrights, trade name or names shall not release Purchaser from payment of royalties.

SEVENTH: The royalties herein provided to be paid by the Purchaser shall be paid on or before the twentieth (20) of each month succeeding each calendar month for each unit sold and invoiced ~~or disposed of~~ during such calendar month, by the Purchaser.

EIGHTH: This agreement is the sole agreement between the parties hereto in relation to the matters herein referred to and all prior conversations, correspondence, memoranda and agreements relative thereto are merged herein.

NINTH: This agreement and all of its terms and provisions shall enure to and be binding upon the parties hereto and their successors, heirs, legal representatives, and assigns respectively.

IN WITNESS WHEREOF, This agreement has been made and executed by the parties hereto as of the day and year first above written.

NATIONAL SKEE BALL COMPANY INC.

THE RUDOLPH WURLITZER MANUFACTURING COMPANY

Agreement between National Skee-Ball Company Inc. and Rudolph Wurlitzer Manufacturing Company, June 19, 1936, p. 7.
(Courtesy Philadelphia Toboggan Coasters, Inc. Archive)

```
STATE OF NEW YORK  )
COUNTY OF Niagara  ) SS:
CITY OF No. Tonawanda
```

On this *19th* day of June, 1936, before me personally came *Maurice Piesen*, to me known, who, being by me duly sworn did depose and say:

That he resides in the City of *Brooklyn* New York, and he is the *President* of NATIONAL SKEE BALL COMPANY INC., the corporation described in, and which executed the above instrument; that he knows the seal of said corporation; that the seal affixed to said instrument is such corporate seal; that it was so affixed by order of the Board of Directors of said corporation and that he signed his name thereto by like order.

W. D. Waterstrat
Notary Public
NOTARY PUBLIC IN AND FOR ERIE COUNTY
CERTIFICATE FILED IN NIAGARA COUNTY

```
STATE OF NEW YORK  )
COUNTY OF Niagara  ) SS:
CITY OF No. Tonawanda
```

On the *19th* day of June, 1936, before me personally came *Farny R. Wurlitzer*, to me known, who, being by me duly sworn did depose and say:

That he resides in the City of *No. Tonawanda* N.Y. and he is the *President* of THE RUDOLPH WURLITZER MANUFACTURING COMPANY, the corporation described in, and which executed the above instrument; that he knows the seal of said corporation; that the seal affixed to said instrument is such corporate seal; that it was so affixed by order of the Board of Directors of said corporation, and that he signed his name thereto by like order.

W. D. Waterstrat
Notary Public
NOTARY PUBLIC IN AND FOR ERIE COUNTY
CERTIFICATE FILED IN NIAGARA COUNTY

- 8 -

Agreement between National Skee-Ball Company Inc. and Rudolph Wurlitzer Manufacturing Company, June 19, 1936, p. 8.
(Courtesy Philadelphia Toboggan Coasters, Inc. Archive)

```
STATE OF NEW YORK    )
COUNTY OF Kings      ) SS:
CITY OF New York
```

On this 22 day of June, in the year Nineteen hundred and thirty-six, before me, the subscriber, personally appeared MAURICE PIESEN, HUGO H. PIESEN, and JULIAN I. BERNHOFFEN, to me known and known to me to be the same persons described in and who executed the within instrument, and they acknowledged to me that they executed the same.

Agreement between National Skee-Ball Company Inc. and Rudolph Wurlitzer Manufacturing Company, June 19, 1936, p. 9.
(Courtesy Philadelphia Toboggan Coasters, Inc. Archive)

or be construed to be an agreement on the part of the Purchaser to manufacture, sell, dispose of or pay royalties on any specific or minimum number of units whatsoever. [4] *(emphasis ours)*

Boiled down, the right to produce Skee-Ball and own the patents and trademark was worth $5,000. But the real cost of the deal was $205,000. The first 3,000 alleys would account for $30,000 in royalties. The next 7,000 alleys at $7.00 each would account for another $49,000.00 for a total of $79,000. To pay off the balance of the royalties for the remaining $121,000 at $5.00 per alley meant selling another 24,200 units.

The company that bought Skee-Ball was The Rudolph Wurlitzer Manufacturing Company, Inc. a subsidiary of The Rudolph Wurlitzer Corporation. It was able to mass produce a large number of their musical instrument products and sell them to millions of people through retail outlets, as well as supplying juke boxes for every coffee shop and restaurant in the country. The royalty agreement with the National Skee-Ball Company may have seemed both reasonable and reassuring as to the number of alleys they would be able to manufacture and sell.

They were to discover, however, that Skee-Ball had a somewhat more specialized market. It had already penetrated the amusement market heavily, and the ability to expand under the circumstances would be limited. The clones were still providing some alternatives to Skee-Ball at a lower price that proved enticing enough to challenge Skee-Ball's expansion at the lower end of the market. These realizations either did not register with the senior managers at Wurlitzer, or they had the confidence that they could dominate the market in games as they had in music. They proceeded with full assurance that this would prove a lucrative opportunity for the company. The sale was finalized on the 22nd day of June, 1936. [5]

The following month, on July 18, The Rudolph Wurlitzer Manufacturing Company of North Tonawanda, New York, ran a full-page ad in The Billboard announcing the formation of its new Games division. Wurlitzer was completely committed to embracing Skee-Ball as a welcome and valued member of the family. However, this ad and several that followed it also became the source of more confusion in the history of Skee-Ball, since Wurlitzer assumed that the National Skee-Ball Company had owned the game from the beginning.

The ad copy read:

> *WURLITZER extends its leadership into GAMES FIELD*

* With the inauguration of a Games Division, Wurlitzer brings to the amusement games field a fresh viewpoint, unfettered by past practices, products, or tradition, plus the same leadership that has made "Wurlitzer-Simplex" the outstanding success in automatic phonographs. A success that witnesses an ever-increasing operator demand for these instruments month after month.

* It will be the aim of this new Department to provide new products designed to win widespread and lasting public acceptance. Back of the new division is the long experience, the vast designing, engineering and manufacturing facilities, the unlimited financial resources and sound merchandising policies of The Rudolph Wurlitzer Manufacturing Company. Factors responsible for its pre-eminent position in the music field--advantages that likewise meet every requirement for leadership in coin-operated games.

* The initial product to be offered by Wurlitzer's Games Division will be "Skee Ball," redesigned from the original coin-operated "Skee Ball"--introduced last fall by the National Skee Ball Company of Coney Island, N. Y.--recently acquired by Wurlitzer. "National" were the creators and original "Skee Ball" manufacturers. Their product which, until its recent perfection as a coin-operated device, required supervision by attendants, has been a big money-maker in the amusement park field since 1908.

* As successors of National Skee Ball Company Wurlitzer can assure its customers not only complete security and protection on patents but, based on the twenty-eight year success of the "Skee Ball" idea in the amusement park field, a permanently profitable investment as well.

* Next month, through the pages of this and other coin machine journals, Wurlitzer will make a complete announcement of its new "Skee Ball"--redesigned by Paul Fuller, whose creation of the beautiful cabinets and lighting effects of the Wurlitzer-Simplex has played no small part in its tremendous and ever-growing popularity. Combining striking eye appeal, intriguing play appeal and a record for permanent sizeable profits, Wurlitzer's "Skee Ball" should prove to be one of the biggest money-makers that has ever been brought to the coin machine industry!

Games Division

THE RUDOLPH WURLITZER MANUFACTURING CO. NORTH TONAWANDA, NEW YORK

WURLITZER...A NAME THAT

STANDS FOR PROFITS IN AMUSEMENT PRODUCTS [6]

Wurlitzer was widely known for excellence in manufacture and design. Throughout the history of the game, all of the Skee-Ball manufacturers were unsophisticated operations, with a focus on producing product without meticulous attention to finish quality or aesthetic design, even though some were well-funded and increasingly reliable.

Wurlitzer had significant manufacturing facilities and a full-time professional cabinet designer, Paul Fuller, who designed all the cabinets for every product Wurlitzer made. [7] He completely redesigned the cabinet for Skee-Ball, incorporating the classic sculpted cabinetry shape into the alley. This incorporated the very distinctive style, rounded sweeping lines, consistent with the other Wurlitzer products. The company brought not only classic beauty to the game design, but consistent manufacturing, mechanical and electrical reliability, and high quality. It was a significant step up for Skee-Ball, and an investment in making it more than a cut above the plethora of "me-too" products that had emerged as the patents for the game expired. Wurlitzer could compete with name recognition and quality, and their company's stellar reputation in the amusement industry.

The competition from clones still looked to be nipping at the heels of Skee-Ball. On July 25, 1936, it was reported in The Billboard that Joe Calcutt ordered 400 Bally-Roll games from the Bally Manufacturing Company. It was said to be the largest order ever of a single game. [8] The Billboard also reported that the first three Skill-Ball games from the Stirling Novelty Company, Inc. had rolled off the new production line and were shipped to Mrs. Sue Silverman. [9]

In the same issue, Bally Manufacturing Company claimed that it was having to revise its production plans for Bally-Roll because the company was receiving more orders than expected. [10]

Wurlitzer was prepared to take on the battle for the game. In the same issue of The Billboard was a big announcement that the Modern Vending Company was preparing an elaborate party for the formal presentation of the first Skee-Ball game built by the Wurlitzer factory. The company noted that Homer E. Capehart, Joe A. Darwin and Paul S. Bennett would be present at the party. [11]

At the same time, the price wars had begun as Skill-Ball made its first price cuts and the clones succumbed to the trap of "chasing zero." In the same issue, The Billboard reported that the Stirling Novelty Company was reducing prices on their Skill-Ball game. [12]

Left to right: Homer Capehart, Vice President in charge of sales, James Broyles, assistant to Mr. Capehart. Other unidentified people are purchasers of juke boxes made at the North Tonawanda plant and installed all over the country.
(Courtesy Historical Society of the Tonawandas)

The Rudolph Wurlitzer Manufacturing Company plant in North Tonawanda, New York.
(Courtesy Historical Society of the Tonawandas)

The Rudolph Wurlitzer Manufacturing Company plant in North Tonawanda, New York.
(Courtesy Historical Society of the Tonawandas)

Wurlitzer threw down the gauntlet. The Modern Vending Company of New York City, eastern factory distributors for The Rudolph Wurlitzer Manufacturing Company ran an ad in The Billboard For Skee-Ball. The ad copy read:

> CAUTION BEFORE YOU BUY . . .
>
> WAIT AND SEE THE NEW SENSATIONAL
>
> *Streamlined*
>
> WURLITZER
>
> SKEE-BALL
>
> A MODERN PRODUCT IS ALWAYS A WINNER
>
> *The ORIGINAL and only SKEE-BALL with mechanism that has been tried and proven order a long period of time--!*
>
> NOW READY FOR DELIVERY EASTERN FACTORY DISTRIBUTORS *Modern Vending Company 656 Broadway, New York City* [13]

According to their manufacturers, the clones continued to sell. On August 1, The Billboard reported that Jim Buckley claimed his company was swamped with orders for Bally-Roll. [14]

That same day, an article in The Billboard titled "George Ponser Enthused Over Roll-A-Ball Results" reported that George Ponser said the following about Roll-A-Ball:

> *"The game has player appeal; it attracts and keeps the crowds. It presents new and exclusive features that make every watcher a player and it gives the player complete control over the ball."* [15]

But Wurlitzer was staking its own, sophisticated, high-class claim to the game. The company did a significant amount of cosmetic work to make it look "Wurlitzer-y" and as part of the process, shortened the alley and discontinued Skee-Roll.

On August 29, Wurlitzer ran a full-page ad in The Billboard for their new, improved version of Skee-Ball.

> WURLITZER'S SKEE-BALL (REG. U. S. PAT. OFF.) *already the accepted* LEADER
>
> *Designed with exceptional play appeal to be the leader . . . styled with added eye appeal to be the leader . . . built more solidly and more substantially to be the leader . . .*
> WURLITZER'S SKEE-BALL *(Reg. U. S. Pat. Off.) has already attained its goal.*

Operators have accepted it as the leader of all coin-operated bowling games because they feel that Wurlitzer's acquisition of the National Skee-Ball Company, creators and manufacturers of the original Skee-Ball, gives Wurlitzer the knowledge necessary to build a game with greatest play appeal--knowledge based on National's tried and proven record extending over a quarter century for big, steady profits in the amusement park field.

Operators recognize Wurlizers Skee-Ball as the outstanding value . . . not a game hurriedly designed to get on the market, but solidly built of fine quality hardwood, weighing 522 lbs.--an investment that will bring them big profits long after games, flimsily built of light woods and weighing some two hundred pounds less are thrown onto the scrapheap.

They know that back of the Wurlitzer's Skee-Ball (Reg. U. S. Pat. Off.) are the same unlimited facilities--the identical fair policies and methods that have led operators to buy more Wurlitzer-Simplex Automatic Phonographs than all other makes combined.

Why not line yourself up with the leader and share the profits of leadership? Confidently we say, "You will make more money with Wurlitzer's Skee-Ball" (Reg. U. S. Pat. Off.) "Write, phone, or wire for details at once."

THE RUDOLPH WURLITZER MFG. CO., N. TONAWANDA, N. Y. [16]

Wurlitzer ran an ad in The Billboard on September 5 for their game Skee-Ball, setting the bar for smart business people.

The Greatest Thing in Business . . .

*THE greatest thing in business is reputation. Nothing else can stand up to it. Nothing else can take its place. Wurlitzer recognizes this fact. This is why Wurlitzer, established since 1856, values its reputation above everything else. And that is the reason why Wurlitzer has not engaged in any grab-all, catch-as catch-can methods of getting business. What you think of Wurlitzer five years from now is more important to us than to force a sale out of you today by unfounded claims and promises. * * * In the midst of the present hue and cry about Skee-Ball, Wurlitzer considers it a duty to give you the actual facts:*

Orders. Wurlitzer has orders on hand for thousands and thousands of Skee Balls. In all likelihood, far more than any other company can boast of. But nothing has been said about this because operators know that

Wurlitzer is doing the biggest business on Skee Balls, just as it is on the Wurlitzer-Simplex Phonograph.

Deliveries. Shipments of Wurlitzer's Skee Balls to all parts of the country are now under way. Quantities could have been shipped ten weeks ago, if we had no regard for the operators' welfare. But we refused to be stampeded or rushed into turning out anything but a quality job. Now that we know the Wurlitzer Skee Ball is right, now that we know it is the most dependable alley on the market, we are stepping up production to big volume figures.

Facilities. Wurlitzer occupies and utilizes 700,000 square feet of floor space. This is probably the largest factory unit in the coin machine industry. Every square inch of space is in actual use, and the 700,000 square feet is an actual figure. And yet, we have not played up our size or facilities for the simple reason that these facts are self-evident and need no exaggerated ballyhoo.

Experience. Wurlitzer's Skee Ball is the only Skee Ball. It is the original. There has been no begging, borrowing, or stealing of ideas. When Wurlitzer decided to build Skee Ball, it went direct to the owner of Skee Ball and purchased the company lock, stock and barrel. Wurlitzer thereby gained the benefit of the National Skee Ball Co.'s 30 years' experience with Skee Ball. That is why you can be sure of Skee Ball. You know it is not a hopeful imitation, born just yesterday.

Quality. In Wurlitzer's Skee Ball, you have more solid quality than any imitation can give you. Wurlitzer's Skee Ball is built to stand up for years. What's more, Wurlitzer's Skee Ball is mechanically dependable. Yet, no wild claims of perfection have been made because operators know they can always depend on a Wurlitzer product.

Price. Wurlitzer's Skee Ball costs you no more than cheaply thrown together imitations and can be bought on Wurlitzer's time payment play by those who desire terms.

What do all these facts mean to you? Just this: that when you do business with Wurlitzer you are doing business with the leader. You are buying the original Skee-Ball-- the genuine article, and not a counterfeit. You are sure of getting the best. You are getting a product that is backed up by a company with millions of dollars in resources, a company whose reputation is worldwide--one that has never broken faith with the operator . . . . and that means complete, permanent satisfaction for you.

Games Division The Rudolph Wurlitzer Manufacturing Co. North Tonawanda, New York [17]

The clone companies continued to advertise, ship and seemed to thrive. Wurlitzer apparently paid no attention and pursued work in its games division, unconcerned. The company, however, made it abundantly clear that it had undisputed rights to the Skee-Ball trademark and to all of the patents still in effect. In this otherwise clear statement of fact, however, is another mis-statement about the automatic coin operation, which had been a key feature on the original Skee-Ball game that Simpson developed, and for that reason was advertised from the beginning as "no attendant needed."

A Plain Statement of Facts on "Skee Ball" (REG. U. S. PAT. OFF.)

by HOMER E. CAPEHART Vice-President, The Rudolph Wurlitzer Manufacturing Company

WITH so much being said and written about "Skee Ball" (Reg. U. S. Pat. Off.), I believe it is time that the industry should know who holds the original patents on "Skee Ball"-- who owns the copyright to the name "Skee Ball" (Reg. U. S. Pat. Off.)--whose experience best fits them to produce the kind of game that will have the greatest play appeal--that will enable you to make the biggest profits as an operator.

* As you may know, last November the National Skee Ball Company, creators [sic] and manufacturers of "Skee Ball" (Reg. U. S. Pat. Off.) introduced a coin operated "Skee Ball". For nearly a quarter century prior to that time their business had been confined to amusement parks, where the game is operated by attendants and has always been a big money maker.

* We became interested in the "Skee Ball" (Reg. U. S. Pat. Off.) because it was a legitimate game that could be placed in the same category as bowling alleys . . . archery . . . bowling on the green and other such games--and the fact that it required a certain athletic skill to play it. This was important because only such type games are of interest to us.

* Our scouts made a careful survey of locations where "Skee Balls" (Reg. U. S. Pat. Off.) were being operated--discovered that it was making big profits for operators--recommended that we engage in the manufacture and sale of "Skee Balls".

* Instead of attempting to infringe the patent rights of others, we then negotiated with and acquired the National Skee Ball

Company. This move by a company as large and successful as Wurlitzer, opened the eyes of the industry, with the result that others have entered the business.

* We have no quarrel with those who wish to enter this field. However, for your own good, we hope they do not make a gambling device out of this wonderful game and that they will produce a well constructed, high class piece of equipment which will lend credit to the industry and the game.

* However, we have not licensed anyone to manufacture or distribute this game or any similar bowling device. Through the acquisition of the National Skee Ball Company we control the original "Skee Ball" patents and copyrights for the name "Skee Ball" and "Skee Roll". No other manufacturer can rightfully imitate this game and call it "Skee Ball" (Reg. U. S. Pat. Off.) or "Skee Roll" (Reg. U. S. Pat. Off.) either in advertising, correspondence or verbally.

* In acquiring the National Skee Ball Company, we also had another motive--namely to eliminate the guesswork and experiment . . . to build the kind of game that experience has taught is essential to the operators' success.

* We learned that electrical operation destroys the essentially athletic character of the game. This is why everything about "Skee Ball" (Reg. U. S. Pat. Off.) except the lighting is mechanical.

* When the player pulls the knob to release the balls--when he bends slightly because our game is made bowling height, he gets the mild exercise which is the basis of this game.

* When he sees his scores mechanically recorded after each ball in white numerals on a black field, he sees it in a form that he is accustomed to seeing scores at baseball games, football games, etc.

* When the player rolls the balls he wants the alley to feel solid--just as in bowling. This is why "Skee Ball" (Reg. U. S. Pat. Off.) is built of heavy red oak and weighs 450 lbs.-- why we refuse to build a game from light wood that would have a hollow sound and lose much of its play appeal.

* Yet, because we make our own cabinets--are not obliged to buy them from outside plants, we can sell a game that will give you years of fine service for no more than what you would pay for a game built from light wood.

In building the highest quality of merchandise and selling it at the right price, we are following the same policy that has proven so successful with the Wurlitzer-Simplex Automatic Phonograph.

It is my belief that Wurlitzer policies and methods will make "Skee Ball" (Reg. U. S. Pat. Off.) a big, profitable business for everybody . . . that Wurlitzer's "Skee Ball" is a worthy companion to the Wurlitzer-Simplex Automatic Phonograph.

Both were the originals. The Simplex phonograph business was purchased by us from the Simplex Phonograph Company of Chicago--established in 1930--which company introduced the first multi-selective type phonograph. The National Skee Ball company were pioneers and the originators [sic] of the game called "Skee Ball" (Reg. U. S. Pat. Off.).

Already orders on hand indicate a tremendous demand for the Wurlitzer "Skee Ball" (Reg. U. S. Pat. Off.)--a demand that promises to tax our production capacity for months to come. So, to insure deliveries when you want them, let me suggest that you wire, write or phone for full particulars without delay.

H. E. Capehart

WURLITZER'S "SKEE BALL" (REG U. S. PAT. OFF.)

The Original "Skee Ball" (REG U. S. PAT. OFF.)

REGULATION SIZE AND CONSTRUCTION. Substantially constructed of high quality red oak. Meets every regulation standard for width of playing field--length and arrangement of alley--size and arrangement of target area and all other essentials.

STREAMLINE DESIGN. Smartly designed for maximum eye and play appeal by Paul Fuller, noted designer of Wurlitzer-Simplex cabinets. Natural hardwood finish attractively set off with black, color and chrome decorative treatment and fittings . . . finished in liquor [sic] and waterproof ship varnish.

DIMENSIONS

    Overall length 14' 2"

    Width 29 1/4"

    Height at rear 6'

    Length of Ball Runway 10'

    Weight Approx. 450 lbs.

PORTABLE. Divided construction permits ease in shipping, transportation to locations and assembly.

POSITIVE ACTION, MECHANICAL COUNTING DEVICE . . . shows score in large white numerals on back field up to 450, the maximum score.

INDIRECT LIGHTING of scoring device for easy reading of scores. *INDIVIDUAL LIGHT BRACKET* floodlights target area.

REGULATION SIZE TARGET area. Target circles made of heavy rubberized machine belting.

HEAVILY CORDED HAND WOVEN NET, supported on heavy tubular steel forms protects tops and side of rear and of alley.

ADJUSTABLE FOR EASIER OR MORE DIFFICULT SCORING. Elevation of "hump" over which balls roll before reaching target area can be adjusted. Front of alley protected with metal strips to prevent wear from players feet.

UNOBSTRUCTED ALLEY. Coin chute and ball release located on the right side out of the way, not in front where they would be bent out of shape and put out of commission by players feet. Nothing in front of alley to cut down on length of playing field--detract the players eye--interfere with his play.

Rear view of cabinet showing location of "Coin" and High Score Meters.

REGULATION SIZE ALLEY Both the alley and target area are covered with heavy green cork carpet, easily cleaned to move dust and ball marks.

HIGH SCORE METER adjustable to any figure the operator wishes to set shows the number of "winning" scores that have been made and is a positive check on the number of prizes given by the location owner.

COIN METER shows how many coins have been taken in as a check on collections.

SILENT. Rubber cushioning on ball return rack--construction and insulation of target area and inclined alley, insures quiet operation. Can be installed in locations where noisy games would not be permitted.

POSITIVE MECHANICAL OPERATION. Everything about this game is mechanical, nothing electrical except the lighting. No contacts, wires, batteries or power packs to get out of order.

Advanced type coin drop -- not coin chute.

Money box located on inside or right front foot with quality lock equipment.

NOTE: No one is licensed by us to manufacture or distribute this game or any other similar bowling device

RUDOLPH WURLITZER MFG. CO. NORTH TONAWANDA N. Y.

READ PRECEDING PAGES FOR IMPORTANT MESSAGE BY H. E. CAPEHART [18]

Wurlitzer's decision to redesign Skee-Ball cabinets and re-engineer parts of the game would pay off handsomely. And Wurlitzer Skee-Ball rolled on.

On December 5, The Rudolph Wurlitzer Company ran an ad in The Billboard for Skee-Ball. The text of the ad emphasized the wisdom of holding out for the real thing, instead of a cheap imitator. The ad read:

"We looked at them all!

... then signed up with WURLITZER'S SKEE BALL as the biggest money-maker and the best investment"

Ben Palastrant Supreme Amusement Co. of N. E.

Ben Palastrant of the Supreme Amusement Company of New England, Boston, Mass. and M. J. Lockwood, his partners at right, signing up with Ben Kulick, Wurlitzer New England representative, for big order of Wurlitzer Skee Balls.

BEFORE investing in any make of bowling game, the Supreme Amusement Company of New England, with headquarters in Boston, "looked at them all". Then they signed up for the Wurlitzter Skee Ball. [sic]

The following statement is from Ben Palastrant of this company: "Operators are in business for profits--consequently we looked at all the bowling games from all the angles--particularly from the standpoint of ability to produce profits over a long period of time. We decided to handle the Wurlitzer Skee ball [sic] and results have already justified our decision.

"Wurlizter's Skee Ball [sic] has greater eye appeal. It attracts crowds on sight. Its design is modern, will not become obsolete. It has greater play appeal. A full-size game that invites continuous operation-- assures more profit. Finally, it is solidly constructed-- mechanically perfect. No service headaches or excessive costs for repairs. It's built to stay in operation for many years.

"We are handling the Wurlitzer Skee Ball [sic], not only because it is the original Skee Ball [sic], but because it is superior to all the others. We felt that the Wurlitzer Skee Ball [sic] has investment value that will pay big dividends for a long time to come.

"Our advice to any operator is simply this. If you want to get and hold the best locations--make and continue to make big profits--do as we did--invest your money in Wurlitzer Skee Balls. [sic] They have everything it takes to pile up permanent profits."

FOLLOW THE ADVICE OF SUCCESSFUL OPERATORS EVERYWHERE. LOOK AT ALL THE BOWLING GAMES. Then MAIL THE COUPON or WIRE FOR FULL PARTICULARS

SOLD ONLY TO OPERATORS

THE RUDOLPH WURLITZER CO.
North Tonawanda, N. Y.

Gentlemen:

I'd like to cash in on the big Skee-Ball profits. Please tell me how I can get into this profitable business.

Name ....

Address ....

City and State ....

Present Occupation .... [19]

On December 12, an article titled, "Wurlitzer-Modern Party Climax To Good-Will Building Program" appeared in The Billboard covering the 1,500-person banquet held by Wurlitzer and the Modern Vending Company. The only speaker of the evening was Homer E. Capehart. After his speech he was the recipient of a Skee-Ball shaped watch. The watch was presented by Lou Rose president of the Amalgamated Vending Machine Operators' Association. [20] This party was held at the opulent and prestigious Waldorf-Astoria Hotel in New York City.

A photograph of Homer E. Capehart, Billy Bolles of Wurlitzer and Nat Cohn of Modern Vending Company appeared in The Billboard. The caption of the photograph read:

A MANUFACTURER AND DISTRIBUTOR LAY PLANS--Left to right: Homer E. Capeheart, vice-president of Rudolph Wurlitzer Company; Bill Bolles, Wurlitzer credit and collection manager, and Nat Cohn, of Modern

Wurlitzer's Skee-Ball Brochure, front cover
(Author's Collection)

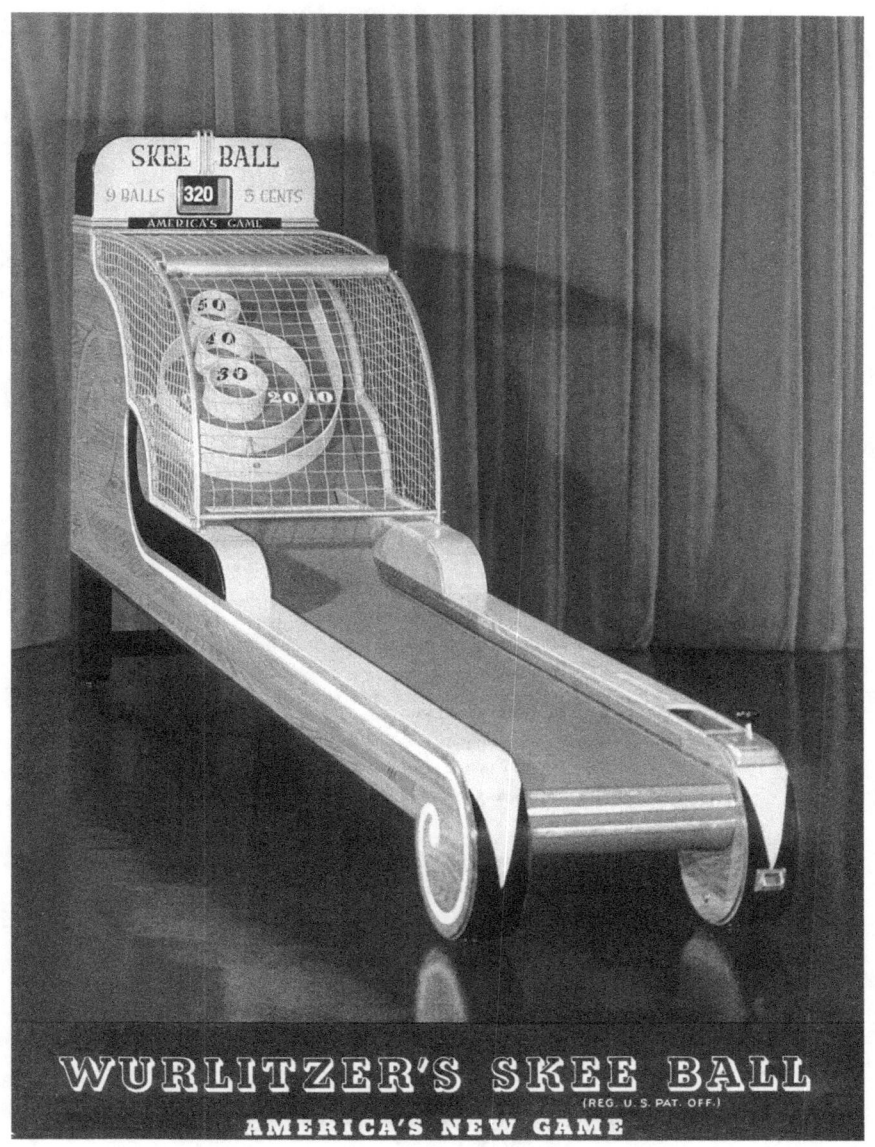

Wurlitzer's Skee-Ball Brochure, p. 2
(Author's Collection)

A PLAIN STATEMENT of FACTS on SKEE BALL
(REG. U. S. PAT. OFF.)

by H. E. Capehart

HOMER E. CAPEHART
VICE PRESIDENT, RUDOLPH WURLITZER MFG. CO.
NORTH TONAWANDA, NEW YORK

WITH so much being said and written about "Skee Ball" (Reg. U. S. Pat. Off.), I believe it is time that the industry should know who holds the original patents on "Skee Ball"—who owns the copyright to the name "Skee Ball"—whose experience best fits them to produce the kind of game that will have the greatest play appeal—that will enable you to make the biggest profits as an operator.

• As you may know, last November the National Skee Ball Company, creators and manufacturers of "Skee Ball" (Reg. U. S. Pat. Off.) introduced a coin operated "Skee Ball". For nearly a quarter century prior to that time their business had been confined to amusement parks, where the game is operated by attendants and has always been a big money maker.

• We became interested in the "Skee Ball" because it was a legitimate game that could be placed in the same category as bowling alleys . . . archery . . . bowling on the green and other such games—and the fact that it required a certain athletic skill to play it. This was important because only such type games are of interest to us.

• Our scouts made a careful survey of locations where "Skee Balls" were being operated—discovered that it was making big profits for operators—recommended that we engage in the manufacture and sale of "Skee Balls".

• Instead of attempting to infringe the patent rights of others, we then negotiated with and acquired the National Skee Ball Company. This move by a company as large and successful as Wurlitzer, opened the eyes of the industry, with the result that others have entered the business.

Page THREE

Wurlitzer's Skee-Ball Brochure, p. 3
(Author's Collection)

A PLAIN STATEMENT OF SKEE

(Continued from preceding page)

- We have no quarrel with those who wish to enter this field. However, for your own good, we hope that no one makes a gambling device out of this wonderful game but that everyone will produce a well constructed, high class piece of equipment that will lend credit to the industry and the game.

- However, we have not licensed anyone to manufacture or distribute this game or any similar bowling device. Through the acquisition of the National Skee Ball Company we control the original "Skee Ball" patents and copyrights for the name "Skee Ball" and "Skee Roll". No other manufacturer can rightfully imitate this game and call it "Skee Ball" (Reg. U. S. Pat. Off.) or "Skee Roll" (Reg. U. S. Pat. Off.) either in advertising, correspondence or verbally.

- In acquiring the National Skee Ball Company, we also had another motive—namely to eliminate guesswork and experiment . . . to build the kind of game that experience has taught is essential to the operators' success.

- We learned that unnecessary electrical operation destroys the essentially athletic character of the game. This is why "Skee Ball" is almost entirely mechanical.

- When the player sees his scores mechanically recorded after each ball in white numerals on a black field, he sees it in a form that he is accustomed to seeing scores at baseball games, football games, etc.

- When the player pulls the knob to release the balls—when he bends slightly because our game is made bowling height, he gets the mild exercise which is the basis of this game.

- When the player rolls the balls he wants the alley to feel solid — just as in bowling.

Page FOUR

Wurlitzer's Skee-Ball Brochure, p. 4
(Author's Collection)

FACTS ON BALL
(REG. U. S. PAT. OFF.)
by HOMER E. CAPEHART

This is why "Skee Ball" is built of heavy red oak and weighs 522 lbs.—why we refuse to build a game from light wood that would have a hollow sound and lose much of its play appeal.

- Yet, because we make our own cabinets—are not obliged to buy them from outside plants, we can sell a game that will give you years of fine service for no more than what you would pay for a game built from light wood.

- In building the highest quality of merchandise and selling it at the right price, we are following the same policy that has proven so successful with the Wurlitzer-Simplex Automatic Phonograph.

- It is my belief that Wurlitzer policies and methods will make "Skee Ball" a big, profitable business for everybody . . . that Wurlitzer's "Skee Ball" is a worthy companion to the Wurlitzer-Simplex Automatic Phonograph.

- *Both were the originals.* The Simplex phonograph business was purchased by us from the Simplex Phonograph Company of Chicago—established in 1930—which company introduced the first multi-selective type phonograph. The National Skee Ball company were the pioneers and the originators of the game called "Skee Ball" (Reg. U.S. Pat. Off.).

- Already orders on hand indicate a tremendous demand for the Wurlitzer "Skee Ball"—a demand that promises to tax our production capacity for months to come. So, to insure deliveries when you want them, let me suggest that you wire, write or phone for full particulars without delay.

H. E. Capehart

VICE PRESIDENT, THE RUDOLPH WURLITZER MFG., CO.
NORTH TONAWANDA, NEW YORK

Page FIVE

Wurlitzer's Skee-Ball Brochure, p. 5
(Author's Collection)

Wurlitzer's Skee-Ball Brochure, p. 6
(Author's Collection)

Wurlitzer Skee-Ball Alley on Display at National Premium Co. Omaha, Nebraska
(Courtesy Philadelphia Toboggan Coasters, Inc. Archive)

Vending Company. Smiles indicate they enjoyed planning the big Wurlizer party which was staged in New York December 6. [21]

On December 12, in an article titled, "Genco-Ponser Hookup To Push Bank-Roll Games" in The Billboard, the following was reported:

> *Working closely with [Nat] Cutler and other promotional-minded operators, Genco and its Eastern distributor, George Ponser Company, of Newark, have evolved a series of sales promotional ideas, declaring that Bank-Roll is out of the short-life class, which has been thought to be a necessary evil among coin machines. [22]*

Rock-O-Ball continued to advertise. December 19, a large full-page display ad appeared in The Billboard for Rock-Ola's Rock-O-Ball and Tom the Mix Radio Rifle. [23]

In the end, Wurlitzer's commitment seemed to have paid off in the big picture of maintaining Skee-Ball's reputation in the market. The low cost clones were lower quality, and could not keep up with the elegance and prestige of Wurlitzer's product. Although there is no evidence that any of the clones achieved the popularity and recognition of Skee-Ball, some clones remained popular for years with the lower end of the market.

After the patents, trademarks and all manufacturing and sales rights were sold to Wurlitzer, Maurice Piesen officially changed the name of the National Skee-Ball Company to Piesen Manufacturing Company, Inc. on October 30, 1937. [24] Piesen continued to operate his manufacturing facility under the new name, Piesen Mfg. Co. but it is unclear whether Piesen ever brought another product to market, and it appears that he may have continued to operate it solely as a vehicle to receive the royalty payments. This was to prove somewhat problematic years later.

Even as they rolled out their newly refined product, Wurlitzer found that all was not as uncomplicated as they would have liked. As they began to sell their machines, another legal matter reared its head in the form of potential patent infringement. The Wurlitzer machines continued to use a scoring device largely inherited from earlier alleys, with an internal count of the number of games played, external display of each 9-ball game score for each player, and a "high score" device that recorded the highest score reached by any player on that particular alley, and continued to do so until reset.

Wurlitzer's manager of patent and trademark matters, Mr. Hokanson, was contacted by representatives of a new patent-holder, who alleged infringement of its recently patented high score feature on it's "Game Totalizer." This was the Durant patent, submitted in 1933 and granted September 15, 1936. [25] The mechanism for the Skee-Ball scoring device operated on a different mechanical principle from the Durant patent, by means of movement of levers triggered by the ball passing through an opening in a target. Durant's mechanism was originally designed for pinball games, and used a channel at different levels that would turn a helical rib a certain distance, depending on how high on the rib the ball started. There was clearly no infringement there.

However, according to the patent attorneys that Wurlitzer requested visited the displayed Skee-Ball alley at an exhibition in Chicago, the attorneys found that the description of the maximum scoring device was more problematic. In a letter written on January 11, 1937 to The Rudolph Wurlitzer Company from the law office of Dyrenforth, Lee, Chritton & Wiles, they quoted four items from the Durant patent. They wrote:

> *Claim 3, however, is quite broadly drawn to cover an indicating device and a maximum score indicator operable thereby. The indicating device is the dial showing the score for one round of balls. The claim, however, specifically includes the following four elements:*
>
> *A, "Means operated by the balls in amounts determined by the hole through which the ball is passed." (The shaft and helical rib)*
>
> *B, "An indicating device registering the totality of said amounts of operation and operated by said means." (The total score indicator 85 for one round of balls)*
>
> *C, "Means for resetting said indicating device."*
>
> *D, "A maximum score indicator operable by said indicating device whenever said latter device is registering scores higher than those previously made, said maximum score indicator being unaffected by said resetting mechanism."*
>
> *If the claim is given a broad construction it is infringed by your apparatus.* [26]

Although they thought it was doubtful that this broad construction interpretation would necessarily hold up if challenged, it was unclear what that challenge might entail in time and effort, and what the consequences might be if Wurlitzer did not prevail.

Thus, non-exclusive licensing agreement seemed a more prudent course of action, through Durant's representative Kenneth

Shyvers. Another royalty agreement was drafted:

> THIS AGREEMENT, entered into this 10th day of May, 1937, by and between KENNETH C. SHYVERS of Chicago, Illinois, LYNDON A. DURANT of Springfield, Massachusetts, and GEORGE H. CAMPBELL of Agawam, Massachusetts, hereinafter jointly referred to as "LICENSORS" and THE RUDOLPH WURLITZER COMPANY, a corporation of the State of Ohio, having a manufactory or plant at North Tonawanda, New York, hereinafter called "LICENSEE", WITNESSETH THAT:
>
> WHEREAS, LICENSORS warrant that they are the sole and exclusive owners of the entire right, title and interest in and to Letters Patent of the United States issued to said DURANT and said CAMPBELL jointly on the 15th day of September 1936, No. 2,054,616, for a Game Totalizer, hereinafter called "Game Device" or "Devices"; AND
>
> WHEREAS, The Rudolph Wurlitzer Company, LICENSEE, is desirous of acquiring a non-exclusive license to manufacture and sell Game Devices under and in accordance with said Letters Patent No. 2,054,616, for the full remaining term thereof throughout the United States and its possessions, including foreign countries, on the following terms:
>
> 1. LICENSEE agrees to pay LICENSORS, as royalty, One Dollar ($1.00) for each Game Device manufactured and sold. Checks to be made payable to all three licensors jointly.
>
> 2. It is agreed that royalties shall be paid hereunder monthly, the royalty being payable on or before the 20th day of each month covering all Game Devices manufactured and sold during the preceding calendar month, said royalty to be accompanied by a statement of the LICENSEE setting forth the total number of devices manufactured and sold during the preceding month upon which royalty is paid.
>
> 3. Upon the execution of this agreement, LICENSEE agrees to pay LICENSOR the royalty covering devices sold between January 1, 1937, and March 20, 1937, such payment is to be accompanied by a statement of the total number of devices sold during such period.
>
> 4. LICENSORS agrees [sic] to deliver LICENSEE, upon the execution of this agreement, a sample of the device embodying

a score totalizer and indicator and drawings showing its adaptation to the Skee Ball Game as manufactured by LICENSEE.

5. It is further agreed that LICENSEE may cancel this license upon giving LICENSORS thirty (30) days written notice of its intention by addressing such notice to the address of said Kenneth C. Shyvers, complying with all provisions hereof and payments hereunder up until the time of such termination; and LICENSORS may cancel this license in event LICENSEE violates any of the provisions hereof upon LICENSORS giving thirty (30) days notice of such violation to the LICENSEE, provided that within said thirty-day period said violation is not fully remedied.

IN WITNESS WHEREOF, the parties hereto have set their hands and seals on the day and year first above written.

s/ Kenneth C. Shyvers
s/ Lyndon A. Durant
s/ George H. Campbell
THE RUDOLPH WURLITZER COMPANY

by /s/ Farny R. Wurlitzer, Pres. [27]

Immediately after they redesigned the alleys, Wurlitzer stepped up production on their production line more than 500%, and flooded the market. They ceased production at the end of 1937. It would be the last time that Skee-Ball alleys were ever produced on an assembly line. [28] Wurlitzer continued to sell their beautiful and refined Skee-Ball alleys all the way up through World War II. Like all of the other major amusement manufacturing companies in the United States, the Wurlitzer Corporation stopped manufacturing amusements and dedicated their manufacturing capacity to support the war effort between 1942 and 1945. As the war continued, Homer Capehart left the company to begin serving as a United States Senator in 1944.

When the Wurlitzer Manufacturing Company restarted normal operations after World War II, the remaining corporate officers took stock of their future.

Clearly, Skee-Ball was not in the class of commodities appropriate for mass production, nor could it even match the volume of jukebox sales. There were orders of magnitude more restaurants and social venues than amusement venues, even if the venues were running multiple Skee-Ball alleys. With their high volume manufacturing and assembly capability, Wurlitzer had rapidly manufactured over 5,000 units in the first year or so of operation. [29]

It was not until 1945 that they sold out most of their stock, 5,022 units—an average of about 600 units per year. [30] As a result, they realized that Skee-Ball Alleys might not fit their business and manufacturing model as well as they had hoped. There was less overlap than expected in the markets they served, and they had lost their appetite to bring more games into the mix. They apparently did not conceal their interest in divesting themselves of the manufacturing.

They were not the only ones taking stock of their direction after finishing their wartime manufacturing commitment. So was another company, with a history of engagement with Skee-Ball, albeit in the distant past: The Philadelphia Toboggan Company.

THIS AGREEMENT, entered into this 10th day of May, 1937, by and between KENNETH C. SHYVERS of Chicago, Illinois, LYNDON A. DURANT of Springfield, Massachusetts, and GEORGE H. CAMPBELL of Agawam, Massachusetts, hereinafter jointly referred to as "LICENSORS" and THE RUDOLPH WURLITZER COMPANY, a corporation of the State of Ohio, having a manufactory or plant at North Tonawanda, New York, hereinafter called "LICENSEE", WITNESSETH THAT:

WHEREAS, LICENSORS warrant that they are the sole and exclusive owners of the entire right, title and interest in and to Letters Patent of the United States issued to said DURANT and said CAMPBELL jointly on the 15th day of September, 1936, No. 2,054,616, for a Game Totalizer, hereinafter called "Game Device" or "Devices"; AND

WHEREAS, The Rudolph Wurlitzer Company, LICENSEE, is desirous of acquiring a non-exclusive license to manufacture and sell devices under the aforesaid patent;

NOW THEREFORE, in consideration of One Dollar ($1.00) and other valuable consideration, the receipt whereof is hereby acknowledged, LICENSORS hereby grant to the said LICENSEE a non-exclusive license to manufacture and sell Game Devices under and in accordance with said Letters Patent No. 2,054,616, for the full remaining term thereof throughout the United States and its possessions, including foreign countries, on the following terms:

1. LICENSEE agrees to pay LICENSORS, as royalty, One Dollar ($1.00) for each Game Device manufactured and sold. Checks to be made payable to all three licensors jointly.

- 1 -

Non-exclusive agreement between Kenneth Shyvers, Lyndon Durant, and George C. Campbell and The Rudolph Wurlitzer Co., p. 1.
(Courtesy Philadelphia Toboggan Coasters, Inc. Archive)

2. It is agreed that royalties shall be paid hereunder monthly, the royalty being payable on or before the 20th day of each month covering all Game Devices manufactured and sold during the preceding calendar month, said royalty to be accompanied by a statement of the LICENSEE setting forth the total number of devices manufactured and sold during the preceding month upon which royalty is paid.

3. Upon the execution of this agreement, LICENSEE agrees to pay LICENSOR the royalty covering devices sold between January 1, 1937, and March 20, 1937, such payment to be accompanied by a statement of the total number of devices sold during such period.

4. LICENSORS agrees to deliver to LICENSEE, upon the execution of this agreement, a sample of the device embodying a score totalizer and indicator and drawings showing its adaptation to the Skee Ball Game as manufactured by LICENSEE.

5. It is further agreed that LICENSEE may cancel this license upon giving LICENSORS thirty (30) days written notice of its intention by addressing such notice to the address of said Kenneth C. Shyvers, complying with all provisions hereof and payments hereunder up until the time of such termination; and LICENSORS may cancel this license in event LICENSEE violates any of the provisions hereof upon LICENSORS giving thirty (30) days notice of such violation to the LICENSEE, provided that within said thirty-day period said violation is not fully remedied.

IN WITNESS WHEREOF, the parties hereto have

Non-exclusive agreement between Kenneth Shyvers, Lyndon Durant, and George C. Campbell and The Rudolph Wurlitzer Co., p. 2.
(Courtesy Philadelphia Toboggan Coasters, Inc. Archive)

set their hands and seals on the day and year first above written.

/s/ Kenneth C. Shyvers
/s/ Lyndon A. Durant
/s/ George H. Campbell

THE RUDOLPH WURLITZER COMPANY

By /s/ Farny R. Wurlitzer, Pres.

State of Illinois :
        SS
County of Cook :

   On this 3 day of May, 1937, before me personally came Kenneth C. Shyvers, to me personally known to be the person described in and who executed the foregoing instrument and acknowledged to me that he executed the same.

/s/ Geo. W. Heich
Notary Public.

(My Commission Expires Nov. 17, 1937)

State of Illinois :
        SS
County of Cook :

   On this 19 day of April, 1937, before me personally came Lyndon A. Durant, to me personally known to be the person described in and who executed the foregoing instrument and acknowledged to me that he executed the same.

/s/ Erwin H. Maack
Notary Public

My commission expires Oct. 13, 1940.

- 3 -

Non-exclusive agreement between Kenneth Shyvers, Lyndon Durant, and George C. Campbell and The Rudolph Wurlitzer Co., p. 3.
(Courtesy Philadelphia Toboggan Coasters, Inc. Archive)

State of Massachusetts :
                            SS
County of Hampden   :

On this 28th day of April, 1937, before me personally came George H. Campbell, to me personally known to be the person described in and who executed the foregoing instrument and acknowledged to me that he executed the same.

/s/ William Pauly
Notary Public

My Commission Expires Nov. 12, 1937

State of New York :
                        SS
County of Niagara :

On this 10th day of May, 1937, before me personally came Farny R. Wurlitzer, to me personally known to be the person described in and who executed the foregoing instrument and acknowledged to me that he executed the same.

/s/ W. A. Waterstrat
Notary Public.

W. A. Waterstrat
Notary Public In and For Erie County
Certificate Filed in Niagara County

— 4 —

Non-exclusive agreement between Kenneth Shyvers, Lyndon Durant, and George C. Campbell and The Rudolph Wurlitzer Co., p. 4.
(Courtesy Philadelphia Toboggan Coasters, Inc. Archive)

Chapter 15

FULL CIRCLE
The Philadelphia Toboggan Company

This is a fascinating, and somewhat ironic turn of events that brought at least one aspect of Skee-Ball's saga full circle. The original owner of the Philadelphia Toboggan Company, Henry Auchy, gave Skee-Ball an important start back in 1911, but originally passed on buying the rights and manufacturing it. It's entirely unclear whether the company realized the historical connection at the time they purchased it from Wurlitzer.

By then, Samuel High Jr. owned the controlling interest in the company. His father, Samuel High Sr. was originally the corporate attorney for Philadelphia Toboggan Company. For his work, he had taken company stock in lieu of payment. Between 1902 and 1930, he gradually acquired all the stock in the company, completing his ownership after founder Henry Auchy passed away in 1922. [1]

By 1930, Samuel High Sr. owned all of the stock in Philadelphia Toboggan Company. In the years after he passed away, his son, Sam High Jr., shared the stock with his two sisters after one was widowed, and the other divorced. After their deaths, they passed the stock on to their sons who were also lawyers, and to a daughter, keeping control of the company firmly in the family. [2] The Philadelphia Toboggan Company continued to manufacture and market elaborately carved carousels, coaster cars, as well as the newer "bumper cars" and outdoor furniture such as bench seating to amusement parks all over the country.

As World War II drew to a close, Clarence M. Gerhart, the Assistant Secretary and the manager of patents and trademarks at Philadelphia Toboggan Company, wrote to the General Manager of the North Tonawanda Manufacturing facility of The Rudolph Wurlitzer Company. Gerhart had operated Skee-Ball Alleys in amusement facilities before he joined the Philadelphia Toboggan Company, and knew how lucrative they could be to operate. With some excess manufacturing capacity that Philadelphia Toboggan Company had developed to support the war effort, he thought adding Skee-Ball manufacturing would be a great fit—swell, in fact.

August 7, 1945

Rudolph Wurlitzer Manufacturing Co., North Tonawanda, New York

Attention: Mr. Michael Hammergren
          General Manager

Gentlemen:

During the past three years our plant was engaged in war work, principally Naval Aircraft parts and assemblies. Our present contracts will probably be completed within the next month or two, consequently we have been seriously studying our post war reconversion problems, having in mind particularly, the utilization of our additional production facilities.

Having been an operator of Skee Ball Alleys at several Amusement Parks with satisfactory and profitable results, brought to our mind the fact that this is an item that would fit in swell with our present production facilities, and we are confident a desirable market exists for a limited quantity of Skee Ball Alleys.

The purpose of this letter therefore is to inquire as to the plans of the Wurlitzer Company in the manufacture of Skee Ball Alleys, and as indicated herein, we are sincerely interested in manufacturing Skee Ball Alleys providing some satisfactory arrangement with your company can be made, extending us such privilege.

Would appreciate the opportunity to come to your office to discuss the matter in person, in the event that there is a possibility of our obtaining your permission to continue the manufacture of Skee Ball Alleys.

Awaiting your kind and prompt reply, we remain,

Respectfully,

PHILADELPHIA TOBOGGAN COMPANY,

C. M. Gerhart, Assistant Secretary [3]

This letter got things off to a rather slow start, and little happened for almost three months. But by November 1, 1945, Gerhart had his answer.

WURLITZER

THE RUDOLPH WURLITZER COMPANY

NORTH TONAWANDA, N.Y.

August 7, 1945

Rudolph Wurlitzer Manufacturing Co.,
North Tonawanda, New York

Attention: Mr. Michael Hammergren,
General Manager

Gentlemen:

During the past three years our plant was engaged in war work, principally Naval Aircraft parts and assemblies. Our present contracts will probably be completed within the next month or two, consequently we have been seriously studying our post war reconversion problems, having in mind particularly, the utilization of our additional production facilities.

Having been an operator of Skee Ball Alleys at several Amusement Parks with satisfactory and profitable results, brought to our mind the fact that this is an item that would fit in swell with our present production facilities, and we are confident a desirable market exists for a limited quantity of Skee Ball Alleys.

The purpose of this letter therefore is to inquire as to the plans of the Wurlitzer Company in the manufacture of Skee Ball Alleys, and as indicated herein, we are sincerely interested in manufacturing Skee Ball Alleys providing some satisfactory arrangement with your company can be made, extending us such privilege.

Would appreciate the opportunity to come to your office to discuss the matter in person, in event there is a possibility of our obtaining your permission to continue the manufacture of Skee Ball Alleys.

Awaiting your kind and prompt reply, we remain,

Respectfully,

PHILADELPHIA TOBOGGAN COMPANY,

CMG:ecm   C. M. Gerhart, Assistant Secretary.

Letter from the Philadelphia Toboggan Company to the Rudolph Wurlitzer Manufacturing Co., August 7, 1945.
(Courtesy Philadelphia Toboggan Coasters, Inc. Archive)

November 1, 1945

Mr. C. M. Gerhart, Assistant Secretary

Philadelphia Toboggan Company
130 E. Duval Street

Germantown, Philadelphia 44, Pa.

Dear Mr. Gerhart:

With reference to your letter of August 7th to Mr. Hammergren concerning the availability of "Skee Ball" patents, drawings, trade marks, etc., I am enclosing herewith a copy of the agreement which was executed by and between our Company and National Skee Ball Company, Inc., on June 19, 1936. This document speaks for itself, but its principal contents and effect can be summarized briefly as follows:

1. National Skee Ball Co., Inc. transferred to Wurlitzer all of National's patent and trade mark rights relating to the Skee Ball business together with some tools and engineering data and the right to use the word "National" in connection with the Skee Balls, Skee Rolls and Alleys to be manufactured.

2. United States Patent No. 2,010,213 issued August 6, 1935, Belgium Patent No. 411,685 issued November 30, 1935, and United States Trade Mark Registration for the mark "Skee Ball", No 256,496 issued May 21, 1929, were formally assigned to Wurlitzer as an incident of the foregoing agreement.

3. Wurlitzer paid National Skee Ball the sum of $5,000.00 and agreed to pay royalties on each Skee Ball, Skee Roll or Alley, embodying any of the features of the patents, or sold under the trade name or names "Skee Ball, Skee Roll, or Skee Ball Alley", of $10.00 each on the first 3,000 units, $7.00 each on the next 7,000 units and $5.00 each on all units above 10,000 until a total sum of $200,000 in royalties should have been paid, when the obligation to pay royalties would cease.

4. At the present, Wurlitzer is in a position to assign its rights under the agreement of June 19, 1936, and to transfer by formal assignment, without warranties, our interest in the two patents above referred to, and in the trade-names and trade mark registration. I believe that we have also some drawings or engineering data which could be turned over to a prospective purchaser of our rights.

The purchaser, of course, must obligate himself to pay the royalties reserved under this agreement and in such event we would get from National Skee Ball Company a consent to the assumption of these obligations by the purchaser and a release of our Company.

I believe that the royalties at the present time are on a $7.00 per unit basis. [ed. there is a handwritten note to the side which reads: Payable to Piesen Mfg Co.

It is possible that an arrangement might be made between Wurlitzer and a prospective manufacturer of Skee Ball by working out a licensing arrangement whereby we would permit the manufacturer to use all patent rights, trade marks, trade names, etc., upon the payment to our Company of agreed royalties. Under this arrangement, our Company would, of course, pay the royalties stipulated by the agreement dated June 19, 1936 to National Skee Ball Co., Inc.

In the event that you are interested in acquiring all of the rights under the agreement with National Skee Ball Co., Inc., or a license agreement from Wurlitzer, we will be glad to consider any proposition which might be offered. Perhaps it would be advantageous to arrange for a meeting at North Tonawanda in order to go into further details. Would appreciate hearing from you as soon as possible.

The above is subject to prior sale.

Thanking you for your interest, I am

Very truly yours,

THE RUDOLPH WURLITZER COMPANY

*O. A. Hokanson, Manager
Patents and New Products Department
North Tonawanda Division [4]*

A week later, Gerhart replied with thanks, and a promise to submit their proposal, and the royalty agreement with Piesen Manufacturing Company to the Executive Committee of Philadelphia Toboggan Company for their approval in principle on November 14. In the meantime, he obtained copies of the original three patents: Simpson's 1908 patent for the game; the Este/Doebrich patent for the scoring device; and the Bergoffen patent for the ball-vending mechanism. In addition they obtained the terms and timing for renewal of the Skee-Ball and Skee-Roll trademarks. [5]

Suddenly, matters heated up on the Wurlitzer side. Handwritten notes on Clarence M. Gerhart's "From the desk of—" stationery of a phone conversation on November 9, 1945 read:

11/9/45 - Mr Hammergren telephoned from Buffalo at the request of Mr Johnson

THE RUDOLPH WURLITZER COMPANY

NORTH TONAWANDA, N.Y.

November 1, 1945

Mr. C. M. Gerhart, Assistant Secretary
Philadelphia Toboggan Company
130 E. Duval Street
Germantown, Philadelphia 44, Pa.

Dear Mr. Gerhart:

With reference to your letter of August 7th to Mr. Hammergren concerning the availability of "Skee Ball" patents, drawings, trade marks, etc., I am enclosing herewith a copy of the agreement which was executed by and between our Company and National Skee Ball Company, Inc., on June 19, 1936. This document speaks for itself, but its principal contents and effect can be summarized briefly as follows:

1. National Skee Ball Co., Inc. transferred to Wurlitzer all of National's patent and trade mark rights relating to the Skee Ball business together with some tools and engineering data and the right to use the word "National" in connection with the Skee Balls, Skee Rolls and Alleys to be manufactured.

2. United States Patent No. 2,010,213 issued August 6, 1935, Belgium Patent No. 411,685 issued November 30, 1935, and United States Trade Mark Registration for the mark "Skee Ball", No. 256,496 issued May 21, 1929, were formally assigned to Wurlitzer as an incident of the foregoing agreement.

3. Wurlitzer paid National Skee Ball the sum of $5,000.00 and agreed to pay royalties on each Skee Ball, Skee Roll or Alley, embodying any of the features of the patents, or sold under the trade name or names "Skee Ball, Skee Roll, or Skee Ball Alley", of $10.00 each on the first 3,000 units, $7.00 each on the next 7,000 units and $5.00 each on all units above 10,000 until a total sum of $200,000.00 in royalties should have been paid, when the obligation to pay royalties would cease.

At the present, Wurlitzer is in a position to assign its rights under the agreement of June 19, 1936, and to transfer by formal assignment, without warranties, our interest in the two patents above referred to, and in the trade-names and trade mark registration. I believe that we have also some drawings or engineering data which could be turned over to a prospective purchaser of our rights.

Letter from Rudolph Wurlitzer Company to Philadelphia Toboggan Company, November 1, 1945, p. 1.
(Courtesy Philadelphia Toboggan Coasters, Inc. Archive)

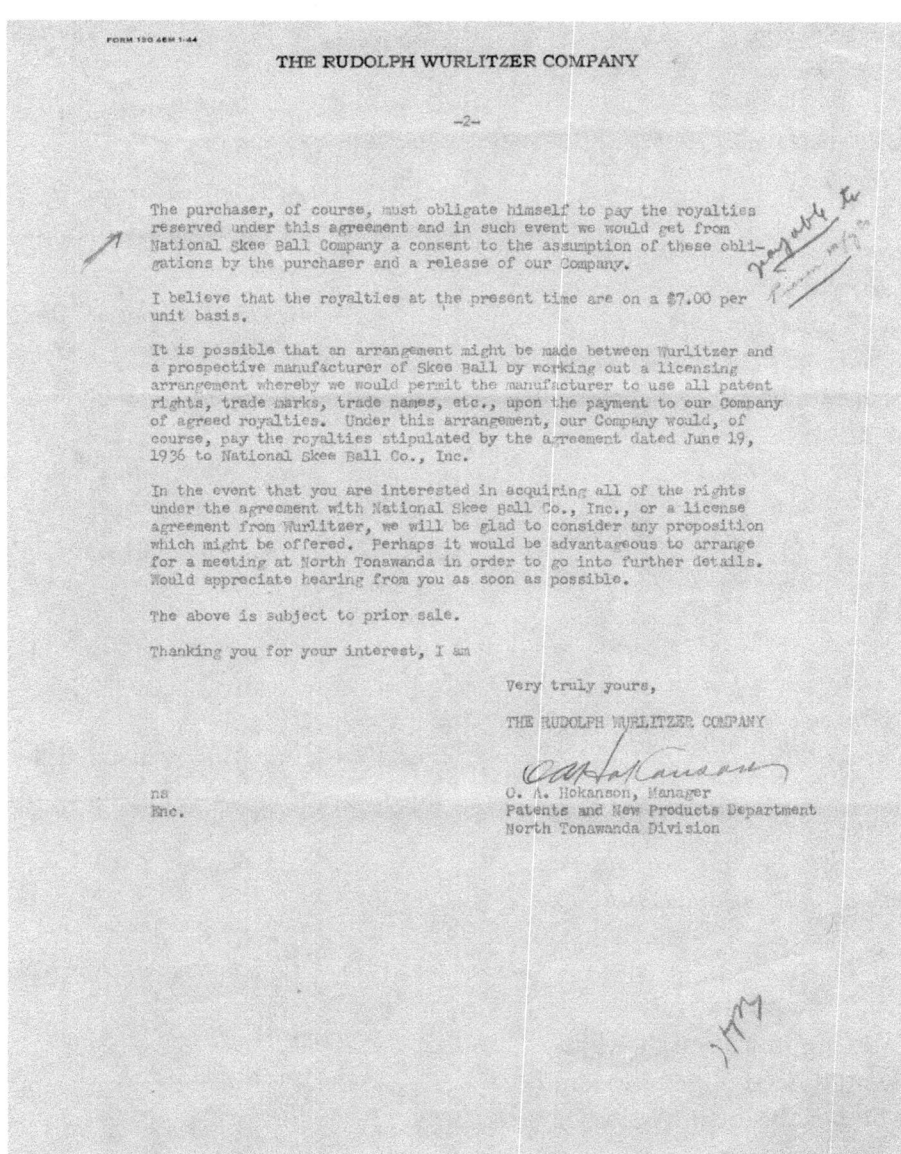

Letter from Rudolph Wurlitzer Company to Philadelphia Toboggan Company, November 1, 1945, p. 2.
(Courtesy Philadelphia Toboggan Coasters, Inc. Archive)

their Vice Pres to inform us relative to our letter dated Nov 7th that they have two proposals from other manufacturers being submitted one on Monday 11/12 and another on Tuesday 11/13 -

Wurlitzer wants $5000 - cash for all privileges such as more extended to them in the National Skee Ball company content[?] - the royalty is now $7.00 per alley payable to the National Skee Ball Co — whoever now controls such company?

They are telephoning us as a matter of courtesy - because I indicated in my letter that our executive committee doesn't meet until next Wednesday 11/14

Its a matter of first come first served with them on the sale of their rights and privileges for $5,000 cash.

We would manufacture and sell the Skee Ball alleys ourselves - Wurlitzer would have no further interest in the distribution or sale. [6]

What followed was a scramble for information—and identification of what questions they would need to get answered to determine whether this deal would be workable.

- *Are there any riders attached to the contract?*
- *Term of years, commissions, territory involved?*
- *Did Wurlitzer obligate itself to any number of sales or distribution agreement?*
- *Were there any patent infringements by other manufacturers, and did Wurlitzer make an effort to restrain their manufacture?*
- *Does the royalty (to Piesen Mfg) apply only to the target? (no!) and*
- *How much has Wurlitzer already paid? [7]*

In a flurry of phone calls, one by one, the questions got answered.

Finally, the meeting was scheduled for November 19, and confirmed with a telegram:

> *Mr. C. M. Gerhart*
>
> *Our Mr. King will pick you up - Statler Hotel, Buffalo 9 A.M., November 19.*
>
> *Rudolph Wurlitzer Company North Tonawanda, N.Y.*
>
> *C. E. Johnson*
>
> *Received: 11:40 A. M. [8]*

Wurlitzer:
Buffalo Office
Cleveland 4072
North Tonawanda 2500

Mr Johnson
Russell
7617
Buffalo
[illegible]

From the desk of—
CLARENCE M. GERHART

11/9/45 – Mr Hammergren telephoned from Buffalo at the request of Mr Johnson their Vice Pres. to inform us relative to our letter dated Nov 7th that they have two proposals from other manufacturers being submitted one on Monday 11/12 and another on Tuesday 11/13 –

Wurlitzer wants $5000 – cash for all privileges such as were extended to them in the National Skee Ball company contract – the royalty is now $7.00 per alley

payable to the National Skee Ball Co – whoever now controls such company?

They are telephoning us as a matter of courtesy – because I indicated in my letter that our executive committee doesn't meet until next Wednesday 11/14

It's a matter of first come first served with them on the sale of their rights & privileges for $5,000 – cash.

We would manufacture and sell the Skee Ball alleys ourselves – Wurlitzer would have no further interest in the distribution or sale

Notes from Clarence M. Gerhart.
(Courtesy Philadelphia Toboggan Coasters, Inc. Archive)

Wurlitzer had a letter of agreement ready, with four points of agreement. They would:

1. Assign patents and trademarks;
2. Assign remaining rights from National Skee-Ball Company;
3. Pay $5,000 from Philadelphia Toboggan Company to Wurlitzer;
4. Get consent of National Skee Ball Company to assume royalty responsibilities.

Gerhart took it back and added four more stipulations.

First, Wurlitzer must assure Philadelphia Toboggan Company that no addition patents had been filed on either Skee Roll or Skee Ball, none were pending, and if any did surface, they would automatically be assigned to Philadelphia Toboggan Company. Second, Wurlitzer would provide all customer names, addresses and purchase information for the 5022 alleys sold, and provide proof of royalty payments. Third, Philadelphia Toboggan Company would be allowed a similar royalty deal with Shyvers and the Durant patent, paying no more than Wurlitzer was paying per unit. And fourth, after the sale was closed, Wurlitzer would advertise the sale in The Billboard and give notice that all violators on infringements of patents or trademarks would be prosecuted according to law—and that Wurlitzer would assist in doing so. [9, 10]

In the end, Wurlitzer agreed to furnish a list of customers and what they bought for the 5022 units they sold, plus proof of payment of royalties. They also freely acknowledged that there were no applications or patents pending, and if there were, they would be assigned to Philadelphia Toboggan Company. However, they would not advertise for them in Billboard and issue notices with references to patents they no longer owned. They also pointed out that Philadelphia Toboggan Company must negotiate their own non-exclusive rights for the Shyvers (Durant) patent.

After a few more rounds of correspondence to smooth out the details, they reached a meeting of minds by November 27, and finalized the agreement. [11]

On December 6, 1945 C. M. Gerhart wrote a letter to Carl E. Johnson. The text of the letter read:

December 6, 1945

Mr. Carl E. Johnson Vice President

The Rudolph Wurlitzer Company
North Tonawanda, New York

Dear Mr. Johnson:

In compliance with your letter of November 29th we now enclose herewith three copies of the three party agreement, between your company, our company, and Piesen Manufacturing Company, having executed all copies on our part.

After you execute these agreements on your part and also obtain the execution by the Piesen Manufacturing Company, kindly let us know and I suggest that in order to conclude the sale, I will come up to your office with a certified check for $5,000.00 and upon surrender of the check you will furnish me with the executed legal instruments involved in this sale, together with plans, blueprints, bills of material and list of customers to whom you sold Skee Ball or Skee Roll alleys, all as referred to and agreed in your formal letter dated November 29th.

Kindly give this matter your prompt attention as we think it very urgent to conclude the sale as soon as possible so as to give us an opportunity to publicly announce our purchase and advertise same in the New Year's issue of the Billboard.

With best wishes, we remain,

Very truly yours,

PHILADELPHIA TOBOGGAN COMPANY,

C. M. Gerhart, Ass't. Secretary.

CMG:ecm

encls.(3) [12]

But the enclosures didn't make it into the mail until Sam High signed off the next day, causing some consternation. On December 7, Carl E. Johnson wrote to C. M. Gerhart. The text of the letter read:

December 7, 1945

Mr. C. M. Gerhart, Ass't. Secretary

Philadelphia Toboggan Company
130 E. Duval St.
Germantown, Philadelphia 44, Pa.

Dear Mr. Gerhart:

I wish to acknowledge your letter of December 3, 1945, enclosing extra copy of our letter dated November 29th, 1945, signed by your President Mr. J. R. Davies as of December 1st, 1945.

As soon as you return to us the three copies of the three party agreement between *your Company, our Company and Piesen Manufacturing Company, properly executed, we will, in turn, execute them and send them to Piesen Manufacturing for final execution.*

We will then be in position to complete the transaction.

Very truly yours,

THE RUDOLPH WURLITZER COMPANY

Carl E. Johnson
Vice President and Manager
North Tonawanda Division [13]

A handwritten note on right side of the letter read: "showed these copies to Sam High and mailed them on 12/6/45 HPS"

After the agreement phase was completed, Wurlitzer launched a final goodwill sendoff to The Philadelphia Toboggan Company, as the new owners were about to begin their manufacturing effort. It had been eight years since the last Skee Ball alley rolled off the Wurlitzer manufacturing floor in 1937. They forwarded the first indication of interest from a new customer.

Philadelphia Toboggan Company
150 E. Duval St.
Germantown, Philadelphia, Pa.

Gentlemen:

We are enclosing an inquiry received at this office from the American Bowling & Billiards Corporation, regarding Skee Ball.

Very truly yours,

THE RUDOLPH WURLITZER COMPANY

Carl E Johnson
Vice President and General Manager
North Tonawanda Division [14]

Subsequently, the correspondence between the two companies took on a more relaxed tone, as in this letter from Gerhart to Johnson.

The Rudolph Wurlitzer Company
North Tonawanda, New York
Attention: Mr. Carl E. Johnson, Vice President and Manager

Dear Mr. Johnson:

First of all, I want to thank you for mailing us, under date of December 19th, an inquiry your office received from the American Bowling & Billiards Corporation regarding our Skee Ball machines. We have written them direct from our office and informed them we were planning to start production as soon as we are able to obtain all of the materials required.

Your Mr. Hokanson telephoned me the other day and informed me that he received the executed agreement from Piesen Manufacturing Company, and that everything was ready to conclude the sale. I informed Mr. Hokanson that our patent attorney was preparing an advertisement to be inserted in the "Billboard". As soon as he has prepared it, I will bring a certified check for $5,000.00. I am now planning to obtain reservations to come up there some time during the second week in January.

Extending our sincere greetings for a Happy and Prosperous New Year, we remain

Yours very truly,

Philadelphia Toboggan Company,
C. M. Gerhart, Sales Manager. [15]

A whole series of legal documents followed to complete the assignments of trademarks, patents, and fulfillment of other transferred materials and documentation. These were painstakingly detailed and fully notarized, including a three-page long agreement for the assumption of royalties owed to what was now Piesen Manufacturing, reflecting the name change applied to National Skee-Ball Company Inc. in 1937. In the end, the two patents had been transferred, both the U.S. and Belgium patents on Bergoffen's ball release mechanism, along with the two United States Trade Mark Registrations, one for the mark "Skee Ball" (No. 256,496 issued May 21, 1929) and the other for the mark "Skee Roll", (No. 304,883 issued July 18, 1933). In addition, the agreement with Shyver had been executed for a $1 per unit royalty, with a minimum annual $250 payment; and Piesen Manufacturing had agreed to assign the royalty agreement to Philadelphia Toboggan Company. The latter required a complicated, three-way contract agreement. Finally, by January 16, 1946, all assignments had been executed, physical assets transferred, and the sale had been completed.

Then followed almost twenty-two months of preparation but no sales for the Philadelphia Toboggan Company, Inc.

Finally, in November of 1947, the 50th Street Amusement Center in New York City placed an order for 10 alleys. [16] At that point, almost belatedly, someone at The Philadelphia Toboggan Company remembered that they owed royalties to Piesen Manufacturing. They pulled the agreement signed almost two years before to determine to whom to make the check, and where to send the payment.

A. R. Ridyard, Office Manager sent identical letters to Maurice Piesen, Hugo Piesen and Julian Bergoffen on November 19, 1947. The text of those letters read:

> *We have analized[sic] the conditions of the Skee Ball and Skee Roll arrangement and sale between the National Skee Ball Company and the Wurlitzer Company, and in turn the Wurlitzer Company sale to Philadelphia Toboggan Company.*
>
> *We want to be sure that we are going to make the payment of royalties of $7.00 per alley to the proper person and we would appreciate an answer promptly to this letter as to whom in your opinion and understanding is to be the receiver of the said royalties.*
>
> *We would appreciate a prompt reply.*
>
> Very truly yours,
>
> PHILADELPHIA TOBOGGAN COMPANY
>
> A. R. Ridyard, Office Manager [17, 18, 19]

Since the contract required payment on the 20th of every month, the checks were cut and mailed before those letters could even arrive at their destinations in New York. [20] This probably caught Maurice Piesen and Julian Bergoffen off-guard, since they had not received royalties in a number of years. Hugo Piesen had passed away in 1942 [21], and it was unclear whether Piesen Manufacturing Company, Inc., was operating with a legal number of directors.

There followed a flurry of activity of phone calls and letters exchanged over the next several months.

Julian Bergoffen wrote back, directing Philadelphia Toboggan Company that "checks for the Skee Ball royalties should be made to the order of Maurice A. Peisen[sic] and Julian I. Bergoffen, attornies." [22] Maurice Piesen and Julian Bergoffen had gone into law practice together in the intervening years. H. P. Schmeck, general manager of Philadelphia Toboggan Company determined that Bergoffen did not have the standing to make that change, according to the contract.

Schmeck replied to Maurice Piesen:

> *January 20, 1948*
>
> *Mr. Maurice Peisen[sic]*
> *Peisen[sic] Mfg. Company*
> *291 Broadway*
> *New York, N. Y.*
>
> *Dear Mr. Peisen[sic]:*
>
> *Sometime ago we had a telephone*

November 19, 1947

Mr. Hugo H. Piesen
Piesen Mfg. Company
291 Broadway
New York, N. Y.

Dear Mr. Piesen:

We have analized the conditions of the Skee Ball and Skee Roll arrangement and sale between the National Skee Ball Company and the Wurlitzer Company, and in turn the Wurlitzer Company sale to Philadelphia Toboggan Company.

We want to be sure that we are going to make the payment of roaylties of $7.00 per alley to the proper person and we would appreciate an answer promptly to this letter as to whom in your opinion and understanding is to be the receiver of the said royalties.

We would appreciate a prompt reply.

Very truly yours,

PHILADELPHIA TOBOGGAN COMPANY

A. R. Eidyard, Office Manager

arr/jd

Letter from Philadelphia Toboggan Company to Hugo H. Piesen, November 19, 1947.
(Courtesy Philadelphia Toboggan Coasters, Inc. Archive)

conversation as to whom the checks for royalties for the Skee Ball Alleys were to be made to in the future. You at that time were to notify us whether they should be paid to the payees as under the contract or whether through a meeting of the payees and proper authorization to us from all of them, to pay some other designated person or persons. This was your suggestion as under the conditions existing now you are compelled to keep alive the National Skee Ball Company. I believe this is the sum and substance of our conversation.

The letter of November 24th from Mr. Julian I Bergoffen is not according to contract and as such we regret not acceptable as authorization.

We at present have only ten more alleys to pay the royalty on but will, right after the 1st of the month be shipping quite a few of them I hope, so if you can give us the proper authorization we will be pleased to work along with you, but such authorization should be of such character that our attorney will be free to pass upon it and approve it. Otherwise, we will have to continue paying as before.

Upon receipt of proper authorization, we will make payment on the ten alleys shipped to Asbury Park last month.

Very truly yours,

PHILADELPHIA TOBOGGAN COMPANY

H. P. Schmeck, General Manager [23]

Maurice Piesen telephoned Schmeck on January 29, 1948 to discuss the issue, and followed up with a letter on Piesen Manufacturing Company letterhead a few days later.

February 3, 1948

H.P. Schmeck

General Manager
Philadelphia Toboggan Co.
130 E. Duval Street
Germantown, Philadelphia 44, Pa.

Dear Mr. Schmeck:

In regard to the royalties for the Skee Ball Alleys which you are now making, we would appreciate your holding them for us on an accrual basis until after July 1st, 1948.

This request is made in order to give us time to determine the future status of our company, which as you know, has been in a dormant position for some time. After the 1st of July we should be in a position to know

January 20, 1948

Mr. Maurice Piesen
Piesen Mfg. Company
291 Broadway
New York, N. Y.

Dear Mr. Piesen:

Sometime ago we had a telephone conversation as to whom the checks for royalties for the Skee Ball Alleys were to be made to in the future. You at that time were to notify us whether they should be paid to the payees as under the contract or whether through a meeting of the payees and proper authorization to us from all of them, to pay to some other designated person or persons. This was your suggestion as under the conditions existing now you are compelled to keep alive the National Skee Ball Company. I believe this is the sum and substance of our conversation.

The letter of November 24th from Mr. Julian I. Bergoffen is not according to contract and as such we regret not acceptable as authorization.

We at present have only ten more alleys to pay the royalty on but will, right after the 1st of the month be shipping quite a few of them I hope, so if you can give us the proper authorization we will be pleased to work along with you, but such authorization should be of such character that our attorney will be free to pass upon it and approve it. Otherwise, we will have to continue paying as before.

Upon receipt of proper authorization, we will make payment on the ten alleys shipped to Asbury Park last month.

Very truly yours,

PHILADELPHIA TOBOGGAN COMPANY

H. P. Schmeck, General Manager

hps/jd

Letter from Philadelphia Toboggan Company to Maurice Piesen, January 20, 1948.
(Courtesy Philadelphia Toboggan Coasters, Inc. Archive)

definitely the dispositions to be made of the royalties that have accumulated by that time.

We are pleased to hear that you are making additional shipments and sincerely hope that your investment will return. With our long experience with alleys, we know that it is still the best amusement game ever developed and have full confidence in its future.

Thanking you for your cooperation in this matter, we remain

Very truly yours,

Maurice Piesen
President [24]

The Piesen Manufacturing Company had been held open as a method for receiving these royalty payments, almost since its inception. The address of the company was Piesen's residence, and the phone number had been let go years before. However, they apparently had not filed taxes with the State of New York for a number of years, and had to determine how to exit the business gracefully and safely, from a financial and legal standpoint.

In the meantime, sales for Skee-Ball alleys had picked up considerably. Philadelphia Toboggan Company was starting to ship a lot of 14 foot alleys, with a handful of shorter (12 foot) and slightly larger (16 foot) alleys to special customers in New York. Sometime around May, 1948, when Philadelphia Toboggan Company had sold its 300th alley, this handwritten note documented a telephone conversation between Philadelphia Toboggan Company and Piesen and Bergoffen:

Piesen Mfg Co wants to let corporation go by default. and as written by J. Berghoffen they want to assign their royalty interest to Berghoffen & Piesen jointly

Check if you think we can safely pay 2100.00 ($7.00 royalty per alley on 300 alley) for payment due to date [25]

Finally, in an agreement dated August 6, 1948, Piesen and Bergoffen, acting as officers of the Piesen Manufacturing Company, Inc., authorized themselves personally as assignees to receive the royalty checks. They had the agreement duly notarized, and informed Philadelphia Toboggan Company of the new arrangement by providing them with an extract of the minutes from their next board meeting, likely consisting of both of them in attendance. [26]

EXTRACT FROM MINUTES

I, JULIAN I. BERGOFFEN, Secretary of PIESEN

Notes from phone call.
(Courtesy Philadelphia Toboggan Coasters, Inc. Archive)

MANUFACTURING CORP., do hereby certify that the following is a true extract from the minutes of a special meeting of the Board of Direcotrs[sic] of the PIESEN MANUFACTURING CORP., held on the 17th day of August, 1948, at the office of Julian I. Bergoffen, 280 Braodway, Borough of Manhattan, City of New York:

WHEREAS this corporation, under its former name of National Skeeball[sic] Co., Inc., entered into an agreement with Rudolph Wurlitzer Corp., which said agreement was subsequently assigned by the said Rudolph Wurlizer Corp. to Philadelphia Toboggan Co., and

WHEREAS the officers of this corporation deemed it in the best interests of this corporation to cause an assignment of royalties due under said agreement to be made to Maurice Piesen and Julian I. Berghoffen, and

WHEREAS the president and secretary of this corporation did on or before August 6, 1948, cause such an assignment to be executed and a copy thereof delivered to Philadelphia Toboggan Co., and

WHEREAS Philadelphia Toboggan Co. has requested that the said assignment be ratified by the Board of Directors of the corporation, it is

Seeking Redemption

> *ORDERED that the said assignment of royalties by this corporation to Maruice Piesen and Julian I. Bergoffen be and the same is hereby ratified in all respects."*
>
> *(signed) Julian I Bergoffen [27]*

Sam High Jr., then the corporate attorney and major shareholder in The Philadelphia Toboggan Company, approved the change. [28]

In 1948, with the alleys selling somewhat more briskly, and standardized (for the time being) at a length of 14 feet, it was time to renew the Certificate of Registration for the Skee-Ball trademark. At this point, it appears that the term Skee-Roll was abandoned, and was subsequently never renewed.

Sales for the next few years were seasonal, picking up in the spring as the amusement venues opened for the summer, and tailing off in the winter. Between November of 1947 and May of 1952, they had sold over 1,600 alleys. About 70% of the alleys went to venues in New York, New Jersey, Ohio, Pennsylvania and Massachusetts. 63 alleys made their way West to California, and the rest were distributed to a smattering of venues across the United States. [29]

At least one clone game seemed not to have gotten the message on the trademark. The Ideal Toy Company of New York was selling its own game, and calling it Skee-Ball. It's likely that Julian Bergoffen discovered this first. Sales of games called Skee-Ball outside of the Philadelphia Toboggan Company agreement meant he and Piesen would lose royalties. In a 1952 letter in response to his concern, Philadelphia Toboggan Company replied that they had not failed to protect the trademark.

> *October 29, 1952*
>
> *Mr. Julian Bergoffen*
> *280 Broadway*
> *New York, N. Y.*
>
> *Dear Mr. Bergoffen:*
>
> *Mr. Piesen in a phone conversation requested Mr. Schmeck to send a copy of your renewal of the trade mark "Skee Ball".*
>
> *In regards to the ads that we have run, the only time we failed to use the words, "Reg. U.S. Pat. Off." was in the N.A.P.A. Yearly Guide of 1952, which came out in December 1951. All the alleys that have been sold have a plate on them, indicating that the game Skee Ball was registered.*
>
> *Very truly yours,*

EXTRACT FROM MINUTES

I, JULIAN I. BERGOFFEN, Secretary of PIESEN MANUFACTURING CORP., do hereby certify that the following is a true extract from the minutes of a special meeting of the Board of Direcotrs of the PIESEN MANUFACTURING CORP., held on the 17th day of August, 1948, at the office of Julian I. Bergoffen, 280 Broadway, Borough of Manhattan, City of New York:

"WHEREAS this corporation, under its former name of National Skeeball Co., Inc., entered into an agreement with Rudolph Wurlitzer Corp., which said agreement was subsequently assigned by the said Rudolph Wurlitzer Corp. to Philadelphia Toboggan Co., and

WHEREAS the officers of this corporation deemed it in the best interests of this corporation to cause an assignment of royalties due under said agreement to be made to Maurice Piesen and Julian I. Bergoffen, and

WHEREAS the president and secretary of this corporation did on or before August 6, 1948, cause such an assignment to be executed and a copy thereof delivered to Philadelphia Toboggan Co., and

WHEREAS Philadelphia Toboggan Co. has requested that the said assignment be ratified by the Board of Directors of the corporation, it is

ORDERED that the said assignment of royalties by this corporation to Maurice Piesen and Julian I. Bergoffen be and the same hereby is ratified in all respects."

Extract from minutes.
(Courtesy Philadelphia Toboggan Coasters, Inc. Archive)

Philadelphia Toboggan Company
R. W. Carroll
Asst. Secretary [30]

Due diligence ensued to rectify the trademark infringement.

On March 2, 1953, The Philadelphia Toboggan Company signed a contract licensing the Ideal Toy Company to finish selling their stocks of games, to pay The Philadelphia Toboggan Company, Inc. $1,000 for the privilege, and to promise never to use the name "Skee-Ball" on its products again. If more than $50,000 worth of games had sold, Ideal would owe 1% royalties to Philadelphia Toboggan Company on the excess sum. [31]

Skee-Ball alleys continued to be ubiquitous in amusement parks, and in the new "Kiddieland" parks designed for children under twelve that were popping up across the United States in the wake of the Baby Boom following World War II, so there were some new venue opportunities. By 1958, The Philadelphia Toboggan Company had grossed approximately $3,000,000 from selling Skee-Ball Alleys.

On the other hand, Skee-Ball Alleys were notoriously well made and lasted for decades. Philadelphia Toboggan Company was already taking trade-ins of old alleys for credit toward new ones. In 1958, they arranged special terms for the purchase of new Skee-Ball alleys.

2 YEAR TERMS ON SKEE-BALL

By a special arrangement with a Philadelphia bank, we are able, for the first time, to offer a deferred payment plan with up to 2 Operating Seasons to pay, when you buy SKEE-BALL.

These terms place SKEE-BALL in the most enviable position in the Amusement Industry as an investment. Anyone who knows anything about SKEE-BALL will tell you "you can't lose on a deal like this". Earnings from SKEE_BALL operations have been on an increase since 1950 until it has become a $3,000,000 business.

WHY NOT GET YOUR SHARE OF THIS PROFITABLE BUSINESS NOW?

There is a Fly in the Ointment, however, because SKEE-BALL Alleys are in short supply; more so now than at any time in our history. Production of Alleys have been curtailed this year to allow us to fill our commitments for riding devices. SO WE'RE NOT KIDDING!

If you have ever wished you could own and

operate SKEE-BALL, now is the time to do it. Now is the time to add to your present Alleys. Now is the time to replace those old Wurlitzer and National alleys.

NOW IS THE TIME TO BUY SKEE-BALL.

Here is the real clincher to make you want to earn with SKEE-BALL.

THERE IS NO INCREASE IN PRICE

In the face of rising material and labor costs, we have made every effort to hold our prices stable. In addition, we have continued to make improvements with the Alley with better, stronger materials and are more than proud of our workmanship. We are so sure these Alleys will operate 100% free of any trouble that we warrant them free of defective material and workmanship for the entire first Season.

Investigate, check, compare SKEE-BALL with any other game, or for that matter, any other device in the Amusement business and you will find that dollar for dollar, square foot for square foot, there just is nothing that comes even close to SKEE-BALL for low cost, for high earnings, for trouble-free operation and for popularity with the public.

WISHING WON'T DO IT - SKEE-BALL WILL. GET 'EM NOW.

Sold Only By

PHILADELPHIA TOBOGGAN COMPANY

*130 E. Duval Street
Phila. 44, Pa.
GErmantown 8-3737 [32]*

One notable improvement that cemented Skee-Ball's ability to become truly independent of an attendant, and still function terrifically as a redemption game, occurred in 1960. On March 1, Patent 2,926,915 was granted to Frank D. Johns for his Automatic Ticket-Dispensing Skee-Ball Machine. [33]

Frank D. Johns was a long-time Skee-Ball customer, well-known to the Philadelphia Toboggan Company sales department, who ran Skee-Ball concessions in Daytona Beach, Florida. The Billboard reported that "In 1955, [Johns] owned the and had upwards of 75 amusement machines and a rooftop golf course." [34] Johns was clearly not one to think small. For as much as Skee-Ball had been known for its "no attendant required" feature since 1909, the truth was that some attendant needed to be present to witness the score and offer tokens that represented credit toward rewards and recognition.

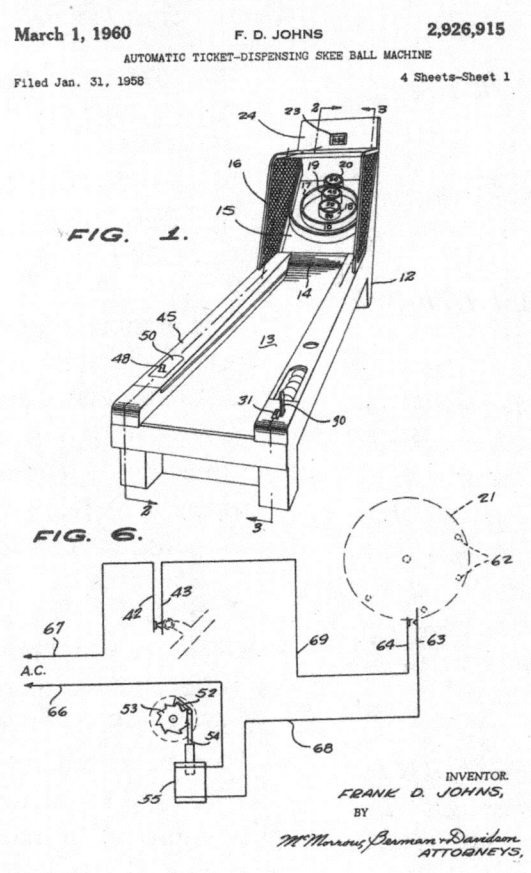

U.S. Patent No. 2,926,915, Automatic Ticket-Dispensing Skee Ball Machine.
(Author's Collection)

Automatic Ticket Dispenser on a Skee-Ball alley.
(Courtesy Philadelphia Toboggan Coasters, Inc. Archive)

Advertisement for Skee-Ball alley that includes an automatic ticket dispenser.
(Courtesy Philadelphia Toboggan Coasters, Inc. Archive)

Skee-Ball tournaments were always associated with prizes, but now the automatic ticket dispensing feature made it easy to turn Skee-Ball into a full-fledged, automated redemption game with prizes for all who earned enough tickets.

The Johns patent, and the devices produced in accordance with it, provided a straightforward addition to new alleys and an easy retrofit of the ticket device onto existing alleys. This made the games more attractive to operators and for the players, it fed that compulsive desire not to settle for the pencil erasers or gaudy trinkets, but to play incessantly and repeatedly until they had enough tickets for that ginormous teddy bear. Everybody wants the teddy bear.

Skee-Ball Alleys continued to sell, and now were easy to incorporate into parks and fairs that had one central location to display and redeem prizes from multiple games of skill and chance.

In 1971, Philadelphia Toboggan Company moved its operations, including Skee-Ball, from Germantown, Pennsylvania to Lansdale, Pennsylvania.

Six years later, in 1977 several interesting things happened. First, a handwritten letter arrived, addressed to Samuel H. High III, owner of Philadelphia Toboggan Company, from Maurice Piesen, regarding the royalties which, apparently, nobody had been keeping track of. The letter read:

275 Central Park W
NY 10024

Oct 27, 1977

Dear Mr. High-

When Julian Bergoffen who was our Secretary and attorney closed his office about twelve years ago he put some of his old records in the under the sidewalk vault in a building of which he was part owner.

We went through these old records and found the Wurlitzer agreements there.

The enclosed is a copy of the purchase agreement.

Our records of royalties however are incomplete so that we do not know if 10,000 alleys have been made.

I will call you on Wednesday Nov 2 to discuss the situation, hoping in the meantime you can determine the number of alleys made by Wurlitzer and yourselves to see if the $7 cut off has been reached.

If it has been reached, royalties should

2 W Central Park W
N.Y. 10024

Oct 27, 1977

Dear Mr. High—

When Julian Bergoffen who was our Secretary and attorney closed his office about twelve years ago he put some of his old records in the under the sidewalk vault in a building of which he was part owner.

He went through these old records and found the Wurlitzer agreements there.

The enclosed is a copy of the purchase agreement.

Our records of royalties however are incomplete so that we do not know if 10,000 alleys have been made.

I will call you on Wednesday Nov 2 to discuss the situation, hoping in the meantime you can determine the number of alleys made by Wurlitzer and yourselves to see if the $3 cut off has been reached.

If it has been reached, royalties should now be at $5 an alley, and we can discuss the matter of the $2 if there has been an overrun of $7 payments.—

Sincerely yours,
Maurice Piesen

Letter from Maurice Piesen to Mr. High, October 27, 1977.
(Courtesy Philadelphia Toboggan Coasters, Inc. Archive)

now be at $5 an alley, and we can discuss the matter of the $2 if there has been an overrun of $7 payments.

Sincerely yours

Maurice Piesen [35]

Mr. Piesen followed up with a phone call on November 2. [36]

It's unknown exactly what was discussed in that call, but it seems to have resulted in a modification of the royalty agreement, suitable to both parties.

Also in 1977, Skee-Ball, Inc. was officially spun off from the Philadelphia Toboggan Company as its own company, since it was unique and different from the amusement rides that were the core of their business. However, Samuel High Jr. remained the Majority Stock Holder, for both Philadelphia Toboggan Company and Skee-Ball Inc. His son Sam High III was president of the Skee-Ball Inc. spin-off and the Philadelphia Toboggan Company. [37]

One more interesting thing happened in 1977: The opening of what became the Chuck E Cheese restaurant chain, which claims that Skee-Ball had been part of its operations since the first one opened in 1977. Skee-Ball has sporadically shown up in restaurants and bars since its first year of sales in 1909, but this was the first time it appears to have been a standard feature of a restaurant chain.

By the end of 1983, the royalty payments were deemed completed with a final set of correspondence, this time with relative Peter Piesen. The new understanding was incorporated into this agreement.

SKEE BALL, INC.

8th & Maple Streets, Lansdale, Pa 19446 - 215-362-0300

December 4, 1983

*Mr. Pete Piesen
C/O Bergoffen & Piesen
375 Park Ave.
New York, NY 10152*

Reference 1983 Skee-Ball Alley Royalty Payment

Dear Mr. Piesen:

Our royalty payment for 1983 is enclosed in the amount of $8,470.50. This remittance was based on 1,210 Skee-Ball Alleys sold at $7.00 per unit.

This 1982 Balance will be reduced accordingly:

1982 Balance	*16,941.00*
Less 1983 Remittance	*8,471.00*
Less 1983 Allowance	*8,470.00*
	-0- Paid in Full

Sincerely,

SKEE-BALL, INC.

Frank

Frank Farnan
Treasurer

FF/lh

Enc: Check enclosed. [38]

A second letter sent the next day followed Farnan's letter regarding the final royalties. This letter, also addressed to Pete Piesen, was from from Samuel High III.

SKEE BALL, INC.

8th & Maple Streets, Lansdale, Pa 19446 - 215-362-0300

December 5, 1983

Mr. Pete Piesen
C/O Bergoffen & Piesen
375 Park Ave.
New York, NY 10152

Dear Pete:

Enclosed is our last royalty check in the amount of $8,470.50. According to our records this would complete our agreed-upon contract.

It hardly seems possible that we have sold enough alleys to pay off the contract. It seems just a few short years ago that we would never be able to sell that many machines. However, times do change and the industry demanded Skee-Ball Alleys at an ever increasing rate.

I am sorry that I missed you on the phone today as I would have enjoyed chatting with you. Frank tells me that you have been sick and I certainly hope that you are on the mend now. I have certainly enjoyed our relationship over these many years and would enjoy having you visit us anytime.

Sincerely:

SKEE-BALL, INC.

Sam

Samuel H. High III
President [39]

SKEE-BALL, INC.

8th & Maple Streets, Lansdale, Pa. 19446 • 215/362-0300

December 4, 1983

Mr. Pete Piesen
C/O Bergoffen & Piesen
375 Park Ave.
New York, NY 10152

Reference 1983 Skee-Ball Alley Royalty Payment

Dear Mr. Piesen:

Our royalty payment for 1983 is enclosed in the amount of $8,470.50. This remittance was based on 1,210 Skee-Ball Alleys sold at $7.00 per unit.

This 1982 balance will be reduced accordingly:

1982 Balance	16,941.00
Less 1983 Remittance	8,471.00
Less 1983 Allowance	8,470.00
	-0- Paid in Full

Sincerely:

SKEE-BALL, INC.

Frank

Frank Farnan
Treasurer

FF/lh

Enc: Check enclosed.

Skee-Ball • Skee-Roll • Amusement Devices

Letter from Skee-Ball, Inc. to Pete Piesen, December 4, 1983.
(Courtesy Philadelphia Toboggan Coasters, Inc. Archive)

8th & Maple Streets, Lansdale, Pa. 19446 • 215/362-0300

December 5, 1983

Mr. Pete Piesen
C/O Berghoffen & Peisen
375 Park Ave.
New York, NY 10152

Dear Pete:

Enclosed is our last royalty check in the amount of $8,470.50. According to our records this would complete our agreed-upon contract.

It hardly seems possible that we have sold enough alleys to pay off the contract. It seems just a few short years ago that we would never be able to sell that many machines. However, times do change and the industry demanded Skee-Ball Alleys at an ever increasing rate.

I am sorry that I missed you on the phone today as I would have enjoyed chatting with you. Frank tells me that you have been sick and I certainly hope that you are on the mend now. I have certainly enjoyed our relationship over these many years and would enjoy having you visit us anytime.

Sincerely:

SKEE-BALL, INC.

Samuel H. High III
President

SHH/lvh

Enc: Check.

Skee-Ball • Skee-Roll • Amusement Devices

Letter from Skee-Ball, Inc. to Pete Piesen, December 5, 1983.
(Courtesy Philadelphia Toboggan Coasters, Inc. Archive)

Chapter 16

FULL CIRCLE AND BEYOND
Skee-Ball Rolls On

Free and clear of the royalty agreement that spanned 47 years, the Skee-Ball, Inc. was sold to Joe Sladek and his three partners, with each partner owning twenty five percent of the stock. Joe Sladek gradually bought out his partners and became the sole owner of Skee-Ball Inc., renaming it Skee-Ball Amusement Games Inc., carefully guarding the patent and trademark rights and shepherding the game forward. [1]

CEO Joe Sladek's words capture the staying power of the game, as well as it's fascination:

> *Skee-Ball has been an amusement tradition since 1909. Its ageless appeal is astounding! It's a game that my father and grandfather spent hours playing with me as a child. Now I play it with my own children and grandchildren! It's obvious - Skee-Ball maintains its popularity from one generation to the next!*
>
> *Skee-Ball's excellent reputation has withstood the test of time. For nearly a century our company has produced games of skill and entertainment that have worldwide appeal!*
>
> *Skee-Ball's corporate mission is to continuously supply the amusement industry with quality games that withstand the test of time. Not only are we committed to maintaining the quality of our existing games, we are committed to introducing exciting new games aimed to thrill players everywhere. Skee-Ball's goal is to introduce a new game concept at every major amusement industry trade show.*
>
> *Skee-Ball is - and will always remain - the game they keep coming back to!* [2]

As Skee-Ball maintained its market and ubiquitous presence in arcades and amusement parks all over the country, it also continued to infiltrate anywhere there were games and a spot big enough to host a few alleys, including child-oriented restaurants and, increasingly, back to bars and more mature recreational venues.

It even made it onto the iPhone, which is how this research project got started. In December 2009, Freeverse, Inc.'s Skee-Ball iPhone app was the best selling paid application in the iPhone App Store. On Christmas Day alone, 47,926 copies of the Skee-Ball app, selling for 99 cents a copy, generated over $33,000 after Apple took their 30% cut of the sales price. [3]

Chuck E Cheese now provides an online version of Skee-Ball that lets kids play the game in the comfort of their own environments, and bring the virtual tickets they earn to the restaurant to redeem their prizes and rewards. [4]

Perhaps due to the relatively recent popularity of the game in kid-friendly restaurants and Kiddielands, Skee-Ball had developed the reputation of being a kid's game, with short alleys, easy play, and plenty of flashing lights. However, one hardy set of more mature players unwittingly restarted the old tradition of tournament Skee-Ball leagues.

The Full Circle Bar located in the Wilmington District of Brooklyn, New York, gets credit for bringing National Skee-Ball tournaments back to the public. Bar owner Eric Pavony, "Skee-E-O," founded the BrewSkee-Ball League after he challenged a friend in Coney Island to a competitive match. He brought that idea back to his Full Circle Bar, installing several Skee-Ball machines, and founding the BrewSkee-Ball league national tournaments.

As that league gained prominence, with games hosted at bars from New York City to San Francisco CA, another legal issue arose. Joe Sladek and the Skee-Ball Company, Inc. discovered that the term "BrewSkee-Ball" infringed on its trademark rights to the name Skee-Ball. [5] This led to a rather unfortunate dust-up, and a series of court cases arose after the Full Circle Bar applied for and received a trademark for their "BrewSkee-Ball" name for the league play in Skee-Ball tournaments. They applied for the BrewSkee-Ball trademark in July of 2006, and it was finally granted in February of 2008. Dimensional Branding Group in Marin County CA was the Skee-Ball Company's exclusive agent for licensing, business development and promotion of the game and the trademark, and they attempted to arrange a licensing agreement with Full Circle Bar to be able to use the trademark. Full Circle Bar did not feel they should have to license the Skee-Ball trademark, since they had been granted the Trademark for BrewSkee-Ball.

Unfortunately for them, the law in this case affirmed that the trademark for BrewSkee-Ball was granted in error, because it did infringe on the original trademark. Failing to challenge this would have put the Skee-Ball trademark in jeopardy. After multiple phone calls and emails, Sladek's company attorneys sent a cease and desist order to the Full Circle Bar, which ignored it, since they maintained that they had been granted the trademark through the United States Patent and Trademark Office. In late 2011, Skee-Ball Company finally filed suit in Federal Court in California, the location of the Dimensional Branding Group. Full Circle Bar filed for a transfer back to the East Coast and in December, the case was transferred back to New York. "You can't be granted a trademark that includes somebody else's trademark," said Richard Idell, an attorney for Skee-Ball Inc., which trademarked the name in 1928. [6]

For years, the two organizations battled it out in court, filing suits and countersuits until finally, an undisclosed agreement-in-principle between the two organizations was reached that seems to have resolved the matter. [7]

What we do know is that the BrewSkee-Ball League is still going strong, and the Full Circle Bar (Full Circle United LLC) is happily sponsoring the League which plays in bars and venues all over the country. Puns have become an intrinsic part of the league enthusiasm, and it's teams names reflect that: Flock of Skee-Gulls, Skee Patrol, and Skee-ven Colbert, for example. Players take novel names. The first national champion of the BrewSkee-Ball League, Ray Carannante, is known as Skee-diddy. [8]

Joey Mucha, competitive Skee-Ball player from San Francisco, and National Champion 2011-2012, is known in Skee-Ball circles as Joey the Cat. He has also been a popular spokesperson for the game. Asked how he became so skilled at the game, he shared his secret. He bought a Skee-Ball machine off eBay, which he kept in his one bedroom apartment, giving him plenty of opportunity to practice and share his love of the game with friends and guests. "Skee-Ball is a state of mind" he says. [9]

Star News Online reported on the first woman to win the national championship, Tracy Townsend from Wilmington, North Carolina in 2015. [10] It has been clear from the game's early history that people of all kinds play Skee-Ball competitively, and it doesn't seem to matter what size, age or physical build the winners are. Some people have observed that short stature players may have an advantage, being close to the level of the alley, but for every example there is a counter-example of winners who are tall. The real take-away is that Skee-Ball has proven to be a universally fascinating game, and has stood the test of time better than any other game of its kind.

Aside from the enthusiasm over the BrewSkee-Ball League, and the brief legal battle that caught some minor headlines, Skee-Ball has remained a quiet but ubiquitous fixture in the amusement market. Thousands of people have played the game every day, though many might not even recognize the name Skee-Ball until the game was described to them.

Once again, in late February 2016, Skee-Ball made the news. Bay Tek Games, Inc. of Pulaski, Wisconsin bought the trademark and manufacturing rights, and all the patents from Skee-Ball Amusement Games Inc. This marked the first time in history that the manufacturing of Skee-Ball alleys moved away from the East Coast. [11]

The Bay Tek Games engineers embraced the challenge of at once retaining the nostalgic feel and fascination of play that has made Skee-Ball a favorite of kids and adults for over a hundred years, while making them attractive, affordable, and contemporary enough in appearance to blend into modern arcades. Redesigning the alleys took months of painstaking work, between the experienced Skee-Ball Company employees, and the Bay Tek Games designers. Bay Tek Games is a compact, lean operation with high tech sensibilities and a focus on optimized manufacturability. Finally, the first alleys were ready to roll off the production line during the first week in June, 2016. [12]

Bay Tek Games, Inc. wasted no time updating the alleys to become fully electronic, with sleek, modern designs and flashing displays to fit in with modern video arcade styles. Now the 10 foot long alleys are ripe to be sold to electronic arcades populated with video games as well more traditional venues.

The Skee-Ball journey rolls on. From the struggle to birth Skee-Ball as "a man's game" in the early years, cashing in on the newly opened amusement park craze, to the survival of the game into the age of electronic and video amusements found at every shopping mall around the country, Skee-Ball continues to have that fascination of play that attracts old and young alike. Alleys that are a half-century old continue to be played, as well as those fresh off the assembly line in Wisconsin. And people still play Skee-Ball on their iPhones.

This once again returns us to the musings of J. F. Simpson, originator of Skee-Ball, as he described the difficulty in recognizing why games have their appeal, and the history of how they were developed.

> "Games that are played when they have become old are rare. Of those that remain, their origin is lost in antiquity."
>
> *Joseph Fourestier Simpson*

Skee-Ball is the oldest surviving game of its kind in modern history. Its story has been shrouded in the fog of time and fanciful tales, some half-true, retold again and again. We hope that this loving story of the beautiful game of Skee-Ball has made an exception to Joseph Fourestier Simpson's observation that the origin of games such as these must be lost to antiquity.

Thanks to Simpson, and to his sister Alice who ensured the survival of that fascinating history when she donated all of Simpson's papers to the Vineland Historical and Antiquarian Society, we have happily been able to rescue that history from the brink of obscurity.

And the balls roll on.

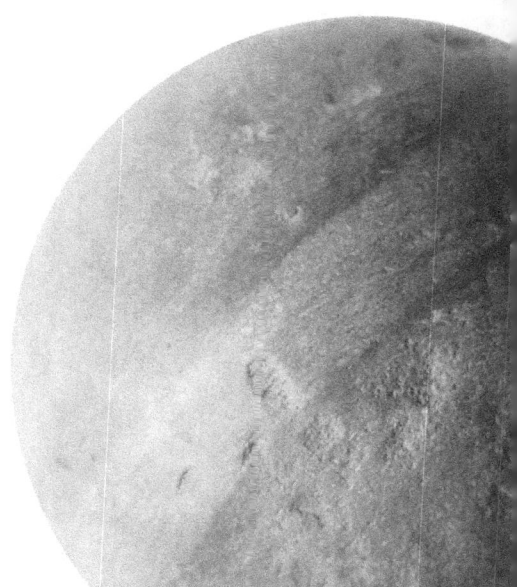

SKEE-BALL OWNERSHIP CHRONOLOGY

1907-8 • Skee-Ball invented and patented by Joseph Fourestier Simpson.

1908 The Skee-Ball Alley Company • Founded by William Nice Jr., and John W. Harper. Nice was awarded 50% ownership of the patent, and both were principals in the company, responsible for manufacture and sales. Simpson retained patent licensing rights.

1914-1919 J. D. Este Company, Inc. • Jonathon Dickinson Este, Arthur Wheeler, Herbert Wheeler, Edwin LeBouttier. Este also incorporated Skee-Ball Alley Company when he purchased the US Patents and rights to the game from Simpson and the Nice Estate, and the interests of John W. Harper, whom he hired as a manager. Skee-Ball Alley Company was allowed to go void in 1916.

1919-1928 Skee-Ball Company, Inc. • Este's partners Edwin V Dougherty, Jr., John W. Harper and Edwin LeBouttier bought out his interest in the J. D. Este Company, Inc. and changed the name to the Skee-Ball Company, Inc. Morris Goldberg joined the company and was general manager and later Vice President and motive spirit for them.

1928-1936 National Skee-Ball Company, Inc. Skee-Ball Company, Inc. sold rights to Hugo H. Piesen, Maurice Piesen, and Herman Bergoffen, who incorporated as The National Skee-Ball Company.

1936-1945 The Rudolph Wurlitzer Manufacturing Company, Inc. • The National Skee Ball Company, Inc., sold Skee-Ball rights, subject to negotiated royalties, including trademarks and patents, to The Rudolph Wurlitzer Manufacturing Company, Inc., a subsidiary of The Rudolph Wurlitzer Company, Inc. which assumed ownership when it discontinued its subsidiary. In 1937, The National Skee-Ball Company, Inc. changed its name to Piesen Manufacturing, Inc., collecting royalties as part of the sales agreement.

Between 1942 and 1945 Wurlitzer, and other game manufacturers, suspended manufacture of amusements and turned to manufacturing to support the war effort. The Rudolph Wurlitzer Manufacturing Company, Inc. formerly a subsidiary, was assimilated back into the parent company, The Rudolph Wurlitzer Company, Inc.

1946 Philadelphia Toboggan Company, Inc. Wurlitzer sold all rights, patents and trademarks for Skee-Ball, and responsibilities for payment of royalties, to the Philadelphia Toboggan Company, Inc. (PTC). Ironically, Philadelphia Toboggan Company is the same company that was started by Henry Auchy, who helped give Skee-Ball it's start at Chestnut Hill Park, but didn't have enough confidence in it to buy the rights to Skee-Ball back in 1912.

1977 Skee-Ball, Inc. • The company is spun off from the Philadelphia Toboggan Company, but retained by the same owners.

1984-5 Skee-Ball, Inc. • Purchased by Joseph Sladek and his partners. Skee-Ball, Inc. is eventually renamed Skee-Ball Amusement Games.

2016 Bay Tek Games, Inc. • Buys Skee-Ball from Skee-Ball Amusement Games. This is the first time manufacturing is moved away from the East Coast, to Pulaski, Wisconsin.

END NOTES

Prologue

[1] —, 'The Beautiful Game of Skee-Ball,' The Billboard, 11 December 1909, p. 48D.

Chapter 1

[1] —, 'The Beautiful Game of Skee-Ball,' The Billboard, 11 December 1909, p. 48D.

Chapter 2

[1] Simpson, Joseph Fourestier. 1928. 'Letter to Mr. Frederick E. Swope,' May 29, 1928, (Vineland, New Jersey), p. 2, from the archive of the Vineland Historical and Antiquarian Society.

[2] —, 'McElroy's Philadelphia City Directory For 1861.' Philadelphia, E. C. & J. Biddle & Co., 1861. p. 1142.

[3] Simpson, Joseph Fourestier. 1928. 'Letter to Mr. Frederick E. Swope,' May 29, 1928, (Vineland, New Jersey), p. 2, from the archive of the Vineland Historical and Antiquarian Society.

[4] —, 'McElroy's Philadelphia City Directory For 1865.' Philadelphia, E. C. & J. Biddle & Co., 1865. p. 620.

[5] Simpson, Joseph Fourestier. 'Family Records-And Traditions. Burr-Smith-Brown-Brognard.,' 1927. p. 19.

[6] Simpson, Joseph Fouerister, 'Improvement in Trunk-Fastenings,' No. 168,677 (United States Patent Office), October 11, 1875, pp. 1–2.

[7] Bureau of Awards, 'International Exhibition. 1876. Report on Awards. Group 10. Catalogue No. Shoe and Leather Building, Patent Trunk Fastener and lock combined.' Philadelphia, 1876.

[8] Okie, Frederick E, and Joseph Fourestier Simpson, 'Wrench,' No. 279,271, (United States Patent Office), June 12, 1883, pp. 1-4.

[9] —, 'Gopsill's Philadelphia City Directory, for 1885.' Philadelphia, 1885. p. 1355.

[10] —, 'Gopsill's Philadelphia City Directory for 1886.' Philadelphia, 1886. p. 1588.

[11] —, 'Gopsill's Philadelphia City Directory for 1888.' Philadelphia, 1888. p. 1341.

[12] Simpson, Joseph Fourestier. 'Family Records-And Traditions. Burr-Smith-Brown-Brognard.,' 1927 p 19.

[13] Ibid.

[14] Ibid.

[15] —, 'Certificate of the Organization of Vineland Knitting Mills Company,' 14 April 1892, pp. 1–6.

[16] —, Injunction (Trenton, New Jersey, 23 October 1894), pp. 1–2.

[17] Gardner, A. K., 'Letter to Joseph Fourestier Simpson,' August 19, 1903. (Rapid City, South Dakota), from the archive of the Vineland Historical and Antiquarian Society.

[18] Simpson, Joseph Fourestier, 'Proposed Plan of the Postal Card Check,' July 1902, pp. 1–9, from the archive of the Vineland Historical and Antiquarian Society.

[19] Wanser, Frank 'Letter to Hon. John J. Gardner,' November 18, 1904, (Vineland, New Jersey), from the archive of the Vineland Historical and Antiquarian Society.

[20] Simpson, Joseph Fourestier, 'Letter to George B. Cortelyou,' August 24, 1905. 'Letter' (Vineland, New Jersey), from the archive of the Vineland Historical and Antiquarian Society.

[21] Hitchcock, F H, 'Letter to Joseph Fourestier Simpson,' October 30, 1905, (Washington, DC), from the archive of the Vineland Historical and Antiquarian Society.

[22] Simpson, Joseph Fourestier, 'Letter to W. Scott Towers,' November 6, 1905. (Vineland, New Jersey), from the archive of the Vineland Historical and Antiquarian Society.

[23] Hitchcock, F. H., 'Letter to Joseph Fourestier Simpson,' November 11,1905, (Washington, DC), from the archive of the Vineland Historical and Antiquarian Society.

[24] Butler, Frank M, 'The Book of the Boardwalk and the Atlantic City Story,' 1st edn (The 1954 Association, Inc.) p. 5.

Chapter 3

[1] Simpson, Joseph Fourestier, Letters Patent Application, 'Improvement in Game.' November 8, 1907. pp. 1467-1473.

[2] Simpson, Joseph Fourestier, Letters Patent Application, 'Improvement in Game.' November 8, 1907. pp. 1471-1472.

[3] Hyatt, R H, 'Letter to Joseph Fourestier Simpson, and Charles A Rutter,' December 18 1907, (Washington, D. C.).

[4] Simpson, Joseph Fourestier, 'Letter to The Honorable Commissioner of Patents,' January 6, 1908, (Philadelphia, Pennsylvania), pp. 1475-1476

[5] Ibid.

[6] Townsend, W. W. 'Letter to Joseph Fourestier Simpson and Charles A Rutter,' February 1, 1908, (Washington, D. C.).

[7] Simpson, Joseph Fourestier by Charles A Rutter, 'Letter to The Honorable Commissioner of Patents,' February 12, 1908, (Philadelphia, Pennsylvania).

[8] Ibid.

[9] Townsend, W W, 'Letter to Joseph Fourestier Simpson, and Charles A Rutter,' March 2, 1908, (Washington, D. C.).

[10] Simpson, Joseph Fourestier, 'Letter to The Honorable Commissioner of Patents,' March 17, 1908, (Philadelphia, Pennsylvania).

[11] Townsend, W W, 'Letter to Joseph Fourestier Simpson, and Charles A Rutter,' April 4, 1908, (Washington, D. C.).

[12] Simpson, Joseph Fourestier and Charles A Rutter, 'Letter to The Honorable Commissioner of Patents,' April 7, 1908. (Philadelphia, Pennsylvania).

[13] Townsend, W W, 'Letter to Joseph Fourestier Simpson, and Charles A Rutter,' April 20, 1908, (Washington, D. C.).

[14] Simpson, Joseph Fourestier and Charles A Rutter, 'Letter to The Honorable Commissioner of Patents,' May 4, 1908, (Philadelphia, Pennsylvania).

[15] The Honorable Commissioner of Patents, 'Letter to Joseph Fourestier Simpson, and Charles A Rutter,' May 16, 1908, (Washngton, D. C.).

[16] Rutter, Charles A, 'Letter to The Honorable Commissioner of Patents,' November 6, 1908, (Philadelphia, Pennsylvania).

Chapter 4

[1] Simpson, Joseph Fourestier, 'Prospectus of the National Skee-Ball Alley Company,' Circa 1907, pp. 1–3, from the archive of the Vineland Historical and Antiquarian Society.

[2] Simpson, Joseph Fourestier, 'Letter to The Brunswick-Balke-Collender Co.,' April 5, 1915, (Vineland, New Jersey), from the archive of the Vineland Historical and Antiquarian Society.

[3] —, 'Advertisement — Skee-Ball Bowling,' The Billboard, April 17, 1909, vol. XXI, No. 16, p. 2.

[4] Ibid.

[5] —, 'Advertisement — Skee-Ball Bowling,' The Billboard (Cincinnati, Ohio), May 8, 1909, vol. XXI, No. 19, p. 54.

[6] —, 'Advertisement — Skee-Ball,' The Billboard (Cincinnati, Ohio), May 15, 1909, vol. XXI, No. 20, p. 47.

[7] —, 'Advertisement — Skee-Ball,' The Billboard (Cincinnati, Ohio), May 15, 1909, vol. XXI, No. 21, p. 51.

[8] —, 'Accounting Ledger.' Circa 1910. 'Accounting Ledger,' p. 1, from the archive of the Vineland Historical and Antiquarian Society.

[9] —, 'Skee-Ball Bowling Game,' Popular Mechanics (Chicago, Illinois), July 1909, Vol. 12, No. 1 p. 80.

[10] —, 'Advertisement — Skee-Ball,' Popular Mechanics (Chicago, Illinois), August 1909, Vol. 12, No. 2, p. 118.

[11] —, 'Accounting Ledger.' Circa 1910. 'Accounting Ledger,' p. 1, from the archive of the Vineland Historical and Antiquarian Society.

[12] Ibid.

[13] Ibid.

[14] Ibid.

[15] The fact that the price paid was $275.00 probably indicates that he bought the scoring device as well.

[16] —, 'The Beautiful Game of Skee-Ball,' The Billboard (Cincinnati, Ohio), December 11, 1909, Vol. XXI, No. 50, p. 48D.

[17] 'Advertisement.' 1909. 'Advertisement,' The Billboard, p. 71.
'Advertisement,' The Billboard (Cincinnati, Ohio), December 11, 1909, Vol. XXI, No. 50 p. 71.

[18] Butler, Frank M, 'The Book of the Boardwalk and the Atlantic City Story,' 1st edn (The 1954 Association, Inc.), pp. 15, 19.

[19] —, 'Commonwealth of Pennsylvania Department of Health Bureau of Vital Statistics. File No. 3030. Certificate of Death. William Nice, Jr.' January 18, 1910.

[20] Nice, William Jr., and Joseph Fourestier Simpson. 1910. 'Alley Board and Ball' (Canada).

[21] 'Accounting Ledger.' Circa 1910. 'Accounting Ledger,' p. 1.

[22] Ibid.

[23] Ibid.

[24] Ibid.

[25] Ibid.

[26] Harper, John W, 'Letter to Joseph Fourestier Simpson,' August 15, 1910, (Philadelphia, Pennsylvania), from the archive of the Vineland Historical and Antiquarian Society.

[27] Harper, John W, 'Letter to Joseph Fourestier Simpson,' August 25, 1910, (Philadelphia, Pennsylvania), from the archive of the Vineland Historical and Antiquarian Society.

[28] Harper, John W, 'Letter to Joseph Fourestier Simpson,' August 27, 1910, from the archive of the Vineland Historical and Antiquarian Society.

[29] Harper, John W, 'Letter to Joseph Fourestier Simpson,' August 27, 1910. 'Letter,' p. 2, from the archive of the Vineland Historical and Antiquarian Society.

[30] Ibid.

[31] Harper, John W, 'Letter to Joseph Fourestier Simpson,' September 17, 1910, (Philadelphia, Pennsylvania), from the archive of the Vineland Historical and Antiquarian Society.

[32] Ibid.

[33] --, 'An Eastern Summer Park That Makes Money,' Electric Traction Weekly, March 16, 1911, Vol. VII, No. 30, pp. 861–65.

[34] Harper, John W, 'Letter to Joseph Fourestier Simpson,' September 19, 1910, (Philadelphia, Pennsylvania), from the archive of the Vineland Historical and Antiquarian Society.

[35] Auchy, Henry B, 'Letter to Joseph Fourestier Simpson,' October 10, 1910, (Philadelphia, Pennsylvania), from the archive of the Vineland Historical and Antiquarian Society.

[36] Harper, John W, 'Letter to Joseph Fourestier Simpson,' October 15, 1910, (Philadelphia, Pennsylvania), from the archive of the Vineland Historical and Antiquarian Society.

[37] Enochs, C. J., 'Letter to Joseph Fourestier Simpson,'

October 20, 1910, from the archive of the Vineland Historical and Antiquarian Society.

[38] Harper, John W, 'Letter to Joseph Fourestier Simpson,' October 22, 1910, (Philadelphia, Pennsylvania), from the archive of the Vineland Historical and Antiquarian Society.

[39] Harper, John W, 'Letter to Joseph Fourestier Simpson,' October 30, 1910, (Philadelphia, Pennsylvania), from the archive of the Vineland Historical and Antiquarian Society.

[40] Ibid.

[41] Harper, John W, 'Letter to Joseph Fourestier Simpson,' November 16, 1910, (Philadelphia, Pennsylvania), from the archive of the Vineland Historical and Antiquarian Society.

[42] Harper, John W, 'Letter to Joseph Fourestier Simpson,' December 2, 1910, (Philadelphia, Pennsylvania), from the archive of the Vineland Historical and Antiquarian Society.

[43] Harper, John W, 'Letter to Joseph Fourestier Simpson,' December 13, 1910, (Philadelphia, Pennsylvania), from the archive of the Vineland Historical and Antiquarian Society.

[44] Harper, John W, 'Letter to Joseph Fourestier Simpson,' December 29, 1910, (Philadelphia, Pennsylvania), from the archive of the Vineland Historical and Antiquarian Society.

Chapter 5

[1] Tom Keels, interviewed by Thaddeus O. Cooper and Kevin B. Kreitman, audio recording, San Jose, CA, August 15, 2015.

[2] Harper, John W, 'Letter to Joseph Fourestier Simpson,' January 9, 1911, (Philadelphia, Pennsylvania), from the archive of the Vineland Historical and Antiquarian Society.

[3] The Skee Ball Alley Company, 'Letter to Philadelphia Toboggan Company,' January 11, 1911, (Philadelphia, Pennsylvania), from the archive of the Vineland Historical and Antiquarian Society.

[4] Harper, John W, 'Letter to Joseph Fourestier Simpson,' January 19, 1911, (Philadelphia, Pennsylvania), from the archive of the Vineland Historical and Antiquarian Society.

[5] Harper, John W, 'Letter to Joseph Fourestier Simpson,' February 2, 1911, (Philadelphia, Pennsylvania), from the archive of the Vineland Historical and Antiquarian Society.

[6] Harper, John W, 'Letter to Joseph Fourestier Simpson,' February 7, 1911, (Philadelphia, Pennsylvania), from the archive of the Vineland Historical and Antiquarian Society.

[7] Harper, John W, 'Letter to Joseph Fourestier Simpson,' March 31, 1911, from the archive of the Vineland Historical and Antiquarian Society.

[8] Harper, John W, 'Letter to Joseph Fourestier Simpson,' June 6, 1911, (Philadelphia, Pennsylvania), from the archive of the Vineland Historical and Antiquarian Society.

[9] Harper, John W, 'Letter to Joseph Fourestier Simpson,' June 4, 1911, (Philadelphia, Pennsylvania), from the archive of the Vineland Historical and Antiquarian Society.

[10] Boogar, William F, 'Letter to Joseph Fourestier Simpson,' June 20, 1911, (Philadelphia, Pennsylvania), from the archive of the Vineland Historical and Antiquarian Society.

[11] Simpson, Joseph Fourestier, 'Letter to J. J. Holcombe,' June 24, 1911, (Vineland, New Jersey), from the archive of the Vineland Historical and Antiquarian Society.

[12] Simpson, Joseph Fourestier, 'Letter to Brandt C. Downey,' June 24, 1911, (Vineland, New Jersey), from the archive of the Vineland Historical and Antiquarian Society.

[13] Downey, Brandt C, 'Letter to Joseph Fourestier Simpson,' July 3, 1911, (Indianapolis, Indiana), from the archive of the Vineland Historical and Antiquarian Society.

[14] Simpson, Joseph Fourestier, 'Letter to Brandt C.

Downey. July 5, 1911, (Vineland, New Jersey), from the archive of the Vineland Historical and Antiquarian Society.

[15] Harper, John W, 'Letter to Joseph Fourestier Simpson,' August 5, 1911, from the archive of the Vineland Historical and Antiquarian Society.

[16] 'Big Redwood Named "Jim Lynch" Head of Typo Union Is Honored,' The San Francisco Call (San Francisco, California), August 12, 1911, p. 16.

[17] Rainier, H W, 'Letter to Joseph Fourestier Simpson,' August 6, 1911, (Pitman, New Jersey), from the archive of the Vineland Historical and Antiquarian Society.

[18] The Brunswick-Balke-Collender Co, 'Letter to Joseph Fourestier Simpson,' August 14, 1911, (Chicago, Illinois), from the archive of the Vineland Historical and Antiquarian Society.

[19] Rath, J, 'Letter to The Skee Ball Alley Company,' September 3, 1911, (Newtown, North South Wales, Sydney, Australia), from the archive of the Vineland Historical and Antiquarian Society.

[20] Bell, A H, 'Letter to The Skee Ball Alley Company,' September 22, 1911, (Saskatoon, Saskatchewan, Canada), from the archive of the Vineland Historical and Antiquarian Society.

[21] Gonder, W A, 'Letter to The Skee Ball Alley Company,' September 11, 1911, (Oakland, Garrett Co., Maryland), from the archive of the Vineland Historical and Antiquarian Society.

[22] Harper, John W, 'Letter to Joseph Fourestier Simpson,' September 20, 1911, (Philadelphia, Pennsylvania), from the archive of the Vineland Historical and Antiquarian Society.

[23] Matthews, Judge, 'Letter to C H Birdsall,' September 26, 1911, (Wildwood Crest, New Jersey), from the archive of the Vineland Historical and Antiquarian Society.

[24] Simpson, Joseph Fourestier, 'Letter to C. H. Birdsall,' September 27, 1911, (Wildwood Crest, New Jersey), from the archive of the Vineland Historical and Antiquarian Society.

[25] Johnson Fare Box Company, 'Letter to Joseph Fourestier Simpson,' September 29, 1911, (Washington, D.C.), from the archive of the Vineland Historical and Antiquarian Society.

[26] Harper, John W, 'Letter to Joseph Fourestier Simpson,' October 3, 1911, from the archive of the Vineland Historical and Antiquarian Society.

[27] Harper, John W, 'Letter to Joseph Fourestier Simpson,' October 19, 1911, (Philadelphia, Pennsylvania), from the archive of the Vineland Historical and Antiquarian Society.

[28] Harper, John W, 'Letter to Joseph Fourestier Simpson,' November 1, 1911, (Philadelphia, Pennsylvania), from the archive of the Vineland Historical and Antiquarian Society.

[29] Harper, John W, 'Letter to Joseph Fourestier Simpson,' November 11, 1911, (Philadelphia, Pennsylvania), from the archive of the Vineland Historical and Antiquarian Society.

[30] Harper, John W, 'Letter to Joseph Fourestier Simpson,' November 17, 1911, (Philadelphia, Pennsylvania), from the archive of the Vineland Historical and Antiquarian Society.

[31] --, 'Advertisement -- Skee-Ball,' The Billboard (Cincinnati, Ohio), Vol. XXXII, No. 49, December 9, 1911), p. 105.

[32] --, 'Advertisement -- Owing To Death,' The Billboard (Cincinnati, Ohio), Vol. XXXII, No. 49, December 9, 1911), p. 71.

[33] Parker, C. W. 'Letter to John W. Harper,' December 19, 1911, (Leavenworth, Kansas), from the archive of the Vineland Historical and Antiquarian Society.

[34] Diamond Novelty Co., Stowell 'Letter to John W. Harper,' December 21, 1911, (Schenedtady, New York), from the archive of the Vineland Historical and Antiquarian Society.

[35] Simpson, Joseph Fourestier, 'Letter to John W Harper,' December 16, 1911, (Vineland, New Jersey), from the archive of the Vineland Historical and Antiquarian Society.

[36] Harper, John W, 'Letter to Joseph Fourestier Simpson,' December 20, 1911, (Philadelphia, Pennsylvania), from the archive of the Vineland Historical and Antiquarian Society.

[37] Smith, Morris Edgar, 'Letter to Joseph Fourestier Simpson,' January 13, 1912, (Philadelphia, Pennsylvania), from the archive of the Vineland Historical and Antiquarian Society.

[38] Ibid.

[39] Simpson, Joseph Fourestier, 'Letter to William Sauter,' January 31, 1912, (Vineland, New Jersey), from the archive of the Vineland Historical and Antiquarian Society.

[40] Ibid.

[41] Ibid.

[42] Harper, John W, 'Letter to Joseph Fourestier Simpson,' February 23, 1912, (Philadelphia, Pennsylvania), from the archive of the Vineland Historical and Antiquarian Society.

[43] Harper, John W. January 10, 1912. Skee-Ball Alley Game Construction Cost Estimate, pp. 1–3, from the archive of the Vineland Historical and Antiquarian Society.

[44] Harper, John W, 'Letter to Joseph Fourestier Simpson,' January 17, 1912, from the archive of the Vineland Historical and Antiquarian Society.

[45] Harper, John W, 'Letter to Joseph Fourestier Simpson,' January 24, 1912, (Philadelphia, Pennsylvania), from the archive of the Vineland Historical and Antiquarian Society.

[46] American Box Ball Co., 'Letter to John W Harper,' January 20, 1912, (Indianapolis, Indiana), from the archive of the Vineland Historical and Antiquarian Society.

[47] Harper, John W, 'Letter to Joseph Fourestier Simpson,' January 22, 1912, (Philadelphia, Pennsylvania), from the archive of the Vineland Historical and Antiquarian Society.

[48] Harper, John W, 'Letter to Joseph Fourestier Simpson,' January 24, 1912, (Philadelphia, Pennsylvania), from the archive of the Vineland Historical and Antiquarian Society.

[49] Harper, John W, 'Letter to Joseph Fourestier Simpson,' January 28, 1912, (Philadelphia, Pennsylvania), from the archive of the Vineland Historical and Antiquarian Society.

[50] Harper, John W, 'Letter to Joseph Fourestier Simpson,' February 28, 1912, (Philadelphia, Pennsylvania), from the archive of the Vineland Historical and Antiquarian Society.

[51] Ibid.

[52] Harper, John W, 'Letter to Joseph Fourestier Simpson,' February 21, 1912, (Philadelphia, Pennsylvania), from the archive of the Vineland Historical and Antiquarian Society.

[53] --, 'To Settle for Big Resort,' The Philadelphia Inquirer (Philadelphia, Pennsylvania), Vol. 166, No. 53, February 22, 1912), p. 5.

[54] Harper, John W, 'Letter to Joseph Fourestier Simpson,' February 21, 1912, (Philadelphia, Pennsylvania), p. 2, from the archive of the Vineland Historical and Antiquarian Society.

[55] Keels, Tom. May 1, 2016. 'Email to Thaddeus O. Cooper' (Philadelphia, Pennsylvania), p. 1.

[56] Rebbie, Tom. April 26, 2016. Personal Communication.

[57] Harper, John W, 'Letter to Joseph Fourestier Simpson,' March 4, 1912, (Philadelphia, Pennsylvania), from the archive of the Vineland Historical and Antiquarian Society.

[58] Ibid.

[59] Harper, John W, 'Letter to Joseph Fourestier Simpson,' March 18, 1912, (Philadelphia, Pennsylvania), from the archive of the Vineland Historical and Antiquarian Society.

[60] --, 'Advertisement -- Chestnut Hill Park, Philadelphia, Sold for Real Estate Development, hence these UP-TO-DATE PARK AMUSEMENTS

& PERSONAL PROPERTY TO BE SOLD AT A SACRIFICE,' The Billboard (Cincinnati, Ohio), Vol. XXIV, No. 11, 16 March 1912), p. 45.

[61] Harper, John W, 'Letter to Joseph Fourestier Simpson,' March 18, 1912, (Philadelphia, Pennsylvania), from the archive of the Vineland Historical and Antiquarian Society.

Chapter 6

[1] Simpson, Joseph Fourestier, 'Shipping Package', No. 1,116,746, (United States Patent Office) Nov. 10, 1914, pp.1-3.

[2] 'Advertisement— SKEE BALL,' The Billboard (Cincinnati, Ohio), Vol. XXV, No. 48, November 29, 1913, p. 162.

[3] Ibid.

[4] —, 'Advertisement -- Skee-Ball,' The Daily Princetonian (Princeton, New Jersey), Vol. XXXVII, No. 162, January 24, 1914, p. 2.

[5] Simpson, Joseph Fourestier, 'Letter to Edward Browning', August 16, 1915, from the archive of the Vineland Historical and Antiquarian Society.

[6] Simpson, Joseph Fourestier, 'Letter to Edward Browning', September 21, 1915, (Vineland, New Jersey), from the archive of the Vineland Historical and Antiquarian Society.

[7] —, 'Advertisement — Skee-Ball', The Billboard (Cincinnati, Ohio), Vol. XXVI, No. 12, March 21, 1914, p. 201.

[8] Simpson, Joseph Fourestier, 'Letter to Edward Browning', August 16, 1915, (Vineland, New Jersey), from the archive of the Vineland Historical and Antiquarian Society.

[9] Ibid.

[10] —, 'Skee-Ball.', The Billboard (Cincinnati, Ohio), Vol. XXVI, No. 36, September 5, 1914, p. 28.

[11] Doebrich, Joseph M., 'Scoring Mechanism for Game Apparatus', No. 1,185,071, assignor to The J. D. Este Company (United States Patent Office), May 30, 1916, pp. 1–9.

[12] Simpson, Joseph Fourestier, 'Letter to H. H. Russell', February 25, 1915, (Vineland, New Jersey), from the archive of the Vineland Historical and Antiquarian Society.

[13] Simpson, Joseph Fourestier, 'Letter to Louis Berni', September 29, 1915, (Vineland, New Jersey), from the archive of the Vineland Historical and Antiquarian Society.

[14] Simpson, Joseph Fourestier, 'Letter to David Tim', October 6, 1915, (Vineland, New Jersey), from the archive of the Vineland Historical and Antiquarian Society.

[15] Burnes, J. J., 'Philadelphia', Variety (New York, New York), Vol. 35, No. 1, June 5, 1914, p. 26.

[16] —, 'Advertisement -- Skee Ball Alleys', Electric Railway Journal, Vol. 49, No. 1, January 6, 1917, p. 32.

[17] 'Skee-Ball Draws Crowds', The Billboard (Cincinnati, Ohio) Vol. XXVII, No. 13, , March 27, 1915, p. 95.

[18] 'Sporting News'. May 6, 1914. The Springfield Union (Springfield, Massachusetts), p. 24.

[19] Burnes, J. J., 'Philadelphia', Variety (New York, New York), Vol. 35, No. 1, June 5, 1914, p. 26.

[20] —, 'Public Ordinances of Atlantic City From Jan. 1, 1914 to Dec. 31, 1914', 1914, p. 79.

[21] Myles, 'Coney Island Chatter', The Billboard (Cincinnati, Ohio), Vol. XXVI, No. 27, July 4, 1914, p. 9.

[22] —, 'Coney Island Chatter', The Billboard (Cincinnati, Ohio), Vol. XXVI, No. 28, July 11, 1914, p. 9.

[23] —, 'New Corporations', Chester Times (Chester, Pennsylvania), 41st Year, No. 11,987, July 17, 1914, p. 8.

[24] —, 'Pacific Coast Skee-Ball Company Letters of Incorporation'. July 15, 1914. Delaware Secretary of State (Dover, Delaware), pp. 1–4.

[25] —, 'Advertisement', The Billboard (Cincinnati, Ohio) Vol XXVI, No. 30, July 25, 1914, p. 51

[26] —, 'Advertisement', The Billboard (Cincinnati, Ohio), Vol. XXVI, No. 31, August 1, 1914, p. 37.

[27] Harper, John W, and J. Dickinson Este, 'Improvements in Game Apparatus', No. 14,173/14 Assigned to The J. D. Este Company (Department of Patents, Australia), pp. 1–3.

[28] —, 'Skee-Ball.', The Billboard (Cincinnati, Ohio), Vol. XXVI, No. 36, September 5, 1914, p. 28.

[29] —, 'Advertisement — Skee-Ball', The Billboard (Cincinnati, Ohio), Vol. XXVI, No. 36, September 5, 1914, p. 99.

[30] —, 'Sun of Austerlitz Sets as "Skeeball" Wins Fame', Evening Public Ledger (Philadelphia, Pennsylvania), Vol. 1, No. 26, October 13, 1914, p. 11.

[31] —, 'This Weeks Entertainments', Electric Railway Journal (New York, New York), Vol. 44, No.15A, October 13, 1914, p. 800.

[32] —, 'High Scores In Skee-Ball Contest', Electric Railway Journal (New York, New York), Vol. 44, No.15A, October 13, 1914, p. 800.

[33] —, 'Daily Prizes for Skee-Ball', Electric Railway Journal (New York, New York), Vol. 44, No.15B, October 14, 1914, p. 800.

[34] —, 'Advertising Literature', Electric Railway Journal (New York, New York), Vol. 44, No. 19, November 7, 1914, p. 1084.

[35] —, 'Holds His Constable's Son', Evening Public Ledger (Philadelphia, Pennsylvania), Vol. 1, No. 50, November 10, 1914, p. 11.

[36] —, 'The Fire Record', Oswego Daily Times (Oswego, New York), Vol. 72, No. 290, January 4, 1915, p. 1.

[37] —, 'Philadelphia Has a 900,000 Blaze.', The Oswego Palladium (Oswego, New York), Vol. 96, No. 1, January 5, 1915, p. 1.

[38] 'Advertisement -- Skee-Ball', Electric Railway Journal (New York, New York), Vol. 45, No. 6, February 6, 1915, p. 17.

[39] —, 'Minutes'. February 8, 1915. Union League (Philadelphia, Pennsylvania), p. 1.

[40] —, 'Advertisement — Concessions To Lease', The Billboard (Cincinnati, Ohio), Vol. XXVII, No. 7, February 13, 1915, p. 36.

[41] —, 'Advertisement — Concessions To Lease', The Billboard (Cincinnati, Ohio), Vol. XXVII, No. 9, February 27, 1915, p. 36.

[42] —, 'Advertisement — Concessions To Lease', The Billboard (Cincinnati, Ohio), Vol. XXVII, No. 10, March 6, 1915, p. 40.

[43] —, 'Advertisement — Wheeling Park', The Billboard (Cincinnati, Ohio), Vol. XXVII, No. 11, March 13, 1915, p. 36.

[44] Falk, Charles, 'San Diego Expo. News', The Billboard (Cincinnati, Ohio), Vol. XXVII, No.7, February 13, 1915, p. 29.

[45] —, 'Directory — Skee-Ball — The J. D. Este Co.', The Billboard (Cincinnati, Ohio) Vol. XXVII, No. 13, March 27, 1915, p. 108.

[46] —, 'Advertisement', The Billboard (Cincinnati, Ohio), Vol. XXVII, No. 13, March 27, 1915, p. 159.

[47] —, 'Skee-Ball Draws Crowds', The Billboard (Cincinnati, Ohio), Vol. XXVII, No. 13, March 27, 1915, p. 95.

[48] —, 'Advertisement -- Skee-Ball', Electric Railway Journal (New York, New York), Vol. 45, No. 14, April 3, 1915, p. 31.

[49] —, 'Untitled', Fitchburg Daily Sentinel (Fitchburg, Massachusetts) Vol. 43, No. 6, May 12, 1915), p. 2.

[50] —, 'At the Theaters Next Week.', Washington Herald (Washington, D. C.), No. 3143, May 20, 1915, p. 10.

[51] —, 'Where to Go and What to See', Washington Herald (Washington, D. C.), No. 3146, May 23, 1915, p. 5.

[52] —, 'Resort Opens Saturday', Washington Herald (Washington, D. C.), No. 3149, May 26, 1915, p. 6.

[53] —, 'Attractions Coming to Washington', Washington Times (Washington, D. C.), No. 8547, May

27, 1915, p. 7.

[54] —, 'Chesapeak Beach Opening', The Washington Post (Washington, D. C.), No. 14,231, May 28, 1915, p. 5.

[55] —, 'Coney [Island], 5/23/15', Photograph, May 23, 1915, (Bain News Service).

[56] —, 'Coney and Tody Back in Their Old Stride', New York Sun (New York, New York), Vol. LXXII, No. 266, May 24, 1915, p. 12.

[57] —, 'Marshall Hall', Washington Herald (Washington, D. C.), No. 3155, June 1, 1915, p. 7.

[58] 'Glen Echo Park'. Washington Herald (Washington, D. C.), No. 3155, June 1, 1915, p. 7.

[59] —, 'Advertisement — Enjoy Today At Marshall Hall', The Washington Post (Washington, D. C.), No. 14,240, June 6, 1915, Magazine Section, p. 3.

[60] —, 'News Notes of the Stage', The Washington Post (Washington, D. C.), No. 14,240, June 6, 1915, Magazine Section, p. 2.

[61] —, 'Marshall Hall', Washington Herald (Washington, D. C.), No. 3164, June 10, 1915, p. 5.

[62] —, 'Coming to the Theaters', The Washington Post (Washington, D. C.), No. 14,243 June 10, 1915, p. 5.

[63] —, 'Advertisement -- Enjoy Yourself At Marshall Hall', Washington Herald (Washington, D. C.), No. 3166, June 12, 1915, p. 3.

[64] —, 'Advertisement — Spend Sunday At Beautiful Historic Marshall Hall', The Washington Post (Washington, D. C.), No. 14,245, June 12, 1915, p. 14.

[65] —, 'Marshall Hall', Washington Times (Washington, D. C.), No. 8564, June 13, 1915, p. 12.

[66] —, 'Marshall Hall', Washington Herald (Washington, D. C.), No. 3167, June 13, 1915, p. 6.

[67] —, 'Marshall Hall', The Washington Post (Washington, D. C.), June 13, 1915), Magazine Section, p. 2.

[68] —, 'Advertisement — Enjoy Today At Beautiful Historic Marshall Hall', The Washington Post (Washington, D. C.), June 13, 1915, Magazine Section edition, p. 3.

[69] —, 'Mass. Park a Comer', The Billboard (Cincinnati, Ohio), June 19, 1915, p. 21.

[70] —, 'Advertisement — Skee-Ball', The Billboard (Cincinnati, Ohio), July 3, 1915, p. 21.

[71] Harper, John W., and J. Dickinson Este, 'Improvements in Game Apparatus', No. 14,173/14 Assigned to The J. D. Este Company (Department of Patents, Australia), pp. 1–3.

[72] —, 'Skeeball the Latest Sport Craze Is Here', Corpus Christi Caller and Daily Herald (Corpus Christi, Texas), Vol. 17, No. 192, July 16, 1915, p. 3.

[73] —, 'Attractions Coming to Washington', The Washington Times (Washington, D. C.), No. 8625, August 11, 1915, p. 6.

[74] —, 'Advertisement — Skee-Ball Tournament Tonight', The New York Times (New York, New York), Vol. LXIV, No. 21,018, August 11, 1915, p. 7.

[75] —, 'Stewart Best at Skee Ball.', The New York Times (New York, New York) Vol. LXIV, No. 21,019, August 12, 1915, p. 6.

[76] —, 'Plate Printers Outing Set for September 11', Washington Times (Washington, D. C.), Vo. 8643, No. 14, August 31, 1915, p. 14.

[77] —, 'Printers Plan Jaunt to Chesapeake Beach', Washington Herald (Washington, D. C.), No. 3244, August 31, 1915, p. 2.

[78] —, 'Advertisement -- Skee Ball Alleys', Electric Railway Journal (New York, New York), Vol. 49 No. 49, March 17, 1917, p. 90

[79] —, 'Advertisement Skee-Ball For The Clubman', Life (New York, New York), Vol. 66, No. 1721, October 21, 1915, p. 776.

[80] —, 'Certificate of Incorporation of the Skee-Ball Operating Company, Inc.', A New York Corporation, Filed October 22, 1915, Book 548, p. 579.

[81] —, 'New Incorporations', The New York Times (New York, New York), Vol. LXV, No. 21097 October

29, 1915, p. 16.

[82] —, 'Certificate of Incorporation of the Skee-Ball Operating Company, Inc.', A New York Corporation, Filed October 22, 1915, Book 548, p. 579.

[83] —, 'Skee Ball Added to White Way's Sports', New York Sun (New York, New York), Vol. LXXXII, No. 250, May 8, 1915, p. 11.

[84] —, 'Tips', The New York Clipper (New York, New York), Vol. LXIII No. 40, November 13, 1915, p. 12.

[85] —, 'New Skee Bowling in Town', New Rochelle Pioneer (New Rochelle, New York), Vol. 57, No. 35, November 27, 1915, p. 3.

[86] —, 'Advertisement — Skee-Ball Alleys', The Billboard (Cincinnati, Ohio), December 18, 1915, p. 186.

[87] The J. D. Este Company, Harold Wade, 'Improvements in or Relating to Game Apparatus', No. 103,532 (Great Britain), February 1, 1917.

[88] —, 'Advertisement', The Billboard (Cincinnati, Ohio), Vol. XXVIII, No. 9, February 26, 1916, p. 32.

[89] —, 'Advertisement', The Billboard (Cincinnati, Ohio), Vol. XXVIII, No. 9, February 26, 1916, p. 33.

[90] —, 'Advertisement', The Billboard (Cincinnati, Ohio), Vol. XXVIII, No. 12, March 18, 1916, p. 149.

[91] —, 'Advertising Literature', Electric Railway Journal (New York, New York), Vol. 47, No. 11, March 11, 1916, p. 524.

[92] —, 'Philadelphia Will Boost Pin Tourney in a Mass Meeting', The Washington Times (Washington, D. C.), No. 8838, March 13, 1916, p. 11.

[93] —, 'Skee-Ball', Electric Traction (Chicago, Illinois), Vol. 12, No. 4, April 1916, p. 352.

[94] —, 'Trap-Shooting as a Park Attraction', Electric Traction (Chicago, Illinois), Vol. 12, No. 4, April 1916, p. 288.

[95] —, 'Rochester Pin Pickers to Have Crack at the Game of Skee-Ball', Rochester Democrat and Chronicle (Rochester, New York), April 6, 1916, p. 23.

[96] —, 'Advertisement -- The J. D. Este Company', Electric Railway Journal (New York, New York), Vol. 47, No. 19, May 6, 1916, p. 37.

[97] —, 'Riverview to Open Tonight', The Des Moines News (Des Moines, Iowa), Vol. 36, No. 191, May 20, 1916, p. 5.

[98] —, 'Advertisement -- Marshall Hall', The Washington Times (Washington, D. C.), No. 8914, May 28, 1916, p. 14.

[99] —, 'Advertisement — Amusement Casino', Evening Public Ledger (Philadelphia, Pennsylvania), Vol. 11, No. 221, May 1916, p. 16.

[100] —, 'Advertisement — Amusement Casino', Evening Public Ledger (Philadelphia, Pennsylvania), Vol. 11, No. 221, May 31, 1916, p. 21.

[101] —, 'Advertisement — Amusement Casino', Evening Public Ledger (Philadelphia, Pennsylvania), Vol. 11, No. 225, June 2, 1916, p. 18.

[102] —, 'Advertisement — Amusement Casino', Evening Public Ledger (Philadelphia, Pennsylvania), Vol. 11, No. 226, June 3, 1916, p. 13.

[103] —, 'Advertisement — Amusement Casino', Evening Public Ledger (Philadelphia, Pennsylvania), Vol. 11, No. 228, June 6, 1916), p. 10.

[104] —, 'Advertisement — Amusement Casino', Evening Public Ledger (Philadelphia, Pennsylvania), Vol. 11, No. 230, June 8, 1916, p. 18.

[105] —, 'Amusement Casino', Evening Public Ledger (Philadelphia, Pennsylvania), Vol. 11, No. 231, June 9, 1916, p. 20.

[106] —, 'Orders for Silent Sunday', The New York Times (New York, New York), Vol. LXV, No. 21,349, July 7, 1916, p. 22.

[107] —, 'Compromise at A. C.', The Billboard (Cincinnati, Ohio), Vol. XXVIII, No. 34, August 19, 1916), p. 62.

[108] Ibid.

Chapter 7

[1] —, 'Revere Skee Ball Men Defeat Poor Aggregation', The Philadelphia Inquirer (Philadelphia, Pennsylvania), Vol. 171, No. 173, December 20, 1914, p. 1.

[2] —, 'Propose Skee Ball League', Evening Public Ledger (Philadelphia, Pennsylvania), Vol. 1, No. 87, December 23, 1914, p. 11.

[3] —, 'Bender's Skee Ball Tourney', Evening Public Ledger (Philadelphia, Pennsylvania), Vol. 1, No. 93, December 31 1914, p. 12.

[4] —, 'Washington Woman Wins at Skee Ball.', The Washington Post (Washington, D. C.), No. 14,298, August 4, 1915, p. 8.

[5] —, 'Stewart Best at Skee Ball.', The New York Times (New York, New York), Vo. LXIV, No. 21,019, August 12, 1915, p. 6.

[6] —, 'Skee Ball Contest at Market Square Billiard Parlors', Lebanon Daily News (Lebanon, Pennsylvania), No. 255, May 18, 1916, p. 7.

[7] —, 'Skee Ball Game at the Market Square Parlors', Lebanon Daily News (Lebanon, Pennsylvania), No. 257, May 20, 1916, p. 5.

[8] Ibid.

[9] —, 'Girls Will Play Skee Ball Game This Evening', The Lebanon Daily News (Lebanon, Pennsylvania), May 26, 1916, No. 263, p. 3.

[10] —, 'Weimar Girls Down Lebanon Quintet in Skee Ball Game', Lebanon Daily News (Lebanon, Pennsylvania), No. 264, May 27, 1916, p. 9.

[11] —, 'Skee Ball Contest at McKinney Parlor', Lebanon Daily News (Lebanon, Pennsylvania), No. 270, June 2, 1916, p. 7.

[12] —, 'Skee Ball Six Defeated the Big Five at Palace', Lebanon Daily News (Lebanon, Pennsylvania), No. 271, June 3, 1916, p. 5.

[13] —, 'Will Open Branch Skee Ball Parlors', Lebanon Daily News (Lebanon, Pennsylvania), No. 278, June 10, 1916, p. 5.

[14] —, 'Will Open New Skee Ball Parlor Tonight', Lebanon Daily News (Lebanon, Pennsylvania), No. 283, June 15, 1916, p. 3.

[15] —, 'Advertisement', New York Herald (New York, New York), No. 29,150, June 14, 1916, p. 22.

[16] —, 'Lebanon Defeated Mt. Gretna Team at Skee Ball', Lebanon Daily News (Lebanon, Pennsylvania), No. 326, July 28, 1916, p. 3.

[17] —, 'Skee Ball Contest at McKinney's Parlors', Lebanon Daily News (Lebanon, Pennsylvania), No. 332, August 3, 1916, p. 7.

[18] —, 'Mt. Gretna Skee Ball Team Defeated the Strong Local Team', Lebanon Daily News (Lebanon, Pennsylvania), No. 334, August 5, 1916, p. 6.

[19] —, 'Mt. Gretna Skee Ball Team Downed Lebanon Big Six', Lebanon Daily News (Lebanon, Pennsylvania), No. 340, August 11, 1916, p. 5.

[20] —, 'Young Ladies to Play Skee Ball at Palace Parlors', Lebanon Daily News (Lebanon, Pennsylvania, No. 347, August 18, 1916, p. 9.

[21] —, 'Mt. Gretna Skee Ball Team Beaten by the Big Six', Lebanon Daily News (Lebanon, Pennsylvania), No. 354, August 25, 1916, p. 3.

[22] —, 'Plate Printers Give Outing', The Washington Post (Washington, D. C.), No. 14,697, September 9, 1916, p. 5.

[23] —, 'Outing of Plate Printers', The Washington Post (Washington, D. C.), No. 14,698, September 10, 1916), p. 5.

[24] —, 'Lebanonians Were at Palmyra for Skee Ball', Lebanon Daily News (Lebanon, Pennsylvania), No. 13, September 20, 1916, p. 7.

Chapter 8

[1] Simpson, Joseph Fourestier, 'Letter to Evelyn Parker', April 7, 1916, from the archive of the Vineland Historical and Antiquarian Society.

[2] Simpson, Joseph Fourestier, 'Game.', Application No.

4422, (United States Patent Office), Filed January 21, 1915.

[3] Simpson, Joseph Fourestier, 'Game.', No. 1,156,438, (United States Patent Office), October 15, 1915.

[4] Simpson, Joseph Fourestier, 'Game', No. 174409, (Canada), January 9, 1917.

[5] The E. T. Burrowes Company, H H Russell, 'Letter to Joseph Fourestier Simpson', February 19, 1916, (Portland, Maine), from the archive of the Vineland Historical and Antiquarian Society.

[6] The Brunswick-Balke-Collender Co., 'Letter to Joseph Fourestier Simpson', March 23, 1915, (Chicago, Illinois), from the archive of the Vineland Historical and Antiquarian Society.

[7] Auchy, Henry B, 'Letter to Joseph Fourestier Simpson', March 26, 1916, (Germantown, Pennsylvania), from the archive of the Vineland Historical and Antiquarian Society.

[8] Berni, Louis, 'Letter to Joseph Fourestier Simpson', September 28, 1915. (New York, New York), from the archive of the Vineland Historical and Antiquarian Society.

[9] Simpson, Joseph Fourestier, 'Letter to The Brunswick-Balke-Collender Co.', April 5, 1915 (Vineland, New Jersey), from the archive of the Vineland Historical and Antiquarian Society.

[10] The Brunswick-Balke-Collender Co., Adler, L. H., 'Letter to Joseph Fourestier Simpson', April 30, 1915, (New York, New York), from the archive of the Vineland Historical and Antiquarian Society.

[11] Simpson, Joseph Fourestier, 'Letter to Edward Browning', August 16, 1915, (Vineland, New Jersey), from the archive of the Vineland Historical and Antiquarian Society.

[12] Simpson, Joseph Fourestier, 'Letter to Edward Browning', September 21, 1915, (Vineland, New Jersey, from the archive of the Vineland Historical and Antiquarian Society.

[13] Sando, Briant, 'Letter to Joseph Fourestier Simpson', April 27, 1916, (Indianapolis, Indiana), from the archive of the Vineland Historical and Antiquarian Society.

[14] Sando, Briant, 'Letter to Joseph Fourestier Simpson', April 28, 1916, (Indianapolis, Indiana), from the archive of the Vineland Historical and Antiquarian Society.

[15] —, 'Briant Sando in New Company', Printers Ink (New York, New York), Vol. XCVI, No. 4, July 27, 1916, p. 90.

[16] R. L. Polk & Co.'s Indianapolis City Directory 1917 (R. L. Polk & Co., 1917) p. 324.

[17] Ibid.

[18] —, 'Advertisement — Big Money', The Billboard (Cincinnati, Ohio), Vol. XXVIII, No. 42, October 14, 1916, p. 33.

Chapter 9

[1] —, 'Advertisement — SkeeBallAlleys', The Billboard (Cincinnati, Ohio), Vol. XXVIII, No. 43, October 21, 1916, p. 31.

[2] —, 'Advertisement — SkeeBallAlleys', The Billboard (Cincinnati, Ohio), Vol. XXVIII, No. 44, October 28, 1916, p. 29.

[3] —, 'Advertisement — SkeeBallAlleys', The Billboard (Cincinnati, Ohio), Vol. XXVIII, No. 51, December 16, 1916, p. 219.

[4] —, 'Advertisement -- SkeeBallAlleys', Electric Railway Journal (New York, New York), Vol. 49, No. 1, January 6, 1917, p. 32.

[5] Simpson, Joseph Fourestier, 'Game', No. 174409, (Canada), January 9, 1917.

[6] The J. D. Este Company, 'Improvements in or Relating to Game Apparatus' No. 103532, (Great Britain), February 1, 1917.

[7] —, 'Advertisement — SkeeBallAlleys', The Billboard (Cincinnati, Ohio), Vol. XXIX, No. 5, February 3, 1917, p. 25.

[8] —, 'Advertisement — Start The Season Right With

Bridge Ball', The Billboard (Cincinnati, Ohio), Vol. XXIX, No. 6, February 10, 1917, p. 67.

[9] —, 'Advertisement -- Skee Ball Alleys', Electric Railway Journal (New York, New York), Vol. 49, No. 7, February 17, 1917, p. 44.

[10] —, 'Advertisement — Shooting Gallery and Skee Ball Alleys', The Chicago Daily Tribune (Chicago, Illinois), Vol. LXXVI, No. 46, February 22, 1917, p. 20.

[11] —, 'Advertisement — $10 To $25 Per Day On One Game', The Billboard (Cincinnati, Ohio), Vol. XXIX, No. 8, February 24, 1917, p. 62.

[12] 'Skee-Ball Alley Company Entity Details', File No. 40827, Delaware Secretary of State. Retrieved June 24, 2011, 8:28PM.

[13] —, 'Tips for the Ad Manager', The Editor & Publisher (New York, New York), March 3, 1917, p. 18.

[14] —, 'Essington School Closes for Season', Aerial Age Weekly (New York, New York), Vol. 4, No. 10, November 20, 1916, p. 248.

[15] —, 'Advertisement -- Skee-Ball is always in the limelight of popularity', Electric Railway Journal (New York, New York), Vol. 49, No. 9, March 3, 1917, p. 56.

[16] —, 'Advertisement -- SkeeBallAlleys', El Paso Herald (El Paso, Texas), March 8, 1917, p. 12.

[17] —, 'Advertisement — $10 To $25 Per Day On One Game', The Billboard (Cincinnati, Ohio), Vol. XXIX, No. 10, March 10, 1917, p. 66.

[18] —, 'Advertisement — $50 To $100 Per Day On Four Games', The Billboard (Cincinnati, Ohio), March 17, 1917, p. 65.

[19] —, 'Advertisement -- Skee Ball Alleys', Electric Railway Journal (New York, New York), Vol. 49, No. 11, March 17, 1917, p. 90.

[20] —, 'Advertisement — Score-Ball', The Billboard (Cincinnati, Ohio), Vol. XXIX, No. 12, 24 March 1917, p. 183.

[21] —, 'Score-Ball a New Game', The Billboard (Cincinnati, Ohio), Vol. XXIX, No. 12, 24 March 1917, p. 182.

[22] —, 'Advertisement — $50 To $100 Per Day On Four Games', The Billboard (Cincinnati, Ohio), Vol. XXIX, No. 12, 24 March 1917, p. 92.

[23] —, 'Advertisement — SkeeBall Always In The Limelight Of Popularity', The Billboard (Cincinnati, Ohio), Vol. XXIX, No. 12, 24 March 1917, p. 95.

[24] —, 'Advertisement — $50 To $100 A Day', The Billboard (Cincinnati, Ohio), Vol. XXIX, No. 13, March 31, 1917, p. 27.

[25] —, 'Advertisement — SkeeBallAlleys, The Billboard (Cincinnati, Ohio), Vol. XXIX, No. 13, March 31, 1917, p. 33.

[26] —, 'Skee-Ball Alleys', Electric Traction (Chicago, Illinois), Vol. 13, No. 4, April 1917, 312.

[27] Parker, Evelyn, 'Letter to Joseph Fourestier Simpson', February 10, 1917, (Atlantic City), from the archive of the Vineland Historical and Antiquarian Society.

[28] —, 'Advertisement — Score-Ball', The Billboard (Cincinnati, Ohio), Vol. XXIX, No. 15, April 14, 1917, p. 67.

[29] —, 'A New Game of Real Merit', The Billboard (Cincinnati, Ohio), Vol. XXIX, No. 17, April 28, 1917, p. 35.

[30] —, 'Obituary', Electric Railway Journal (New York, New York), Vol. 50, No. 26, December 29, 1917, p. 1184.

[31] —, 'Record of J. Dickinson Este, Cl. of 1909 Undergraduate Alumni File, box 351. [Princeton University Seely G. Mudd Manuscript Library]', p. 1.

[32] —, 'Advertisement — SkeeBallAlleys', The Billboard (Cincinnati, Ohio), Vol. XXX, No. 2, January 12, 1918, p. 35.

[33] —, 'Advertisement — SkeeBall', The Billboard (Cincinnati, Ohio), Vol. XXX, No. 26, June 29, 1918, p. 88.

[34] —, 'Advertisement — Make Big Money With Whirl-O-Ball', The Billboard (Cincinnati, Ohio), Vol. XXX, No. 11, March 16, 1918), p. 33.

[35] —, 'Advertisement — Skee Ball For Trolley Parks', Electric Railway Journal (New York, New York), Vol. 51, No. 11, March 16, 1918, p. 104.

[36] —, 'Fascinating Game of "Skee-Ball"', Electric Traction (Chicago, Illinois), Vol. XIV, No. 4, April 1918, p. 230.

[37] —, 'Este Games', The Billboard (Cincinnati, Ohio), Vol. XXX, No. 18, May 4, 1918), p. 33.

[38] —, 'Woodside Park, Philadelphia', The Billboard (Cincinnati, Ohio), Vol. XXX, No. 21, May 25, 1918, p. 29.

[39] —, 'Coney Island, a Cincinnati Park, Suffers Damage by Fire', The Billboard (Cincinnati, Ohio), Vol. XXX, No. 20 May 18, 1918, pp. 3, 61.

[40] —, 'Advertisement — Spend July 4th at Summit Park', Utica Herald-Dispatch (Utica, New York), Vol. 74, No. 189, July 2, 1918, p. 3.

[41] —, 'Two Big Syracuse Picnics Draw 500 Persons to Lake', The Auburn Citizen (Auburn, New York), August 17, 1918, p. 6.

[42] —, 'Guests at Manchester', Brooklyn Daily Eagle (New York, New York), August 18, 1918, p. 7.

Chapter 10

[1] —, 'Record of J. Dickinson Este, Cl. of 1909 Undergraduate Alumni File, box 351. [Princeton University Seely G. Mudd Manuscript Library]', p. 1.

[2] Ibid.

[3] Ibid.

[4] Este, Jonathan Dickinson, 'Princeton University War Records Form', October 28, 1924.

[5] —, 'Record of J. Dickinson Este, Cl. of 1909. [Princeton University]', p. 1.

[6] 'Certificate of Death, Commonwealth of Pennsylvania - Charles Este', (August 10, 1917), File No. 86889 Registered No. 166.

[7] —, 'Record of J. Dickinson Este, Cl. of 1909. [Princeton University]', p. 1.

[8] Este, Jonathan Dickinson, 'Princeton University War Records Form', October 28, 1924.

[9] —, 'Record of J. Dickinson Este, Cl. of 1909. [Princeton University]', p. 1.

[10] Ibid, p. 2.

[11] Ibid.

[12] Ibid.

[13] Ibid.

[14] Ibid.

[15] Este, Jonathan Dickinson, 'Reconnaissance Report M199', September 13, 1918.

[16] Pvt. Shaw, S. C., 'Lt. Gen. Hunter Liggitt awarding the D.S.C. to Capt. J. D. Este of the 13th Squadron, P.S. Group, 1st Army Air Service.' (Remicourt, France), November 10, 1918, NARA 111-SC-30942.

[17] Este, Jonathan Dickinson, 'Princeton University War Records Form', October 28, 1924.

[18] 'Marriages Este-Taber' New York Times (New York, New York), Vol. LXVIII, No. 22,293, February 6, 1919, p. 11.

[19] 'Certificate of Amendment of Certificate of Incorporation of The J. D. Este Compay', A Delaware Corporation, June 17, 1919.

[20] 'Skee Ball Company, Philadelphia, Pa.', Electric Railway Journal, 54 (1919), p. 780.

'Skee Ball Company, Philadelphia, Pa.', Electric Railway Journal (New York, New York), Vol. 54, No. 16, October 18, 1919, p. 780.

Chapter 11

[1] —, 'Advertisement — For Sale Two Bridge Ball Games', The Billboard (Cincinnati, Ohio), Vol. XXXI, No. 47, November 22, 1919, p. 68.

[2] —, 'Coney Island Chatter', The Billboard (Cincinnati, Ohio), Vol. XXXII, No. 19, May 8, 1920, p. 63.

[3] 'United States Federal Census', (Department of Commerce—Bureau of the Census, Cumberland, New

Jersey, Supervisors District 2, Enumeration District No. 152, 3 Precinct), Sheet No. 23B.

[4] Death Certificate for Joseph Fourestier Simpson, 17 June 1930, Registered No. 394, State of New Jersey Bureau of Vital Statistics.

[5] —, 'Advertisement Skee Ball Score Ball Baseballite', The Billboard (Cincinnati, Ohio), Vol. XXXII, No. 4, January 24, 1920, p. 71.

[6] Al. Ballyhoo, 'Coney Island Chatter', The Billboard (Cincinnati, Ohio), Vol. XXXII, No. 18, May 1, 1920, p. 61.

[7] —, 'Advertisement — Jazz Ball', The Billboard (Cincinnati, Ohio), Vol. XXXII, No. 23, June 5, 1920, p. 61.

[8] —, 'Noblett Hold Barmann's Notes', Kingston Daily Freeman (Kingston, New York), August 20, 1921, p. 1.

[9] —, 'Advertisement -- Skee-Ball Company', Association Men (New York, New York) Vol. XLVI, No. 6, February 1921, p. 252.

[10] 'Coney Island', Wikipedia, https://en.wikipedia.org/wiki/Coney_Island retrieved, September 4, 2016.

[11] —, 'Coney Island Chatter', The Billboard (Cincinnati, Ohio), Vol. XXXII, No. 24, 12 June 1920, p. 63.

[12] —, 'Advertisement — Rocky Glen Amusement Resort', The Billboard (Cincinnati, Ohio), Vol. XXXII, No. 25, June 19, 1920, p. 4.

[13] —, 'Coney Island Chatter', The Billboard (Ciincinnati, Ohio), Vol. XXXII, No. 25, June 19, 1920, p. 63.

[14] —, 'Advertisement' — Havana, Cuba, The Billboard (Cincinnati, Ohio), October 9, 1920, Vol. XXXII, No. 41, p. 75.

[15] —, 'Advertisement', The Corsicana Daily Sun (Corsicana, Texas), Vol. XXIII, No. 69, November 1, 1920, p. 7.

[16] —, 'Advertisement', The Corsicana Daily Sun (Corsicana, Texas), Vol. XXIII, No. 69, November 1, 1920, p. 6.

[17] 'Young Mens Christian Association', The Social Welfare History Project, Virginia Commonwealth University Libraries, retrieved September 4, 2016 (http://socialwelfare.library.vcu.edu/youth/young-mens-christian-association/).

[18] —, 'Advertisement -- Skee-Ball Company', Association Men (New York, New York) Vol. XLVI. No. 6, February 1921, p. 252.

[19] 'Dissolution of Skee Ball Operating Co. Inc.' (A Corporation of the State of New York), Filed June 2, 1921.

[20] —, 'Patents and Design Acts, 1907 and 1919 -- Application for Restoration of Lapsed Patent Under Section 20', The Edinburgh Gazette, 1921, No. 13,766, p. 2121.

[21] —, 'Harry Tudor', The Billboard (Cincinnati, Ohio), Vol. XXXIII, No. 50, December 10, 1921, p. 127.

[22] —, 'Arnold Neble in England', The Billboard (Cincinnati, Ohio), Vol. XXXIV, No. 5, February 4, 1922, p. 76.

[23] —, 'Advertisement — Bargain Skee Ball Alleys', The Billboard (Cincinnati, Ohio), Vol. XXXIV, No. 6, February 11, 1922, p. 98.

[24] —, 'Mid-City Park', The Billboard (Cincinnati, Ohio), Vol. XXXIV, No. 8, February 25, 1922, p. 86.

[25] —, 'White City, Little Rock', The Billboard (Cincinnati, Ohio), Vol. XXXIV, No. 9, March 4, 1922, p. 78.

[26] —, 'Advertisement — Games May Come And Games May Go', The Billboard (Cincinnati, Ohio), Vol. XXXIV, No. 11, March 18, 1922, 19.

[27] —, 'Advertisement Best In 1914 Skee Ball', The Billboard (Cincinnati, Ohio), Vol. XXXIV, No. 12, March 25, 1922, p. 108.

[28] —, 'New Skee-Ball Factory Running to Full Capacity', The Billboard (Cincinnati, Ohio), Vol. XXXIV, No. 12, March 25, 1922, p. 107.

[29] —, 'Advertisement — It Was In The City Of

Bridgeport', The Billboard (Cincinnati, Ohio), Vol. XXXIV, No. 13, April 1, 1922, p. 3.

[30] —, 'Advertisement — Out In Sunny California!', The Billboard (Cincinnati, Ohio), Vol. XXXIV, No. 14, April 8, 1922, p. 75.

[31] —, 'Cincinnati Parks Get Away to Excellent Start', The Billboard (Cincinnati, Ohio), Vol. XXXIV, No. 23, June 10, 1922, p. 68.

[32] —, 'Advertisement — Grand Opening, June 3, 1922, Mid-City Park', The Billboard (Cincinnati, Ohio), Vol. XXXIV, No. 23, June 10, 1922, p. 68.

[33] —, 'Schuykill Park', The Billboard (Cincinnati, Ohio), Vol. XXXIV, No. 23, June 10, 1922, p. 67.

[34] —, 'Advertisement — Wanted At Once For Paradise Park Opening June 16th.', The Billboard (Cincinnati, Ohio), Vol. XXXIV, No. 23, June 10, 1922, p. 6.

[35] —, 'Advertisement -- Faulkner's Novelty Store', Evening Public Ledger (Philadelphia, Pennsylvania), Vol. VIII, No. 234, 14 June 1922, Travel And Resort Section, p. 7.

[36] —, 'Advertisement — Wanted — Skee-Ball Alleys.', The Billboard (Cincinnati, Ohio), Vol. XXXIV, No. 45, November 11, 1922, p. 63.

[37] 'Certificate of Incorporation of Skee Ball Sales And Security Co. Inc.' (State of New York, Filed December 16, 1922).

[38] —, 'Advertisement — White City Park', The Billboard (Cincinnati, Ohio), Vol. XXXV, No. 5, February 3, 1923, p. 82.

[39] —, 'Advertisement — Will Lease Box Ball Or Skee Ball Concession', The Billboard (Cincinnati, Ohio), Vol. XXXV, No. 11, March 17, 1923, p. 104.

[40] —, 'Advertisement — Announcing The Opening Of Ontario Lake Park Saturday, May 19th', Oswego Daily Palladium (Oswego, New York), Vol. LX?, No. 118, May 18, 1923, p. 7.

[41] —, 'Advertisement — A Surprise For You!', Republican Watchman (Monticello, New York), Vol. 99, No. 24, May 25, 1923, p. 2.

[42] —, 'State Coal Men at Sacandaga to Hear Noted Spears and Take Part in Varied Program', The Morning Herald (Gloversville And Johnstown, New York), Vol. XXVII, No. 134, September 1, 1923, p. 12.

[43] —, 'Advertisement — Silver Spray Pleasure Pier, Long Beach, California', The Billboard (Cincinnati, Ohio), Vol. XXXV,, No. 50, December 15, 1923, p. 187.

[44] —, 'Advertisement — Skee Ball', The Billboard (Cincinnati, Ohio), Vol. XXXV, No. 52, December 29, 1923, p. 87.

[45] —, 'Morris Goldberg in Florida', The Billboard (Cincinnati, Ohio), November 12, 1927, p. 70.

[46] —, 'Great Progress Made in Preparing Rye Beach as a County Park', The Daily Argus (Mount Vernon, New York), No. 11,580, November 16, 1927, p. 3.

[47] —, 'Morris Goldberg Home From Fla.', The Billboard (Cincinnati, Ohio), Vol. XXXIX, No. 47, November 19, 1927, p. 70.

[48] —, 'Advertisement — Skee-Ball The International Game Of Skill', The Billboard (Cincinnati, Ohio), Vol. XXXVI, No. 12, March 22, 1924, p. 99.

[49] —, 'Advertisement — 762 Amusement Centers Now Operating Skee-Ball', The Billboard (Cincinnati, Ohio), Vol. XL, No. 11, March 17, 1928, p. 70.

[50] 'Certificate of Incorporation of National Skee Ball Company, Inc.', (State of New York, Filed 30 March 1928), pp. 1-10.

[51] —, 'Advertisement — 762 Amusement Centers Now Operating Skee-Ball', The Billboard (Cincinnati, Ohio), Vol. XL, No. 12, March 24, 1928, p. 104.

Chapter 12

[1] 'Certificate of Incorporation of National Skee Ball Company, Inc.', State of New York, Filed March 30, 1928.

[2] —, 'Bergoffen Dies Suddenly on Trip to Atlantic City', Brooklyn Daily Eagle (Brooklyn, New York), June 2, 1935, A Section, p. 15.

[3] 'Herman Bergoffen Petition for Naturalization District Court of the United States For The Eastern District of New York', July 1, 1903.

[4] —, 'Teacher Arrests Driver at School Fire Drill', The Brooklyn Standard Union (New York, New York), Vol. XLIV, No. 316, May 15, 1908, p. 1.

[5] —, 'Vacation School Teachers.', The Brooklyn Daily Eagle (New York, New York), Vol. 71, No. 150, June 9, 1910, Picture and Sporting Sections edition, p. 2.

[6] —, 'School Teacher Seeks Injunction', The Brooklyn Standard Union (New York, New York), Vol XLVII, No. 196, January 16, 1911, p. 1.

[7] —, 'Community House Campaign Is Begun', The Brooklyn Standard Union (Brooklyn, New York), Vol. LVI, No. 143, November 21, 1919, p. 11.

[8] —, 'Hebrew Societies Buy Site for Home', The Brooklyn Standard Union (New York, New York), Vol. LVL, No. 153, December 2, 1919, p. 10.

[9] Fourteenth Census of the United States: 1920 Population, 15 January 1920, p. 1A.

[10] —, 'Williamsburg Y.M.H.a. to Give Big Ball', The Brooklyn Standard Union (New York, New York), Vol. LVII, No. 195, January 16, 1921, Second Section, p. 9.

[11] —, 'Degrees Given to 116 Law Students', The Brooklyn Standard Union (New York, New York), Vol. XLVII, No. 339, June 7, 1912, p. 9.

[12] 'R. L. Polk & Co. Trows General Directory of New York City Embracing The Boroughs of Manhattan and the Bronx 1916' Volume 129 (New York, R. L. Polk & Co. Inc., Publishers) p. 258.

[13] R. L. Polk & Co.'s 1917 Trow's New York City Directory Boroughs of Manhattan and Bronx Vol. 130 (New York, R. L. Polk & Co. Inc., Publishers) p. 350.

[14] —, 'News of Brooklyn Students in Schools and Colleges', The Brooklyn Daily Eagle (New York, New York), February 26, 1917, p. 10.

[15] R. L. Polk & Co.'s 1918 Trow's New York City Directory Boroughs of Manhattan and Bronx Vol. 131 (New York, R. L. Polk & Co. Inc., Publishers) p. 324.

[16] R. L. Polk & Co.'s 1920-21 Trow's New York City Street and Avenue Directory Borough of Manhattan (New York, R. L. Polk & Co. Inc., Publishers) p. 313.

[17] —, 'Jewish Bodies Unite', The Brooklyn Daily Eagle (New York, New York), Vol. 81, No. 141, May 22, 1921, Section 1, p. 13.

[18] Bergoffen, Herman, 'A Visit to Coney', The Billboard (Cincinnati, Ohio), Vol. XLVI, No. 30, July 28, 1934, p. 52.

[19] —, 'Elect Dr. P. I. Nash C. I. Chamber Head', The Brooklyn Daily Eagle (New York, New York), Vol. 85, No. 12, January 13, 1925, p. 5.

[20] —, 'Work on $2,000,000 Hotel for Coney Island to Start May 1; to Have 300 Rooms', The Brooklyn Daily Eagle (New York, New York), Vol. 85, No. 87, March 29, 1925, p. 18A.

[21] —, Bergoffen, Herman, 'A Visit to Coney', The Billboard, Vol. XLVI, No. 30, July 28, 1934, p. 52.

[22] —, 'Apartment Plans for Montgomery St. Involve $600,000', The Brooklyn Daily Eagle (Brooklyn, New York), Vol. 87, No. 359, December 29, 1927, Section 1, p. 5.

[23] —, 'Elect Dr. P. I. Nash C. I. Chamber Head', The Brooklyn Daily Eagle (New York, New York), Vol. 85, No. 12, January 13, 1925, p. 5.

[24] —, 'Chamber to Oppose Anti-Parking Plan', The Brooklyn Standard (Brooklyn, New York), Vol. LXII, No. 289, April 20, 1926, p. 4.

[25] —, 'Nash Renominated by Coney Chamber', The Brooklyn Daily Eagle (New York, New York), Vol. 86, No. 325, November 23, 1926, p. 3.

[26] —, 'Coney Complains About Insurance', The Brooklyn Standard Union (Brooklyn, New York), Vol. LXIII, No. 274, April 5, 1927, p. 3.

[27] —, 'End of Parking Ban in Surf Ave. Urged', The Brooklyn Daily Eagle (New York, New York), Vol. 87, No. 139, May 20, 1927, p. 7.

[28] —, 'Charity Committee Is Formed in Coney', The Brooklyn Standard Union (Brooklyn, New York), Vol.

LXIII, No. 323, May 24, 1927, p. 2.

[29] —, 'Twelve Thirty Club Luncheon', The Brooklyn Standard Union (New York, New York), Vol. LXIV, No. 118, October 28, 1927, p. 10.

[30] —, 'Coney Island', The Brooklyn Standard Union (New York, New York), Vol. LXIV, No. 126, November 5, 1927, p. 7.

[31] —, 'Coney Relief Group Plans Dance Feb. 4', The Brooklyn Standard Union (New York, New York), Vol. LXVII, No. 167, January 16, 1931, p. 15.

[32] Weber, Michael John, "Nine Balls For One Thin Dime A brief history of Skeeball", New Jersey Monthly, June 1979, pp. 77, 113.

[33] —, 'Advertisement — Coney Island Spaces', The Billboard (Cincinnati, Ohio), Vol. XL, No. 13, March 31, 1928, p. 70.

[34] —, 'Advertisement — 762 Amusement Centers Now Operating Skee-Ball', The Billboard (Cincinnati, Ohio), Vol. XL, No. 13, March 31, 1928, p. 70.

[35] —, 'Advertisement — Skee-Ball', The Billboard (Cincinnati, Ohio), Vol. XL, No. 38, September 22, 1928, p. 67.

[36] —, 'Coney Island Plot Sold, Plan for Hotel Hinted', Brooklyn Daily Eagle (New York, New York), Vol. 33, No. 115, April 25, 1928, p. 16.

[37] —, 'All Set for Greatest Outdoor Conventions', The Billboard (Cincinnati, Ohio), Vol. XLI, No. 47, November 30, 1929, p. 173.

[38] Ibid.

[39] —, 'Advertisement — Skill-Ball', The Billboard (Cincinnati, Ohio), Vol. XLII, No. 16, April 19, 1930, p. 64.

[40] —, 'Advertisement — Skee-Ball The Most Popular Amusement Device In The World', The Billboard (Cincinnati, Ohio), Vol. XLIII, No. 4, January 24, 1931, p. 53.

[41] —, 'Advertisement — Skee-Ball For 1931', The Billboard (Cincinnati, Ohio), Vol. XLIII, No. 11, March 14, 1931, p. 39.

[42] —, 'Advertisement — National Skee-Ball Co., Inc.', The Billboard (Cincinnati, Ohio), Vol. XLIII, No. 13, March 28, 1931, p. 85.

[43] —, 'Crystal Beach Opens May 28', The Billboard (Cincinnati, Ohio), Col. XLIII, No. 13, March 28, 1931, p. 97.

[44] —, 'Advertisement — To The Members of The N.A.A.P.', The Billboard (Cincinnati, Ohio), Vol. XLIII, No. 34, August 22, 1931, p. 35.

[45] 'Layman M. Sternbergh', New Jersey, Births and Christenings Index, 1660-1931, (Ancestry.com. New Jersey, Births and Christenings Index, 1660-1931 [database on-line]. Provo, UT, USA: Ancestry.com Operations, Inc., 2011.).

[46] Paterson Directory 1914 (Paterson, N. J., The Price & Lee Co.) p. 694.

[47] Polk's Asbury Park New Jersey Directory 1924 p. 523.

[48] —, 'Along the Way', The Ocean Grove Times (Ocean Grove, New Jersey), December 5, 1924, Vol. XXXII, No. 49, p. 5.

[49] —, 'Along the Way', The Ocean Grove Times (Ocean Grove, New Jersey), March 19, 1926, Vol. XLIV, No. 12, p. 5.

[50] Sternbergh, Layman M., 'Skee Ball Apparatus', No. 1,826,964, (United States Patent Office), October 13, 1931.

[51] —, 'Advertisement — To The Members of The N.A.A.P.', The Billboard (Cincinnati, Ohio), Vol. XLIII, No. 34, August 22, 1931, p. 35.

[52] —, 'Henry Guenther Dines NAAP in Climax of Three-Day Meet', The Billboard (Cincinnati, Ohio), Vol. XLIII, No. 35, August 29, 1931, pp. 44,47.

[53] —, 'Petition', Application No. 276901, (United States Trademark Office), December 14, 1928.

[54] —, 'Advertisement — Skee-Ball', The Billboard (Cincinnati, Ohio), Vol. XLIII, No. 49, December 5, 1931, p. 72.

[55] Peccerillo, Dominick, 'Game', No. 1,834,317,

(United States Patent Office), December 1, 1931.

[56] —, 'Manufacturers Seek Way Out From Present Credits Burden', The Billboard (Cincinnati, Ohio), Vol. XLIII, No. 50, December 12, 1931, p. 36.

[57] —, 'Advertisement — Visit The New Skee-Ball Stadium', The Billboard (Cincinnati, Ohio), Vol. XLIV, No. 10, March 5, 1932, p. 35.

[58] Weber, Michael John, "Nine Balls For One Thin Dime A brief history of Skeeball", New Jersey Monthly, June 1979, p. 113.

[59] —, 'Advertisement — Visit The New Skee-Ball Stadium', The Billboard (Cincinnati, Ohio), Vol. XLIV, No. 11, March 12, 1932, p. 39.

[60] —, 'National Skee-Ball Tourny at Atlantic City, October 1 and 2', The Billboard (Cincinnati, Ohio), Vol. XLIV, No. 11, March 12, 1932, p. 38.

[61] —, 'Rock Springs Park Has Heavy Opening Attendance', The Billboard (Cincinnati, Ohio), Vol. XLIV, No. 25, June 18, 1932, p. 36.

[62] —, 'Park Gleanings', The Billboard (Cincinnati, Ohio), Vol. XLIV, No. 25, June 18, 1932, p. 38.

[63] —, 'Change A. C. Playoff Dates Account Holiday Conflict', The Billboard (Cincinnati, Ohio), Vol. XLIV, No. 25, June 18, 1932, p. 37.

[64] —, 'Playland Skee Ball Tourney', The Billboard (Cincinnati, Ohio), Vol. XLIV, No. 25, June 18, 1932, p. 38.

[65] Van Valkenberg, W. D., 'Covering Coney', The Billboard (Cincinnati, Ohio), Vol. XLIV, No. 26, June 25, 1932, p. 46.

[66] —, 'Paris Men Have Arcades', The Billboard (Cincinnati, Ohio), Vol. XLIV, No. 34, August 20, 1932, p. 37.

[67] —, 'Advertisement — Skee-Ball Marches On!', The Billboard (Cincinnati, Ohio), Vol. XLIV, No. 35, August 27, 1932, p. 63.

[68] —, 'Crown Skee Ball Champ', The Billboard (Cincinnati, Ohio), Vol. XLIV, No. 41, October 8, 1932, p. 36.

[69] Bergoffen, Herman, 'Game', No. 2,010,213, Assignor to National Skee Ball Company, Inc. (United States Patent Office), August 6, 1935.

[70] —, 'Fansher New Dealers' Head', The Billboard (Cincinnati, Ohio), Vol. XLIV, No. 50, December 10, 1932, pp. 38,40.

[71] —, 'Exhibits Show a Wide Range', The Billboard (Cincinnati, Ohio), Vol. XLIV, No. 50, December 10, 1932, p. 39.

[72] NATIONAL SKEE-BALL CO., INC., V. SEYFRIED, Court of Chancery. 110 N.J. Eq. 18 (N.J. 1932).

Chapter 13

[1] —, 'Advertisement — Just Out! Whirl-O-Ball', The Billboard (Cincinnati, Ohio), Vol. XXX, No. 2, January 12, 1918, p. 39.

[2] —, 'Machinery Markets and News of the Works', Iron Age (New York, New York), Vol. 101, No. 4, January 24, 1918, p. 306.

[3] R. L. Polk & Co.'S Indianapolis City Directory 1918 (Indianapolis, Indiana: R. L. Polk & Co.), 1918.

[4] —, 'Advertisement — Bank Ball', The Billboard (Cincinnati, Ohio), Vol. XLIV, No. 17, April 23, 1932, p. 39.

[5] —, 'Advertisement — Skill Ball', The Billboard (Cincinnati, Ohio), Vol. XLVIII, No. 15, April 11, 1936, p. 142.

[6] —, 'Advertisement — Bank Roll', The Billboard (Cincinnati, Ohio), Vol. XLVIII, No, 33, August 15, 1936, p. 77.

[7] —, 'Advertisement — Roll-A-Ball', The Billboard (Cincinnati, Ohio), Vol. XLVIII, No. 24, June 13, 1936, p. 81.

[8] —, 'Advertisement PAMCO TANGO', The Billboard (Cincinnati, Ohio), Vol. XLVIII, No. 27, July 4, 1936, p. 79.

[9] —, 'Advertisement — Bally-Roll', The Billboard (Cincinnati, Ohio), Vol. XLVIII, No. 28, July 18, 1936, p. 90.

[10] —, 'Advertisement — Hurdle Hop', The Billboard (Cincinnati, Ohio), Vol. XLVIII, No. 31, August 1, 1936, p. 87.

[11] Peccerillo, Dominick, 'Game', No. 1,834,317, (United States Patent Office), December 1, 1931.

[12] —, 'Advertisement — International Mutoscope Reel Co. Inc.', The Billboard (Cincinnati, Ohio), Vol. XLVIII, No. 33, August 15, 1936, p. 78.

[13] —, 'Advertisement — Bowl-A-Game', The Billboard (Cincinnati, Ohio), Vol. XLIV, No. 17, April 23, 1932, p. 69.

[14] —, 'Advertisement — Sensationally Presenting ROCK-OLA'S Superb ROCK-O_BALL', The Billboard (Cincinnati, Ohio), Vol. XLVIII, No. 35, August 29, 1936, p. 120.

[15] —, 'Advertisement — Gyro', The Billboard (Cincinnati, Ohio), Vol. XLIV, No. 18, April 30, 1932, p. 77.

[16] —, 'Advertisement — Acknowledged - "the best game of all!" KEENEY'S BOWLETTE', The Billboard (Cincinnati, Ohio), Vol. XLVIII, No. 31, August 1, 1936, p. 92.

[17] —, 'London', The Billboard (Cincinnati, Ohio), Vol. XLVIII, No. 30, July 25, 1936, p. 88.

[18] —, 'British Coin Machine Show', The Billboard (Cincinnati, Ohio), Vol. XLVIII, No. 14, April 4, 1936, pp. 64, 74, 75.

[19] —, 'How Visitor Can See "Whole Show" at World's Fair for Only $15', Seneca County News (Waterloo, New York), Vol. 61, No. 28, May 25, 1939.

[20] —, 'Advertisement — Proof Of Solid Merit', The Billboard (Cincinnati, Ohio), Vol. XLIV, No. 24, June 11, 1932, p. 56.

[21] —, 'Advertisement — Skee Roll', The Billboard (Cincinnati, Ohio), Vol. XLVII, No. 17, April 27, 1935, p. 39.

[22] —, 'Advertisement — Skee Roll', The Billboard (Cincinnati, Ohio), Vol. XLVII, No. 21, May 25, 1935, p. 39.

[23] —, 'Advertisement — Skee Roll', The Billboard (Cincinnati, Ohio), Vol. XLVIII, No. 4, January 25, 1936, p. 83.

[24] —, 'Advertisement — An International Institution', The Billboard (Cincinnati, Ohio), Vol. XLVIII, No. 15, April 11, 1936, p. 58.

[25] —, 'Advertisement — There Is Only One Skee Roll', The Billboard (Cincinnati, Ohio), Vol. XLVIII, No. 16, April 18, 1936, p. 65.

[26] —, 'Advertisement — There's Long Life and Consistent Earning Power In Skee Roll', The Billboard (Cincinnati, Ohio), Vol. XLVIII, No. 26, June 27, 1936, p. 129.

[27] Bergoffen, Herman, 'Game', No. 2,010,213, Assignor to National Skee Ball Company, Inc. (United States Patent Office), August 6, 1935.

[28] Traube, Leonard, 'Coney Island', The Billboard (Cincinnati, Ohio), Vol. XLVII, No. 21, May 25, 1935, pp. 40, 57.

[29] Traube, Leonard, 'Coney Island', The Billboard (Cincinnati, Ohio), Vol. XLVII, No. 24, June 15, 1935, p. 43.

[30] —, 'The Final Curtain', The Billboard (Cincinnati, Ohio), Vol. XLVII, No. 24, June 15, 1935, p. 30.

[31] National Skee Ball Company, Inc., 'Improvements in or Relating to Apparatus for Playing a Game', No. 459,521, (Great Britain) January 8, 1937.

[32] Bergoffen, Herman, 'Game', No. 2,010,213, Assignor to National Skee Ball Company, Inc. (United States Patent Office), August 6, 1935.

[33] —, 'Exhibit Space Demand Soars', The Billboard (Cincinnati, Ohio), Vol. XLVII, No. 44, November 2, 1935, pp. 36–37.

[34] —, 'NAAPPB Program Is Ready', The Billboard (Cincinnati, Ohio), Vol. XLVII, No. 48, November 30, 1935, pp. 52, 54.

[35] —, 'Advertisement — Skee Roll', The Billboard (Cincinnati, Ohio), Vol. XLVII, No. 48, November 30, 1935, p. 54.

[36] —, 'Exhibits Are Listed', The Billboard (Cincinnati, Ohio), Vol. XLVII, No. 50, December 14, 1935, p. 41.

[37] Certified copy of proclamation of dissolution by the State of New York Department of State.

[38] Weber, Michael John, "Nine Balls For One Thin Dime A brief history of Skeeball", New Jersey Monthly, June 1979, p. 113.

[39] —, 'Candid Camera Shots at the Show', The Billboard (Cincinnati, Ohio), Vol. XLVIII, No. 4, January 25, 1936, p. 76.

Chapter 14

[1] —, 'Agreement between National Skee Ball Company Inc. and The Rudolph Wurlitzer Manufacturing Company', June 19, 1936, from the archives of Philadelphia Toboggan Coasters Inc.

[2] Weber, Michael John, "Nine Balls For One Thin Dime A brief history of Skeeball", New Jersey Monthly, June 1979, p. 113, from the archives of Philadelphia Toboggan Coasters Inc.

[3] —, 'Wurlitzer in Game Field; Buys National Skee-Ball Co.', The Billboard (Cincinnati, Ohio), Vol. XLVIII, No. 28, July 18, 1936, p. 68.

[4] —, 'Agreement between National Skee Ball Company Inc. and The Rudolph Wurlitzer Manufacturing Company', June 19, 1936, from the archives of Philadelphia Toboggan Coasters Inc.

[5] Ibid, p. 10.

[6] —, 'Advertisement — Wurlitzer extends its leadership into Games Field', The Billboard (Cincinnati, Ohio), Vol. XLVII, No. 28, July 18, 1936, p. 86.

[7] —, 'Wurlitzer in Game Field; Buys National Skee-Ball Co.', The Billboard (Cincinnati, Ohio), Vol. XLVIII, No. 28, July 18, 1936, p. 68.

[8] —, 'Calcutt Orders 400 Bally-Rolls', The Billboard (Cincinnati, Ohio), Vol. XLVIII, No. 30, July 25, 1936, p. 101.

[9] —, 'First Skill-Balls to Woman Op', The Billboard (Cincinnati, Ohio), Vol. XLVIII, No. 30, July 25, 1936, p. 89.

[10] —, 'Great Welcome for Bally-Roll', The Billboard (Cincinnati, Ohio), Vol. XLVIII, No. 30, July 25, 1936, p. 84.

[11] —, 'Modern Prepares a Big Party for New Wurlitzer Skee-Ball', The Billboard (Cincinnati, Ohio), Vol. XLVIII, No. 3, July 25, 1936, p. 89.

[12] —, 'Stirling Announces Price Reduction on Skill-Ball', The Billboard (Cincinnati, Ohio), Vol. XLVIII, No. 30, July 25, 1936, p. 95.

[13] —, 'Advertisement — Caution Before You Buy…', The Billboard (Cincinnati, Ohio), Vol. XLVIII, No. 30, July 25, 1936, p. 103 (BackCover).

[14] —, 'To Be Biggest Summer Yet, Says Jim Buckley, of Bally', The Billboard (Cincinnati, Ohio), Vol. XLVIII, No. 31, August 1, 1936, p. 78.

[15] —, 'George Ponser Enthused Over Roll-a-Ball Results', The Billboard (Cincinnati, Ohio), Vol. XLVIII, No. 31, August 1, 1936, p. 89.

[16] —, 'Advertisement — Wurlitzer's Skee-Ball already the accepted Leader', The Billboard (Cincinnati, Ohio), Vol. XLVIII, No. 35, August 29, 1936, p. 134.

[17] —, 'Advertisement', The Billboard (Cincinnati, Ohio), Vol. XLVIII, No. 36, September 5, 1936, p. 75.

[18] —, 'Advertisement — A Plain Statement Of Facts On Skee-Ball', The Billboard (Cincinnati, Ohio), Vol. XLVIII, No. 31, August 1, 1936, pp. 79–82.

[19] —, 'Advertisement — We looked at them all!', The Billboard (Cincinnati, Ohio), Vol. XLVIII, No. 49, December 5, 1936, p. 100 (BackCover).

[20] —, 'Wurlitzer-Modern Party Climax to Good-Will Building Program', The Billboard (Cincinnati, Ohio), Vol. XLVIII, No. 50, December 12, 1936, p. 77.

[21] —, 'Photograph — A Manufacturer And Distributor Lay Plans', The Billboard (Cincinnati, Ohio), Vol. XLVIII, No. 50, December 12, 1936, p. 82.

[22] —, 'Genco-Ponser Hookup to Push Bank-Roll Games', The Billboard (Cincinnati, Ohio), Vol. XLVIII, No. 50, December 12, 1936, p. 90.

[23] —, 'Advertisement — Look to Rock-Ola For Leadership', The Billboard (Cincinnati, Ohio), Vol. XLVIII, No. 51, December 19, 1936, p. 91.

[24] Certificate of Change of Name of National Skee Ball Company, Inc. to Piesen Maufacturing Co., Inc., State of New York, Department of State. Filed 1 November 1937.

[25] Durant, Lyndon A., 'Game Totalizer', No. 2,054,616, Assignor of one half to George H. Campbell, (United States Patent Office), September 15, 1936.

[26] Dyrenforth, Lee, Chritton & Wiles, 'Letter to The Rudolph Wurlitzer Mfg. Company, Sherman Hotel, Chicago, Illinois, Attention Mr. Capehart', January 11, 1937, from the archives of Philadelphia Toboggan Coasters Inc.

[27] —, 'Agreement between Kenneth C. Shyvers, Lyndon A. Durant, George H. Campbell and The Rudolph Wurlitzer Company', May 10, 1937, from the archives of Philadelphia Toboggan Coasters Inc.

[28] Weber, Michael John, "Nine Balls For One Thin Dime A brief history of Skeeball", New Jersey Monthly, June 1979, p. 113, from the archives of Philadelphia Toboggan Coasters Inc.

[29] —, 'Notes — The Rudolph Wurlitzer Company', circa 1937, from the archives of Philadelphia Toboggan Coasters Inc.

[30] The Rudolph Wurlitzer Company, 'Letter to The Philadelphia Toboggan Company', November 19, 1945, from the archives of Philadelphia Toboggan Coasters Inc.

Chapter 15

[1] Rebbie, Tom, 'Email to Thaddeus O. Cooper', April 6, 2016.

[2] Ibid.

[3] Gerhart, C. M., 'Letter to Rudolph Wurlitzer Manufacturing Company, Attention: Mr. Michael Hammergren, General Manager,' August 7, 1945, from the archives of Philadelphia Toboggan Coasters Inc.

[4] Hokanson, O. A., 'Letter to Mr. C. M. Gerhart, Assistant Secretary, Philadelphia Toboggan Company,' November 1, 1945, pp 1-2, from the archives of Philadelphia Toboggan Coasters Inc.

[5] Pitcher, E., Howson and Howson, 'Letter to Philadelphia Toboggan Company Att: Mr. Gearhart,' November 9, 1945, from the archives of Philadelphia Toboggan Coasters Inc.

[6] Gerhart, Clarence M., 'Notes', November 9, 1945, from the archives of Philadelphia Toboggan Coasters Inc.

[7] —, 'Notes', circa 1945, from the archives of Philadelphia Toboggan Coasters Inc.

[8] Johnson, C. E., 'Telegram to Mr. Cm. Gerhart', November 15, 1945, from the archives of Philadelphia Toboggan Coasters Inc.

[9] Johnson, C. E., "Letter to The Philadelphia Toboggan Company," November 19, 1945, pp. 1-2, from the archives of Philadelphia Toboggan Coasters Inc.

[10] Gerhart, Clarence M., "Notes", circa 1945, pp 1-3, from the archives of Philadelphia Toboggan Coasters Inc.

[11] The Rudolph Wurlitzer Company, C. E. Johnson, 'Letter to The Philadelphia Toboggan Company', November 19, 1945, from the archives of Philadelphia Toboggan Coasters Inc.

[12] Philadelphia Toboggan Company, C. M. Gerhart, 'Letter to Mr. Carl E. Johnson, The Rudolph Wurlitzer Company', December 6, 1945, from the archives of Philadelphia Toboggan Coasters Inc.

[13] Johnson, Carl E., 'Letter to C. M. Gerhart Assistant Secretary, Philadelphia Toboggan Company', December 7, 1945, from the archives of Philadelphia Toboggan Coasters Inc.

[14] Johnson, Carl E., 'Letter to Philadelphia Toboggan Company', December 19, 1945, from the archives of Philadelphia Toboggan Coasters Inc.

[15] Gerhart, C. M., 'Letter to The Rudolph Wurlitzer Company, Attention: Mr. Carl E. Johnson, Vice

President and Manager', circa 1945, from the archives of Philadelphia Toboggan Coasters Inc.

[16] —, 'File of Skee-Ball Purchases 1948-1952 of the Philadelphia Toboggan Company', 1948-1952, from the archives of Philadelphia Toboggan Coasters Inc.

[17] Ridyard, A. R., 'Letter to Mr. Maurice Piesen, Piesen Mfg. Company', November 19, 1947, from the archives of Philadelphia Toboggan Coasters Inc.

[18] Ridyard, A. R., 'Letter to Mr. Julian I. Berghoffer, Piesen Mfg. Company', November 19, 1947, from the archives of Philadelphia Toboggan Coasters Inc.

[19] Ridyard, A. R., 'Letter to Mr. Hugo H. Piesen, Piesen Mfg. Company', November 19, 1947, from the archives of Philadelphia Toboggan Coasters Inc.

[20] Ridyard, A. R., 'Letter to Piesen Manufacturing Company', November 20, 1947, pp 1-2, from the archives of Philadelphia Toboggan Coasters Inc.

[21] —, Death of Hugo Piesen, Find A Grave (http://www.findagrave.com/cgi-bin/fg.cgi?page=gr&GRid=96124526&ref=acom), retrieved September 10, 2016,

[22] Bergoffen, Julian I., 'Letter to Philadelphia Toboggan Co., Attention: Mr. A. R. Ridyard, Office Manager', November 24, 1947, from the archives of Philadelphia Toboggan Coasters Inc.

[23] Schmeck, H. P., 'Letter to Mr. Maurice Piesen', January 20, 1948, from the archives of Philadelphia Toboggan Coasters Inc.

[24] Piesen, Maurice, 'Letter to H. P. Schmeck, General Manager, Philadelphia Toboggan Co.', February 3, 1948, from the archives of Philadelphia Toboggan Coasters Inc.

[25] Bergoffen, Herman, 'Notes', circa 1948, from the archives of Philadelphia Toboggan Coasters Inc.

[26] —, 'Contract between Piesen Manufacturing Corp. & The Philadelphia Toboggan Company', August 6, 1948, from the archives of Philadelphia Toboggan Coasters Inc.

[27] —, 'Extract From Minutes', August 7, 1948, from the archives of Philadelphia Toboggan Coasters Inc.

[28] Ibid.

[29] —, 'File of Skee-Ball Purchases 1948-1952 of the Philadelphia Toboggan Company', 1948-1952, from the archives of Philadelphia Toboggan Coasters Inc.

[30] Carrol, R. W., "Letter to Mr. Julian Bergoffen", October 29, 1952, from the archives of Philadelphia Toboggan Coasters Inc.

[31] —, 'Contract between Philadelphia Toboggan Company & Ideal Toy Corporation', March 2, 1953, pp. 1-5, from the archives of Philadelphia Toboggan Coasters Inc.

[32] —, '2 Year Terms on Skee-Ball', March 1958, from the archives of Philadelphia Toboggan Coasters Inc.

[33] Johns, Frank D., 'Automatic Ticket-Dispensing Skee Ball Machine', No. 2,926,915, (United States Patent Office), March 1, 1960.

[34] —, 'Florida Spot Grows / Fun Business Booming at Daytona Shoreline', The Billboard, July 9, 1955, pp. 51,53,

[35] Piesen, Maurice, 'Letter to Mr. High', October 27, 1977, pp. 1-2, from the archives of Philadelphia Toboggan Coasters Inc.

[36] —, 'Notes', November 2, 1977, from the archives of Philadelphia Toboggan Coasters Inc.

[37] Rebbie, Tom, 'Email to Thaddeus O. Cooper', April 6, 2016,

[38] Farnan, Frank, "Letter to Mr. Pete Piesen C/O Bergoffen & Piesen", December 4, 1983, from the archives of Philadelphia Toboggan Coasters Inc.

[39] High III, Samuel H., 'Letter to Mr. Pete Piesen C/O Bergoffen & Piesen', December 5, 1983, from the archives of Philadelphia Toboggan Coasters Inc.

Chapter 16

[1] Rebbie, Tom, 'Email to Thaddeus O. Cooper', April 6, 2016.

[2] Skee-Ball Inc. Website (http://skeeball.com/), pulled

April 2016.

[3] Frommer, Dan, 'Skee-Ball iPhone App Has A Huge Christmas', Business Insider - Tech, Dec. 28, 2009 (http://www.businessinsider.com/skee-ball-iphone-app-has-a-huge-christmas-2009-12).

[4] —, 'Play Online Games, win in-store tickets', (https://www.chuckecheese.com/kids-corner/games), pulled September 10, 2016.

[5] Wickham, Allissa, 'Skee-Ball Maker Settles Trademark Row With League', Law 360, June 18, 2014, (http://www.law360.com/articles/549583/skee-ball-maker-settles-trademark-row-with-league%5D), pulled September 10, 2016.

[6] —, 'New York game league Brewskee-Ball fights trademark case', Reuters, May 8, 2014, (http://www.reuters.com/article/us-usa-new-york-skee-ball-idUSBREA470OL20140508), pulled September 10, 2016.

[7] Wickham, Allissa, 'Skee-Ball Maker Settles Trademark Row With League', Law 360, June 18, 2014, (http://www.law360.com/articles/549583/skee-ball-maker-settles-trademark-row-with-league%5D), pulled September 10, 2016.

[8] Schweber, Nate, 'Skee-Ball, Played for Fun and Money', New York Times, May 29, 2011, (http://cityroom.blogs.nytimes.com/2011/05/29/skee-ball-played-for-fun-and-money/?_r=0), pulled September 10, 2016.

[9] National Public Radio's All Things Considered, 'In New York City, Skee-Ball For Grown-Ups', February 18, 2010, (http://www.npr.org/programs/all-things-considered/2010/02/18/123618418/), pulled September 10, 2016.

[10] Moore, Laura, 'Tracy Townsend is a champion who has put Wilmington on the map', Star News Online, July 17, 2015, 7:15 AM, (http://www.wwaytv3.com/2015/06/05/wilmington-skee-ball-lets-the-good-times-roll/), pulled September 10, 2016.

[11] Brubaker, Harold, 'Skee-Ball maker in Chalfont sold to rival; production to move', philly.com, February 24, 2016 (updated February 25, 2016), pulled September 10, 2016 (http://www.philly.com/philly/business/20160225_Skee-Ball_maker_in_Chalfont_sold_to_rival__production_to_move.html).

[12] Bollier, Jeff, 'Arcade classic Skee-Ball finds home in Pulaski', USA Today Network-Wisconsin (June 6, 2016, 12:28 PM CDT), pulled September 10, 2016, (http://www.greenbaypressgazette.com/story/money/2016/06/03/skee-ball-bay-tek/84497632/).

PHOTO CREDITS

Chapter 1

P. 1, Skee-Ball, Argun Tekant, author's collection. Skee-Ball Alleys, Thaddeus O. Cooper, author's collection.

P. 2, Ginormous Teddy Bear, Argun Tekant.

Chapter 2

P. 5, Joseph Fourestier Simpson, Unknown, Courtesy Vineland Historical and Antiquarian Society.

P. 8, Historic American Buildings Survey, Creator. Pennsylvania Railroad Station, Broad Street Station, Broad & Market Streets, Philadelphia, Philadelphia County, PA. Documentation Compiled After, 1933. Pdf. Retrieved from the Library of Congress, https://www.loc.gov/item/pa1046/. (Accessed September 11, 2016.).

P. 9, Joseph Fourestier Simpson, unknown, courtesy Vineland Historical and Antiquarian Society.

P. 14, Joseph Fourestier Simpson and sisters, unknown, courtesy Vineland Historical and Antiquarian Society.

P. 18, 919 Landis Avenue, unknown, courtesy Vineland Historical and Antiquarian Society.

P. 25, Midway Plaisance and balloon, World's Columbian Exposition, Chicago, Ill. ca. 1893. Image. Retrieved from the Library of Congress, https://www.loc.gov/item/2006680017/. (Accessed September 11, 2016.).

P. 28, Willow Grove, Montgomery Co., Pennsylvania. ca. 1907. Image. Retrieved from the Library of Congress, https://www.loc.gov/item/91787559/. (Accessed September 11, 2016.).

Chapter 3

Pp. 46-47, Skee-Ball Alley blueprint circa 1909, Jack Carr, courtesy Vineland Historical and Antiquarian Society.

Chapter 4

P. 53, Early Skee-Ball alleys, unknown, author's collection.

P. 56, Joseph Fourestier Simpson posing with two Skee-Ball Alleys in Atlantic City, NJ near Young's Pier, unknown, courtesy Vineland Historical and Antiquarian Society.

P. 62, Detroit Publishing Co., Publisher. [Steeplechase Pier amusement park and boardwalk, Atlantic City, N.J]. [Between 1900 and 1915] Image. Retrieved from the Library of Congress, https://www.loc.gov/item/det1994024051/PP/. (Accessed September 11, 2016.).

P. 66, Wildwood Crest Pier, Wildwod Crest, NJ, unknown, courtesy Wildwood Crest Historical Society.

P. 67, Detroit Publishing Co., Publisher, Jackson, William Henry, photographer. [Salt Air i.e. Saltair Pavilion, Great Salt Lake, Utah]. [ca. 1900] Image. Retrieved from the Library of Congress, https://www.lcc.gov/item/det1994014832/PP/. (Accessed September 11, 2016.).

Pp. 74-75, Chestnut Hill Park, unknown, courtesy Philadelphia Toboggan Coasters, Inc. Archive.

Chapter 5

P. 87, Henry B. Auchy, unknown, courtesy Philadelphia Toboggan Coasters, Inc. Archive.

P. 90, Philadelphia Toboggan Company Carousel, code named Excelfi, unknown, courtesy Philadelphia Toboggan Coasters, Inc. Archive.

P. 91, Henry Auchy, Arnold Aiman and others, unknown, courtesy Philadelphia Toboggan Coasters, Inc. Archive.

Pp. 92-33, Philadelphia Toboggan Company Duval St., Germantown, Philadelphia, Pa., unknown, courtesy Philadelphia Toboggan Coasters, Inc. Archive.

P. 102, Box Ball alleys in operation circa 1908, unknown, author's collection.

Pp. 148-149, The Wheel Pump Inn across from Chestnut Hill Park, unknown, courtesy Springfield Township Historical Society.

Chapter 6

P. 158, The J. D. Este Company Skee-Ball token, Thaddeus O. Cooper, author's collection.

P. 160, Mechanical Skee-Ball Scoring Device, unknown, courtesy Philadelphia Toboggan Coasters, Inc. Archive.

P. 163, [Charles Albert Chief Bender, of the Philadelphia Athletics baseball team, three-quarter length portrait, seated, facing forward]. [1909] Image. Retrieved from the Library of Congress, https://www.loc.gov/item/89714132/. (Accessed September 11, 2016.).

P. 164, Pacific Coast Skee-Ball Company token, Thaddeus O. Cooper, author's collection.

P. 173, Attendant outside Playland in San Francisco, California, unknown, courtesy James R. Smith Collection.

Chapter 7

P. 190, Skee-Ball alleys and players at Harvey's Lake in Luzerne County, Pennsylvania, circa 1915, unknown, courtesy Luzerne County Historical Society.

Chapter 9

Pp. 244-245, Playland, San Francisco, California, unknown, courtesy James R. Smith collection.

Pp. 246-247, Playland, San Francisco, California, unknown, courtesy James R. Smith collection.

Chapter 10

P. 250, Aviation officers just prior to their decoration with Distinguished Service Cross, by Lieut. Gen. Hunter Liggett. Left to right: Capt. Jonathan Dickinson Este; Capt. "Eddie" Rickenbacker; Capt. Sollers; Lieut. Hugh Brewster; Lt. Charles R. D'Oliver; Lt. Bradley J. Gaylord; Lt. James Knowles, Jr; Lt. Howard G. Rath; Lt. L. C Somon. Rembercourt, Meurthe et Mosselle, France, Pvt. Clyde L. Eddy, S. C., courtesy National Archives and Records Administration.

P. 252, First pilots of Liberty Plane in France. Left to right: Lt. Jonathan Dickinson Este and Lt. H. C. Boricon, Aviation Supply Field, Romorantin, France, June 8, 1918, Pvt. L. P. Goldshlag, S. C., courtesy National Archives and Records Administration.

P. 254, Skee-Ball Company, Philadelphia, PA token, Thaddeus O. Cooper, author's collection.

Chapter 11

P. 256, Skee-Ball alley, unknown, courtesy Philadelphia Toboggan Coasters, Inc. Archive.

P. 259, Skee-Ball Company, Coney Island, NY token, Thaddeus O. Cooper, author's collection.

P. 260, Bain News Service, Publisher. Coney Island, in Luna Park. [between and Ca. 1915, ca. 1910] Image. Retrieved from the Library of Congress, https://www.loc.gov/item/ggb2004009490/. (Accessed September 11, 2016.).

P. 271, Battery of 8 Skee-Ball alleys at Playland San Francisco, California, unknown, courtesy James R. Smith Collection.

P. 272, Playland San Francisco, California, unknown, courtesy James R. Smith Collection.

P. 273 Close-up of Skee-Ball signs at Playland San Francisco, California, unknown, courtesy James R. Smith Collection.

P. 274, Close-up of Skee-Ball prize cabinet at Playland San Francisco, California, unknown, courtesy James R. Smith Collection.

Chapter 12

P. 277, Bain News Service, Publisher. "The Teaser", Coney Island in Luna Park. 1911. Image. Retrieved from the Library of Congress, https://www.loc.gov/item/ggb2004009286/. (Accessed September 11, 2016.).

P. 283, Skee-Ball button, Thaddeus O. Cooper, author's collection.

P. 284, Skee-Ball tokens from Layman M. Sternbergh's Ocean Grove Alleys in Ocean Grove, N. J., Thaddeus O. Cooper, author's collection.

P. 291, First National Skee-Ball Tournament at Skee-Ball Stadium in Atlantic City, NJ, Fred Hess & Son, courtesy Philadelphia Toboggan Coasters, Inc. Archive.

P. 294, Skee-Ball Alley placard that showed the license number that the alley was operating under. This license was used to limit where the alley could be operated, Argun Tekant, author's collection.

Chapter 13

P. 300, Chime Ball at Asbury Park, New Jersey, unknown, courtesy Philadelphia Toboggan Coasters, Inc. Archive.

P. 301, Miniature Skee-Balls, London, England token, Thaddeus O. Cooper, author's collection.

Chapter 14

P. 326, Homer Capehart, Vice President in charge of sales, James Broyles, assistant to Mr. Capehart. Other unidentified people are purchasers of juke boxes made at the North Tonawanda plant and installed all over the country, unknown, courtesy Historical Society of the Tonawandas.

P. 327, The Rudolph Wurlitzer Manufacturing Company plant in North Tonawanda, New York, unknown, courtesy Historical Society of the Tonawandas.

P. 328, The Rudolph Wurlitzer Manufacturing Company plant in North Tonawanda, New York, unknown, courtesy Historical Society of the Tonawandas.

P. 344, Wurlitzer Skee-Ball Alley on Display at National Premium Co. Omaha, Nebraska, unknown, courtesy Philadelphia Toboggan Coasters, Inc. Archive.

Chapter 15

P. 379, Automatic Ticket Dispenser on a Skee-Ball alley, unknown, courtesy Philadelphia Toboggan Coasters, Inc. Archive.

Chapter 16

P. 391, Skee-Ball, Argun Tekant, author's collection.

INDEX

A

Aiman, Arnold 87, 89, 91, 96, 146
Alamac Pier 186
Albany, New York 263
Allen and Sparks 63
Allentown, Pennsylvania 143, 288, 290
American Box Ball Company 101, 107, 138, 164, 211, 214
American Electric Railway Association 167
American "Flexible" Egg Crate Carrier Company 195
amusement parks 1, 24, 27, 55, 63, 72, 88, 143, 183, 184, 185, 225, 242, 255, 265, 267, 289, 332, 355, 376, 387
Anderson, J. C. 181
Animated Game And Toy Company 257
Appleton, George A. 263
Arcachon, France 251
arcades 1, 27, 242, 255, 281, 299, 307, 387, 390
Archer, Mark E. 214
Arkansas 263, 266, 301
Arnolds Park, Iowa 287
Arverne, New York 288
Atlantic City Boardwalk 9, 223, 233
Atlantic City Convention 240
Atlantic City, New Jersey 9, 15, 24, 56, 60, 62, 155, 162, 166, 167, 174, 185, 186, 187, 191, 205, 206, 208, 209, 230, 234, 258, 268, 281, 285, 287, 288, 289, 290, 291, 305
Auburndale, Massachusetts 288
Auchy, Henry B. 72, 73, 77, 85, 87, 88, 89, 91, 95, 96, 97, 116, 143, 144, 145, 198, 199, 201, 355
Auchy's Facility 96
Auchy's operation 110
Auchy's Shop 88
Auditorium Pier 61
Australia 114, 164, 177
Australian Patent No. 14.173/14 177
automatic coin device 166, 280, 299, 306, 335
Automatic Games Company 298
automatic scoring device 3, 60, 158, 166, 198, 234, 335, 345, 346, 359
Automatic Ticket Dispenser 379, 380
Automatic Ticket-Dispensing Skee-Ball Machine 377

Aviation Section Signal Corps 249

B

Bachman 192
Bachman, C. 192
Baker, Philip 84, 85, 101, 209
Bally Manufacturing Company 297, 325
Bally-Roll 297, 325, 329
Baltimore Country Club 171
Bank-Roll 297, 345
banks of Skee-Ball alleys 268
Barkham, Joseph 11
BaseBallLite 256
Bay Tek Games designers 390
Bay Tek Games engineers 390
Bay Tek Games, Inc. 390
Beach Haven, New Jersey 288
Beam 192
Beamesderfer 192
Belgium 299, 301, 306
Belgium Patent No. 411,685 358, 367
Bell, A. H. 113, 114
Belmar, New Jersey 287, 288
Bender, Charles 191
Bender, Charles "Chief" 162, 163, 191
Bender, Charles Playoffs 189
Bender, Charles Skee-Ball Alleys 189
Bender, Charles Skee-Ball Competitions 191
Bender, Charles Tournament 170
Bender, "Chief" Sporting Goods Store 171, 189
Benicia, California 63
Bennett, Paul S. 311, 325
Bergoffen 268, 275, 276, 278, 279, 283, 284, 287, 289, 290, 292, 304, 305, 306, 307, 310, 311
Bergoffen and Michaels Law Firm 276
Bergoffen, Herman, obituary 305
Bergoffen, Julian I. 311, 312, 368, 370, 372, 373, 374, 381
Bergoffen Patent 359, 367
Bergoffen & Piesen 372, 383, 384

Berni, Louis 158, 201, 202
Berni Organs 201
Bethlehem Pike 144
bicycle seat 20, 24
Big 5 192
Big Five Rollers 192
Big Six 193, 194
Birdsall, C. A. 116, 118
Bittler, George A. 214
Blue Laws 145, 186, 187
boardwalk 1, 9, 24, 110, 158, 162, 170, 178, 186, 234, 242, 255, 299
Boardwalk and Florida Ave. 285
Bolles, Billy 337
Bollinger 192, 193, 194
Booth, Bummy 181
Bowery 162, 258, 269
Bowl-A-Game 298
Bowlette 298
Box Ball 73, 77, 101, 102, 103, 110, 116, 118, 124, 138, 189, 211
Bradley Beach, New Jersey 287, 288
Bradshaw 96
BrewSkee-Ball League 388, 389
BrewSkee-Ball trademark 388, 389
Briant Manufacturing Company 214, 218, 219, 220, 224, 225, 227, 228, 229, 231, 232, 238, 295. *See also* Briant Specialty Company
Briant Specialty Company 214, 238, 242, 243, 290, 295. *See also* Briant Manufacturing Company
Bridge Ball 196, 198, 199, 201, 204, 205, 206, 208, 209, 210, 211, 214, 218, 219, 220, 223, 224, 225, 227, 228, 229, 231, 232, 233, 240, 256, 295
Bridgeport, Connecticut 265
British Skee-Ball Company 265
Brognard, Mary 7
Brognard, Sophia 7, 15, 96, 97, 256
Brôn, France 249
Browning, Edward 155, 201, 204, 207, 208
Brunswick-Balke-Collender Co. 114, 199, 201
Brussels Exposition 307
Buckley, Jim 329
Buffalo, New York 281, 359, 362
Burlholder 192
Burlington, North Carolina 60
Bury, Edmund 68
Butter Kist Popcorn machine 211
Byrne, John T. 158, 178
Byrne, John T. Endorsement 220, 229
Byrne, John T. Poolroom 169

C

cabinet designer 325
Calcutt, Joe 325
California 58, 63, 115, 173, 183, 265, 267, 271, 272, 273, 274, 301, 374, 389
California Amusement Zone 267
Camden, New Jersey 9, 164, 169
Cameron Auto Sales 89
Campbell, George H. 348. *See also* Shyvers, Durant and Campbell Agreement
Campion, Kenneth 287
Camp Kelly 249
Canada 206, 255, 261, 279, 280, 301
Canadian Patent, Bridge Ball 223
Canadian Patent, Bridge-Ball 198
Canadian Patent No. 174,409 223
Canadian Patent Skee-Ball 125
Canadian Patent, Skee-Ball 61, 63, 136, 157, 198
Canadian rights to Skee-Ball 157, 206
Canarsie Coaster Co. Inc. 179
candy company 20
Capehart, Homer E. 311, 312, 325, 326, 332, 334, 337, 348
Cape May 174, 266, 288
Captell, Celeste 179, 259
Carannante, Ray 389. *See also* Skee-diddy
Carty, Andy 191
Cedarhurst, Long Island, New York 290
Centennial Exposition 10, 12, 13, 17
Central Park 288, 289
Certificate of Incorporation 179, 253, 268
Charles Este Lumber Company 153, 154, 169
chattels 293
Chesapeake Beach, Virginia 174, 177, 194
Chester Park 265
Chester, West Virginia 287, 288
Chestnut Hill Park 72, 75, 76, 87, 88, 103, 110, 143, 144, 145, 146, 149, 186
Chestnut Hill Park Sale 143, 145
Chevy Chase Club 171
Chicago, Illinois 24, 25, 26, 177, 185, 297, 307, 334, 346, 347
Chime Ball 299, 300
Chuck E Cheese restaurant chain 383, 388
Church Element 186
Chutes at the Beach 268
Cincinnati, Ohio 142, 145, 240, 265
Clements 189, 191
Cleveland, Ohio 164, 174, 177, 185, 266, 288, 289

Cliff House 268
Clone Games
    Bally-Roll 297, 325, 329
    Bank-Roll 297, 345
    Bowl-A-Game 298
    Bowlette 298
    Chime Ball 299, 300
    Gyro 298
    Hurdle Hop 297
    PAMCO Tango 297
    Rock-O-Ball 298
    Skee Shot 299
    Ski-ball 299
    Skill-Ball 279, 283, 284, 296, 297, 325
Coast Holding Company 276, 305
Cohen, A. 240
Cohen, Morris 290
Cohn, Nat 337
coin box 1, 55
coin-freed hand lever 183
coin-operated machines 304, 324, 330
coin-operated Skee-Ball 324, 332
coin-operation mis-statement 332
Collins, Eddie 256
Columbia Park 287
Compton, George 290
Coney advisory committee 306
Coney Island Ave. 162
Coney Island Boardwalk 305
Coney Island Chamber of Commerce 276
Coney Island Chatter 162, 256, 258
Coney Island, Cincinnati, Ohil 265
Coney Island, Cincinnati, Ohio 240
Coney Island Emergency Relief Committee 276
Coney Island, New York 61, 162, 166, 174, 185, 186, 204, 206, 240, 257, 258, 260, 264, 265, 266, 267, 268, 269, 276, 277, 278, 279, 280, 281, 284, 285, 288, 289, 299, 301, 305, 306, 307, 324, 388
Coney Island of the West 63
Cooke III, Jay 145
Copenhagen 307
Cortelyou, George B. 24
Cossey, Fred J. 63
Crespie, Sam 258
Crolius, Fred 181
Crystal Beach, Buffalo, New York 281
Cuba 258
C. Von Voigt's Pool Parlor 155

D

Dakota Wyoming and Missouri River Railroad Company 20
Dallas, Texas 298
Danerch, Pennsylvania 287
Dartmouth College 181
Darwin, Joe A. 325
Davies, J. R. 365
Daytona Beach, Florida 377
Deering, H. 240
de Fourestier, Joseph Martin 6
Dehn, F. B. 306
Dentzell, E. P. 186
Dentzel, William H. 186, 187
Des Moines, Iowa 186
Dimensional Branding Group 388, 389
Distinguished Service Cross 250, 253
Doebrich 159, 359
Doebrich, Joseph M. 158
Dougherty Jr., Edwin V. 227, 254
Downey, Brandt C. 107
Durant, Lyndon A. 346, 348. *See also* Shyvers, Durant and Campbell Agreement
Durant Patent 346, 364
Dyer, M. P. 225, 231
Dyrenforth, Lee, Chritton & Wiles 346

E

Eastern Pennsylvania Railways Company 266
Edgemere 288, 290
Edson 64, 77, 82, 84, 85, 95, 96
Edward K. Tryon Company 132, 143
Edwards, Big Bill 181
egg crate 157, 195, 196. *See also* Shipping Package
Electric Railway Journal 169, 170, 171, 183, 223, 224, 228, 229, 234, 240
Electric Traction Journal 184, 185, 233, 240
Ellen 11
Elm Beach Park 288
Enochs, C. J. 77, 80, 81, 82, 85
Equinox House 242
Erdenheim, Pennsylvania 143, 144
Este, Charles 153
Este Company style 181
Este Cup 191
Este Family 153
Este, Jonathan Dickinson 153, 154, 155, 157, 158, 164, 165, 167, 169, 170, 172, 176, 177, 179, 181, 184, 189, 195, 196, 198, 204,

205, 206, 208, 209, 210, 214, 219, 220, 223, 224, 227, 228, 231, 238, 240, 249, 250, 251, 252, 253, 254, 259, 359
Este Jr., Charles 170, 227, 228
Este Sr., Charles 170, 249
E. T. Burrowes Company 146, 158, 198
Euclid Beach Park 174

F

Faber, Nathan 287
Fansher Amusement Company 287
Fansher, Fred 287, 290
Farnan, Frank 384
Far Rockaway, Long Island, New York 290
Faulkner's Novelty Store 266
Fieldston Gardens 290
5th Aviation Instruction Center 249
50th Street Amusement Center 367
fire 169, 240, 295
firemen 169
fire-proof 281
First flight to London 251
First National Skee-Ball tournament 285
First National Skee-Ball Tournament 285, 287, 288, 289, 291
first repeat customer. *See* Noell, James T.
Fitterer (Capt.) 193
Fittery 192
Flint, Michigan 266
Flint Park & Amusement Company 266
Flock of Skee-Gulls 389
Florida 177, 267, 377
folding ten foot alleys 69
Fortress Monroe 249
Foury 6, 7, 9, 10, 11, 14, 15, 19, 21, 24, 29, 33, 35, 37, 41, 42, 44, 52, 55, 61, 63, 68, 69, 73, 77, 80, 81, 82, 84, 85, 89, 95, 96, 97, 101, 107. *See also* Simpson, Joseph Fourestier
Fox 192
Fox, H. 192
Frank Wilcox Company 287
fraud 257, 258
Full Circle Bar 388, 389
Full Circle United LLC 389
Fuller 189, 191
Fuller, Paul 324, 325, 334

G

Gardner, Harry M. 290
Gates 194

Genco 297, 345
George Ponser Company 297, 345
Gerhart, Clarence M. 355, 356, 358, 359, 362, 363, 364, 365, 366, 367
Germantown, Philadelphia, Pennsylvania 95, 97, 381
ginormous teddy bear 2, 381
Glen Echo Park 174, 177
Gloniger, J. H. 290
Gloversville, New York 58
Goldberg Award 279
Goldberg, K. 258
Goldberg, Minnie 266
Goldberg, Morris 257, 258, 259, 264, 266, 267, 276, 278, 279, 287, 307, 310
Goldman, Julius 186
gold pieces 290
Goldsmith, Edward 287
Gonder, W. A. 115
Good, John 51
Grand View Park 287
Great Depression 275, 279, 285, 287, 293
Great Neck, Long Island 285
Great Salt Lake 63
Greenville, Pennsylvania 289
Griffith & Crane 132
Grookert, T. Wooster 186
Gustav, Andrew F. 58
Gyro 298

H

Haenie, Walter 287
Half Moon Hotel 283
Hallman 192
Hammergren, Michael 356, 358, 359
Hansell, F. R. 164
Harbaugh 193, 194
Harkins 193
Harper, Anna 52
Harper, D. Walter 52, 89
Harper, Henry Clay 52
Harper, John Washington 51, 52, 57, 61, 63, 64, 68, 69, 72, 73, 77, 80, 81, 82, 84, 85, 88, 89, 97, 103, 110, 115, 118, 122, 123, 125, 128, 132, 135, 136, 138, 142, 143, 145, 146, 153, 157, 164, 177, 195, 205, 227, 254, 259
Harper, Susan 52
Harvey's Lake 174, 190
Haulman 192
Havana 258

Headquarters, Air Service 249
Henderson's Walk 258
Hershbeck Building Corporation 276
Heverling 192, 194
High III, Samuel 381, 382, 383, 384
High Jr., Samuel 355, 374, 383
High, Samuel 365, 366
High Sr., Samuel 355
Hoffman 194
Hokanson, O. A. 345, 359, 367
Hoke, Fred 101, 107, 110, 124, 138
Holcomb and Hoke 101, 210, 211
Holcomb, J. J. 101, 124
Hotel Weimar Girls 192
Hoy 194
Huber, Miss S. 193, 194
Hughes. F. P. 191
Humphrey's Euclid Beach 301
Humphreys, H. C. 287
Hurdle Hop 297, 298
Hurtig & Seamons Apollo Theater 181

I

Ideal Toy Company 374, 376
Improvements in or relating to Apparatus for Playing a Game 306
Indiana 103, 107, 138, 295, 301
Indianapolis, Indiana 101, 103, 107, 124, 138, 214, 295
Indianapolis News 107
Inman, Mark 60
iPhone 388
Ireland, Thomas 186
Issoudun, France 251

J

Jackson 189, 191, 192, 193, 194
Jackson, John A. 192
Jazz-Ball 257
J. D. Este Company, The 157, 158, 164, 165, 167, 169, 170, 171, 174, 179, 180, 181, 182, 183, 184, 185, 205, 219, 220, 221, 223, 226, 227, 228, 229, 230, 231, 233, 234, 235, 239, 240, 241, 253, 257
Jewish High Holidays 287
JFS. *See* Simpson, Joseph Fourestier
J. H. Keeney and Company 298
Joey Mucha. *See also* Joey the Cat
Joey the Cat 389
Johns, Frank D. 377

Johnson Farebox Company 116
Johns Patent 381
Jones' Walk 162

K

Kates 189, 191
Kawamath, J. 186
Kennedy, D. J. 181
Kenneywood Park 288
Kentucky Derby Company 261, 263
kiddie park 257
Klopp, Dr. E. L. 138
Kolar, Hilda M. 191
Kortonic, Grover 266

L

Langford, J. E. 63
Lansdale, Pennsylvania 381, 383, 384
Larken, Henry 186
L. A. Thompson Scenic Railway Corporation 186
Law Degree, Herman Bergoffen 276
Leavenworth, Kansas 128
Lebanon Big Six 193
Lebanon, Pennsylvania 193, 194
Lebanon Skee-Girls 192
LeBoutillier, Edward H. 254
Levi, I. N. 138, 139, 140, 141
Lewis, Isaac A. 214
Lianerch, Pennsylvania 288
Lianerch Swimming Pool 288
Liberty bomber 251
Liberty bombers 238
licensing tax, Skee-Ball 162
Lichty 193
Lincoln, California 63
Link 189, 191
Lipkin, Laurence 290
List 189, 191
Lombard, Mrs. M. E. 63
London Coin-Operated Machine Exhibition 299
London, England 261, 299, 306
London Olympia Christmas Carnival 261, 265
London World's Fair 10
Long Beach, California 177, 267
Long Beach, Long Island 287
Long Beach, New York 288
Long Branch, New Jersey 287, 288

Long Island, New York 290
Los Angeles, California 63, 183
Lukens, Bill 84
lumber 11, 51, 52, 157, 169
lumber business 52, 170, 249
lumber industry 6
lumber merchants 52, 153
lumber planing mill 153
lumber yard 51, 52, 142, 146, 153, 157, 169, 170
Lunenburg, Massachusetts 174
Luzerne County 190

M

Macgley (Capt.) 193
Manasquan, New Jersey 292
Manchester, Pennsylvania 288
Manchester, Vermont 242
Mangold, Charles 186
Manitou Beach 185
Manny 258
Maple Company 145
Margut 194
Marley 192
Marshall Hall 174, 177, 186
Marshall Jr., Robert 290
Martin, G. H. B. 164
maximum scoring device 346
Maxwell Roadster 266
Mays 194
McBride, W. 191
McKinney, Paul B. 193
Meeker, George 191
Merrill, John 110, 116, 118, 122, 123, 124, 135
Michigan 265, 266
Mid-City Park 263, 265
Midland Beach 288
Midway Recreation Center 377
Millburn, New Jersey 290
Million Dollar Pier 155, 210
Modern Vending Company 325, 329, 337
Monticello Amusement Park 266
Monticello, New York 266
Montsko, Frank 266
Moorish Palace in Zion 63
Mormon 63
Morris Edgar Smith 136
Moses, Paul E. 287
Mt. Gretna 193, 194

Mucha, Joey 389
Munn, Jack 181
Mutoscope 298, 303

N

N.A.A.P.. *See* National Association of Amusement Parks
N.A.A.P.P.B.. *See* National Association of Amusement Parks, Pools and Beaches
National Association of Amusement Parks 278, 281
National Association of Amusement Parks, Pools and Beaches 278, 306
National Skee-Ball Company 54
National Skee-Ball Company Inc. 275, 276, 279, 282, 283, 284, 285, 286, 292, 298, 299, 301, 302, 303, 305, 306, 307, 310, 311, 313, 314, 315, 316, 317, 318, 319, 320, 321, 322, 323, 330, 345, 364, 367
National Skee-Ball Company, Inc. v Seyfried 292
Neble 261, 263
Neue, "Tacks" 181
Neumarkt, Austria 275
New Cape May Hotel 206
New Jersey 5, 9, 15, 19, 29, 51, 89, 158, 164, 178, 186, 187, 220, 222, 266, 269, 281, 283, 285, 287, 289, 290, 292, 299, 300, 301, 374
Newport News 249
Newport News flying school 249
Nice, Budd Good 51, 61, 80, 82, 97, 101, 115, 122, 124, 135, 138
Nice Estate 63, 64, 68, 69, 103, 126, 157
Nice Family 51, 61, 63, 68, 77, 82, 101, 157, 227
Nice, John 51
Nice Jr., William 44, 51, 52, 57, 61, 63, 64, 68, 73, 77, 84, 96, 103, 114, 122, 138, 153, 312
Nice Sr., William 51
Nice Town 51
Noblett, Edward Arden 257
Noell, James T. 57
North Bergen, New Jersey 287
North Carolina 60, 389
Norumbega Park 288

O

Ocean Beach 268
Ocean City, New Jersey 174, 287, 288
Ocean Grove, New Jersey 283, 287
Okie, Frederick E. 14, 15
Okie, Howard 207
Ontario Lake Park 266

origin of the Skee-Ball 168
outdoor version 69
Oyen, Joseph 52, 95, 96

P

Pacific Amusement Manufacturing Company 297
Pacific Coast 265
Pacific Coast resorts 264
Pacific Coast Skee-Ball Company 164, 171
Pacific Coast states 206
Palace Skee Ball Parlors 194
Palais Berlitz 289
Palisades Amusement Park 287
Palmer, Charlie 258
Palmyra, Pennsylvania 194
PAMCO Tango 297
Pana, Illinois 60
Panama-Pacific Exposition 162, 174
Paradise Park Amusement Company 266
Paris, France 249, 251, 289
Parker, Evelyn 195, 196, 234, 236, 237
Park Island, Michigan 265
Patents
  Australian Patent No. 14.173/14 177
  Belgium Patent No. 411,685 358
  Canadian Patent No. 174,409 223
  U.S. Patent No. 1,116,746 154
  U. S. Patent No. 1,185,071 158
  U. S. Patent No. 1,834,317 285
  U. S. Patent No. 2,010,213 306, 308, 309, 358
  U. S. Patent No. 2,054,616 347
  U. S. Patent No. 2,926,915 377, 378
  U. S. Patent No. 168,677 11, 12
  U. S. Patent No. 279,271 14
Paterson, New Jersey 281
Paul B. McKinney's Market Square Billiard Parlors 191, 192
Paul McKinney's Billiard Parlor 193
Paul McKinney's Billiard Parlors 193
Paul McKinney's Market Square Billiard Parlor 192
Paul S. Keller Brokerage 19
Pavony, Eric 388
Peccerillo, Dominick 285, 298
Pennsylvania Railroad 7, 8, 169
Phelps, Mrs. R. G. 290
Philadelphia Athletics 162
Philadelphia City Directory 6
Philadelphia Evening Public Ledger 191
Philadelphia Inquirer 142, 144

Philadelphia, Pennsylvania 5, 6, 8, 11, 14, 15, 19, 28, 51, 52, 55, 58, 61, 64, 72, 87, 88, 89, 103, 110, 132, 136, 138, 143, 146, 153, 157, 162, 164, 166, 169, 170, 171, 178, 183, 184, 186, 189, 191, 206, 240, 253, 258, 288
Philadelphia Racquet Club 171, 191
Philadelphia School of Aviation 227, 249
Philadelphia Skee-Ball Title 162
Philadelphia Stock Exchange 162
Philadelphia Toboggan Company 73, 88, 90, 145, 199, 349, 355, 357, 358, 359, 360, 361, 364, 365, 366, 367, 368, 369, 371, 372, 374, 376, 377, 381, 383, 387
Piesen family 311
Piesen, Hugo H. 268, 275, 276, 278, 311, 368, 369
Piesen Manufacturing Company, Inc. 345, 359, 362, 365, 366, 367, 368, 370, 372
Piesen, Maurice 268, 275, 278, 283, 285, 292, 306, 307, 310, 311, 345, 368, 370, 371, 372, 373, 374, 381, 382, 383
Piesen, Peter 383, 384, 385, 386
Piesen Residence 372
Pitman, New Jersey 112
Pittsburgh, Pennsylvania 288, 290
planing mill 11, 14, 51, 153
Plate Printers' Union 194
Playground of the Coal Fields 266
Playland, Rye Beach, New York 267, 288
Playland, San Francisco, California 173, 268, 271, 272, 273, 274
Poor 189, 191
Popular Mechanics 57, 58, 59, 60, 103, 126
Postal Check 20, 21
Potte, Wilson 145
Pottsville, Pennsylvania 177, 266
Pressed Steel Manufacturing Company 51, 61
Princeton, New Jersey 155, 205, 209, 253, 254
Princeton University 153, 155, 165, 181, 227
prizes 1, 2, 167, 169, 174, 181, 193, 258, 268, 275, 285, 287, 289, 290, 335, 381, 388
Production Center No. 2 251
Prospect Hotel 257
prospectus 52, 54
Pulaski, Wisconsin 390
Puns 389

R

Rainier, H. W. 112
Ramsay, W. H. 15, 19
ratchet wrench 14
Rath, J. 114
Revere Beach, Massachusetts 269, 285, 287, 288

Revere Rubber Company 189, 191
Ridyard, A. R. 368
Ringler 194
Ritter 189, 191
Riverdale, New York 290
Riverview Park 174
Roanoake, Virginia 57
Rockaway Beach, New York 174, 287, 288
Rockaway, New York 288
Rockaway Park, New York 288
Rock-O-Ball 298, 312, 345
Rock-Ola 298, 311
Rock Springs Park 287, 288
Rocky Glen Amusement Resort 258
Rogers & Four 289
Romorantin, France 251, 252
Rosatto 146
Roush, Frank 265
royalty agreement, National Skee-Ball Company 323
royalty agreement, Piesen Manufacturing Co. 359, 367, 383, 387
royalty agreement, Shyvers, Durant and Campbell 347
Rudolf Wurlitzer Company 337
Rudolph Wurlitzer Company 345, 346, 347, 348
Russell, H. H. 158
Rutter, Charles A. 23, 24, 29, 44, 45, 207
Rye Beach, New York 266, 267, 288

S

Saldein, George M. 186
Saltair Park 63, 67
Salt Lake City, Utah 63, 67
San Diego, California 170, 174
San Diego Exposition 170
Sando, Briant 210, 211, 212, 213, 214, 215, 216, 290
Sando, Mrs. 210
San Francisco, California 173, 268, 271, 272, 273, 274, 388, 389
Santa Cruz Beach Boardwalk 110
Santa Cruz, California 110
Saskatoon 114
Sauter, William 132, 135, 136, 142, 143, 146
Savin Rock, Westhaven, Connecticut 287, 288
Schmeck, H. P. 368, 370, 374
Schoenfeld, Al 290
Schreiber 194
Schroon Lake, New Jersey 288
Schuykill Park 266
Score-Ball 230, 231, 234, 235, 238, 239, 256
scoring device. *See* automatic scoring device

Sea Isle City, New Jersey 288
Seal Beach 183
Seaside Heights, New Jersey 288
Seaside Park, Ocean County, New Jersey 292
2nd Pursuit Group 251
Seyfried, Mr. 292
Sheepshead Bay, New York 174, 288
Shields, J. 287
Shipping Package 153, 154
shorter alley 69, 285
Shyvers and Durant Patent 364
Shyvers, Durant, Campbell Agreement 350, 351, 352, 353
Shyvers, Kenneth C. 347, 348
Signal Officers Reserve Corps 249
Silverman, Mrs. Sue 325
Silver Spray Pleasure Pier 267
Simpson, Alice 6, 211, 256, 391
Simpson, Henry Evans 6, 7
Simpson, Henry Rowland (Brother) 6
Simpson, Joseph Fourestier 5, 6, 7, 9, 10, 11, 12, 14, 15, 19, 20, 23, 29, 42, 44, 45, 51, 52, 56, 57, 60, 61, 69, 70, 71, 78, 79, 82, 83, 88, 98, 99, 100, 101, 103, 107, 110, 112, 114, 116, 117, 118, 120, 121, 127, 132, 136, 137, 145, 146, 147, 153, 155, 157, 158, 164, 195, 196, 198, 200, 201, 202, 204, 211, 212, 213, 214, 215, 216, 219, 223, 227, 230, 234, 236, 237, 256, 295, 297, 332, 359, 390, 391
Simpson, Josephine 6, 15, 256
Simpson, Josephine (Sister) 6
Singac, New Jersey 287
Skee-Ball 1, 2, 3, 5, 20, 24, 27, 29, 32, 37, 44, 45, 47, 48, 49, 50, 51, 52, 53, 54, 55, 56, 57, 59, 60, 61, 63, 64, 65, 69, 77, 80, 81, 82, 88, 89, 95, 96, 97, 101, 107, 110, 115, 116, 118, 125, 132, 136, 138, 139, 140, 141, 143, 145, 146, 153, 154, 155, 156, 157, 158, 159, 160, 161, 162, 164, 165, 166, 167, 168, 169, 170, 171, 174, 175, 177, 178, 179, 181, 183, 184, 185, 186, 187, 189, 190, 191, 192, 193, 194, 195, 196, 198, 199, 201, 208, 214, 219, 220, 222, 223, 224, 225, 226, 227, 228, 229, 230, 231, 233, 234, 238, 240, 241, 242, 243, 249, 254, 255, 256, 257, 258, 259, 261, 263, 264, 265, 266, 267, 268, 269, 270, 271, 273, 274, 275, 276, 278, 279, 280, 281, 282, 283, 284, 285, 286, 287, 289, 290, 291, 292, 293, 294, 295, 296, 297, 298, 299, 301, 302, 303, 304, 305, 306, 307, 310, 311, 312, 313, 314, 315, 316, 317, 318, 319, 320, 321, 322, 323, 325, 329, 330, 331, 332, 336, 337, 338, 339, 340, 341, 342, 343, 345, 346, 348, 349, 355, 356, 359, 364, 367, 372, 374, 376, 377, 379, 380, 381, 383, 384, 385, 386, 387, 388, 389, 390, 391
Skee-Ball Alley Company 51, 52, 64, 69, 81, 89, 110, 115, 146, 153, 154, 155, 157, 161, 227, 278, 292

Skee-Ball battery 230, 234, 268, 281, 282
Skee-Ball Bowling Game 57
Skee-Ball Company 253, 254, 255, 256, 257, 258, 263, 264, 265, 267, 268, 269, 270, 275, 276, 278, 279
Skee-Ball Company, Inc. 388, 389, 390
Skee-Ball Company of Illinois 184
Skee-Ball Construction Co. 77, 80
Skee-Ball Exhibition Co. 77, 80
Skee-Ball iPhone app 388
Skee-Ball, online game 388
Skee-Ball Operating Company 179, 259, 261
Skee-Ball Patent Infringement
   Ideal Toy Company 374, 376
Skee-Ball, perfect scores 181
Skee-Ball Sales and Security Company 257, 278, 310
Skee-Ball, scores 167, 174, 181, 189, 191, 268
Skee Ball Six 192
Skee-Ball Stadium 281, 287, 289, 290, 291
Skee-Ball trademark 310, 323, 332, 374, 388, 390
Skee-Ball trademark application 286
Skee-Ball trademark infringed 374
Skee-Ball trademark infringement 376, 388
Skee-Ball trademark rights 387
Skee-diddy 389. *See also* Carannante, Ray
Skee-E-O 388
Skeel Game 298
Skee Patrol 389
Skee-Roll 288, 290, 292, 296, 299, 301, 302, 303, 307, 311, 329, 359, 374
Skee-Roll (under license) 299
Skee Shot 299
Skee-ven Colbert 389
Ski-ball 299
Skill-Ball, Stirling Novelty Company 296, 325
Skill-Ball, Washington Bowling Billiard Company 279, 283, 284
Sladek, Joe 387, 388, 389
Smith 192
Scoy, William F. 186
Sousa, John Phillip 61
South Africa 301
South Beach 288
Sporting Goods Dealer 126
Springfield Lake, East Akron, Ohio 174
Springfield, Massachusetts 174, 177, 347
Springfield Township, Montgomery County, Pennsylvania 143
S. S. Poor Cup 189
Stahley 192, 193, 194
Star Manufacturing 298

Staten Island, New York 288
State of New Jersey 19
Steeplechase Pier 60, 61, 62
Steeplechase Pier, Coney Island 61
Sterbergh, Layman M. 287
Sternbergh, David H. 281
Sternbergh, Layman M. 281, 283, 289
Stewart, Herbert W. 191
Stine 192
Stirling Novelty Company 296, 325
stock market crash 275, 279, 287
Stohler 193
Stohler's Slide Easies 192
Stone 189, 191
Storms, Edgar A. 285, 287
St. Paul, Minnesota 298
Stuhley 192
Sukerman, R. 290
Summit Park 242
Surf Avenue, Asbury Park, New Jersey 281
Surf Avenue, Culver Depot 258
swindled 257
swindler 257
Sydney, Austrailia 114

T

Taber, Lydia Richmond 253
Taxier, Morris 258
tax run over my yard 69
teacher, Herman Bergoffen 275, 305
teddy bear 2, 381
Tennessee 225, 231
Tenpinnet 110, 189, 201, 211
Tenpinnet Co. 107
Terrell, Frank S. 287
Texas 177, 249, 298
The Beautiful Game of Skee-Ball 1, 60
The Billboard 1, 55, 57, 60, 103, 126, 128, 129, 130, 131, 132, 135, 146, 150, 154, 155, 162, 164, 165, 170, 171, 174, 176, 181, 183, 184, 186, 193, 214, 218, 219, 220, 221, 223, 224, 225, 229, 230, 231, 233, 234, 235, 238, 240, 243, 255, 256, 257, 258, 261, 263, 264, 265, 266, 267, 268, 269, 270, 278, 279, 280, 281, 282, 283, 284, 285, 287, 288, 289, 292, 295, 298, 299, 301, 302, 303, 304, 305, 307, 312, 323, 325, 329, 330, 336, 337, 345, 364, 367, 377
The Electro-Ball Company of Dallas 298
The J. D. Este Company. *See* J. D. Este Company, The
The Neptune Operating Company 171

The Philadelphia Ledger 178
The Philadelphia School of Aviation 227, 249
The Rudolf Wurlitzer Co. 350
The Rudolf Wurlitzer Manufacturing Company 310, 312, 313, 314, 315, 316, 317, 318, 319, 320, 321, 322, 323
The Rudolph Wurlitzer Co. 351, 352, 353, 355, 359, 360, 361, 362, 364, 366, 368, 373, 381
The Rudolph Wurlitzer Corporation 323
The Rudolph Wurlitzer Manufacturing Company 311, 323, 324, 325, 327, 328, 329, 330, 331, 332, 333, 334, 336, 337, 356, 357, 358
These alleys are going to make money someday for somebody 115, 116, 195
3rd Aviation Instruction Center 251
13th Aero Squadron 251, 253
32nd Aero Squadron 249
Thomas Jr., George C. 145
Tilyou, George C. 61
Tim Esq., David 158
Times Square 179, 181
Tivoli Gardens 307
Tonner, George V. 261, 262
Toul, France 251
Townsend, Dr. William Wilder 35, 37, 41, 42
Townsend, Tracy 389
"toy" sized tabletop version 69
trade items for Skee-Ball Alleys 164
Trademarks
    U. S. Trademark No. 256,496 358, 367
    U. S. Trademark No. 304,883 367
Trainer, Newlin 201, 204
Trenton, New Jersey 208, 287, 290
Trolley Parks 27, 72, 224, 225, 240
trunk 11, 12, 13
Tudor 261

U

Ukiah, California 58
Union League 153, 170, 171
U. S. Patent No. 1,116,746 154
U. S. Patent No. 1,185,071 158
U. S. Patent No. 1,834,317 285
U. S. Patent No. 2,010,213 306, 308, 309, 358
U. S. Patent No. 2,054,616 347
U. S. Patent No. 2,926,915 377, 378
U. S. Patent No. 168,677 11, 12
U. S. Patent No. 279,271 14, 15
U. S. S. Tire Company 189

U. S. Trademark No. 256,496 358, 367
U. S. Trademark No. 304,883 367

V

Vanell, E. T. 164
Varholy, Miss 194
Venice, California 177, 265
Vineland Knitting Mills Company 15, 19
Vineland, New Jersey 5, 15, 18, 19, 23, 29, 50, 55, 64, 69, 80, 81, 84, 88, 95, 126, 136, 164, 210, 256
Vineland Postmaster 21
Virginia 57, 174, 194, 249
virtual tickets 388

W

Walford, Richard 179
Waltz, Miss E. 193, 194
Warren, John Clifford 58
Washington Bowling Billiard Co. 279
Watson, William S. 15, 19
Welsh, Charles N. 145
West Haven, Connecticut 287, 288
West Philadelphia 166, 167
West Philadelphia, Pennsylvania 6, 7, 15
West Virginia 170, 287, 288
Whalom Park, Fitchburg, Massachusetts 177
Whalom Park, Lunenburg, Massachusetts 174
Wheeler, Arthur L. 165, 205, 206, 234, 259
Wheeler, Arthur, obituary 234
Wheeler, Herbert 179, 181, 238
Wheel Pump Inn 144, 149
Whidden 189, 191
Whirl-O-Ball 238, 240, 242, 243, 255, 279, 295
White City Park, Erdenheim, Pennsylvania 72, 73, 118. *See also* Chestnut Hill Park
White City Park, Little Rock, Arkansas 263, 266
White, Will L. 287
Wildwood 64, 84, 89, 158, 174, 178, 204, 205, 206, 208, 209, 220, 222, 225, 288
Wildwood Crest, New Jersey 66, 101, 116
Wildwood Crest Pier 61, 65, 66, 101, 208
Wilkesbarre, Pennsylvania 177
William D. Rogers Carriage Business 14
Williamson, F. J. 60
Williamson, North Carolina 389
Willow Grove Park 27, 28, 240
Wilson, Lester 181

Woltemate 192
Women's National Championship 290
Woodlawn Park 287
Woodside Park 174, 240, 288
Wurlitzer Corporation 348
Wurlitzer, Farny R. 348
Wurlitzer in Game Field; Buys National Skee-Ball Co. 312
Wurlitzer Manufacturing Company 348
Wurlitzer-Modern Party Climax To Good-Will Building Program 337
Wurlitzer Skee-Ball 331, 334, 336, 337, 338, 339, 340, 341, 342, 343, 344, 345, 377
Wyndmoor, Pennsylvania 143, 144

Y

Yale 181
YMCA. *See* Young Men's Christian Association
Young, Abby 52
Young Men's Christian Association 258, 259
Young Men's Christian Association 258
Young Men's Hebrew Association 275, 276
Young's Old Pier 191
Young's Pier 56
Young Women's Hebrew Association 275, 276

www.ingramcontent.com/pod-product-compliance
Lightning Source LLC
Chambersburg PA
CBHW080404300426
44113CB00015B/2401